Praise for *Big Impact Without Burnout*

"This is a guidebook full of practical steps, tools and strategies showing women how to transform manic busyness into meaningful productivity, both at home and at work."
Arianna Huffington, Founder & CEO, Thrive Global

"A refreshing guide for women seeking to succeed without sacrificing themselves in the process. Dive in and discover how to make a big impact without burnout."
Shelley Zalis, Founder & CEO, The Female Quotient

"A genuinely groundbreaking answer to burnout for any woman looking to follow their passions and achieve greatness."
Nicola Mendelsohn CBE, Head of Global Business Group, Meta

"With warmth and honesty, Bianca generously shares her hard won experience to help you tap into your leadership and power. Keep this book on your desk and turn to any page for instant inspiration."
Katherine Morgan Schafler, author of *The Perfectionist's Guide to Losing Control*

"An essential read if you are someone who wants to thrive in life without sacrificing your health in the process. Read it, apply it and witness your life transform."
Simon Alexander Ong, bestselling author of *Energize*, Keynote Speaker, Life Coach and Business Strategist

"With empathy and insight, Bianca guides us through the challenges women face in balancing leadership, personal life, and wellbeing. This is a must-read for any woman seeking to thrive in her career while staying true to herself."
Neha Dakwala-Shah, Global Director & Women's ERG Lead, Google

"*Big Impact Without Burnout* is a beacon of hope, offering practical strategies and a much-needed dose of inspiration for women at all stages of their careers. This book is a must-read for any woman who dares to dream big, lead with purpose, and embrace new beginnings."
Nishma Robb, Glittersphere Founder, ex Marketing Lead, Google UK

"*Big Impact Without Burnout* is a wonderful book that combines inspiration with practical actionable steps to help the reader achieve their true human potential. Highly relevant for these transformative times."
Rishad Tobacowalla, bestselling author of *The Soul of Business*

"This is an effervescent and inspiring read that will offer support to any woman who dreams big but who is spinning lots of plates"
Theresa Cheung, bestselling author of *The Dream Dictionary from A to Z*

"A brilliant sum of inspiration and actionable advice, for any person who feels it's time for them to take back the remote control of their life."
Severine Charbon, International Chief Talent Officer, Publicis Groupe

"A powerful and personal story of how preventing or overcoming burnout is not just about improving work-life balance, but about living the life you believe in and making a real difference in the world."
Dr. Dina Glouberman, author of *The Joy of Burnout* and Co-Founder of Skyros Holidays

"A magic mix of empowering messages and practical advice from a true trailblazer, with a healthy dose of kindness and empathy."
Jacqueline O'Sullivan, Head of Global Agencies, EMEA, Yahoo Inc.

"A must-read for any woman seeking inspiration to have it all without sacrificing themselves. Bianca's practical steps will guide today's women of impact to a life of limitless success and personal wellbeing."
Solance Scholey, Founder & CEO, The Best Ever Brownie Company

"*Big Impact Without Burnout* is an essential toolkit for anyone looking to thrive in modern business."
Richard Britton, Founding Partner, CCV Group

"A great read for anyone aiming to excell in their career while maintaining balance. With actionable insights and practical strategies, Bianca offers a blueprint for sustainable success."
Claire Valoti, Co-Founder Haylo Ventures, ex VP Snap Inc.

"Fast-paced, easy to follow and uplifting ... This is a must-read and copies are going to all of my friends this holiday season!"
Laura Preslan, Founder and Lead Coach, Advoture, Inc.

"Bianca is not only a wise, strong and accomplished businesswoman, she has a lovely soft energy, warm heart and great sense of humor! You're in good hands with someone who can keep it real and embrace vulnerability while also encouraging you to live your potential."
Tanya Carroll Richardson, author and professional intuitive

"Bianca Best masterfully illuminates the path to success without sacrifice, offering ambitious women a blueprint for achieving their dreams with grace and vitality."
Lizzie Burton, Global Partnerships Head, Google

"I simply devoured this book. It was an absolutely gift for me and I am putting what I have learnt into practice every single day as well as using the tools to create my vision and plan for the future. Read it, read it, read it!"
Charlotte Dahl, Managing Director, Woodreed Consultancy

"The power of this book lies in its truly holistic approach to health, wellbeing and mindset. Truly life-changing."
Wendeline de Bruijn, CMO, Candid Group

"To be devoured alongside your favourite morning coffee as you achieve one goal at a time."
Leila Siddiqui, Director of D&I, Institute of Practioners in Advertising

"This book is business critical, because 'how' we succeed is business critical. I am delighted Bianca is offering some guidance and tools from her own personal journey."
Tracy De Groose, CEO, Coach & Advisor, Reiki Master

"In a world that often demands more from women than it gives, Bianca Best's *Big Impact Without Burnout* is a breath of fresh air ... A must read for any woman seeking to balance ambition with self care!"
Claire Higgon, Global Account Manager, Amazon

"The difference between *Big Impact Without Burnout* and other books I've read is that the author totally understands what it's like to be a real, flawed, trying to do it all, working woman in the twenty-first century."
Joanne Brenner, Founder, Ten27 Communications

BIG
IMPACT
WITHOUT
~~BURNOUT~~

8 Energizing Strategies to Stop Struggling and Start Soaring

Bianca Best

WATKINS
1893

Big Impact Without Burnout
Bianca Best

First published in the UK and USA in 2025 by
Watkins, an imprint of Watkins Media Limited
Unit 11, Shepperton House, 83–89 Shepperton Road
London N1 3DF

enquiries@watkinspublishing.com

Commissioning Editor: Ella Chappell
Project Editor: Brittany Willis
Head of Design: Karen Smith
Production: Uzma Taj

A CIP record for this book is available from the British Library

ISBN: 978-1-78678-926-6 (Hardback)
ISBN: 978-1-78678-927-3 (eBook)

10 9 8 7 6 5 4 3 2 1

Typset by Lapiz
Printed and bound by CPI Group (UK) Ltd, Croydon, CR0 4YY

www.watkinspublishing.com

MIX
Paper | Supporting
responsible forestry
FSC
www.fsc.org
FSC® C171272

Lovingly written for every woman with a glittering dream,
and especially my daughter, an eternal ray of divine light
as yet unaware of her radiant magnificence.
Darling Scarlett, may you forever sparkle.

*"Your most important work is always
ahead of you, never behind you..."*

— Stephen Covey

CONTENTS

Dear Ambitious Soul,

In every wish upon a star, every first kiss, business launch, pregnancy test, interview, vision board and every laminated corporate mission statement blue-tacked to a wall, tinkles hope. Hope is the billowing, elevating wind beneath the wings of our dreams. In hope there is bounty, optimism and golden energy. In hope soars all the intentions of our hearts, propelling us to persist, persevere and honour our soul's longings. Hope is a force to cling to when the going gets tough, which it inevitably will. Hope glistens and floats gently alongside us, co-creating our journeys with imagination, motivation and invigoration, guiding us to course correct when needs be. Hope blows our flickering flame of ambition into a roaring beacon, illuminating all the light beyond the shadow.

I wish you hope. I wish you brilliance. I wish you love.

Here's to you being the dazzling star of your own story.

Bianca

X

INTRODUCTION

"In the midst of winter, I found there was, within me, an invincible summer. And that makes me happy. For it says that no matter how hard the world pushes against me, within me, there's something stronger – something better, pushing right back."

— Albert Camus

"Entire physical shut down," the doctor asserted, a grave expression on his face. "You're on the brink of total immune collapse."

"Damn!" I sighed petulantly, slumping into his unwelcoming plastic chair. "Why did this happen?"

Why indeed? I was in my late twenties. I had a thriving, rapidly expanding business to manage, two exuberant toddlers, a home to run, obligations everywhere and a defiant resistance to being told I was on the brink of a dangerous health malfunction. But, I also now had seriously noticeable hair loss, was a skinny wisp of a woman with hollow eyes and a pallid, blemished complexion. I constantly caught tonsillitis, conjunctivitis, bronchiolitis, every-itis. I was swarming with allergies, skin disorders, insomnia, IBS, PMS, you name it, I had it, and I was permanently oscillating between hyper wired and bone-achingly tired.

I was, I reluctantly admitted, whopperly chopperly burnt out. I had hit my first rock bottom. Many more of these impromptu health crises followed. Then, I eventually cracked the code. I uncovered how to commit vibrant and consistent impact to all the realms in my life that matter most to me, without burning out.

Burnout is torture for the ambitious woman. It's the nemesis of every high achiever. It's crippling, harrowing and life-jolting. Burnout creeps up on us gradually, lurking, until suddenly, slap bang in the middle of one of our superbly productive output crescendos we collapse, floored into inertia, plans abruptly awry. There we lie, imprisoned in our own flailing bodies, tormented by the listlessness of unexpected life paralysis, bleakly lamenting our energetic, ambitious selves now forced into stillness, ashamed, useless, exhausted. Almost 60 per cent of working women today lie there.[1]

Obeying medical instruction, I surrendered, took a break, healed and once strong again, went back to embracing my never-ending to-do lists with my usual gusto. Naively though, I hadn't paid attention to the lessons within the crisis. I'd failed to notice the reasons I'd ended up so inconveniently incapacitated. I had brushed the incident off as bad luck, embarrassed to retrospectively dwell on my own vulnerability, inwardly humiliated by what I perceived as weakness. Foolishly, back onto life's treadmill I rushed, donning my numerous hats once again, obstinately denying the blip's occurrence. "Woohoo Life, I'm back!" said the mother, entrepreneur, techie, wife, daughter, boss, socialite, fitness queen, domestic goddess, erm no scrap that last one, you get the gist though, lots of hats, and on and on I jogged.

Over the next decade, as my life, family, homes, businesses, busyness and hat collection expanded, I repeatedly broke down in similar circumstances, whacked by burnout episode after burnout episode; each unexpected calamity rendering me reliant on generous friends, family and colleagues to pick up the charred shadows of my unfinished work projects, uncared-for children and unfulfilled obligations. Each crash sending me into a spiral of self-loathing, fear and frustration; "Why am I so weak? When will I recover? I've got so much to do. I need to be well!".

Gradually, I awoke to patterns at play, recognizing certain precursors to impending burnout cascades, and slowly I acknowledged my own inadvertent self-destruction. With interrogative self-awareness I came to understand the role I held in my frequent demises, which were not misfortune, but a toxic blend of overzealous productivity, incessant stress and suffocation in too many areas simultaneously. I respected that while some of the whirlwinds were squarely out of my control, there were vast aspects of my life and lifestyle that were 100 per cent within it. And although my abundant ambitions were motivating, I was pushing too hard, too consistently, too reactively and careering relentlessly into my own breaking points time and time again, ignoring signals that could have been neat alerts to change route or halt. As pennies started to drop and I examined my behaviours, attitudes and circumstances, I bubbled with optimism and ever-expanding hope. I could see and feel the misadventuring afoot with increasing clarity.

The Myth of the Mastered To-Do List

We live in an age where it's busy. Sure. There's loads to do and loads to distract. White boards, family planners and diaries are chock-a-block. There's public celebration in this as much as there's private despair. "Get you Girl and how much you accomplish, wowey!" and by sheepish contrast, "Thank you, Dentist, apologies if I nod off while you do the root canal, this is my secret spa time these days." And within this twizzly polarity of "busy is cool but exhausting" pervades a naivety that assumes the magnitude of demands slamming into our multifaceted life realms are both manageable and happily satisfying. Not necessarily, my friend, not necessarily.

Perhaps, like younger me, you view life's freneticism as a battle to be won, assuming you will eventually reign victorious over a utopian state of calm, where the to-do list is enticing, gently stimulating and delightfully untroublesome. For years, I ploughed through the mayhem of work, family and self-care, fervently trying to manage, sedate and control it all, to get to an ethereal tomorrow where I would no longer be exhausted or overwhelmed, but would still realize all of my tantalizing ambitions and goals and be the perfect mother, entrepreneur, wife, daughter, social butterfly, employee, and, and, and ... But, as I repeated each day in an identical pattern to the day before, the stress and intensity never waned, that transcendent tomorrow never came, my fairy godmother never appeared and the cuddly nirvana of "Balance" never cradled me, instead those repeated burnouts did.

Despite the violent life bumps, I kept recovering and hopping eagerly back up onto that treadmill, exuberantly leaning into the next business expansion, corporate promotion, home to renovate, party to plan, exercise regime to adhere to, nutritional overhaul to implement, meditation practice to learn, twins to breastfeed, cupboard to clean, book to write, gift to give, homework to assist with, puppy to train, divorce to broach, on and on and on ...

This continued until I finally recognized a physical tweak here – for example, prioritizing less caffeine for better sleep – or a mental tweak there, such as committing to daily meditation, wasn't enough. There needed to be emotional and attitudinal tweaks too. And for the record, mere tweaks weren't enough either. Holistic, systemic and definitively radical change was required. If I wanted to keep on doing all these juicy things without breaking myself, I needed to break the repetitive cycle itself. My very life approach needed an overhaul. I realized that Balance as a concept was as ethereal as a mastered to-do list and as unlikely as a fairy wielding her magic wand with the words, "I'm here. I'll protect you now, Darling. Have a little sleep in this four-poster snuggle-nest while I do your thing for you." Surprisingly (like a serious, drop the mic and look in the mirror moment), I also realized I didn't even want Balance in its steady, ploddy, safe sense after all, despite all the books and courses and hopelessly chasing it over the years. I startled with the acknowledgement that I loved life's fizziness, adored its buoyant fullness, exciting undulations and never wanted any of it to quieten, or in fact, anyone to do it for me, but the thing I loathed and would no longer tolerate was self-compromise. This was what was broken and breaking me time and time again. Self-compromise.

To be compromised means being "impaired or diminished in function: weakened, damaged or flawed", according to Merriam Webster. It also means being "made vulnerable by unauthorized access, revelation or exposure".[2] The Oxford Dictionary's definition is "the expedient acceptance of standards that are lower than is desirable." So, universally, compromise is suboptimal – weakness, vulnerability, exposure, low standards, diminishment. By my observation, a compromised life can manifest when, for example, you're lonely in your marriage, stifled in a work culture, riddled with ill health or excessively indulging because everyone else is. I see it when clients are niggled, unsure why unrest is swirling. There's a disharmony percolating they can't quite put their finger on. My carefully cultivated definition of compromise is "being and doing something that doesn't chime authentically with your soul; departing from one's integrity." I see self-compromise as suppressing who you are, what you want and what matters most. I see it as the most debilitating aspect of Success today. You cannot have Big Impact Without Burnout if you are compromising your essence.

Corporate experiences have hurt me. I've had a chair thrown across an office at me (I swerved). And a teaspoon come to think of it (that one struck!). I was only 22 years old that time. I've had a man put his hand over my mouth while I was speaking in a boardroom meeting to shush me. Aged 42 that time. I've been invited into a 7am central London office meeting where two senior male executives, who bizarrely felt threatened, warned me to no longer have a relationship with another more influential and senior female colleague. I've been chastised so loudly in the middle of an open-plan office that I've cried in humiliation, witnesses surreptitiously agog. I've been unfairly blamed, criticized and insulted, both overtly and behind my back. I've suffered the bitter toxicity of corporate survivors' manipulative and self-serving cat's play. I've been deliberately overlooked, blocked, ignored and bypassed in both remuneration and promotion. I've been told to avoid mentioning I'm a mother. Disappointingly, women have occasionally tripped me up, more venomous and conniving than men who play similar games. I've been undermined. I've been frightened. I've been burned.

I've been challenged as an entrepreneur too, making it all up as I went along, learning how and when to trust myself. Opening doors then having them slammed in my face, belittled by big players diminishing me as too "cottage industry", not established, nor global enough. Working on the business and in the business, never enough time, nor skill, nor certainty that this or that direction was the best one. Not knowing which of the raft of potential suppliers or advisors to believe. Who to hire, where to locate, which expansion to prioritize, how much to pay, how much to invest, how much risk to gamble, how much family security to jeopardize.

My reaction to adversity used to be more work, more productivity, more effort, more contortion to fit whatever round hole I was suddenly required to distort myself to. I even once cut a blunt fringe and darkened my wardrobe, a fish very much out of water in black blazer and heels, innocently hoping an austere exterior would embolden me as I flipped and flapped ashore, urgently moulding into a tough, egoic culture. I've set my alarm to work between midnight and 3am trying to fit in a bit more work between bedtime and the school run, hoping over-delivery will impress and prove my substance. I've left my family asleep in the hotel room to do a 5–10am stint in the lobby keeping on top of my entrepreneurially-driven workload before breakfast on holiday. I've wept in HQ toilet cubicles ashamed at my apparent incompetence. I've taken on more, more, more, endlessly people-pleasing to validate my self-worth – "Yes, to that extra project, of course", "I've had another idea," "How about I do this?" I've chased endlessly cavernous proof-of-self, desperately seeking a proud boss, organization, parent, social group or society even. I've been lost in swirls of painful, unyielding success-hunting.

I've felt afraid of redundancy during corporate stints, equally as afraid of my own lack when running my own enterprises. Sometimes at night, masked assailants would chase me through looping, derelict underground tunnels as I ran for my life, subconsciously urgently seeking an escape route. There have been tough times for sure. But mainly it's been exhilarating and, despite the knockbacks, I have progressed and ascended. I've grown. Gradually, while initially warier, I eventually became wiser. Success in all those above scenarios were never actually my success ideals. I had warped and mulched my personal version of success into something exploitable and malleable, and inadvertently squashed it into that which other people wanted, suppressed and compromised. I had shrunk my very essence and damaged myself repeatedly with all that squeezing. Is it any wonder I kept burning out despite the decaf pledges and meditation retreats?

The Light

Over time, as I leaned, wide-eyed and curious, into those pockets of my life where I felt emotionally compromised and addressed them, tuning into what my purest, non-egoic, heartfelt self needed, gently adjusting situations accordingly – changing jobs, businesses, relationships, habits, behaviours, homes, parenting style, leadership style and more – this became the transcendent elixir enabling me to soar.

It took years of experimentation addressing physical, mental and emotional imbalances, years to understand and hone the effects of my various life adjustments, but gradually, as I focused on obliterating self-compromise and finding my way back into my version of integrity, I woke up. I stepped into self-accountability and self-leadership, recognizing I am the one wholly responsible for my present-day reality. If I don't like a situation, a culture, a relationship, or whatever aspect of my life is a niggle, I shouldn't wonkily bend into it, compromising who I am, morphing into what others want. Nope, the epiphany slowly emerged. It was up to me.

With decisive confidence, I decided no more burnout. No more overwhelm. No more debilitating, insurmountable energy depletion. No more inability to consistently perform. No more shame of under-delivery through collapse. No more peaks and troughs of excited highs followed by depressive lows. No more bursts of activity followed by crippling inertia. No more satisfying others' demands before my own. No more compromise. No more.

The notion of my imaginary fairy godmother and her make-all-the-crap-disappear wand dissolved. My imaginary knight in his shining armour heralding my talents to the world with his tooty trumpet, a red carpet lined with opportunities and wealth aplenty, evaporated in puffs of wispy wafty smoke. The empty pursuit of that supposedly glinting pot of gold at the end of the rainbow ended. "Fake it to make it" became a nonsense as no amount of pretending would make any inwardly uncomfortable situation sustainable, easy, manageable or okay, however hard I buckled and bent. Suddenly, all those assumptions I'd been making about what was around the corner, the fictional successful tomorrow I had clung to in my nightly visualizations, where it would feel easier, the 16-hour days would end, a mentor would scoop me up and rescue me, crystalized into sharp focus. No one was coming to make it better. No wishing and wanting would change anything. And working harder, longer and faster certainly was not the answer.

The problem of operating in the fog of a mythological success ideal, an unwittingly delusional busy buzzy life of what others expect of us, is that we can be so ensconced in fear, fatigue and running on that hamster-wheel that we forget to rise up and observe, with eagle vision looking down, who we are, what we are spending time on and what we could, in fact, more rewardingly be contributing to our one precious life. It's too easy in our bouncy, overcommitted days to be mouse-like, trapped in the detail on the ground, shrinking, scurrying, trying to satisfy others, focusing only on the next task on the list, ignoring inner shrieks of, "Erm, excuse me, why?? Not sure that's best serving you, Lovely. Little bit of time wasting afoot here, me thinks." Breaking ourselves through emotional suppression, channeling unrest through scattered, whizzing helixes of misdirected effort, working harder and harder, later and longer, trying to produce and please is self-compromise and wrong.

We're responsible for our level of empowerment, indeed our in-power-ment, and for protecting our self-authority. If we find ourselves disempowered, we are the ones to re-empower ourselves. It's all up to us. We can choose to give away our power or retain and protect it. Our decisions determine our destiny.

And within this truth lies the key to unlocking that most magnificent, iridescent and majestic you. There is a simple route to your shiniest ambitions being realized. When you fully step into self-accountability and self-leadership, I promise you will be en route to your biggest, brightest and very best impact, all without burnout. And though it requires bravery and a strong will, it's not even that hard, it just takes strategy, awareness and application.

It was the final piece in my burnout management puzzle. Master the physical, tick. Master the mental, tick. Master the emotional, at last, tick. Zoning in on obliterating self-compromise, finding my way back into integrity, became my thing. I hope this book will make it yours too. As I truly believe this is where myths melt and reality sparkles.

Radiant Success

Only once I finally understood the delicate and fragile interplay between my physical, mental and emotional realms and the harm of compromise anywhere at any time, was I able to immaculately hone how to stay well while being gracefully productive. My north star became how to succeed healthily. I observed any inner sirens blaring, paid attention to the compromise afoot and took instant action. I carefully, incrementally learned how to achieve goals without hurting myself (and those around me). With heartening delight, I discovered that establishing inner strength laid a solid foundation for apparently limitless impact. It came down to consciously and intuitively adjusting activities and approaches to honour what mattered most, when it mattered most and to respecting my own truth, my own wants and needs and, ultimately and most powerfully, my integrity.

I learned to preserve mind, body and soul equilibrium as the core priority, fastidiously being self-reflective throughout and always focusing on positive personal evolution. I listened to the niggles, leaned into triggers and course corrected. Achieving my visions without intermittent, interrupting health disasters at last became a reality and after a tumultuous decade of boom-bust impact, my burnout cycle ended. In 2015 I suffered my last crash and am proud to have honoured and maintained vibrant vitality since. In happy consequence, I've also delivered unfaltering levels of strong contribution to work, family, love, life, the lot.

Did my life shrink or recede in any way? Not one jot. Did I eliminate any of my dreams? Not one. Did I compromise anything at all? Not one single thing. Conversely, I am tingling to acknowledge that life is fuller, richer and more satisfying in so many beautiful ways. I have found a delicious blend of power, progress and peace, which I'll forever nurture and be grateful for.

This book is a shortcut to your biggest impact without burning out. It describes what worked for me so you can give it a whirl too and avoid wasting the decade I did yo-yoing from energized to depleted, productive to useless, from exuberant to desperately low with crushing frustration and fatigue. My intention is for you to find your productivity zen too. I have proved it absolutely exists for all of us. There does not need to be strife in a life of impact. In these pages you will learn how to build your Foundational Imperatives, your inner solidity, to then expand out into your Expansion Phenomenon, unleashing your best out into the world.

Hi, It's Me

As I finally refined my way of navigating everything I cherish without compromising myself, I realized I hadn't only ended cycles of physical, mental and emotional diminishment, but that operating inauthentically was now in the past too. Protective metaphorical masks fell away as I seized the courage to drive who I truly was and what I really thought up to the surface, for the first time, consistently, in all environments. Ironically, the more "me" I became, the easier and more fun the whole of life's breadth became, with work, relationships and even wealth flowing more abundantly. Without compromise, my entire spirit felt freer and lighter. In this space of personal integrity, I'd also identified and liberated myself from warped success ideologies that I hadn't previously recognized weren't even mine in the first place, so at last I was gliding toward what made me feel most content at a soul level, my very own version of success. It didn't end there though, as once I found my voice and clarified what I wanted and needed, amazingly there also exploded more confidence and influence. My whole way of being became simpler, more effective and naturally energized. And this magic all arose because I stepped back into myself, my purest self.

The three epiphanies that led me to this way of integrity, this way of Big Impact Without Burnout – the physical, the mental and the emotional – are interwoven throughout the eight strategies you will learn in this book.

The Physical Epiphany

Initially, I viewed my burnouts as a call to improve my physical strength. I would come out of the collapses, which usually took the form of bouts of flu, pneumonia, colds, a "nasty" virus, and so on, with a renewed interest in fitness and nutrition, chasing all the trending diets – low inflammation, alkaline, low glycemic index, etc. I drank more water and exercised more regularly. Oh, the cookbooks, juicers and steamers I bought, not to forget the treadmill in the garage, but no matter how much I fed my body good stuff, cut back on toxins like caffeine, alcohol and processed gunk, I didn't feel more energized. It took me years to understand sleep's role in physical restoration too. This is lunacy with hindsight, but I'm an 80s kid of the "work hard, play hard" ilk and newborn twins had trained me to push through sleep deprivation, so I had a warped regard for sleep. For years, I failed to experience any sense of energetic balance and was always shattered, reliant on fast fake energy fixes to get my productivity highs.

The Mental Epiphany

Gradually, I started to recognize that I didn't have only a tired body, but a tired mind. That I was always busy thinking, even when I wasn't doing. That I was forever buzzing with plans and agendas and task lists and had a full calendar from dawn until dusk and then some, with no space for rest. While I had always been proud of my "yes to everything!" enthusiasm, I came to respect the power of a firm but considered and kind "no". I learned that the brain needs to recharge too, and that artful time-management was not about cleverly fitting things in, but filtering stuff out. That rest, meditation and space to mentally float were actually core facets of productivity. This rocked my world. I had always regarded a busy life as eponymous with a fulfilling life. I discovered it was absolutely not so.

The Emotional Epiphany

Probably most important in my journey to burnout mastery, and something that is surprisingly under-addressed in common wellbeing guidance, was the realization that when we compromise our heartfelt values anywhere in our lives – and let me emphasize this again, *anywhere* – we are inwardly contorted with emotional stress whether yet demonstrably visible or not. That any whisper of discontent about any aspect of your life is an intuitive caution that you're suppressing an essential part of you in a damaging way. It's your soul calling you to realign and get back on your truer path. That this unacknowledged stress will be sapping your very essence, debilitating your energy, thoughts and general ability to embrace life authentically. This could be where you live, where you work, who you're married to, what work you do, who your friends are, whatever – if a niggle is rumbling that this situation doesn't feel right, no matter how much you fervently try to ignore it, it's going to erupt later, potentially explosively. Any emotional disquiet causes such subtle but potentially devastating effects laser beaming through your mind, body and soul, that it is only once this aspect is bravely cleansed that you will be able to unleash your best out into the world.

My Impact Journey

In spite of the burnouts, I've had super impact too, realizing dreams and ambitions along the way, steadily and persistently manifesting my success goals. I'll share some favourite highlights here, briefly illustrating where leaning into my passions has taken me over the years before we get into the meat of building your strategies (I call my CV a "chronology of passions explored", is yours?).

My impact story includes founding businesses, being a global corporate executive, passionately creating – writing books, filming vlogs, producing courses and more, certifying in healing therapies, travelling the world for speaking gigs, hosting Flourish retreats and Big Impact workshops inspiring delegates to unleash their brilliance and, most proudly, mothering my four now-all-taller-than-me children.

I'll start just after my second child was born, when I tripped into entrepreneurialism, impassioned by a simple idea to make unique, custom-made, truly personalized gifts (like weaving memories into poetry), which quickly became a pioneering tech business that effectively transformed the personalized gift industry. This was back in the days when consumer confidence in online shopping was just beginning and retailers were hungry to satisfy the fresh demand. Enter, me. The Bespoke Gift Company became an invigorating, thrilling ride where I learned how to excel as a business owner with the added twist of simultaneously raising four children under the age of seven. I self-directed every minute, learning as I went, trusting hunches, and exploring where my ideas and inspiration took me. The company went from trade manufacturing in my garage and nursery to a vast e-commerce platform, from selling a small range of personalized poem products to thousands of gifts with hundreds of artistic gift designers and freelance creatives working for me, from one cute local retail outlet to concessions in high street department stores and a gazillion happy customers. I sold the company a decade later, after what had turned out to be an incredible personal growth period where I proved repeatedly that with the right energy, focus and intention literally anything you dream of is possible. Highlights included showcasing my wares on ITV's *This Morning*, being the only gift manufacturer to make personalized magnetic memo boards in the entire world and selling over 10,000 personalized letters from Father Christmas one year.

Less glitter sprinkled, but perhaps just as impactful, and certainly rich in steady personal development every time, I've navigated the corporate world, applying my skills to companies from burgeoning digital startups with 100 staff to scaling the international advertising industry, ascending to my latest role as a global leader within Publicis Groupe, one of the world's largest communications conglomerates, where I work alongside 110,000 colleagues.

I've written several books, interviewed and cohosted events with some of the most inspiring leaders in business today and launched my international wellbeing business to ignite high performers into their brightest potential, a privilege I'm endlessly grateful for. I've graced stages at Amazon and Google, hosted leadership retreats for companies like Snap and WPP, worked with brands like Spotify and *The New York Times*, brainstormed with Arianna Huffington in her Thrive Global New York City office, and I feel a "pinch me, thank you so much, Universe" rush every time I step in front of an audience, most recently addressing 1,500 people from a dramatic stage in Poland's largest cinema!

Over years of study and hands-on practice with clients, I've certified as an executive coach, hypnotherapist, neurolinguistic practitioner and timeline therapist, been accredited by the International Coaching Federation and am honoured to cultivate clients' dreams with them through my work as a Success Strategist. I've designed a six-step, patented Energy-Scape™ programme, mentoring thousands of women around the world into their best selves through a video series and live workshops. I'm blessed to have hosted female empowerment retreats from my cherished sanctuary of a forever home in Surrey, welcoming hundreds of women to push their personal boundaries (by literally soaring on a zipline! Huge energy stimulant, I tell you!), reflect in tranquil woodland and design their "maximum impact without burnout" lives.

I'm grateful to have won awards from entrepreneur categories to the advertising industry's "Woman of Tomorrow". I've renovated several homes, tenderly navigated divorce after 26 years of togetherness, always given my all, loved hard and laughed a lot.

My biggest achievement, though, is without doubt that I'm a proud and present mother to four vibrant teenagers, raising them single-handedly. Our home is a bustling hive of school blazers, Pot Noodles, body spray, fake tan, weights, odd socks, muddy shoes, endless laundry cycles, broken or missing-when-you-need-them biros, crumbs and cereal flakes on every surface, damp towels, chargers and far too many explosive (and expletive-ridden) gaming meltdowns. With three boys, one girl and a bouncy dalmatian, the energy dynamically flows throughout our English home with the comings and goings of everyone's "mine is the most important" agendas.

I adore the undulation of chaos and calm, and the sheer unpredictability of each moment. Just when the home feels orderly, freshly made soup simmering on the hob, kids nestled in their respective bedrooms and clean uniforms ready for the morning, the dog will vomit all over the plush carpet in the lounge and there's something new to attend to.

On it all rolls. And on and on it will all keep rolling. This I've learned over the years. So I don't sweat the small stuff anymore: the vomit, the spilt milkshake splashed all over the stairs en route to a bedroom, the sibling squabbles, the obscene rap music, the late taxis, the blocked drains, the broken dishwasher, the blown fuses, the dead fish, the shrunk designer t-shirt – "Mum, you've ruined my life!", the smashed frame, the stained sofa, none of it even prompts a raised eyebrow. I've learned to accept the undulations, observing their incessant quirkiness and inevitability, occasionally irked, but generally letting it all melt into the background, because I figure, "This too shall pass". And indeed it does.

Like our home, but without the frenzy, my mind is currently bustling. At the time of writing, I've recently been promoted into another gargantuan corporate role with increased responsibility, budget, targets, team and expectations. I'm ensconced in that steep new-girl learning curve, figuring out how best to apply my strengths to lead growth across the 15,000-strong digital division I'm now overseeing. I'm rereading *The First 90 Days* by Michael D Watkins, intent on making strategic and impactful moves quickly. My wellbeing business continues its ever-accelerating momentum as I pay forward my knowledge around architecting high performance through keynote and dinner speaker bookings, corporate workshops, VIP client sessions and bespoke programmes. I'm nearing completion of another coaching certification (always intent on learning and uplevelling) and have two whopper exams looming. Plus, of course, I'm writing this book, with a tight deadline to completion. My childhood dream of becoming an international published author has materialized, my biggest lifelong wish realized at last and I am abuzz with the thrill of it all!

I appreciate that I've just described a high-volume workload, which isn't for everyone. I also appreciate, however, that you've picked up this book because the title chimed with you and you're a woman who is not afraid of hard work and enjoys reaching for the stars. You're a woman who leans into life with zeal. You are proud to spin numerous plates. You are excited by life and say "yes" a lot. Your life overflows with people, opportunities, fun, work, ideas and invigoration aplenty. You feel busy, your diary is full, your days pass quickly. You're ambitious. You've already tasted or dreamt of success. You know there's more glory ahead, but sometimes as you snuggle into bed, you realize you're absolutely brain-dead, body-zonked exhausted, and you wonder if all of this toil and relentless juggling is worth it.

It is. All of the fizzy living you're doing just needs a system, mindful honing and constructive tweaks here and there to iron away this busy-ness into your highest impact contribution through artful productivity. I firmly believe you can have majestic impact without struggle. With careful strategic application of your efforts directed in the right way, in the right time, in your unique style, you can manifest both your most magnificent ambitions *and* fulfilment all at once. Success and peace can co-exist.

With the humblest sincerity, I can honestly declare that the work, children, love, chaos, deadlines, domesticity and the sheer amount of stuff I describe above bring me peace. It all makes me smile. Within the fullness of my life, with its unpredictability and variety, I feel an overriding, grounding sense of purpose and satisfaction every day. I feel awake, conscious, present and grateful. I feel empowered by choice. For I have indeed chosen this and proactively created this present reality. Today unfurls as a manifestation of those choices and decisions I made yesterday, the day before, the month before and the year before. I get that "Balance" is nonsense when you have a frothy, dynamic life. Yes, I do a lot, but in my time, on my terms, in my way. I love my lot. I glide through the roll, very steadily, very deliberately and with excitement and effervescent joy along the way. I have worked very hard to get to this point. As my burnout tales describe, it has taken years to finesse my ability to consistently achieve my ambitions, and do my thing, without compromising myself.

My wish, and the reason I'm writing this book, is to share my lessons and endow you with the strategies that will imbue you with the joy you deserve as you roll through life. It's up to you how much you take on and how far you choose to stretch, but with practice it will become progressively easier, with success becoming more readily accessible without inner or outer friction. After years of struggling, I am free; and I firmly believe I am living proof that a rewarding, abundant life does not need to be excruciatingly tough.

I will not lie to you; it is not always easy. I still occasionally hit a wall and feel lost sometimes. Imposter syndrome strikes, nervous fears bubble up, inner-child wounds stunt me, my voice shakes, external bombs explode, derailing me unexpectedly. I still get tired. I still get wired. I question my own substance and ability to show up as I've promised I will. But, nowadays, I understand this is all just part of life's undulating flow and I can detach from its drama and stop it from inhibiting me and my progress. I know exactly when and how to pause, rejuvenate, recharge and break from the doing to honour the stillness of being, and then get on with getting on again. I've found the way to have what I've crafted as my personal "all" and I religiously implement the eight strategies you will learn in these pages constantly.

Of course, I know I'm not perfect and am still learning fervently as I go. We all are. I also know perfectionism is not a beneficial nor sustainable trait when obsessively clutched, so don't cling to it as a holy grail (but it can be deliciously propelling when cleverly harnessed, more on that later!). I don't for one moment want you to shrink any of your dreams, park any aspirations, or keep any of your true essence in the shadows because you're afraid you're not enough. Too many of us do. Let's not. Ever. Anymore. Please. My intention for you is to harness your unique drives and passions with zest, so your work, relationships, wealth and overall life energize you and those around you, and that, as you step into your realm of highest contribution, graceful productivity and impact, it is never destructive nor self-sabotaging.

The Choice Paradox

So, what about you? Perhaps you've got young children and you're juggling nursery drop-offs, school runs plus a newly enforced Return to Office protocol. Or maybe you're an entrepreneur, invigorated by your acorn of an idea now flourishing into that oak, delicately balancing ageing parents and children as well as the business expansion. Maybe you're single, energized, dependent-free but rising so fast in your organization that the daily requests and pressure are spiralling into 100-hour work weeks and it's hard to fit your spin classes in. Maybe your kids have flown the nest, your big dream is bubbling and it's time to shift priorities away from domesticity back into the business arena and you're terrified. Maybe your partner is sick and you need to work and care for the little people as well as you both. Maybe you're freshly divorced and surging with Personal Reinvention Fantasies but paralysed with how to begin. Maybe you're at uni, overwhelmed by part-time work as well as the lectures, assignment deadlines and distracting flatmates. Maybe your ambition is being suffocated by too many priorities distracting and diluting you all at once.

Whatever your circumstance, today's "Age of Acceleration", with its unprecedented technological progress, is full of pressure for women. It's an age of accelerated choice. And too much choice inevitably leads to overwhelm. On the one hand, yes, there's a wonder to our modern working life with its "have it all" potential, equal opportunities, shared parental leave, female STEM (Science, Technology, Engineering, Maths) initiatives, childcare incentives, entrepreneur grants, global villages, working-from-home flexibility and so on, but for all of the women in boardrooms today, championing higher/equal salaries and leading by cool-sneakered or stiletto-heeled example, outside of the office bubble a million and one other choices to make, manage and lead. Having it all has come to mean plenty in work and out. Yes, we're empowered. Yes, we're decision-makers. Yes, we can call so very many shots. But with all this empowerment comes the practicality of ever more weight on our shoulders, as we still hold the bulk of the domestic load and childcare responsibilities for the main part too.

Just take a moment to consider the choices we face. Not just where we work, but where we live, where we educate our children, who we marry, if we marry, if we conceive (whose egg or sperm even?), if we spend time with our parents, if we emigrate, if we study while we work, if we study even after school, if we run a side hustle, if we cook, if we take the bins out, if we work, if we work out, if we donate money or blood, if we eat sugar or go vegan, if we watch Netflix or Amazon, if we vote, if we drive, if we worship a god, if, if, if.

We proudly and defiantly boss our lives, making the big and little decisions, but with each, we gradually start to suffer their multifaceted, subtly emerging consequences. The "have it all" fallacy gradually presents an energy crisis, a burnout emergency that poses the question "have all what, exactly?"

The Burnout Saga

In 2019, the World Health Organization classified burnout as a global epidemic, acknowledging that industrialized society is in serious trouble. (And this was before the pandemic, when new levels of mental-health trauma hit ever-worsening lows.) Burnout is calculated to cost the global economy in the region of 1 trillion dollars per year in lost work time,[3] and it's estimated that 75–90 per cent of healthcare costs are lifestyle-based and preventable. Some 88 per cent of UK workers have experienced burnout since 2020[4] and Glassdoor's economic research team have established that the UK's burnout cases more than doubled from 2021 to 2022.[5] Britain has a staggering 2.5 million people economically inactive because of the rise of long-term sickness (up by 400,000 since the pandemic).[6] Sadly, the burnout trends hit women hardest, with 43 per cent of female leaders experiencing burnout compared to 31 per cent of male leaders.[7] It's a sorry plight for too many of us trying to make our dent in the world.

A further disappointing twist is the revelation that, despite the prevalent growth of burnout affliction, as working societies, we're ludicrously passive at structuring our lives around optimal work and rest. Bizarrely, research shows we're not even using up the entirety of our allocated holiday allowance. Despite three-quarters of UK workers believing annual leave is an effective way to reduce burnout, last year only three in five employees used all their holiday entitlement, and one in five workers aged under 25 took no holiday at all.[8] We're basically burnout bonkers!

However, organizations are introducing wellbeing initiatives aplenty and every shareholder letter includes a "People First" pledge, but I firmly believe true change starts with individual accountability (like taking our holiday!). Burnout can be avoided when we personally decide to avert it. Period.

Recognizing Burnout's Grips

Let's do a little deep dive into how burnout feels. What are the signs and symptoms? Well, in my years of research, personal experience and client evidence, it starts with a pervasive feeling of overwhelm. There's a sense of not having enough time to get on top of things, a little flurry of panic as we look at our to-do list, then up across our wider stream of life demands, and the list doesn't even fit onto one page anymore. We need multiple lists, and they're all long, and it's all just a little bit hard to prioritize. That's a clue that things are going awry. When you're attacking your to-do list in war mode, this is a sign you are slipping out of your healthy and balanced state of being. Warning sign number one.

Sign number two: you start dropping balls. Perhaps you are managing the workflow at the office, but you forgot about the school trip, so your beloved spends the day alone in the library (true story). Or maybe home life is calm, but you realize too late that you inadvertently missed an entire section of your work presentation just as you walk into the boardroom. Or maybe you're on the train, look down and suddenly spot yesterday's knickers protruding from your trouser ankle (also a true story). These are the signs of cognitive overwhelm.

Foggy thinking starts dominating. Your keys are in the fridge between the blueberries and avocadoes and you're losing your power-woman grip.

Sign three: you feel physically exhausted. Anxiety dominates your wakeful thoughts, distracting you from efficient productivity. Challenges feel insurmountable and enlarge into all-consuming disasters. Bedtime sees you comatose within moments, yet at risk of insomnia, with even more fatigue the following day. There's no burst of rejuvenation in your 24-hour rhythm and you turn to artificial energy boosts in desperation as you strive to cope with demand after never-ending, nerve-jangling demand.

Sign four is the crashing crescendo where body and mind give up. It may manifest as a nasty virus committing you to bed for a few days, or it could be something much more serious and debilitating. At this point your brain and body have resigned from duty. The onslaught has been too extreme, your nervous system too strung out for too long. (If you feel this describes you right now, please urgently prioritize yourself and your health by consulting a doctor asap to stay safe and well.)

The body always knows the score. The expectation to be "always on" is unrealistic and needs challenging. Radically. Health is absolutely the only wealth, and if we fail to put our metaphorical oxygen masks on first, we're not going to be having any impact at all, beyond wearing out our woolly bed socks. It's up to us to recognize these dangerous descents into burnout and adjust our lifestyles and thinking to address them. We're going to learn how in the following pages. With conscious planning, I believe burnout is absolutely combatable, but I want us to focus on prevention rather than war. This book is about stepping into graceful productivity not battle zones, be they inner or outer. No conflict anywhere please. Harmony is the goal.

You Hold All the Power

Modern life presents constant disruption and challenge, but within this lies so much opportunity and potential. Be ready for change. It's up to each one of us to adapt to our circumstances to ensure we thrive and not, as the cliché goes, merely survive. We can direct change ourselves, more prolifically than at any other time in human history, but it all starts from within. Once you clarify who you are, what matters most to you and what you actually want, you prime yourself to unleash your work most powerfully into the world. You will never have the impact you desire if you dance through life reactively, passively or in a chaotic manner. Unsustainable speed, lack of a plan and a victim mindset are also common pitfalls.

No, the path to your greatest self and greatest life lies in your ability to stop being swept up by the tornado swirling around you, to stop drifting nonchalantly downstream, to take charge, refocus and rekindle all those glimmering passions simmering inside you. Remove any excuses you've baked into your daily thinking and truly step into your most positive impact yet. Your special rays of brilliance deserve to shine bright in this exquisite life of yours.

This book is about your dreams, seizing them and making them real. Yourself. On your terms, in your way, in your style, in your time. In these pages you will never read about someone or something else having power over your happiness, determining your success, dictating what you can or can't pursue. You will never read about ways to limit yourself by depending on others for your life's ambitions to unfurl.

No, this book is about your glossiest dreams becoming ever more wonder-full as we bring them into vibrant technicolour. As you feel into your desires – elaborating on them, fine-tuning them, getting behind the shiny idealism into why they feel so compelling – you will figure out exactly what your callings are about. Then you can proactively design plans to honour those tingles of "What if ...?" and make them deliciously, tangibly, "Let's get cracking'ly" real.

This book is about action, energy and effort working toward achieving your biggest ideas and boldest imaginings. It is about feeling the tantalizing progress of being plugged in to what you know is your liveliest potential. It's feeling harmoniously aligned in head and heart, knowing you're on the right path, doing the most soulfully resonant things that make you explode with joy and sleep peacefully at night, replete with enriched relationships, vitality and the gentle satisfaction of a day lived with meaning and purpose.

And within all this, there is no striving, no suffering, no interminable struggle. Yes, there will be rewarding graft, and invigorating good stress bursts here and there, but I know you're reading this book because you're not afraid of exertion and pushing beyond your comfort zone.

For fun, I invite you also to trust in little fluttery senses of the magical, which I hope you'll start to notice. I see and feel magic everywhere. Why not? Call me mad or join me in relishing the miraculous. As Einstein guided, "There are only two ways to live your life. One is as though nothing is a miracle. The other is as though everything is a miracle." I choose the latter. Are you with me?

You Are a Creator

We are all in constant evolution, creating and recreating. Not one cell in your body today was there when you were born. Our cells renew unconsciously and our hearts beat without concerted effort. Every thought creates a ripple of either good or bad out into matter. Language has potency to create or destroy. What happens when we apply conscious intention, thought and action can be truly transformational. I believe in the magical potential that exists when we conscientiously direct our inner and outer worlds positively.

We each hold the power and grace to redefine our personal success map and take action to create a new, desired reality that includes more calm flow and optimized productivity. The eight strategies you will discover in this book will guide you to fulfil your wishes and contribute in meaningful ways. This is a book about stepping out of any plight and into peaceful progress. It's about leaving a legacy, sparkling your way through life with kindness and positivity, and waking up motivated, stimulated and purposeful every day. It's about energy and vitality and mostly about reclaiming who you are, knowing what your gifts are and using them to full effect, because at last, you know why you're here and what you need to do.

As a high-performance coach, I work intimately with my clients exploring both the spoken and unspoken, the energy present and what I refer to as "the energy of possibility". As a businesswoman, I do this too (but, shh, please don't tell anyone as it wasn't in my job description). While coaching by its very nature invites clients to tap into more of their "whole-self" (the entirety of your glorious, innermost essence) and to work with "heartfelt desire" (doing what feels right), my experience has taught me that when our work worlds are equally infused with whole-self stuff and earnest wishes, then we all get a lot further, a lot quicker, a lot more impactfully and, delightfully, a lot more harmoniously. When we weave integrity into how we operate in the world, both personally and professionally, progress, impact and joy are omnipresent.

This book brings together all of those lessons for you, in one place. You will learn how to respect and revere yourself inwardly and outwardly, honouring your unique talents, interests and spirit with tenderness and self-awareness. You will learn how to courageously share your gifts and how to extend compassion and understanding toward others. I promise that when you do, your world will fill with even more magnificence. An expansion will occur.

Being plugged in to your flow is a buzzy thrill, animated with the pulse of your universal destiny. Your work will become prolific in volume and quality, abundantly pouring forth. Your relationships will deepen and become more enriching and interesting. Your sense of success will settle satisfactorily at last, as enchantment in the here and now melts all that stress and fear. And finally, I promise you, waves of blissful inner peace will pervade as the magic of life enshrouds you. All at once, Big Impact, without even the remotest glimmer of burnout, will be your fantastic, exhilarating, reality. You will come home.

THE DESIRE TO MATTER

"Every moment there are a million miracles happening around you: a flower blossoming, a bird tweeting, a bee humming, a raindrop falling, a snowflake wafting along the clear evening air. There is magic everywhere. If you learn how to live it, life is nothing short of a daily miracle."

— Sadhguru

I have a diary from 1990 in my loft. It's battered and tatty, swollen with rave flyers, gig tickets, fading photos and pen-pal letters wedged between ink-adorned pages chronicling my sixteenth year. This one relic, sandwiched between a wobbly stack of similar journals, stands out because of the magazine tear sheet I stuck to its cover all those years ago. At aged 16, I privately decided this image depicted the me I wanted to be. This image symbolized my ambitions and would be the guiding light to take me into my boldest and brightest future. It struck such a deep chord that it became my front cover for the year. I connected to the image, and I wanted my subconscious to absorb and own it.

The photograph captures a snow-white trouser-suited businesswoman in a city scene. She's oozing radiance, luminous in confidence and power, an olive-skinned brunette with thick, wavy shoulder-length locks. She's striding purposefully, smiling. She embodies success, independence and happiness. She's probably just left a board meeting she chaired and is heading to her latest book-signing before she swoops up her children for snuggles and love. I see her as a woman as playful as she is professional, as serene as she is serious, as intellectual as she is inspiring. I decided that she epitomized who I would become. I would be that woman one day. I would have the impact she had on me.

This image enchanted me then and, as I re-examine it 30 years later, it enchants me again, triggering a "well whadayaknow" kind of smile and eye twinkle. I've just today delivered a keynote in the bustling heart of London's West End, wearing a snow-white trouser suit, hair gently curled, my olive skin luminous courtesy of Charlotte Tilbury. I feel deliciously serene, joyful, purposeful, confident and successful. I signed copies of my last book for members of the audience who queued for over an hour to meet me – *serious wow* – and headed back to my West London office to host my monthly town hall meeting before later cocooning into the warm glow of home with my four children. I feel independent, professional and inspiring. With a wave of incredulity, I realize I fit my teenage image of success. I bask in a delicate dewy wonderment that I made the big impact I planned, exactly as I'd planned to.

Now, I'm not saying the advice in this book will take 30 years to take effect. Nope, we're going to get you there a lot faster. This little "well blow me down" moment is simply to demonstrate the magnitude of impact possible when you have a clear vision and apply yourself determinedly.

Ever since reading Barbara Taylor Bradford's *A Woman of Substance* aged 12, I was inspired to believe that I too would be a woman of substance and positively impact the world through my work. I too would live with integrity and awareness, follow my heart, lead with kindness, love with passion and, of course, make a whole lot of money. Babs and her rags-to-riches tale excited me with the potential of what is possible when hard work and an earnestness to do the right thing are put into action. She sparked my ambition. I remain just as motivated today to always lean into life with ardour.

Defined by the Cambridge Dictionary as "A strong wish to achieve something,"[9] ambition can also be perilous. There's a delicate balance to ambition: to stay positive and not become self-destructive or alienated. I meet too many clients in my coaching practice who suffer from workaholism, addicted to punchy daily progress, grinding themselves into the ground. Similarly, I have met too many business peers along the way who have tangled ever-swelling egos with ambition, ruining relationships, opportunities and, alas, even their personalities.

Ambition is a positive thing when it is about making progress every day toward a goal, feeling determined, creative and impassioned. It breeds energy, enthusiasm and output. However, if that ambition becomes all-consuming, driving an unhealthy lifestyle, imbalanced productivity and eventual burnout, this is purely negative. And when someone's ambitions are realized and their ego engorges, it's unpleasant to witness and excruciating to experience. Success is far healthier and magnetic when doused in humility.

When ambition sees you progressing toward your goals while enjoying the growth and the stimulation along the way, the journey as well as the destination, you are sampling the juice of life! The trick is figuring out what it is that you want to create and what will bring you joy and satisfaction as you advance into your dreams. We'll get to that in these pages.

There's also the question of timing. JK Rowling didn't write *Harry Potter* until she was in her 30s. Vera Wang didn't design her first wedding dress until she was in her 40s. Arianna Huffington was 54 when she launched *The Huffington Post*. And Colonel Sanders of KFC-founder fame had his idea after "retirement" at age 65! Most hardy, relentlessly optimistic entrepreneurs finally succeed in their mid-40s. It's a small minority of widely heralded inventors, business leaders, politicians, athletes, performers and intellectual prodigies who identified and followed a calling from childhood (or were cajoled and Tiger-parented into their golfing majesty or the like, pun intended). The majority of us stumble and fumble our way into working life, often having lengthy, meandering careers before we pivot to follow a passion, usually once the mid-life niggle erupts into a bubbling lava; enter Melissa's Magnificent Muffin Metropole, Belinda's Bikini Range, every eBay vintage clothing store ever, most Balinese Surf Shacks and an awful lot of "consultancies".

Our work experience varies according to our life path, family lineage, geography, demography, gender and capabilities, and in addition to this, we're witnessing the evolution of work once again. Our fourth industrial revolution is impacting how we work as well as what we do. Technology enables hybrid workplaces, squiggly careers, side hustles, communities everywhere and an unprecedented pace of output and connectivity.

What is unchanged, however, is the burning desire twinkling in each and every one of us to do work that matters, work that feels rewarding and meaningful as well as providing us security to live comfortably. We're wired to want our work to have impact. Primeval neurology programmed us to demonstrate our value to the tribe, to protect us from ostracization. If we were outcast for what was perceived as redundant, seemingly nonessential work, we wouldn't survive. It became essential to demonstrate to our community that our work was enhancing life for the collective. We needed to, and just as passionately wanted to, belong and prove our usefulness daily. The work we did needed to matter so that we mattered.

And so it still is. Beyond the cave-dweller graft, us lovely homo sapiens were also gifted with brains designed to create, not just do. It's our imagination that sets us apart from animals and what keeps us endlessly advancing through the ages. Progress is innate in all of us, not just something to read about in history books. We make impact and thus individually and collectively progress.

So, impact can stem from wanting to belong, but what else triggers the desire for impact? It can be the ego's craving for applause, a spiritual quest or the desire to continue a family legacy. It could be sheer enthusiasm for a craft or talent, honing it to perfection and launching it out into the world, as per my writing forays (first short story penned aged 8).

How impact manifests varies in form and size. One person's impact might be encouraging more women in the West to have home births; another's to parent so devotedly that all her children flutter out into the world confident, courageous and kind; another's to create gigantic bronze sculptures; and another's to exemplify compassionate leadership in the finance sector.

I once shared the stage with an incredible man, Hugh Evans, also known as the Global Citizen, who devotes his life to eradicating worldwide poverty. Inspired on a school trip to the Philippines at age 14, he was aghast at the appalling living conditions of his respective Filipino peers and has been a man on a (hugely successful) mission since, with over 1.2 billion lives positively impacted, multiple government policies established and millions and millions of dollars of charitable donations raised. His contribution to our planet is vast.[10]

You'll meet more amazing men and women trailblazing similarly inspiring paths throughout this book as they share their impact journeys, ambitions and guiding principles. You'll also meet clients working their way into impact at different stages of their journeys. (These are fictional women based on amalgamations of amalgamations of real-life case studies to illuminate strategies, emotions and responses. Confidentiality is rigidly and respectfully unbreakable in my coaching practice. Thank you to all my clients, your stories remain your own.)

In all its variety, it is essential to understand that impact ultimately feels satisfying only when it meets an individual's sense of meaning and fulfilment. When the work that we do is tied to a purpose that resonates deeply within us, we are propelled to contribute more and, in turn, do indeed have more impact. Studies have shown that when soldiers are released from the military, they often trip into depression (non-PTSD related) because the army's communal thrust is gone.[11] The satisfaction of contributing collectively (albeit to war), united through common agenda, was more invigorating and enlivening than the mundanity of solitary civilian life devoid of "protect thy nation" purpose.

When children dream of their future selves, they dream fantastical, limitless dreams. They will save the orangutans, be pioneering palaeontologists, revolutionizing inventors, inspiring leaders, brave astronauts, remarkable scientists. They will be busy. They will change or protect the world. They will work hard in honour of their dreams. They will be happy and kind. Children naturally think big, follow what interests them, are saintly in how they show up in future projections, and assume that's how life will unfold. There's real wisdom here.

But despite our youthful intentions, life happens and external influences contort our dreams. Our vision becomes blotted by layers of ever-sprouting, often self-limiting belief systems. That spirited ambition to be something, or someone, often becomes cloudy. We may be streamed into polarized lanes at school where we are labelled "academic" or "creative". Our families may pressure us to conform to their lineage as lawyers or medics, say, or they make nonchalant comments such as, "Don't be silly, you're not [smart/funny/confident] enough to do that!" Our self-esteem is diminished, as what others think and say about us makes us feel paranoid and scared. And there are other pressures, particularly for women: from staying at home and raising the family, right through to the glass-ceiling inequalities and exhausting reality of 131 years to close the gender pay gap.[12] Yes, you read that correctly.

All too often, we emerge into adulthood with childhood intentions buried, as we fall into careers that society and our families deem appropriate, popping out of college into the first open arms to catch us (aka our first successful interview). We tentatively step onto that bottom rung of the career ladder. Even if we have determinedly followed a passion or interest, we still slot lockstep into where society affords us opportunity and hook onto that ladder gratefully. From there, we all too often settle into a comfortable trudge upward while the rest of life distracts us with all the glossy, alluring stuff outside of work, like love, marriage, children, home, friends, fun, fashion, fitness and any more fabulously alluring Fs that tantalize us in our 20s.

Procter & Gamble conducted a Global Dreams Index Survey (a commercial endeavour to sell more of their skincare brand SK-II)[13] to ascertain the level of life fulfilment in women across the world. Surveying over 5,000 women in 14 countries spanning 6 continents, the results were disheartening as they led to the crushing (if deliberately attention-grabbing) PR claim: "Over half the world's women population have given up on their dreams". Reasons cited included lack of financial support and lack of confidence. Western countries were not as bleak as the global average, with 59 per cent of Western women apparently actively pursuing dreams. That's still a whole lot of wasted dreams.

Female ambition is reportedly on the rise, however, with a 2023 Women in the Workplace McKinsey & LeanIn study[14] finding US women "more hungry to ascend" post-pandemic and rising in C-suite boardroom numbers, up 28 per cent year on year. Flexible working is benefiting women, especially mothers. Fact.

But still, study after study tells us that most businesses are not holding on to talented and skilled women after they have children. The UK's 2023 Careers After Babies Report showed that 85 per cent of mothers leave the full-time workforce within three years of having their first child, with 19 per cent leaving the workforce altogether for good.[15] More wastage.

This book is written in the hope that no more flickering dreams fade, that more pulsing ambition is seized and no brilliant talent goes to waste for fear of burnout. Ambition and peace can coexist. This is success.

Creation is the Secret of Success

Today's mainstream, populist culture celebrates unhealthy versions of success, oriented around financial and material gain; think insta-bragging "self-made" entrepreneurs, posed jet-set glamour, get-rich-quick schemes and vain Kardashian-esque hype. But this is vacuous, shallow and appealing to egocentricity, with these projections thrust out into the world devoid of soulful substance. These trending icons and representations of apparently "having it all" might trigger envy – oh that butt filler, those MTV cribs, the bank balance of that 17-year-old Bitcoin trader extraordinaire – but they do not create inspired action. They create hollow desire and a sense of lack. They do not offer action or opportunity for the wistful voyeur. The core problem with this shallow approach is that there's a *take, take, take* culture, swirling with entitlement, instead of fostering what really matters: to give, create and contribute.

In scientific terms, hedonic theory is at play. Hedonism is our instinctive motivation to pursue and create pleasure (comfort) and avoid pain (discomfort). This is what drives endless psychological expansion. But within our endless pursuit of happiness – the master quest of humanity – is what's known as the Hedonic Treadmill. This is when all the new materialistic stuff and achievements that initially felt amazing quickly fade into "Hmm, I think I need another designer bag now" or "Yeah, yeah, that award was so last month, thanks. Let's get a more prestigious one next ..." Each uplevelling soon becomes the norm, and then the desire for bigger hits hard again. The pursuit of expansion is core to each of us. We will forever chase more life experience, knowledge, growth and, ever-pressingly as we mature, impact. The magic, however, lies in the pursuit itself, way above the achievements.

Motivation is where the striving begins. Without motivation, we won't even start pursuing our ambitions. How rewarding achievement feels depends on where the motivation originated from in the first place. Generally, motivation is driven by either one of two forces – an intrinsic urge to master an ability, or an extrinsic urge to gain recognition and status. Think of extrinsic motivations as driving toward something outside of ourselves, and intrinsic within.

Intrinsic motivations are always resonant with our values, so pursuing and achieving them will invariably feel more satisfying than those extrinsic success metrics like money and power. When we chase any version of success oriented toward status and symbols thereof, not only is there risk of failure, rejection, competition, etc., but even once the goal is smashed, this type of success eventually feels shallow. Think of the old "money can't buy you happiness" adage and many a midlife crisis pivot (career, relationship, hair colour or otherwise!). Regardless of commensurate financial reward, and however high the bank balance is creeping, if the goal isn't an intrinsic one, you won't feel satisfied.

Importantly and interestingly though, motivation is also affected by whether or not our goal is promotion-oriented or prevention-oriented, whether we are compelled to chase success for the sheer thrill of the goal, or to avoid the shame of failure. Pay attention to this as you work through this book, as you want to hone your goals and motivations around the promotion-oriented type. Promotion-oriented motivation is deemed adaptive and healthy because we learn as we go, build skill in the seeming struggle and enjoy the striving as much as the achievement (if not more). On the other hand, a prevention-oriented attitude is maladaptive because we are driven to succeed only to avoid failure. An entirely different beast. Maladaptive motivation can be exhausting as we become riddled with anxiety, fearing any threat of failure. Instead of pleasure in the pursuit, there's panic.

So, when you look at your goals, are they promotion- or prevention-oriented? Is your approach to success adaptive or maladaptive? Katherine Morgan Schafler, queen of perfectionism management, suggests it's far more enriching when we adapt from the inside out, stating, "As you learn the skills to adapt inwardly, to *your* version of success, based on *your* values; your striving takes on more excitement, more meaning and – most significantly – more joy."[16] So, when we're adaptive and playing to win, we are fuelled by optimism and reward-seeking, but when playing *not to lose*, fear means we'll experience more stress and worry and thus risk burning out. When doing work because it feels satisfying and aligned with our values, the doing itself gives us pleasure because we know on the other side of the apparent struggle lies the ability to soar. So the "struggle" by its very nature isn't painful, it's just effort, and effort feels worthwhile. We feel wealthy through sheer pursuit.

It's the maladaptive amongst us, the women who are prevention-oriented and predominantly extrinsically motivated, who may endlessly seek a version of "other-dependent" success, finding the pursuit itself stressful and, once the goal is accomplished, that there's a heavy emptiness, an uncomfortable itch of "Is that all?" It's baffled therapists, psychiatrists and researchers aplenty, why when the goal is achieved it doesn't always feel satisfying. Described as an "inverse ratio" between success and insecurity, if there's been maladaptive striving at play, once we get the material success we've been obsessed with for so long, that final accomplishment can actually increase anxiety rather than feel satisfying. As Schlafer states, "The experience of winning forces you to realize there are no substitutes for self-worth or presence. Not one."[17] Success is thus very much an internal state deeply connected to self-worth and how intentionally we are pursuing our overarching purpose in life, intrinsically motivated and promotion-oriented.

There's bounty in impassioned effort and becoming besotted with the doing and creating. Once you're empowered by your motivation perspectives, inner goals aligned with outer effort, and are persistently diligent, worshipping effort as though it's your religion, please don't ever then waste any energy feeling jealous of those who seemingly instantaneously get what they want, those "overnight successes" or the "got rich quick-ers". As happiness and leadership professor Dr Tal Ben-Shahar puts it: "Talent and success without the moderating effect of failure can be detrimental, even dangerous."[18] Think of the privileged few who are born into wealth who fall into addictions or obesity, lustfully living with every whim indulged, never seemingly happy, always on the edge of emptiness. They haven't learned resilience. Haven't had to persevere, overcome adversity and get gritty. And so they keep seeking thrills, pills and anything to build a feeling of substantiality. Don't envy them; they secretly envy you.

Within my eight Big Impact strategies, my hope is that you learn to find joy in the sheer creation of you and your beautiful life. That you experience a sweet satisfaction in the doing as much as the having. The joy of work, I believe, lies in both the substance of what you achieve and how you achieve it, not the riches and the lifestyle the achievement brings you (although of course that's a silk-ribboned embellishment wrapped around the gift of life too). Ambition is an invigorating, propelling force that lies in your creation of things that matter to you, and exuberantly putting your heart and soul into creating is a rush. A strong wish to achieve something, to create something; that's ambition. And, funnily enough, when that ambition is focused in accordance with your values, that is when wealth consequently abounds anyhow. Life's truest, purest treasure lies within creating not consuming. And I promise that where there's devout belief and pride in creation, there's motivation and energy in abundance. Chasing gold is not the point; it's creating it. You can create your own magic.

What You'll Learn

I invite you now to journey into deepening your passions, honouring your values, prioritizing with your heart and living authentically always. When you respect your innermost substance, stand your ground and follow your instincts with solid systems, life becomes simpler, you become more effective, happier and fulfilled. You have your biggest impact without burnout. I know you will soar.

The eight strategies taught in the pages ahead will build your courage and confidence, expanding you, the beautiful ambitious soul that you are, in the directions that matter most uniquely to you. After implementing these simple steps, you'll feel energized, motivated and become even more high-performing in the most invigorated ways. The strategies will lead you into your new reality of being a conscious creator, no longer a passive consumer, and guide you on how to live and breathe graceful productivity – never flurried, burnout-inducing doing.

In that sweet intersection of what you're good at, what you do effortlessly and what the world wants, sparkles your guiding star. We've all got one. Do the work to stabilize yourself mentally, emotionally and physically then expand into your most powerful, vibrant self and experience the magnificence unfurling.

The eight foundational and expansive realms are: Energy, Mindset, Purpose, Time, Work, Connection, Wealth and Fulfilment. These are divided into two parts. Energy, Mindset, Purpose and Time are your Foundational Imperatives. Once you've stabilized those, your foundations are set, and you are ready for your Expansion Phenomenon to occur through Work, Connection, Wealth and Fulfilment.

The Foundational Imperatives

In **Energy**, we will explore how to respect your natural rhythms and energetic flows across your body, mind and soul to ensure you work with your energy instead of pushing against it, and learn ways to ground yourself in times of stress, maintaining graceful balance.

In **Mindset**, we will embrace the adventurer in you, liberating you from limiting beliefs, expanding into a growth mindset, establishing accountability and a state of curiosity and self-awareness.

In **Purpose**, we will discover why a meaningful life is healthier and happier than a hedonistic one. You will discover how to create your life purpose, by identifying and honouring your values, ensuring they inform your decision-making, habits and your very vision of yourself.

In **Time**, we will investigate the perils of joyless urgency and busywork, learning how to fall back in love with time, flowing with it expansively instead of chasing it and packing it to the brim. You'll learn where and how to work optimally, and the power of subjective attention in realizing your dreams.

The Expansion Phenomenon

In **Work**, your professional contribution will abound fluidly as your sense of self and your value tighten. You will confidently produce high-quality work in abundance, having fun, knowing where to focus, how to manage stress and never dilute your innate gifts.

In **Connection**, you'll learn to understand the power held within your Positive Relational Energy; this is how you make people feel, and how to positively influence your impact objectives and expand your network. We will dive into a 101 of communication, how to build your own brand and perfect the art of public speaking.

In **Wealth**, you will learn the intricacies of self-esteem and self-identity and the importance of chasing your own success ideologies, never anyone else's. You will cultivate a positive money mindset to encourage abundance to stream forth.

In **Fulfilment**, you will refine what contentment means to you, spiritually and emotionally, honouring your integrity by speaking and honouring your truth. You will listen to your intuition's whispers and practice presence and gratitude.

How to Use This Book

- Each chapter will examine the different life realm and why it is important, inwardly and outwardly. The explorations within each life realm will evolve into solid strategies that will help you identify and make decisions that will transform your impact in that particular area.
- Every chapter includes a variety of Big Impact Reflection exercises. These are designed to process what you're learning through your own lens. You will be asked to consider the topic from every angle with application to your own life. The majority of the reflections end with a dedicated visualization of what embodied enlightenment in this area feels like and means for you. So, with every exercise you have the opportunity to both consciously and subliminally step into a place of expansion where bigger and better impact is natural.
- I invite you to indulge in these reflections with your favourite things that nourish your soul, such as a candle, aromatherapy scents, a special cushion, your coziest socks and, as best as you can, organize losing yourself in your own, uninterruptable, private world for the expansion moments.

- You will not necessarily consider all the reflections essential for you. That's fine. They may be useful later. Do those you are drawn to and those you recognize as most pivotal to release you from any significant "stuckness" you may be experiencing.
- You will need a journal for these reflections. I suggest as a second step toward committing to your life of Big Impact Without Burnout (reading this book is your first step, thank you!), that you make this journal special, a new one if you can, and ensure you have a favourite pen. If you prefer typing that's okay, you do you, but physically putting pen to paper improves focus, absorption and memory, so is more transformational.
- Occasionally, I will reference deepening and expanding your reflections by listening to meditations or visualizations I have created for you. This is complementary, optional work and part of a suite of free supplementary resources available for download on my website biancabest.com if you choose to go beyond this book.
- Each strategy includes a summary expansion grid, describing where you've moved from and to, encouraging you to step into the positivity of expansion through affirmative mental programming, which will also accelerate your growth.
- You will learn from inspiring role models, client stories and my own life experience, whenever illuminating.
- Each chapter consecutively builds on the chapter before, establishing and unleashing your potential through positive decision-making and action declarations.

Part One invites you to make Decision Pledges. Part Two solidifies commitment and timelines with Priority Actions. Then conclusively, at the end of the eight strategies, all your work comes together in a celebratory crescendo with the creation of your 12-month Big Impact Without Burnout Master Plan – a powerful, exciting and inspiring visual display of exactly what you intend to manifest!

WHY IMPACT REQUIRES STRATEGY

"When you do things from your soul, you feel a river moving in you, a joy."
— Rumi

Deciding to divorce was, without doubt, the toughest decision I've ever made. It took six years, endless counselling sessions, heart-breaking conversations and shattering, challenging consequences, but once the decision was finally made, both my ex-husband and I felt a sense of relief, which almost enshrouded the devastating sadness. The interminable mire of that indecision over so many years, oscillating backward and forward from "should we, shouldn't we, what's right, what's wrong, what about you/me/the kids", took its toll on us both physically and mentally. Ultimately, we mutually came to the final decision from a place of integrity. We knew we could look our children earnestly in the eyes and say, "We didn't take this decision lightly."

Big decisions dramatically altering life's course require significant thought, time and energy. We need space to consider all options, assess all information and evaluate all potential future scenarios. In business, big decisions often need to be made rapidly, affecting whole organizations, risking entire product lines, shareholder value, company stability and more. There's an impetus in the work arena to decide quickly to facilitate progress. The more we elongate the process of decision-making itself, the more we will delay advancement, sometimes usefully – for example, we need to be 100 per cent sure France is the right country to emigrate to – sometimes detrimentally, but always with impact.

We make an average of 35,000 decisions a day and 90 per cent of those decisions are the same as the day before.[19] "Shall I have sugar in my tea?", "Shall I take the lift or stairs?", "Do I need to wash my hair?". As we proceed through our days, we enter into decision fatigue; our willpower and energy are depleted, and we find it harder to make good, positive decisions. Layer in the larger, more impactful decisions such as, "Should I pivot the business?", "Should I leave him?", "Should I buy that house?", and there's a lot of energy expended just in deciding, never mind creating and delivering great work, great parenting, and the rest.

Studies of judicial decision-making have identified that in 65 per cent of cases assessed in the morning, judges grant parole, dropping to a moody 0 per cent by the end of the day.[20] The judges' brains gradually become more mentally depleted, worn to exhaustion through all the analysing, evaluating and deciding, so the outcomes for those end-of-day prisoners are already negatively biased merely on account of their afternoon time slot. The judges will invariably be crashing into decision fatigue.

Think of your own resolve upon waking not to have that glass of wine, bowl of pasta, Netflix binge – but how by 8pm, after all your clever working, parenting, arbitrating, strategizing, deciding, deciding and deciding, you unconsciously slide into doing exactly that which you had mentally pledged not to do earlier. The tank is empty, so we default to the easy option and gorge.

Neuroscience has identified that the higher your IQ, the more energy you expend solving challenging problems, so apparently you actually think harder the cleverer you are. For the majority of us, brain crunching uses up 20 per cent of the body's energy each day, 86 billion neurons firing backward and forward.[21] Thinking takes effort and drains energetic supply. This is the reason why you'll hear lots of celebrity entrepreneurs and Forbes 100 stalwarts barking on about minimizing decision-making to maximize themselves. Think Steve Jobs in his black polo shirt, Mark Zuckerberg in his jeans-and-t-shirt combo, Barack Obama in his identical shirt-suit-tie ensemble – why, even Albert Einstein wore the same grey suit daily.

Baroness Karren Brady CBE told me that when she's in her office, she eats the same chicken salad sandwich for lunch every day, without deviation. She won't waste brain power on food choices when there are critical business decisions to be made. Annie Grace, in *This Naked Mind: Control Alcohol, Find Freedom, Discover Happiness & Change Your Life*, says it's more exhausting to decide between having one or two alcoholic drinks than deciding to give up entirely. "Hmm, just one more?", "Maybe tonight I'll cab home?" – these are useless brain-drain contemplations when a resolute commitment to abstinence could provide a more energy-saving, one-time decision option.

Your Decision-Making Profile

Whether making big or small decisions, how we instinctively make them is useful to understand as we commit to our Big Impact strategies and design fresh decision pledges. Our personalities are awash with unique tendencies, which we can profile using any one of the popular frameworks around. If we take a behavioural structure like DiSC,[22] often used in business training to help teams empathize with each other's distinctiveness so they collaborate better, we will find we each have a preponderance toward one of four personality types and colours – Dominant (Red), Influential (Yellow), Steady (Green) and Conscientious (Blue). Each type has a different decision-making style:

- Dominant (Red) individuals generally prefer making quick decisions based on logic and assertiveness.
- Influential (Yellow) individuals may prioritize inspiring and motivating the team with gut-instinct decisions to maintain momentum.
- Steady (Green) individuals may emphasize harmony and take more time to consider the impact of decisions on relationships and team dynamics.
- Conscientious (Blue) individuals may focus on gathering detailed information, analyzing data and ensuring accuracy before reaching a decision.

To work out your DiSC profile, here's a quick way to estimate your style.

First, do you consider yourself more questioning and sceptical, or more accepting and warm? If the former, you will be either a D or C style, the latter, an I or S style. Now, do you consider yourself fast-paced and outspoken, or more cautious and reflective? If the former, you will be either a D or I style, the latter, you will be either a C or S style. Combine the two answers, and you have your personal DiSC style.

So, when my clients sit before me deliberating over a decision, I see clouds of colour billowing around them. "Yup, 'twas the red in you that now sees you unemployed, poppet. It would have been wiser to be less impetuous when you resigned in that huff," or "You didn't make the offer quickly enough and now you've lost the house? Aha, I see. I see a little too much green wafting here."

We are not taught decision-making in school, and I see this as a glaring gap. Decisions are crucial to our impact, so understanding any bias we may have toward making decisions a certain way and when to bend this into a mix of alternative decision-making strategies – for example, to seek a variety of advice, which may feel unnatural to us initially – is crucial to evolve successfully into our lives and worlds. Too much of red, yellow, green or blue doesn't always work. Just because knee-jerk red helps you feel in control, it doesn't mean you're making the right judgement calls and perhaps a little more blue is needed in this scenario to slow down and evaluate what else and who else your decision will affect. Equally, poring over swathes of information, getting stuck in analysis paralysis, won't serve your company, nor your career. It's up to you to become acutely aware of how you decide and when you need to flex from your default method, to bring in more colours from the primary palette.

Identifying When It's Decision Time

It is also important to learn to identify when a decision needs to be made in the first place. Yes, we can eliminate micro decisions by introducing habits; yes, we can observe our styles of decision-making to hone them; but the most skilful impactors in the world know when decision time has arrived and become ultra-conscientious about progress through decision.

BIG IMPACT REFLECTION: YOUR BIG DECISIONS TIMELINE

Reflect on your life, looking at what has led you to where you are today through the lens of decisions made. When you left home, where you've lived, worked, whether you've had children, got fit, learned something, found someone, you will have invariably made a decision to invite that expansion in. Draw a timeline on a large sheet of paper, a straight line from left to right, and label a spike up or down representing each milestone along the roadmap of your life, from birth to today.

You'll see your pattern of decision-making emerge: each milestone, each life-changing occurrence, will have been predicated by a strong decision, or not. Whether consciously or unconsciously, you decided to direct your life a certain way and it unfolded thus.

Taking your DiSC profile identified above, analyse the decisions you made firmly, those you drifted into and those you felt happened to you, observing where a dominant style of decision-making benefited you or not. With my clients, generally the big life moments they feel most positive about arose because of both firm decision-making and a strong strategy implemented.

Journal Reflection: What have you learned about your decision-making style and how will you evolve this into your next chapter of Big Impact?

Too often, an increasingly loud life niggle is accompanied by passiveness or suppression. And that's no good. Especially because I know you're reading this book hungry for more, intent on bigger, bolder, better. Any niggles are calling you to change tack, to make different decisions. Let me emphasize again here and now that Big Impact is only possible once you decide unequivocally it's what you want and commit to making it happen. It's about recognizing what your impact visions are and deciding now is the time to make necessary changes to go about achieving them. It's about intelligent strategy.

Within business, there's gargantuan power in making strong decisions. Leaders who soar do so because they finesse their decision-making skills. It's plain fact: without decisions there won't be progress. Lack of progress will always be more frowned upon (and feel more frustrating) than a wrong decision. As Teddy Roosevelt, moustachioed 26th US president, put it, "In any moment of decision, the best thing you can do is the right thing, the next best thing is the wrong thing, and the worst you can do is nothing."[23]

The Modern Working Mother Conundrum – To Be, Not To Be, or Hoooowwwww???

I coach many ambitious women. Two of the biggest decisions I hear them ponder is: "What if I want to be a mother as well as have a phenomenal career?" and "How will I ever have the energy to work and parent?" If this applies to you, read on; if not, skip to the next chapter.

My client Angelique, a 27-year-old high-performing, "30 under 30" award-winning advertising superstar, announced in one of our sessions that she and her husband had decided they wouldn't be starting a family after all as they felt her career was too important and "It's either career or baby, and I love my job." Really? Is that what society has led us to? Such extreme dichotomous thinking that family planning becomes a career choice? Sadly so, it seems. A quick online search reveals masses of articles, blogs, research studies and forums on this very topic. Take this subreddit thread in r/workingmoms with (at last count) 112k mums chatting "Career or Baby? When is the right time?"[24] Buoyant debate and advice from the community all (mercifully) conferring that there is never a right time and just follow your heart. Hear, hear.

I investigated across my network.

"My career isn't as successful as it could be because I had my son and lost a year in the workplace."

"I would never risk a corporate role. I love my freelance freedom because I can prioritize my children."

"I never wanted children because I knew it would distract me from my business and serious wealth is my goal."

"I won't have children as I know I won't be a good mum but do know I'm good at my job."

This small splattering of responses indicates how much of a pickle we're in societally with such a polarized "either/or" realm bucking against biology.

Perspectives on the topic of motherhood and work are myriad, and that's to be expected, but what about the action taken? Egg freezing is on the rise as women take bold action. More women each year are choosing to get pregnant with a sperm donor and do the whole shebang alone. Panels on female empowerment in the workplace celebrate women who are proud to have avoided motherhood. Women are sharing parental leave with partners, sometimes choosing to return to work immediately, leaving the newborn in their partner's care. One client created a strategy to have a summer baby to hack the British school system (and indeed her body), because, in the UK, the first day of September in the year a child turns five marks the hop out of expensive private childcare into state-funded school. And here I am, proud to be a working mother exemplifying the reality that it is possible to single-parent four children and have a career (although it can be a lonesome and difficult plight, for sure, hence my eight strategy pearls to come).

The decision funk doesn't stop at "baby or not", but also applies to the number of children they have. I have several clients wishing they'd had more than one child, a decision that sometimes wrecks mental wellbeing, marriages and creates all sorts of dark resentment.

What all of this tells us is that today women have choice. We are empowered like never before to decide what suits us and when. And, as with all big decisions in life, we need to ensure we make them strategically, consciously and from the heart.

But ... and there is a big but: when women feel subjugated to choose career over motherhood, and this choice does not come from a place of power but instead fear, that is another story. Similarly, when women feel penalized by maternity leave with its threat of an anticipated lower salary, lower likelihood of promotion, less respect, less opportunity, that is a problem. And if ever women feel pressured to go back to work outside of their own time frame, or coerced to stay at home, there's nothing positive about that.

Let's take it back to basics. We're designed to procreate and nurse infants. It's our mammalian design. For women who choose to opt out, good for you; celebrate your powerful decision. I respect you. For women who tragically struggle with infertility, my heart weeps with you, and I wish I could magic it all away, truly. For those of you with choice, let's get you to resonant choice, to where head and heart align. This should not be as hard a choice as your swirling brain is befuddling you into believing. Please choose based on your value set. Choose consciously, based on what matters most to you. Try to access your longing.

We're going to address fulfilment throughout this book, but take heed here on this delicate, personal, important decision that will impact the course of your destiny irrevocably: you will never, ever, ever experience fulfilment if you dishonour your values. If you rationalize decisions away with your head and don't listen to your heart, one day that suppressed urge will rise up as a regret, a devastating new issue to deal with. When you make big life decisions in honour of your values, when you decide with integrity not duplicity, with love not fear, in terms of creation not destruction, the dilemma always radically simplifies itself and the decision appears to be more obvious. In the Mindset chapter ahead you'll be invited to do a reflection exercise exploring your values, which will hopefully clarify your decision if you're feeling torn in the debate of Motherhood or Not.

Combining Motherhood with Ambition

It is possible to work and parent simultaneously. Almost 75 per cent of mothers in the UK and 70 per cent of mothers in Northern America work.[25] We're doing it. We're combining raising family with a rising career. We're navigating and, more often than not, embracing the journey. By and large, employers are making it easier for us and respecting the juggle. The pandemic was marvellous for proving to reticent employers that flexible working actually works. Equality reports have forced companies to reveal gender splits per employee levels, so there's public revelation in any gender disparity per volume of workers, and shareholders devour the stats of annual women's initiatives as reassurance that the business is looking after its women and all the rich emotional intelligence and compassionate leadership they bring.

When Claire Valoti, ex-VP International at Snapchat, applied to Snap Inc. for this gig, her dream role, she introduced herself and announced in their first conversation that she was pregnant. Claire was certain she wanted the role and certain she wanted an honest discussion. To Claire's delight, Snap congratulated her and were happy to continue conversations, even respecting Claire's decision to hold off signing the contract until she'd passed a key developmental pregnancy milestone, having suffered previous miscarriages and a premature firstborn. Timelines meant that Claire's baby was due two weeks after her scheduled start date with Snap and this too was not an issue. Snap made interim management plans, announced Claire's impending arrival in the press, then waited and eventually welcomed Claire. "I could focus 100 per cent on growing our family, secure in the knowledge that the work, my dream job in fact, was there waiting on the other side," Claire said. "I wish this for every woman."

In the UK's marketing sector, a full year off for maternity is common, and generously often at 80 per cent pay. Breastfeeding mothers have private rooms to express milk in the office. Some companies have onsite crèches, childcare vouchers offered as benefits and more. There is definitely more concession for working mothers today than previous generations can fathom. It's not perfect, but that's a whole other book.

For entrepreneurs, it's less clear-cut. You'll often fudge your way through, making it work your way, based on your needs and priorities. I had a warped belief that using childcare meant I was failing as a mother, so I ludicrously struggled through the first couple of years of my first business without childcare. I bedevilled myself into believing running a rapidly growing business from home with staff dotted around the house amid the potties and toys, with most of my focused work done through the night while the kids slept, was me being a gold-star modern entrepreneur. One burnout later, I admitted that something had to give and maybe childcare was actually an essential part of successfully running a business. (It took a lot of therapy for me to get over the inner disgrace I felt at my self-perceived weakness, my disconcerting inability to sustain the energy to do it all – see what I mean about warped belief systems and how deeply they penetrate?!)

I had a similar experience to Claire, although I was working for myself at the time; I found out I was pregnant with the twins just as I was about to launch my long-planned, omni-channel franchise model – a deliriously exciting new chapter for my business. As shock became ecstasy, exuberance and endless gratitude for my two miracles, I decided the surprise pregnancy was a cue from the universe to pause on business expansion, let it tick along, and focus primarily on family for a bit. I figured I'd have the rest of my life to grow businesses, get jobs, work and earn money, but only this one small window of time to nurture little people. It meant an overhaul of life, finances, business management, priorities and a total pivot of emphasis, but it felt easy and a no-brainer decision that I was determined to make work. This is a solid example of a time when I put my values first.

Outside of corporate and startup entrepreneurialism, there are still ways to make a job alongside having kids work. I'm lucky to know an angel of a woman who is spirited, positive, grafting, determined and, despite a harrowing history of abuse, no family nearby and living in a one-room refuge home with her two young children, sleeping all in the same bed, set herself up as "Mrs Mop". Taking it one day and one house at a time, and with the requisite branded bucket, she now runs a housekeeping service to provide for her family without a single grumble, tear or mention of a sleepless night. She will rise far. How does Mrs Mop do it? Her youngest is in nursery, she leans on friends when her eldest is off school (or brings him to work) and she's at the top of the council list for permanent housing, being sure to keep all formal correspondence with authorities upbeat, respectful and hopeful. She doesn't create a fuss about her disruptive neighbours, choosing always to trust it will all come good in the end. She plays her uplifting music while she works, stays in a positive vibe come rain or shine, and I invite her and the little ones to stay in my home whenever I'm away, knowing what it means to them while also helping me and keeping our dog Rex showered with love.

The key to succeeding in honouring your ambitions as a mother and in your line of work simultaneously is to be very careful in your decision-making and planning. There is no winging it when it comes to being a working mother. Once again, I'm going to emphasize that it comes down to strategy, and just as importantly, your values. This is about you owning your choices and avoiding any risk of being swept along by others' demands or time disappearing in unmeaningful ways. Always be conscious of what you want, designing your week, work and life accordingly.

BIG IMPACT REFLECTION: CONSCIOUS CHILDCARE

Ask yourself the following questions. You will see that I use the word "want" to frame the questions. If there's a disconnect between your wants and your actuality, address it. Be conscious.

What I want for my week:

- How many hours do you want to work?
- Are there any preferred hours of the day you like to work? e.g. is 8–10am a sacred flow-state productivity slot for planning/writing/thinking time?
- If you have children, how many hours do you want to spend with them?
- What are the non-negotiables, e.g. bed/bath/homework time?
- How many hours do you want to yourself, with your partner, friends, etc.? Doing what?
- How many locations do you need to travel to and from each week e.g. between work, school, nursery, gym, etc.?
- How can you improve the flow between locations?
- What does a balanced working and parenting life look like to you? And to your partner? And to your children?

- What are the childcare solutions available to you? Could there be better ones?
- What do the financial implications of work income plus childcare costs mean for you/your family?
- Where is there tension in any current set-up? How can it be alleviated?
- Are there tasks on the domestic to-do list you can delegate?
- Are there home tasks you enjoy and want more time for? e.g. gardening?
- Are there tasks on the work to-do list you can delegate to create more time for the children?

Now take these wants and wishes, build your plan and share it. Share it with your family, with your partner (who may co-create it with you), share it with your children if they're old enough so they understand the plan is considered care (not abandonment), and share it with your employer and colleagues. Evidencing your life organization demonstrates your leadership and earns respect. Put this plan on the wall and live by it. Review with the family cyclically to check it's working for all or to hone elements. You are consciously creating how you work and mother, so lead, own and honour this plan as you would a work project.

There will of course be curveballs – when children are sick, or nursery is closed, or the trains are cancelled, or the twins are tantrumming because their favourite cereal has run out so they won't get dressed – but we'll deal with that under stress-management and communication later in the book. For the main part, you can enjoy a sense of relative calm knowing there is an optimal plan to be executed.

And do please note that I'm expecting you to make this *your* plan, not anyone else's. Yes, sperm made these little people as well, and the owner of the sperm can and absolutely should share responsibility for the plan and the childcare if he's around, or whoever your partner is if you have one, but never automatically assume they are thinking the same way as you. Bring them into your planning and set out clear rules of responsibility and fair play from the off. Take charge, so you're not disappointed further down that windy road.

A Final Word on Decision-Making

Micro or macro, our decisions can influence both what shows up in our lives and how we show up. When you respect and understand the power of your decisions, and that with every decision made you alter your destiny in some way, you start making decisions more considerately.

Howard Thurman, the inspiring philosopher and theologian, was always excited by the voltage of our big, life-changing decisions: "It's a wondrous thing, that a decision to act releases energy in the personality. ... In the wake of the decision ... energy is released. The act of decision sweeps all before it, and the life of the individual may be changed forever." I know you know and feel this too.

Life does indeed feel more electric and exciting once we make decisions firmly. We become supercharged. Think of a friend empowered by her fresh resolve to secure a new job, or the one invigorated by their resolution to workout daily, or the one firmly determined to learn a new skill. Once a decision is made consciously and commitment honoured, the psyche literally buzzes, aglow with newfound empowerment. Our power grows and our impact expands. Life feels purposeful and fulfilling, and you might find that weirdly wonderful coincidences start thrusting progress forward in exciting directions, like a little bit of magic at play.

Wayne W Dyer, one of my go-to mentors, taught, "Make your future dream a present fact by assuming the feeling of the wish fulfilled."[26] So, when you decide, go beyond a literal pledge into a full-on, emotionally rich plan, and when you commit, commit heart and soul, body and mind, and mean it. Decisions determine your destiny. Fulfil those wishes!

PART ONE

THE FOUNDATIONAL IMPERATIVES FOR BIG IMPACT

FIRST, GO WITHIN

"Beginnings are fragile things. They're made of gossamer threads of hope and shimmer with the faint light of potential grace. It's in the human heart that we begin weaving our designs and dreams of experience yet to come. We live our entire lives within chrysalises. As soon as we emerge from one, life sculpts another around us. Within manifest reality, everything is in a constant state of becoming, even God."

— Dana Hutton

What my cyclical boom-bust experience taught me most radically is that without solid foundations, you risk falling over any time things aren't just so. When crisis strikes, when our status quo is disrupted, when bad news comes in, when a hope is dashed or when a raw nerve is hit, we crumble if we're not inwardly stable. We won't necessarily know that we're unsteady until hardship sends us a' wobbling. Our ability to deal with incoming adversity, artfully deflecting suffering with firm resilience, will be entirely down to how much we've invested in prepping ourselves for life when it's not all ponies and kittens.

To prepare for Big Impact, we start the work by going within, by bravely revealing, acknowledging, then healing barriers and perhaps pain, secure that on the other side of this inner work lies that great future we've been dreaming about for flipping ages now.

So, before we progress into the all-important Expansion Phenomenon, we start here in Part One, removing blockers and making space for the glory ahead. We become accountable. We build our power and ground ourselves into who we are, what matters most and compassionately learn where our vulnerabilities lurk. Once we address, understand, manage and pragmatically design our foundations, weaving these first four strategies optimally into our daily existence, only then do we become ready for sustainable, un-derailable impact.

Progress will not be possible fixing one realm alone. It's not just about our Energy, how physically strong, fit, rested, nutritionally bouncy and gym toned we are. Neither is it just about Mindset and those six sessions we had with a psychotherapist years ago when we sussed that inner-child wound. Nor is it solely about how intentional we are in living on Purpose, and that we've got a mission statement so know exactly what we're doing and why. And nope, it's not all okay just because we've got an excellent grip on Time planning so can fit in crisis management no worries. None of these realms in isolation will permit you to soar beyond struggle.

No, Energy, Mindset, Purpose and Time are all interconnected aspects of unique and lovely You, all operating as one delicate and defining ecosystem. The impact of emotional stress can be as debilitating as physical exhaustion, meaning Mindset + Energy are in need of attention. Lack of meaning in daily existence can be as frustrating as yearning for 27-hour days, suggesting Purpose + Time are in need of attention. Old wounds unhealed may mean we're locking ourselves in turrets of limiting belief systems we're not even aware of, detrimentally impacting Energy, Mindset, Purpose and Time all at once. Your vibrancy and shining essence will only protect and empower you when respected as a connected blend of all four realms.

In the next four chapters to come, as you build your Foundational Imperatives, you're going to conclude each strategy by making three Big Impact Decision Pledges, (part of the 10 per cent of conscious decisions that make up your life – those non-autopilot ones). You are about to begin your journey to soar.

YOUR BIG IMPACT STRATEGY NO. 1: ENERGY

"You can do amazing things, but only if you have the energy to do them."
— Simon Alexander Ong

Energy is everything. It's the difference between walking into a room and inspiring levels of collaboration, enthusiasm and interest, or not. It's the power you possess to magnetize others to hear you, see you and look forward to spending time with you, or not. It's the stillness of calm, contemplative floaty zendom, and of excited, rapidly flowing rushes of thoughts and emotions. It's a sensory reading of another as you absorb their energetic vibe, attractive or repulsive, addictive or impartial, interesting or meh. It's fundamental to how you contribute to the world. It's the most elemental essence of your impact.

In this strategy you will learn how to stop viewing energy as a binary push-pull lever with an "in then out" mechanism. My intention is that you will understand more about the delicate dynamism of energy and how to gracefully work with it, not against it.

You cannot assume your energy system is a cycle you can hack through tipping energizers into your energy bucket, filling it to the brim ready for action, then draining it empty and trudging back to the well to replenish it once again. This endless careering from full to empty, the extremes of brim-full to bone dry – that's not how energy flows. You will learn to revere your energy. Just as the most successful, impactful people on the planet understand that only with a respect for their natural, highly personal energetic rhythms and sensitivities can they realize their ambitions, you too will learn to unlock your energy as a superpower. You will hone the elegance of consistent energy management, protecting your very life force as it pulses, enabling it to dynamically flow, expanding and contracting in harmony with your intentions.

You will learn about the "whole-istic" approach to your energy and the unique, ever-undulating interplay between your physical, intellectual and soulful elements. How to honour these intertwining connections and maintain what I call your Harmonic Energy State. You will learn not about filling a bucket, which then empties, but filling a well that endlessly self-replenishes, enabling you to focus on your biggest impact without burning out.

Modern Energy Crimes

Alexis looked dreadful. I mean truly dreadful. The bags beneath her eyes told tales of extreme self-neglect. Her skin was pale, translucent, almost greyish in hue. Her hair was scraped back into a severe, tight low knot, enforcing a stern look. And those eyes, oh those eyes. The puffy shadows beneath those bloodshot pools were haunting.

Dressed immaculately in a chic, gun-metal, flared trouser suit, she was accessorized to perfection with striking bangles and a demure diamond pendant necklace. With elegantly heeled feet and French-manicured hands, to the outside world she looked successful, in control and powerful. Sitting opposite me, up close and personal, on my coaching couch, however, she exuded a dark aura of a woman experiencing significant trauma.

"I collapsed," she mumbled. "I'm so worried they're going to fire me. I passed out at work and now I'm sure they want to get rid of me." In a nonsensical stream-of-consciousness monologue she described a tale of boardroom politics, inequality, bullying and, more recently, her belief of an oncoming deliberate ousting. She described her 17-hour workdays, the lack of anything or anyone in her life except work, incidents leading up to her collapse, her intense paranoia at the threat of job loss and her harrowing admission of the workaholism that she acknowledged had led to her breakdown.

"When my insomnia wakes me, I immediately start work, and the warmth of my laptop on my thighs in bed soothes me. It's actually comforting. I'm so ashamed to even admit this." She started to cry and her tough exterior melted into the Kleenex. "I'm so tired. So, so tired."

Alexis is one of thousands of women I've worked with one-to-one, in global online workshops and at large corporate events, who is suffering an extreme energy crisis. While Alexis is a severe case of chronic workaholism, too many women are living in a similar state of perpetual struggle, pushing on despite the body saying enough is enough. Too many women believe it is normal to be devoid of energy and that the only available solution is simply to push on through. One of my clients pushed on to the gym despite feeling light-headed, over-worked and sleep deprived, hoping some adrenaline would fuel the rest of her day, only to pass out in the changing room and come round in an ambulance. "Where am I? Where's my laptop? I've got a press release to finish writing by midday."

One woman queued to meet me after an event, apparently inspired by the hope I'd offered, asking if she could hug me, weeping into my arms with the admission that she felt "So lost, so tired of the juggle and so stuck." Far too many of us believe and accept that strife and an unrelenting work pace is the norm.

Google "Human Energy Crisis" and around 200 million results ping up. These results are not about climate issues but our human ones. We are struggling. Annually, statistics show our wellbeing, personal effectiveness and quality of life are all declining year on year globally.[27] The pandemic hugely accelerated our energy strife, as abnormal productivity surged, with new organizational expectations, the always-on mentality, blurred home and work boundaries, not to mention the gross slide into 1950s housewifery many of us experienced. Despite our supposed return to post-Covid normality, the alarming burnout statistics continue today. I'm passionate we address this energy crisis urgently. For you, for me, for our kids, the planet.

Energy is our most precious resource. There's a reason your expansion into Big Impact starts with an Energy Strategy. If your energy isn't in balance, you can forget impact, and certainly ever being able to deliver *sustainable* impact. But that is my wish. That you understand this exquisite resource as self-replenishing and potentially abundant once it's respected and not abused. When you learn how to measure and monitor your personal energetic cadence, what enriches your supply and what depletes it, and master how to produce more energetic juice, oozing your bespoke zing, you're in a strong space. Once you can self-regulate and produce renewable energy through rejuvenation and thus be able to maintain your peak equilibrium consistently day in day out, harnessing rest to negate the exhilarating good stress that ambitious women get kicks out of, you're in an exceptional zone of high performance. You have got to learn to work with your energy, not against it.

What Is Energy?

In my executive mentoring, when I talk about energy, I am not just referring to how tired you feel but something much broader than that. I focus on your vibe, your frequency, your zing or your zen. Your energy is your enthusiasm for and connection with a moment, a task, a person, a place and how it invigorates or depletes you. Energy is your rhythmic flow across the day, waxing and waning as you eat, work, sleep, repeat. It is that indescribable sense you get when someone lights you up, or creates shadow, how they infectiously expand your own energy, elevating and inspiring you into a better, more optimistic mood, or repel you with something you can't quite put your finger on.

I'm talking about an invisible realm that science can't yet quantify with finitude. The type of energy that can't be measured with metrics and fitness trackers. I'd like you to think about energetic realms we can't yet gauge or rationalize with fact or data sets, but that you can absolutely feel. To think about your energetic realms in an intuitive way. The wonder you experience as an energetic surge arises with an emotion, the high of expansive abundance compared to a sludgy low. Your ability to read a room or a person and just know something. How you can tap into your own energetic well by trusting how you feel and how you respond.

Even the most brilliant physicists acknowledge that we only partially understand the laws of energy within our universe. With each new discovery, the world becomes ever more intriguing and complex all at once. Look at quantum physics with its mind-bending, subatomic particle-jigging revelations, which have been baffling and intriguing scientists for years.

In healing modalities, particularly within the integrative health realm, there's emerging science around remedying sickness through our biofields, a generally invisible, interconnected web of our physical and energetic systems. Biofield studies are, ever so slowly, becoming increasingly mainstream with medical journals peppered with concrete evidence sounding less woo-woo and more worthy of exploration and serious application. Pioneering doctors like Mark Mincolla and Shamini Jain purport that when our biofields are flowing in balance, we maintain immunity with optimized physical, mental and emotional function. Their evaluation of hundreds of patients over years shows "miraculous" healing occurs when the biofield is harmonized. Technically speaking, the biofield is the "electromagnetic, biophotonic, and other types of spatially-distributed fields that living systems generate and respond to as integral aspects of cellular, tissue, and whole organism self-regulation and organization."[28] Basically, the many internal and semi-external systems that keep us functioning and energized, some empirical and deeply understood (i.e. we can test and measure them like cardiovascular or gut health), and others that still perplex and excite science with their sheer complexity (like the connection between emotional wellness and physical dis-ease).

The abounding evidence and growing interest in alternative healing modalities mean that the biofield is increasingly being explored by the open-minded masses, no longer just unconventional minorities. Here's a quick history lesson. Back in the 1930s, Kirlian photography apparently captured the auras of living things as proof of a life force as yet undescribed by science. Plants, in varying degrees of health, as well as humans, were photographed. Picture a leaf, a tree or a human body with a mist around it. The mist is consistent in density and colour when the living being is healthy, but patchy and nonuniform around a "broken" part of the body, tree or leaf. There are many who believe they see or sense these energy fields, also known as auras, and can heal any broken mist patches. Reiki, sound baths, chanting and many other healing techniques are used by biofield healers to address these leaky gaps.

Chakras are another, as yet, unscientifically proven system of energy channels, with chakra healing growing in popularity. The chakras impact the strength and solidity of the biofield and are the body's seven radiating energy centres affecting mental, emotional, physical and spiritual power. From root, located in the perineum, to "third eye", situated in our forehead, to crown, just above our heads, these much-revered energy points were first mentioned in The Vedas, ancient sacred texts of Indian Hindu origin, dating from around 1500 BC. The texts describe the kundalini energy flow, which allows energy that may have been stale and clogging to be released all the way from our seats to the top of our head, through the pineal gland and beyond. This flow has struck a chord among modern East meets West "new age" philosophies. Beyond the mystical into the chemical, the seven centres are based on hormone glands in the body, and scientific study has observed the effects these focal points have on our entire physical ecosystem. Psychoneuroimmunology and epigenetics are burgeoning emerging sciences proving the delicate connection between our minds and bodies, the influence of our thoughts and emotions on our physical state, and thus our energy.

If we acknowledge that, as recently as 50 years ago, neuroplasticity hadn't been discovered, look how far brain science has progressed and how previous suppositions have been proved incorrect. Only as recently as our parents' or grandparents' generations, it was believed that by the time we turned 20, we were stuck with our neural wiring, our thought patterns locked into obstinate adolescent know-it-all thinking, and limited by the capabilities we had learned by then. Mercifully, we now know that our brain is highly elastic and can create new neural networks at any stage or age to increase our skills, expand perspectives and build new belief systems. Even more impressively, brain scans evidence that we can activate entirely new regions of our brains,which only yesterday were dormant, unused folds of "un-birthed" brain tissue, to grow vast new knowledge centres just by feeding the tissue with new evidence – new matter to wake up the sleeping grey matter. Neurogenesis, as this is known, continues throughout our lifetimes.[29] So, having never played the piano before, we can learn afresh in our 70s and become a world prodigy if talent is awaiting unused and perseverance keeps our fingertips a' tapping.

As with the brain, and so many other areas of science, we still have eons more to explore and understand when it comes to energy.

With all of this in mind, we will take a holistic approach to your glorious replenishing and vibrant energy. As a bio-individual, you are a unique and complex, multi-pinging disco of feedback signals blasting around your one and only ecosystem. Both obvious and sometimes subtle signs alert you to what feels energizing and what doesn't. The intention with this strategy is for you to become tuned into these signals, effortlessly able to trust your feedback loops and modify how you optimize your bespoke bio-individuality, elevating energy levels by embracing body, mind and soul.

Your Beautiful Body

How you nourish and nurture your physical self will inevitably impact your energy levels – whether that be detrimentally or beneficially is up to you.

Exercise

Exercise is good for you. Of course. Have you noticed how even if you drag yourself to that gym session feeling sluggish and resistant beforehand, afterwards you buzz with a newfound force for life, energized by the exercise? It's fact that exercise triggers your body into producing more energy. There are various internal mechanisms at play, starting with cellular-level changes. You make more mitochondria when you exercise, the powerhouses of cells linked to how well we age. These little bullets create fuel from glucose, manufactured from the food we eat and oxygen from the air we breathe, so the more of them you have, the more energy-rich you feel. Exercise also bolsters your oxygen circulation, meaning not only does your skin glow, but you actually use energy more efficiently. Plus, of course, you get that surge of feel-good hormones, endorphins, that elevates your mood.[30] There's also a link between exercise and happiness because it's an experience and experiences, according to a study by the University of Texas,[31] make us happier than material things. So, exercise makes us feel more energetic and happy, and we'll live longer: win-win.

Food

Our bodies are also obviously acutely sensitive to food. Each substance we consume triggers a cascade of responses as we process the "fuel". The level of processing required (i.e. take the nutrients and eliminate the waste via the digestive system) alters depending on the quality of our fodder. Have a Sunday morning brunch of orange juice, white toast and cereal and you'll need a nap after the meal as the insulin spikes then crashes. Make it a vegetable smoothie with a side of avocado on sourdough or chopped fruits with a sprinkling of seeds and you'll be set to power on through the Sunday papers. We are in a crisis of ultra-processed food consumption right now with the modern diet quite literally killing us,[32] so it is key to remember that you are what you eat and design an energizing diet that works for you. We'll explore both what and when to eat later in this chapter.

Rest

Finally, overexertion and working too hard for too long take their toll on us, mentally and physically. The brain uses ferocious amounts of energy to process incoming data as well as think those brilliant thoughts of yours. It's arguably the hungriest organ in the body, using up around 20 per cent of your energy each day,[33] so needs rejuvenation from pondering as much as your body instructs you to lie down after physical exertion. Allow that brain to swirl endlessly with stressful thoughts that trigger continuous surges of cortisol and adrenaline and you put yourself in a heightened peak state, alert for danger always. Your body simply cannot tolerate this long term, so will eventually become "dis-eased" and malfunction. Too long spent in a stress state absolutely wrecks your beautiful body, visibly and disastrously, potentially fatally. Stress is multiple signals blaring simultaneously, all screaming, "Help, stop, halt, please." Our bodies literally know the score, and it's for us to pay attention to the alarm.

Your Marvellous Mind

What you think creates what you feel, and this impacts the body's homeostatic state. Let me explain. Our minds are wonderful for their imaginative abilities, but the "monkey" mind as Buddhists term it, or the "reptilian/lizard" brain as modern psychology speaks of, can send us through loops. Remember your last insomniac night swirling in repetitive mental noise, going over and over a triggering event? For example, how that annoying colleague embarrassed you this morning. On a rational level, you know it's not healthy to be stuck in the same thought cycle, but you can't halt it, and the more your frustration and rage remain, the more your body reacts, locking you into a chemically maladaptive state. The thought of the annoying colleague and what happened creates emotions of anger and shame, and your neurotransmitters then go wild releasing cortisol, norepinephrine and more, waking up all the stress responses of the body, suppressing the soothing nighttime magic of melatonin and flipping your parasympathetic nervous system into gear.

What's happening here is that your amygdala is activated. The amygdala is part of the brain's limbic system responsible for emotions, motivation and memory. It's designed to protect you from threat by activating fear sensations and alerting the body to danger with a cascade of defensive responses. It has a vital role to play in our survival but can become maladaptive in our perpetually demanding modern lives. When this happens we are experiencing what's known as an amygdala hijack.

You have two congruent systems flowing through you, which keep you in your healthy baseline state known as homeostasis. This is when everything is in balance and your body is functioning as it should. The first system, the sympathetic nervous system, keeps your heart beating, blood flowing, cells renewing, organs functioning and so on. System two, the parasympathetic nervous system, is there for emergencies, swooping in to save the day when the environment unexpectedly deviates from the norm, think fight or flight. In these moments the amygdala flashes with an "emergency" signal and the body is flooded with protective chemicals such as adrenaline to ensure you run fast and escape the tiger or boss, or make the train, prove your sister wrong, and so on. When our minds perpetually spiral into negative emotions, unconsciously of course (we'll learn about managing thoughts in our Mindset Strategy), the parasympathetic nervous system is hijacked and activated continuously, which is not what it was designed for. It's exhausting. It's absolutely unsustainable and wrecks our energy levels. This has severe long-term consequences and is why stress management is so important.

Your gut also influences brain activity. More and more studies are proving a healthy ecosystem in the stomach equates to a healthy mind, with scientists like Dr Natasha Campbell-McBride suggesting learning difficulties can be improved once the gut is healed, and copious studies showing how wheat and meat impact immunity and brain function. What's becoming increasingly clear is that for super performance, cognitive or physical, super attention needs to be paid to feeding the gut microbiome so it, and thus we, flourish.

Your Soul's Energy Spring

Your soul is your inner guide, your infallible, trust-worthiest BFF whispering directional pointers, always. Your soul's stirrings signal which way you should travel, when to pivot, when to be still. Your spiritual radar, your intuitive compass; by soul I'm referring to your heart, your spirit, your inner knowing.

The soul is defined by the Oxford Dictionary as "Emotional or intellectual energy or intensity, especially as revealed in a work of art or an artistic performance." I like to think of your life as the work of art your soul is revealing. That when you listen to your soul, and follow your heart's truest desires, you allow destiny to develop, unfurling beautifully with every aligned and brave step. When you ignore the sweet, inner rumblings, life becomes a struggle as you push against it as opposed to gliding along with it, trusting, flowing and synchronizing. There's a heart and mind congruence that I believe stimulates powerful "Yes!" feedback when you feel "plugged in" to your path, aligned, serene, "home". You know this feeling; it's buttery, like being in love. Soothing and magical, seemingly everything you touch turns to gold, you see beauty and goodness everywhere; you know with absolutely certainty you're on the right road.

There's abundant energy when your soul is ignited. A brightly burning soul that's flickering intensely will affect your levels of motivation and enthusiasm as well as outcomes. Your soul may become inflamed to signal something is right, but equally if something is wrong. Trust its intensity. The louder the murmurs, the deeper you need to peek inside yourself and at your situation. Ignore the flames and do work your soul doesn't chime with, or spend time with people or in places that elicit inner disharmony, and regret will surface later. Trust the flickers.

When my daughter applied to do a psychology degree and we sat together to write her personal statement – the essay to universities that makes up a large part of the application – it was an agonizing couple of hours spent crafting clunky reasons why she wanted to attend the course. After a gap year of soul searching, she decided to follow her passion and apply for a music production degree, and this time the words poured out effortlessly; her heart's wishes and knowns gushing onto the paper, producing a moving testimony to her true why. An entirely different level of impact, a congruent heart, an inspired soul and bountiful energy!

Bespoke Bio-Individuality

There is only one of you, and you are bio-individual. There is no one-size-fits-all in energy management; we are all unique and have our own DNA, gene pools, life experiences and belief systems, which mean we energetically respond – in mind, body and soul – differently to extrinsic and intrinsic stimulus.

What is common to us all, however, is that energy expands and contracts. Energy is dynamic. You can make it as fast as you deplete it. Understanding our chemical and hormonal responses and our circadian rhythms to optimize our energy levels is up to each one of us to learn, honour and protect religiously and respectfully. The power to make energy and affect its frequency – high vibes and all that jazz – comes down to achieving a harmonic energy state 100 per cent bespoke to you.

How to Reach Your Harmonic Energy State

To ensure the energy cascading between your body, mind and soul, enlivening and stabilizing your biofield, is balanced, you need to understand where you currently sit on the scale of Energized or Depleted against a range of life factors that influence your productivity. Once we've evaluated this, then we can build your tailored Big Impact Energy plan. You will complete your scorecard at the end of this strategy, after learning about different energy zones, to then design your Energy Decision Pledges accordingly.

To maximize your energy, to be able to produce it and honour it, to have enough to relish purposeful living instead of feeling exhausted, like daily life is just an uphill battle, you need to master how to bring yourself into homeostasis as your golden zen. That's the ultimate goal here.

So, we're going to explore three energy zones which I've identified through my client work and my own life experience as the most important, then analyse how much of a harmonic energy state you are in, or not, to create your bio-individual strategy.

To reach your Harmonic Energy State, we will focus on three energy zones:

- Nourishment
- Rejuvenation
- Maintenance

Energy Zone No. 1: Nourishment

What you consume matters. From food and drink, to pharmacology, to media messages, every input, both physical and mental, will have an effect. These effects may be subtle and gradual or explicit and immediate; either way, the cause may be hard to pinpoint.

Our modern consumption trends are clearly harmful. Obesity levels continue to rise stratospherically, brain dysregulation abounds, from an explosion of neurodiversity at birth, to midlife mental health afflictions, to dementia in old age, skin disorders, allergies, cancers, addictions; there's a lot of suffering. There's also a lot of pharmacology trying to fix the problems with pills, creams and surgeries for everything, so there's a lot of dependence on healthcare treating symptoms and not the cause.

For example, the opioid crisis in the US is horrifying. Despite representing only 5 per cent of the world's population, Americans consume 80 per cent of the world's opioids with catastrophic mortalities as a consequence. According to the Centers for Disease Control and Prevention (CDC), in the 12-month period ending in April 2021, over 96,000 drug overdose deaths occurred in the United States, and the majority of these deaths involved opioids.[34]

I'm all for modern medicine and food efficiency, but any lack of self-accountability in our own healing and vitality is not on. I believe we have to take individual responsibility for our base level of health, as complex as it is today with the media confusing what "healthy" actually is. Is it okay to eat that "vitamin-enriched" cereal, better to choose the gluten-free bread and the low-fat hummus? Or is that cereal, bread and hummus so manufactured and far from Earth's source, we may as well be eating cardboard slathered with some E numbers and sprinkled with an array of un-processable toxins for the body to try and deal with? It's very easy to be swept up by cultural norms and consume coffee like water, believing that's hydration, assume a sandwich, crisps and a soda are a healthy lunch because they're packaged up on offer with a "low calorie, low fat" badge, and indulge in fast food often because, well, it's handy and everyone else is.

Let's bring it back to what we do know. We're getting sicker globally. My new clients arrive energy deficient. Sales of artificial energy kicks, from caffeinated drinks to sugary snacks, continue to rise. We're in yo-yo cycles of up then down, and the downs are worsening according to the burnout stats. We also know that what we consume is the most fundamental way to fuel our energy.

Microbial Marvels

The gut microbiome is a complex community of microorganisms residing in the digestive tract. Think of it as an another one of our incredible internal ecosystems, diverse and intricate. It aids in the digestion of compound substances, supports immune system function, contributes to metabolic processes and protects against harmful pathogens. It influences the synthesis of vitamins and neurotransmitters and maintains the integrity of the gut barrier (meaning less risk of allergies through leaky gut). It basically does an abundance of imperative physical stuff to keep our bodies functioning in homeostasis, but most fascinating are the medical observations that it has vast impact on our brains and how we feel too.

Serotonin, the neurotransmitter primarily known for its role in mood regulation and making us feel happy, has intricate connections with the wonderworld of our gut microbiome. The majority (suggestions of 90–99 per cent) of serotonin in the body is found in the gastrointestinal tract.[35] This is a staggering revelation of recent science. There's a gut-brain axis that operates as a bidirectional communication system between the gut and the central nervous system, which is pinging signals from the gut microbiome up into the brain, impacting mood, stress and mental wellbeing. The brain is pinging back down to the gut too (think nervous diarrhoea or stress cramps). Enter new sciences such as nutritional psychiatry diving into how healing a diet can heal mind and body respectively.

If the microbiome is responsible for how we feel (serotonin) and how well we are (immune system), then feeding our microbiome what it needs to flourish has to be key. And what does our delicate but all-powerful microbiome need? A nutritionally dense and varied diet of high-fibre, plant-based organic food. We should be eating at least 30 different types of fruit or vegetables including nuts and seeds across any one week with a focus on alkalinity, healthy fats and, for stable energy management, low glycemic index foods. Hardcore microbiome feeders will regularly eat fermented foods like kefir, sauerkraut and yogurt, and maintain high levels of foods rich in polyphenols, such as berries, nuts, seeds and dark chocolate (polyphenols have antioxidant properties which support a diverse microbial environment).

How to Embrace a Plant-Based Diet

Stuffing your lovely digestive tract with an abundance of fruit and veg is of course going to make you look and feel fantastic. A plant-based bias toward your meals means emphasizing whole foods while minimizing or excluding animal products. It doesn't mean you eat only kale. Think superfoods like avocadoes, blueberries, sweet potatoes, leafy greens, nuts and seeds, oily fish, ginger, turmeric, garlic, cruciferous delights like broccoli and the raft of delicious tomato varieties. Nature's bounty is abundant with choice, colour, variety, flavour and nutritional wealth. And as high fibre satisfies the biome, so it promotes satiety, thus being great for weight management too. There are numerous health advantages to predominantly eating this way, from the low yet nourishing calories, to blood sugar regulation, reduced risk of cancers, lowered blood pressure and cholesterol levels, stable hormone production, long-term wellbeing and of course more energy!

When shopping for your rainbow fare, organic is best if available. Reducing exposure to pesticides and herbicides, common in modern, industrialized agriculture, puts less strain on the body as there will be less toxicity to eliminate. Make the effort to do your research. For example, the widely used herbicide Glyphosate, spamming supermarkets shelves in anything from fresh fruits to oat milks, has sparked concerns due to its 2015 classification as a "probable human carcinogen" by the International Agency for Research on Cancer (IARC).[36] As I say, please do your research. Logically, organic foods often have lower levels of synthetic additives too, so it's another tick if you're planning to minimize artificial substances, which again is a recommendation for our bodily temple. Generally, organic farming's focus on soil health and biodiversity yields crops with richer nutritional density and more flavour. And let's not forget, organic animal products are free from antibiotics and growth hormones.

Why Inflammation Needs Attention

When your microbiome is out of kilter and the microbial forest within isn't flourishing, it can trigger the immune system to dysfunction and trip into chronic inflammation. This basically means that the protective, short-term response of inflammation to manage injury or infection is triggered ,inadvertently causing all manner of unwanted symptoms. Inflammation is associated with a range of health issues from cardiovascular disease, diabetes, autoimmune disorders, neurodegenerative diseases, arthritis, allergies and various chronic conditions. The World Health Organization classifies inflammation as "the greatest threat to human health", warning three out of five people worldwide will die of a chronic inflammation-based disease.[37]

A common inflammatory response is the wine flush you see after a few too many. It's not a healthy rosy glow, but a sign of the body failing to operate homeostatically. Similarly, rashes or eczema outbursts are all indications of inflammation. Inflammation may not always be seen, but will definitely be felt as energy is depleted while the body focuses on stabilizing the inflammation. In your pursuit of maximum energy, don't hamper yourself at the first hurdle with a needlessly poor diet.

Additionally, there's also a direct link between inflammation and blood sugar levels, as elevated glucose levels can stimulate the release of pro-inflammatory molecules, triggering inflammation while also negatively interfering with insulin resistance. So, prioritizing low glycemic index (low-GI) foods – slow-release carbohydrates like porridge or potatoes (rather than high-GI white bread or doughnuts) – improves blood sugar control.

Studies through continuous glucose monitoring (patches on your arm connected to an app on your phone, like the UK-founded Zoe, for instance) link low-GI diets with enhanced energy levels and sustained physical and mental performance, as well as positive effects on heart health, hormonal balance and insulin regulation. You're more likely to lose or maintain weight too, because low-GI foods, often rich in fibre, promote feelings of fullness, support better appetite control and reduce the likelihood of between-meal snacking. I've recently discovered the biochemist and now Instagram star @glucosegoddess, who teaches hacks to flatten the glucose curve which are easy, simple and I find super effective.

BIG IMPACT REFLECTION: INTUITIVE EATING

I invite you now to tune into your body and the vibrational energy of food. Reflect on your relationship with food and your body image. How have dieting rules or societal expectations influenced your eating habits and perceptions of your body? Consider moments when you ignored your hunger or felt guilty about eating certain foods. How might embracing intuitive eating principles, such as honouring your hunger and respecting your body, change your approach to food and self-care? Think about a time when you genuinely listened to your body's cravings (not your mind's) – perhaps choosing a crisp apple over a chocolate biscuit, and if it felt more satisfying? Write about any fears or reservations you have about letting go of diet mentality and explore the potential benefits of truly listening to and trusting your body's natural cues. Experiment for a week by conscientiously not consuming anything without asking the question "Does my body want this?" After the week, reflect again on the prompts here and imagine a life where intuitive eating feels totally natural and the kindest, most energizing way to eat.

The Wonderful World of Water

We are 80 per cent water and need a lot of it. An ample amount is vital for maintaining overall health, contributing to essential physiological functions in our bodies. Water is a fundamental component of cells, tissues and organs, ensuring optimal cell function and supporting biochemical reactions. Adequate water intake aids in temperature regulation through the body's natural cooling mechanism, sweating. It serves as a lubricant for joints, facilitating smooth movement and preventing discomfort. Water plays a crucial role in nutrient transportation, facilitating absorption in the digestive system and distributing essential substances to cells. Additionally, it supports detoxification by flushing out waste products through urine and promotes healthy urinary function.

Water is essential for digestion, preventing constipation, and supporting regular bowel movements. Proper hydration positively influences cognitive function, including concentration, alertness and memory. It contributes to healthy skin, maintaining elasticity and your glowy, youthful appearance. Drinking water before meals can aid in weight management by promoting a feeling of fullness. For optimal physical performance, athletes particularly rely on adequate hydration to prevent fatigue and support endurance, so if you want to perform at maximum impact, hydrate well too. Try starting your day with a glass of water upon rising, and as you drink, envisage the water waking up your cells as it flows through you, nourishing your body with a cascade of hydrating new-day zing!

Bogus Energy Boosts

Reliance on "fake" energy is the scourge of today. Caffeinated drinks are everywhere, even for tots. Coffee culture is normalized with a Starbucks on every high street. Alcohol is endlessly glamorized. And pharmacology pervades with prescriptions issued before lifestyle advice. We're experiencing a human energy crisis at a time when there are apparent energy "solutions" everywhere. Of course there's a connection.

Safe caffeine levels vary person to person, as bio-individuality means we each respond differently. Just because your best friend can drink an espresso before bed and sleep through, it doesn't mean you'll be okay if your last coffee was at 10am. Likewise, your boss might present like Beyoncé when she's had a coffee supercharge, but you might shake with the adrenaline response and be subpar on stage after the same brew. Take notice of how you react and monitor your intake. There's a plethora of alternatives to tea and coffee, from herbal teas to turmeric lattes, to my favourite: a giant mug of hot water infused with fresh mint leaves, a teaspoon of coconut oil and slices of lemon, lime and ginger. Play with new tastes and monitor how you feel if you take a break from your usual pick-me-ups. Always remember the logic that messing with your system to boost energy artificially is robbing Peter to pay Paul – however hard the energy hit initially, it's temporary and the crash will inevitably come.

If you're tired, your body is beseeching you to slow down, to pause and recharge, and if you have another coffee, reach for a Red Bull or go out for a bottle of Prosecco with your girlies instead, eventually it all catches up with you. Being wired and motoring on is unhealthy and unsustainable. But for the manufacturers of these potions, it's boom time as we all sluggishly try to claw back energy and buy another shot. It's an endless cycle of wiring ourselves up, struggling to come down, then wiring back up again.

BIG IMPACT REFLECTION: FAKE ENERGY – YOUR BODY ALWAYS KEEPS THE SCORE

Write a list of all the quick fixes you consume when you have an energy dip, noting where and when you tend to go for the item. Ensure you include everything from caffeinated sodas, "energy" drinks and coffees, to medication, alcohol, sugary snacks, anything that peps you up immediately and you recognize you use as a crutch when you're tired or low. Now, as you assess this list, are there any revelations that surprise you? Anything that prompts you to make change? If so, what are they? Are you clear what the chemicals are that give you the energy rush each time? Do you check the ingredients on pharma products as well as food stuffs? Which are the situations that tire you the most and make you reach for the emergency boost? What could you do in those moments to avoid harmful energizers and get a nourishing boost? What happens if you listen to your body and rest to rejuvenate instead of the quick fix? Are there patterns in your days that trigger dips cyclically that you could address? Free-write about an imaginary future without fake energy, describing how you'll feel, how you'll manage and the impact of this change.

The Role of Alcohol in Energy Management

British culture is sadly infamous for its alcohol consumption with booze-related accidents, crimes and health issues rife. Consumption of course varies across the world by country, region and demographic, but it's hard for any Western working woman to calculate what's normal and what's healthy. Drink whisky to think; drink red wine to be sophisticated; drink champagne to celebrate; drink cream liqueur while putting up the Christmas tree; drink brandy in your coffee because it's winter; drink gin in your soda because it's summer, and so on. The philosophy is the same: however you feel, go on and have a drink and you'll feel better. This is not so.

Alcohol is neurotoxic, which means it is poisonous to the nervous system and thus takes an energy toll. Because I have so many clients seeking help with their energy, and because alcohol is so omnipresent in Britain, I am focusing on it here. Some considerations to bear in mind before your next tipple:

1. We build an association with alcohol before we ever even taste our first drop.

As children we soak up everything going on around us and our innocent, pliable minds build belief systems about the world, capturing what we understand as right and wrong, good and bad, how to behave, who to trust, and so on. Part of our social awakening includes observing our carers and unconsciously replicating their patterns. So, if you idolize a parent or primary caregiver and they are a wild, party-loving character permanently carrying a beer or glass of wine, we respect and revere that aspect of them as equally as the rest. We instinctively absorb all that is seemingly great and good about them and thus, where booze is concerned, may subconsciously take on the desire to drink like them, to be apparently great and good like them. It's that simple. We literally become our caregivers as we expand out into the world as young adults, treading the path they've paved before us.

When you understand the impression that was made on you as a child around alcohol, it's preferable to look at your own relationship with alcohol afresh today. When you deconstruct your Booze Beliefs you can look them squarely in the eye and appraise them through an adult lens. What do you, with your own life experience and current value set, think about alcohol? Is it playing a positive role in your life today? Does it bring you joy and fun and all that glamour and positivity you associated with it from the media depictions and earlier life observations? What does "adult you" honestly think?

2. Nobody likes the taste of alcohol because the taste is pure poison. We like the taste of the copious chemicals flavouring and masking the ethanol.

William Porter, ex-army officer cum straight-talking health informant, says it best in his best-seller *Alcohol Explained*: "Alcohol in its pure form is a highly poisonous chemical. It is a toxin that kills living things, from human beings to single cells and microorganisms, which is why it is used to preserve food and to sterilize."[38]

To repeat, alcohol is pure poison and the human body is designed to be repulsed by poison. Sniffing neat alcohol makes our eyes water, our nose run and a sip triggers retching, then if you do swallow any, you will start vomiting. Our bodies know what is good for us and innately protect us from anything highly toxic.

We don't drink neat alcohol because we can't. It would literally kill us. Instead, we drink small percentages of the stuff (ethanol) dressed up in a multitude of strong flavours diluting it. It's a fallacy to ever say that we like the taste of alcohol. No, we don't. In fact, we like the taste of the sugar, grapes, hops, barley and all the other flavours obfuscating the repugnant taste.

So, why do we force ourselves to mask the taste of something to drink it? Well, beyond the taste, there's a whole emotional association going on around what that drink represents to us per our belief systems. I'm Popular, I'm Fun, I'm Grown Up, I'm So Executive, My Friends Love Me More, fill in the blanks ... when I drink. The emotional motivation to drink is thus also a highly prevalent factor in our taste perception, which we dull down and slowly over the years build tolerance to. We anesthetize ourselves to the fact that alcohol tastes horrible and makes us feel awful.

3. The destabilization alcohol wreaks on our homeostatic state places a ferocious pressure on the body to return to normal function and lasts around five days. That's five long days of our bodies needing to make adjustments and burn energy trying to restabilize us back to homeostasis. The burdens that alcohol brings to our bodies include:

i) **Dehydration** – alcohol is a diuretic and tricks our brain into thinking we're overhydrated while we're drinking. It triggers abrupt chemical reactions that shut down our active hydration system, which then take days to re-regulate.

ii) **Disturbed sleep** – as glutamine levels attempt to restabilize hours after our last alcoholic drink, our body wakes to begin the complex chain of activities required to remove toxins and attempt to rebalance disrupted hormonal and chemical settings the body needs for normal function. In blasts tedious insomnia.

iii) **Emotional dysfunction** – alcohol is a depressant and an anesthetic. Fact. And it's a nonsense myth that your true feelings are revealed when you're drunk; these are, in fact, befuddled, deranged, very unclear, unowned thoughts. You are not yourself when drunk.

iv) **Cravings** – we may develop a craving for alcohol in certain moments, situations, with particular people, or at key life stages. It is very easy to build habits that lead to cravings, which lead to serious problems.

v) **Metabolic imbalance** – our whole system is disrupted chemically when we drink alcohol. Alcohol is an appetite stimulant making us feel hungry even when we are not. Also, its anesthetic properties deaden our natural alert to tell us when we are full. Furthermore, alcohol is not an energy humans can use as it cannot be stored as fat. However, it does ensure what we eat while we are drinking is immediately and urgently stored as fat. Enter an increased risk of obesity for heavy drinkers.

The most important point here is that we are forcing our bodies to cope with a myriad of additional processes and functions just to get back to baseline functioning. We disrupt our chemical, physical, emotional, intellectual and hormonal systems with each sip. The more sips we have the more extreme the disruption.

If you are committed to healthy productivity and making impact in your family, your work, your world, alcohol can seem like sabotage. It's absolutely possible to be sober and to still go out socializing and carrying on with life as before, just without booze. Why deplete energy reserves when life demands so much energetic balancing already? How about choosing Energy?

BIG IMPACT REFLECTION:
AN ALCOHOL-FREE LIFE VISUALISATION

Take the time to reflect on these questions:

1 Where did alcohol feature in your life in early childhood, from your first encounter observing adults with it to your own first sips?
2 What did alcohol do to your relationships throughout your teens and early adulthood e.g. did relationships with caregivers strengthen through alcohol or diminish?
3 What can you learn from these memories about your own drinking patterns today?
4 What do you feel about alcohol today?
5 What would your life look like without alcohol in it? Free-write about an imaginary future where you are sober and happy, healthy and thriving.

Energy Zone No. 2: Rejuvenation

Sir Dave Brailsford transformed team sport forever. Taking the role as head of British Cycling in 2002, he inherited a team with almost no record of success: in 76 years, Britain had only won a single gold medal in its history. Under Sir Dave's leadership, that quickly changed. The squad won seven out of ten track cycling gold medals at the 2008 Beijing Olympics, impressively matching this achievement at the London Olympics four years later.

A former professional cycler who holds an MBA, Sir Dave applied a theory of marginal gains to cycling. He wagered that if the team itemised every single thing that goes into competing on a bike, and then improved each element by 1 per cent, the impact would be a significant aggregated increase in performance. So, he reduced the risk of dust in equipment by painting transport truck floors white, enabling microscopic visibility, hired surgeons to teach the team proper hand-washing to avoid germs, and modified diet per cyclist. He also, and most relevantly for us, focused on sleep by studying the optimal mattress, pillow and room condition for each cyclist to maximize their shut-eye. It all worked to improve performance consistently and the team have enjoyed numerous Tour de France victories since.[39]

Similarly, sleep can be one of your super uplevelling marginal gains in your Big Impact Energy Strategy. Decent sleep absolutely plays a role in your performance and your impact. Sleep deprivation or low-quality sleep would risk your cycling team not winning the race, but could also impact your promotion, passing your exam or getting the kids in the car without raging on the school run. Having grown up in the 80s where the "work hard, play hard" mentality of the day was all pervasive, it took multiple burnouts for me to understand that sleep needs to be revered. It also took me a while to learn that sleeping tablets are not the answer.

Arianna Huffington, a renowned advocate for wellbeing and founder of Thrive Global is a prolific ambassador for sleep, after her dramatic head injury from burnout mid-career. When we met in her New York Thrive Global HQ, over our lemon and cucumber infused water, she told me, "Sleep is a nonnegotiable aspect of overall health and productivity. Once individuals recognize the transformative power of sufficient, quality sleep both wellbeing and performance improve." She underscores the importance of establishing a consistent sleep routine, with a set bedtime and wake-up time, to regulate the body's internal clock. Her tips include minimizing exposure to screens before bedtime, keeping the bedroom dark and cool and using comfortable bedding. She recommends (and religiously practices herself) disconnecting from electronic devices at least 30 minutes before sleep to facilitate relaxation and engaging in calming activities such as reading or meditation.

Like Arianna, I know sleep matters. I know we need a sleep routine and to prioritize enabling decent, deep and rejuvenating sleep. But what happens when menopausal hormones disrupt nocturnal serenity? What happens when baby twins are awake every forty minutes all night and you've still got a business to run? What happens when your partner snores like an ogre? What happens when your bladder wakes you but you can't get back to sleep for hours knowing the alarm will go off soon and you're going to have a horrific day because you'll be so tired?? What then?

Oh, Mr Sandman, Bring Me a Dream, Please ...

If we have periods in life where sleep disruption is commonplace, we must do everything in our power to establish the best conditions to both fall asleep and stay asleep, silencing any insomniac mental screams by trusting we have done all we can to enable rest and acknowledging that even just stillness in bed is rejuvenating.

Try these tips:

- **A pre-bedtime bath.** This is a comforting habit for stimulating the parasympathetic nervous system, soothing anxious thoughts, lifting mood, slowing heart rate and aiding recovery from the stressors of the day.[40] Add in lavender or other aromatherapy oils you're drawn to, perhaps some Epsom salts (absorbing magnesium through the skin accelerates detoxification and lowers inflammation), light a candle and enjoy the recuperating effects of warm water immersion. When your body temperature slightly elevates, a state of healing envelops the body, so this is a good transition from your workday freneticism into gentle rejuvenation. I sometimes hop in mine as soon as I walk through the door and spend my evening hours at home in pjs, freshly scrubbed and moisturized, the day neatly junctured into the past.
- **Make going to bed the start of your new day.** Bedtime really is the start of your tomorrow. Mess these eight hours up and the next day has the potential to be rotten. So gear up to gear down with sanctity. Invest in sumptuous bedding and bed clothes, get black-out curtains (IKEA have made this easy and affordable), ensure the temperature is optimal for your sleep preferences and for goodness' sake don't have any screens in the bedroom.
- **Maximize melatonin.** Melatonin is a magical little hormone produced by the pineal gland, which follows a daily pattern during your 24-hour circadian rhythm. At low levels during daylight, melatonin increases in the evening as

sunset then darkness descend, making you drowsy, then asleep, peaking in the middle of the night during deep slumber. As the sun rises, our melatonin levels diminish, and we wake up. Mess this cycle up with different time zones, blue light exposure or acute stress and melatonin deregulation means bad sleep and low energy. If you can't get into the dark or avoid screens and travel long-haul frequently, melatonin supplements are an option, but ensure you consult a practitioner for advice. Certain foods from teas to nuts to olive oil and fruits also encourage melatonin production.

- **Honour a sleep routine.** Weekends or otherwise, go to bed and get up at the same time every day. Calculate the optimal number of hours you need to function fantastically and allow that amount of time in bed, including drifting off time. For 14 consecutive days, go to sleep at the same time and see what time you naturally wake up, make a note and that will be your average. Generally, it's between seven to eight hours.
- **Prioritize early bedtimes.** Go to bed at around 10pm without having consumed stimulants. The 90-minute sleep phase before midnight is one of the most powerful and double the value of sleep after midnight as it's a key replenishment phase physically, mentally and emotionally within natural human circadian rhythms.
- **Calm your mind.** Allow yourself to be still in silence. Read fiction. Journal to capture today's activities and dump any tomorrow worries. Meditate or listen to guided hypnosis before sleep or upon waking (or if you wake in the night to get back to sleep).
- **Halt consumption.** Stop drinking liquid several hours before bed to ensure your bladder doesn't wake you in the night. Avoid eating three hours before you plan to sleep as digestion wakes up your body.

BIG IMPACT REFLECTION: THE GIFT OF SLEEP

Let's analyse your current sleep set-up to assess how optimal your routines are for deep, restorative sleep. Consider your current sleep habits. How many hours of sleep do you typically get, and how restful is it? Think about your bedroom's comfort, darkness, noise levels and temperature. Is anyone next to you disturbing your sleep? Are little ones interrupting your sleep? Reflect on your wind-down routine before bed. Do you have practices that help you relax like meditation, reading, journalling or taking a warm bath? How might these routines be improved or adjusted to enhance your sleep quality? Free-write about a reality where you sleep wonderfully every night and the impact this will have on your life.

Work Breaks

In the two weeks before Roger Bannister made history by cracking the four-minute mile, he was on holiday. He wasn't pounding the track daily, focusing body and mind religiously on 6 May 1954's race day goal. Nope, he was on holiday, hiking in Scotland with some non-runner pals strictly briefed not to mention the below-four-minute target.

Was he slacking? Lazily meandering off his life's raison d'etre? Absolutely not. Well aware of the positive impact of rest, he decided to grant himself a full two weeks away, deliberate and tightly scheduled as part of his success plan.

He decided in advance to courageously strategize rest before reward. And it was well strategized indeed, as in 3 minutes, 59.4 seconds, Roger Bannister did magnificently break one of the greatest sporting barriers in human history.

His decision is one reflective of most athletes who've learned to perceive rest as integral to their training plan. The best athletes in the world, in fact, all prioritize sleep just as much as they prioritize their hardest training sessions and their most important competitions. They've decided rest matters as much as the physical exertion.

Now, let's flip this into our modern corporate working worlds. We aren't as tuned in to our bodies as professional athletes to know when rest periods need to be prioritized. In fact, as you learned earlier, not only are we burning out but we're not even bothering to take our holiday allowance.

It's surely common sense that to be productive we need to blend healthy, stimulating stress (work) with rejuvenation periods (leisure) to maintain good energy levels. In their book, *Peak Performance*, Brad Stulberg and Steve Magness teach that the only equation we need to master is "Stress + Rest = Growth", and they assert, "This equation holds true regardless of what it is that you are trying to grow".[41] If we take the analogy of building bicep muscles by lifting weights, we exert, exert, exert, 15 reps at a time, then rest, repeat the reps, then rest further for several days. The muscles have been stressed, and it's during the subsequent rest and recovery period that the muscles repair and grow stronger. It's in the balance of intense effort (stress) with adequate recovery (rest) that optimal performance and consistent growth can be achieved. And so it is with our mental ability and pushing ourselves toward sustained success and wellbeing, we have to factor in rest.

So, let me ask you, how do you rest? Do you truly rejuvenate when you're not working or is your time filled with buddies, booze and buzz? Are your holidays hectic city tours dashing from one itinerary to the next? Do you turn into Supermum, hosting pumpkin-carving parties and sewing flamboyant Halloween costumes for everyone? Or do you nourish your soul with restful leisure? That's the ideal; finding the zen that enables you to mentally divert thought away from the cognitive focus of the day-to-day work, and instead float into reading or hiking or paddling on the shoreline with your toddler. The break needs to truly be a mind shift away from work, and a pause from incessant productivity. Just shifting location won't necessarily do it. If the to-do list travels to the new destination too, that is not switching off. Equally, just because you've switched on your OOO (Out of Office), doesn't mean you're resting if the sewing machine is going 100 miles per hour and the kitchen floor is being endlessly mopped for pumpkin goo.

I'm sure you'll be in two camps here: those who attest to loving work so much it's bliss to be on a beach responding to emails, and those who absolutely know how to set boundaries to recharge adequately and have a holiday. But, who do you think is less likely to burnout further down the line? However much you love your work and apparently need to attend to the business at all times, if you don't create space for your brain and body to relax, you will eventually collapse. It is not sustainable to only work, and however much you love it – yes, I whole-heartedly know ambition and boss-babeing can become addictive – it will be triggering harmful stress hormones, using brain energy and pulling you away from that heavenly present you worked hard to get yourself to.

Breaktimes are necessary, and more than a few weeks a year, of course. There are known benefits to breaking across the day with both microbursts – petting the cat or grabbing a snack – and proper time away from work like the traditional lunch hour. Biologically, it's imperative to rest our brains to be able to contribute intelligently and impactfully. Abundant research on naps, meditation, nature walks and the habits of exceptional artists, as well as athletes, has evidenced how mental breaks replenish attention spans and, by default, increase productivity later.

Think about the way you take breaks – are you moving from one task straight to another, pausing only to scroll through emails or text messages, browse an online store or post to social media? These "breaks" may actually be wearing you down.

The Learning Center at the University of North Carolina at Chapel Hill suggests new ways to take a break that may be more energizing:

- getting creative (daydreaming, colouring, learning)
- moving (going outside, stretching)
- nourishing (drinking water or hot drinks)
- and socializing (calling a pal)[42]

When a brain is exhausted by one task, it can be rejuvenating to flit to something entirely different. Nick Hall, loveable Aussie author of *I Know What To Do, So Why Don't I Do It?*, teaches us that when growing weary of a left-brain analytical task (for example, number crunching the week's sales data), it's a useful leadership hack to quickly change work theme entirely and flip to a creative, right-brain task (for example, writing the comms for your launch announcement). Sparking the other side of the brain gives us a surge of energy, which is healthy and creates renewed motivation, concentration and reinvigorates general cognitive function.

Do please bear in mind, however, that when we dart too rapidly from unconnected task to unrelated, challenging task, then back again, zig, zag, zig, zagging, we dangerously risk plunging into total cognitive shutdown. Our brains simply cannot cope with the frenzied oscillation of this then that, over and over without a break. Eventually we fizzle as our energy is violently depleted after too much cognitive bouncing. We hit mental burnout (which quickly descends into the physical). Thinking becomes fuzzy, we become irritable and decision-making starts to become ineffectual. So, yes, hop from your pipeline analysis mid-morning and work creatively on your tag line until lunch, but don't ever assume you can maintain flitting constantly, every 30 minutes, no way. Focus and flow are key to productivity and we'll learn more about this in the Time chapter.

The Relaxation Conundrum

"People look for retreats for themselves, in the country, by the coast, or in the hills. There is nowhere that a person can find a more peaceful and trouble-free retreat than in his own mind. ... So constantly give yourself this retreat, and renew yourself."

— Marcus Aurelius

Catherine, a cool, blonde creative director in her early 40s, erupted into giggles opposite me, her eyes creasing as she shook her head saying, "Oh well, goodness, how do I relax? Now, there's a question!" There indeed was the question, but should an enquiry like that make someone laugh? Has relaxation become such an alien occurrence that it's plain funny?

Researching this book, I interviewed lots of women (clients, colleagues, industry peers and networkers) about their relaxation habits. Responses often included driving, cooking, gardening, ironing (yes, seriously, with the radio on apparently), putting makeup on and going to the gym. There were also many mentions of ice baths and making time to journal. I heard a lot about performative "relaxation" and effortful and determined fitting in of "me time". Only one true role model stood out for me: someone who set aside deliberate and conscious crochet time as a daily pleasure in life, gently organized into every day without a finite objective to complete anything, simply to relax.

The point around relaxation is that it should bring stillness and tranquillity. I'm a fan of making soups, slicing and peeling my way into relaxation while listing to an audio book. I know it soothes me to connect soulfully to Nature's harvest, maternally feeding my rabble as the tribal elder and all that, but actually, I'm still abuzz with doing stuff. Even in that version of "relaxation", I'm very active: listening, learning and doing. Pure relaxation, in its most rejuvenating form, comes when the mind is still, when quietness descends and inner serenity blooms. This can't happen when you're busy being *and* doing. We'll learn about mindfulness and meditation later, but let's see if you can answer the question that made Catherine laugh so hard, without laughing.

BIG IMPACT REFLECTION: HOW DO YOU RELAX?

Reflect on how well you incorporate relaxation into your life. How do you recharge? Think back to your childhood and the activities that brought you joy and pleasure. Think about what you gravitate toward when you find yourself alone today with unfilled time and what you look forward to doing most? Do you honour holidays as true downtime? What totally rejuvenates you? Who? Where? Design your dream life with an abundance of relaxation in it. Let your mind wander into the mists of fun, serenity, soul restoration and good times. How can you bring more of this into your everyday reality right now?

Nature's Energetic Abundance

The Japanese have a practice, *shinrin yoku*, "forest bathing", where one observes nature and breathes deeply to relax. Just bask in that for a minute please. What an intoxicating description of strolling beneath a leafy canopy, inhaling the damp freshness, twigs cracking underfoot. They've captured it perfectly: soothing, relaxing and, like a bath, washes away any pesky stress. Being in the great outdoors is a tonic bursting with benefits for our energy and wellbeing, rolling into our bodies, minds and souls like moss caressing a stone.

Scientists have long heralded the stress-reducing effects of being outside, with countless studies espousing how exposure to nature enhances mood, creativity and even problem-solving abilities. We're not limited to woods here either. Think parks, coastlines, your own courtyard with its flower boxes; getting close to nature has a way of lifting us out of our heads, away from the bustle of the day and into a different, calmer energetic space. Even just looking at the sky momentarily and truly taking it in can produce a sense of awe. When absorbed in the majesty of the kingdom of the birds and the bees, suddenly that email you accidentally sent to the wrong person won't seem as big and cringy. We shrink beneath the incredulity of Mother Earth, and it's humbling. Sara Blakely, hilarious, inspiring and legendary billionairess founder of Spanx, divinely flattering underwear creations, says that before any big speaking event, she grounds herself by looking up at the sky and remembering how miniscule and irrelevant she is in the grand scheme of things. "Before I speak I try to connect with nature ... it reminds me of how small I am (in the best way). So the next time you're nervous ... look at the sky and remember you're just one of eight BILLION people flying through space. You got this."[43]

When you pop the Lycra on for the hilltop bootcamp, or partake in "green exercise" as outdoor workouts are referred to, the sheer greenness means your exercise has longer and more positive impact afterwards than inner city or indoor workouts[44]. Not only will you increase your overall vitality and improve cardiovascular function, but your circadian rhythms regulate meaning better sleep, you become more mindful and it all bolsters the immune system and increases energy. Engaging in outdoor activities, even in short breaks, boosts productivity, concentration and overall mental energy. So, whether a walking meeting, a lunchtime jog, a weekend dog walk or just commuting to the office the long way round through the park, being in nature is a holistic and rejuvenating experience easy to access.

Energy Zone No. 3: Maintenance

We can eat well, rest well, and then a curveball hits. A new crisis needs managing, a deadline shortens, the unexpected slams into us and we lose our cool. It is in these inevitable moments that happen "to us" when we need strategies to maintain homeostatic equilibrium, to protect us from the destabilizing impact of stress. It's not only external events that can tip us into energy misalignment. We can do it to ourselves with impassioned over-work as we excitedly embrace a new idea, working through the night to birth it. Equally, we can deplete mental energy overthinking and overanalysing ourselves into exhaustion, literally creating physical stress in our bodies through thought alone. So, becoming aware of our own emotional, mental and physical stress levels (and don't forget that we're all bio-individual) is essential to preserving energy.

There's a bell curve called the Peak Performance Curve, identified by scientists Yerkes and Dodson, that depicts optimal levels of stress against productivity. If we're understimulated, we become bored and apathetic and performance suffers. If we're overstimulated, then performance suffers but equally so do we, as we flail downward toward burnout. The peak of the curve represents perfect productivity balance. This is where there's healthy, invigorating stress, fused with high performance and excellent output.

Yerkes Dodson Peak Performance Curve

Good stress is when is when we feel our heart quicken, pulse race and hormones change, but there's no threat or fear. Think how you feel when heading into a negotiation, going in for that first kiss or about to jump into an ice bath! It's excitement or nerves: short, fast and momentarily intense. There are many triggers for this type of good stress, and it keeps us feeling alive and enthusiastic about life; it's motivating and pure. On the other hand, chronic bad stress comes when we repeatedly face stressors that take a heavy toll, weighing heavily, feeling inescapable: an unhappy marriage, a sick loved one or unrelenting work pressure, for example. This is categorized as long-term, serious stress.

Brené Brown, the down-to-earth queen of vulnerability and shame research, identified that our personality types mean we either over- or under-function in moments of extreme stress. The under-functioners become so overwhelmed, they simply stop. The over-functioners keep propelling onward and upward, saying yes repeatedly, taking on more and more. The latter "do instead of feel". In *The Gifts of Imperfection*, Brené writes, "Over-functioners tend to move quickly to advise, rescue, take over, micromanage, and get in other people's business rather than look inward."[45]

Typical warning signs of over-functioning are when you start feeling self-righteous and better than others, becoming judgemental and critical, frustrated when things don't happen your way with an exasperated, "Oh I'll do it myself then!", and so on. Under-functioners tend to get less competent under stress. They invite others to take over and often become the focus of family gossip, worry or concern.

Interestingly, couples comprising one over- and one under-functioner can be driven apart without the self-awareness of these stress-coping mechanisms. However, if identified and acknowledged, the couple can grow stronger together, so it's wise to look at yourself and your partner's respective patterns here.

The Slippery Slope into Adrenal Fatigue

Let's take a moment for a quick biology lesson building upon what we learned earlier about the amygdala hijack. Emotionally, stress can trigger fear, anxiety and anger, and when prolonged can lead into depression and apathy. As we know, this is because stress activates our fight or flight response, the prehistoric neurological "save me" alarm, which of course tires out eventually as it's designed for emergencies not perpetuity.[46]

Physiologically, the cascade of chemicals that stress incurs travels rapidly through our body, sending messages to our organs and glands, large muscles and even our immune system. The flood begins with the release of epinephrine and norepinephrine by our adrenal glands and continues with the release of cortisol. Fabulous initially, cortisol elevates attention and alertness and prepares our organs to withstand stress, pain or injury (the left side of the performance curve), but if this potent little hormone sticks around too long, our immune system is suppressed, making us super vulnerable to infection and burnout (the right side of the curve). This immunological impact is so significant: it's why, for organ transplants, the recipients' bodies are pumped full of cortisol to ensure the new organ won't be rejected; the immune system is mechanically switched off.

Our autonomic nervous system is designed to ensure we manage stress adequately. Flowing nerve cells between our brain and spinal cord, the ANS branches into two – our sympathetic nervous system (SNS) and our parasympathetic nervous system (PNS). The SNS accelerates responses that protect us from danger, and the PNS is like a brake, calming us down and returning us to our harmonious homeostatic state. So, think SNS – fight or flight, and PNS – appetite, sleepiness, sex and fun stuff.

Our amazing bodies also have one more safety valve in the form of our vagus nerve. If the SNS doesn't work in an emergency, this is stimulated and, instead of fighting or flighting, we freeze – think of a deer in headlights, or a car about to hit us – we don't have time to act, so we shut down, literally immobilized. If the situation is extreme, you may feel faint, dizzy or even lose consciousness.

The shutting down response of the vagus nerve can become a learned helplessness to threats like rejection, failure or overwhelm. So, in modern times of great stress, as well as our ego feeling battered and protective, luring us into a safety zone of inertia, we may suffer physically with an uncontrollable paralysis. The cure here is training our brains for resilience.

When neurons in our brains send and receive chemical messengers, like dopamine, linked to motivation and reward-seeking, we are primed for peak performance, surging with energy to produce brilliant and plentiful work. Neurotransmitters like dopamine, serotonin and GABA, also activate our memory centres. When helpful, we can easily recall good memories about how we've managed stressful situations and calm ourselves, but when detrimental, we can inadvertently make ourselves feel even more stressed by recalling bad memories and assuming this situation will slide into negativity as before, thus spiralling into more extreme physical and emotional responses. How do we avoid this? Again, it comes down to training our brains for resilience.

Later, in your Big Impact Work Strategy, you will zone in on resilience and learn an eight-step Stress Success System to ensure your work output is never inhibited by stress and that your stress response isn't maladaptive. Here, we're focusing on maintaining your energy levels for maximum impact. This requires nourishing your adrenals and avoiding sliding into adrenal fatigue.

Loving Our Witless Adrenals

We will inevitably face negative health effects, physical, mental and emotional, if we deal with chronic stress for an extended period of time. Prolonged periods of excessive cortisol have a range of negative impacts, including raised blood pressure, higher risk of cardiovascular disease, osteoporosis, muscle weakness and weight gain. They obviously hamper cognitive function, too, which fosters anxiety, moodiness and potentially shoddy decision-making. Think about that flash that you feel when you're hot and flappy in those high-stress moments. That is the cortisol surge. (It's also when you should be locked in a cupboard away from people before you say, do or decide anything rash.)

When our adrenal glands are pumping like a vigorously firing water pistol, pelting our system with those emergency chemicals to combat stress, they're just doing their job, bless them. Sitting above the kidneys, we have two of them, and they activate when our brain subconsciously reads a situation as dangerous. Overuse of these little innocent glands tips the entire hormonal system out of balance, triggering the extreme physical, mental and emotional slumps we experience with burnout.

So, make a concerted effort to nourish your adrenals. Everything you've learned so far in this strategy will contribute, and here are some specific tips for steadying and negating the impacts of an overflow of cortisol.

1. Adaptogens are herbs, roots and other plant substances (like mushrooms) that help our bodies manage stress and restore balance after a stressful situation has occurred. A supplement like ashwagandha is meant to enhance sleep and athletic performance. Research the different options and seek practitioner advice to find your most appealing remedy to try.

2. Caffeine stimulates the adrenal glands, so avoid it altogether or switch to low-caffeine options like matcha tea (it comes in a potent green powder form, unbleached by the sun in its preparation, so is packed with pure goodness) that has a gazillion additional health benefits, from antioxidants to calming properties. I've even sourced some in pods to run through my coffee machine and still have the frothy milk indulgence of a latte without any coffee twitchiness. Matcha has around 35mg of caffeine in a standard cup versus coffee's 200mg.

3. Drink loads of water, ideally 2 to 3 litres per day (70–100 fl oz/4–6 pints).

4. Choose herbal teas that support liver cleansing, like liquorice, milk-thistle and dandelion, and do regular liver cleanses. In Eastern philosophy, the liver was always considered a part of the digestive system.

5. Beware of the toxic fumes from cleaning products and air pollution as well as chemicals in makeup and moisturizers as the skin absorbs everything.

6. Get out into nature daily and absorb it fully with all your senses. Really soak it up.

7. Try chakra cleansing visualizations – I've made one for you to download at biancabest.com.

8. Prioritize sleep by following the best-practice tips taught earlier on in this chapter to promote hormone balance and the natural repair processes that occur while we sleep.

9. Soothe the adrenals with fibre and seeds – chia, hemp, pumpkin, etc., and salmon, chicken, eggs, leafy greens and cruciferous vegetables.

10. Use coconut oil for cooking (to roast sweet potatoes, for example) or mixed with your herbal teas –experiment. It's a good, healthy fat, rich in triglycerides that support brain function and nourish the adrenals. Avocadoes are wonderfully beneficial for the adrenal glands, too.
11. Turmeric and ginger are great for reducing fatigue, inflammation and pain, and the adrenals love them. Take as supplements or freshly sliced or ground in teas, cooking, however creative you can get.
12. Trial intermittent fasting (with your healthcare practitioner's guidance) as pausing the body from digesting allows the adrenals to settle, as well as stabilizing blood sugar, lowering inflammation and being great for the microbiome. I'm a huge fan of 16:8, where I do all my eating in an eight-hour window per day, and know that from 6 or 7pm, I'll be stopping for 16 hours to let my body rejuvenate.
13. Get moving and breathe. Deep breathing exercises stroke the vagus nerve and motion is key to energy cadence throughout the body (and mind).

Motion and Energetic Flow

The more science evolves, the more we're learning about our biofields' energetic flow throughout the body. Yogis, reiki healers and enlightened scientists teach that energy blocks can form and there are clever mental efforts that can get the flow regulated once more – think Kundalini yoga classes and chakra-clearing meditations. Regardless of what you're into, you can probably recognize when you feel stuck. Stuck in a mind loop over a situation, creatively blocked on a workstream or in a funky mood just because you woke up that way, just stuck.

Exercise is excellent at shifting energy and lifting mood. Emotion is quite simply energy in motion: "e-motion". David R Hawkins cleverly plotted an energy scale associated with emotions in his ground-breaking book *Power vs Force: The Hidden Determinants of Human Behaviour*. His "Levels of Consciousness" study, based on applied kinesiology, or muscle testing, with millions of calibrations over several years, produced a logarithmic scale ranging from 1 to 1,000 measuring energy values per emotion. The spectrum ranges from low energy states such as Shame, Apathy and Guilt, sliding up to Willingness, Love and Joy, the high energy ones. We apparently reverberate at a certain energetic vibe per emotional state and obviously the lower states have negative impact, inside and out. However, there is always fluidity up and down the scale (depending on our thoughts) and physical movement helps emotions propel along the scale, ideally upward.

Strong emotions tend to last only 60 to 90 seconds, but if our thoughts keep triggering the emotion to reappear, we can feel trapped in our own minds, which is exhausting. So, if you're not enjoying the emotions you're feeling right now, move. Do it. Work out. Find your thang. Get in the gym, get outdoors, tidy your bedroom, clean the kitchen, get moving. Basically, move yourself happy!

Remember the mitochondria, those powerhouses of cells vibrantly activated during exercise? Well, they're gagging to effervesce inside your muscle cells, increasing available fuel from glucose and oxygen, catapulting energy upward. When you exercise, you literally increase your body's energy supply. And bring on those delicious little endorphins that get surging as you pump iron, not only do they feel fantastic in the moment but are healthily addictive and more likely to lure you back to more exercise again.

Try to get into a regular rhythm of incorporating exercise into your life. Twenty minutes every day is a good goal. This can be a simple as walking instead of catching the bus, taking the stairs instead of the lift, lifting dumbbells at your desk while watching a webinar, or as hardcore as 5km raced at 13kmph on the treadmill, it's entirely up to you. If you don't prioritize exercise, please don't moan about low energy.

BIG IMPACT REFLECTION: YOUR EXERCISE EXUBERANCE

Reflect on your favourite exercise/s. Think back to physical activities you loved as a child, whether sport, dance or tree climbing. What made you feel most alive? What about now? What exercise do you enjoy? Is there anything you particularly gravitate toward – high impact or gentle, indoors or outdoors, alone or in a group? Envisage your utopian fitness routine with your dream fitness levels making you surge with energy and vibrant vitality. Are there any steps you can take to incorporate that vision into your reality today?

Honouring Your Bespoke Energetic Rhythms

Identifying your levels of stress against productivity is important and something you need to assess regularly. Building a sense of you in your good, energized, brilliantly productive mode and maintaining this is the ideal. To avert a potentially flailing, over-extended, non-thriving, adrenally fatigued mode requires acute awareness of when you're at the peak of the curve, precariously teetering toward the downward slope. You are accountable for where you allow yourself to sit on the performance curve, so let's assess and ascertain if you're on the left or the right, the positive or the negative side.

BIG IMPACT REFLECTION: YOUR PEAK PRODUCTIVITY

Reflect on where you currently sit on the Yerkes-Dodson Stress Performance Curve based on your life today. Consider your recent experiences: have you felt consistently energized and motivated, or often overwhelmed and exhausted? Zone in on a previous moment when you were operating in peak productivity; thriving, feeling focused, accomplishing tasks efficiently and feeling satisfied. What was happening at that time to see you flourishing so? How were you able to accomplish what you did without sliding down the negative side of the curve? What was the encouraging stress guiding and motivating you?

Now, think of a time you were unhealthily stressed and if there were warning signs prior, like increased irritability, fatigue or procrastination. What were the pressures creating stress at this time and who, what or where did they come from? Examine your experiences on both sides of the curve and observe any obvious adjustments you can make to your routine or environment to find and sustain your peak balance between stress and productivity. Now, free-write about you living and operating in that peak state consistently forever more. How will you feel? What will you do? Where will you be? What will your days be filled with? How well will it all flow? Let your mind wander into the dream fully. This is your life of Big Impact Without Burnout.

Now that you have a sense of stress that healthily stimulates you and provokes you to do your best work, as well as the stressors that trigger you unhealthily, you have a clear sense of what to move toward and what to avoid. Your Harmonic Energy State gracefully rests at your peak productivity. Next, for your energetic maintenance for Big Impact, I invite you to score yourself as currently Energized or Depleted based on components of each of the energy zones you've learned about in this strategy. This will empower you to start working with your energy instead of against it, understanding how and what enlivens you and what drains you, to ensure you modify your lifestyle to embrace more of the zingy stuff. A reminder: we're not meant to be exhausted all the time, the clues are all in your map.

BIG IMPACT REFLECTION:
YOUR HARMONIC ENERGY STATE MAP

Reflecting on each of the questions below, score yourself as honestly as you can. 1 is Poor, 5 is Excellent. So, if you drink too much alcohol and you know it's taking its toll on you, then score yourself a 1. Pop an X in the relevant box. Once complete, you have your Harmonic Energy State map of where to focus attention to improve. Any items that scored 3 or lower need addressing to shift you into Big Impact Energy consistently.

	1	2	3	4	5
ENERGY ZONE 1: NOURISHMENT					
How well do you feed your gut microbiome?					
Do you eat a low inflammation diet?					
Are you aware of the GI index of food?					
Do you drink enough water?					
Is fake energy an issue for you (caffeine, sodas, etc.)?					
Do you drink any/too much alcohol?					
ENERGY ZONE 2: REJUVENATION					
How do you rate your sleep quality?					
Do you take regular breaks (daily and holidays)?					
How effective is your relaxation?					
Do you spend plenty of time in nature?					
ENERGY ZONE 3: MAINTENANCE					
Is your lifestyle stressing your adrenals?					
How's your exercise routine?					
How stressed do you feel?					
How productive are you?					

Your Big Impact Energy Expansion Grid

We've covered a lot of ground in these pages and it's time to take stock and evaluate what you understand, what you'd like to research further and what pledges you will make to embrace a conscious and empowered Energy Strategy into your life.

By now, you have all the tools necessary to shift from an overriding sense of being drained into a place of being energetically balanced.

In the grid below is what you now know how to manage.

It's time to translate this into solid action to make your expansion a reality.

Once again, grab your journal and review the statements below, focusing on the "Expanding To" column. Spend 30 minutes free-writing on everything that comes up for you when you read the expansion statements. Elaborate on them where you see fit and make them entirely yours. As well as writing the "what", dive into the "how" and "why". Really explore the statements, applying your newfound knowledge, and have fun immersing yourself in all the life-altering ways you're going to feel and how you're going to get there. Let the inspiration pour forth and capture everything that comes to mind.

FROM	EXPANDING TO...
I have depleted energy reserves.	I have regular and abundant zing.
I suffer from poor quality and duration of sleep. I am an insomniac.	I respect my bodily rhythms enabling nocturnal balance and rejuvenating slumber through routine and melatonin regulation.
I am wired most of the time.	I feel grounded and honour my homeostatic state, enjoying a feeling of harmony within.
I don't pay much attention to nutrition. I am reliant on fake energy.	I am nourished. I respect my brain and gut connection and feed myself well.
I push beyond "normal" output levels.	I honour my productivity balance consciously.
I am stressed and burning out/burned out.	I am acutely aware of my peak performance tipping point and preserve myself from sliding negatively down the scale.
I am physically drained and look exhausted.	I am glowing and radiate a vibrant aura. I feel fit and energetically abundant.

(Continued)

FROM	EXPANDING TO...
I stay cosy and sluggish in my comfort zone and things tend to stay the same.	I am enlivened by new experiences and have the energy and drive to explore. I feel alive!
My habits are self-sabotaging but I'm too busy to change them.	I am conscious of everything I consume and do and how it impacts my energetic rhythms. I take full accountability for how energized I feel.
I don't exercise, it's not for me.	I have found a way to integrate exercise into my life and enjoy moving my body and energy daily.
I don't have enough energy.	I have all the energy I need to fully embrace my life!

Your Big Impact Decision Pledges

It's decision time. You've explored the energy zones of Nourishment, Rejuvenation and Maintenance that take you to your Harmonic Energy State, you are clear on the interconnectedness of body, mind and soul in energy management and you've gathered positive intention in your journal reflection exercises.

Now, harnessing the power of decision, write down three Energy Pledges you will make to ensure your expansion unfurls.

I pledge to work with my energy to create my biggest impact without ever burning out by ...

_____

_____

_____

YOUR BIG IMPACT STRATEGY NO. 2: MINDSET

"Set your ambitions, even if you are uncertain about what they should be. The better ambitions have to do with the development of character and ability, rather than status and power. Status you can lose. You carry character with you wherever you go, and it allows you to prevail against adversity."

— Jordan B. Peterson

Life is an adventure. Well, it should be. It can be. Your state of mind will influence how you respond to life's undulations, and if you're in adventuring mode or not. Let's face it, life will undulate. Oh boy, will it ebb and flow, carrying us along whether we like it or not. How we roll with its currents, rapid then steady, violent then gentle, swirling then still, endlessly fluid and changing, will be the difference between being a brave, swashbuckling hero or a shackled prisoner.

When we honour our thought patterns and are self-reflective enough to acknowledge limiting belief systems, there's liberty around every corner. In each new life situation lies adventure if we choose to courageously view it that way instead of shying away from it, retreating into the cave of our minds, snug and comfy, but enshrouded in darkness and probably a bit bored.

If we learn to discover our brave self that our ego is trying to protect, we can become more responsive in our reactions to our world. As adventurers, there are endless new horizons to explore. In this chapter, you'll learn how to assess your life through the lens of limiting beliefs and flip them, releasing the locked thoughts that keep you stuck. You'll learn how to shift away from blame into accountability, from self-sabotage into self-compassion, and what positive, nonresistant self-direction looks and feels like. You'll learn the fundamentals of a mindset primed for adventure, courageous, excited and ready for Big Impact!

When Life Hurts

Melinda, a 38-year-old mother and part-time sales director, arrived for our session dishevelled and teary, the opposite of her usual vibrant, confident self. Our sessions, which had paused a year or so ago, usually left little room for true coaching, as they generally comprised her upbeat monologue, blustering about herself. Ego-centric by nature, she gained most of her self-esteem from extrinsic sources (I suspect even seeking this from me). She needed to feel valued to feel valuable. Praise and positive feedback were her fuel to motor out into the world. Obsessed with her looks, her status, her handbags, her perfect family, home, finest champagnes sweetie darling, luxurious trips, rah rah rah, she needed others' high regard to make her feel worthy. But beneath the conceited sheen lay crippling insecurity and lack of self-esteem, as is so often the case with the ego's grippy claws. Her altered demeanour today was because her husband had tragically died a year earlier, abruptly leaving her to support herself and their two young children alone, and now, as the life insurance petered out, she was terrified about what lay ahead, not least the impossibility of how to deliver her usual puff to me in these exceptional circumstances.

All those work ambitions she had previously merrily lauded at me during our working hours together (and inevitably with friends and family, too) – her grand potential, the income she would be earning if she chose to work full-time, the clients she would secure if she chose to launch her business, chose to focus on her career as well as children, chose to unleash her vast talents onto the world – were about to be tested. She was quivering with fear, utterly destabilized, timid and, at last, actually ready. Finally, the ego had shattered, and finally we were able to start work on her self-worth and prepare her to step into the reality of her true potential.

Feeling a sturdy sense of "being enough" does not come easily to everyone, especially women. However, full self-acceptance and self-authority are the base foundations from which to pursue our ambitions. There's a psychologist named Martin Covington, who suggests in his Self-Worth Theory that an individual's focus in life is reaching self-acceptance, and that this can be found through self-achievement. This makes sense: we achieve stuff and thus we feel we can better rely on ourselves. Sure.

His model centres around four interconnected elements of achievement: ability and effort, which when combined affect performance and consequently self-worth. Agreed. We have an innate talent for something (ability), we practise (effort) and – lo and behold – performance improves, and, as we realize we're getting better, our self-esteem strengthens (self-worth). Again, sure. But his theory is based on competition with others. We compare our achievements with others'. We compete. We win. We feel a sense of superiority. We feel proud and thus, according to Covington, accept ourselves.

This is interesting, but ... I don't buy that self-worth is relative. Well, I don't any longer. Nowadays, I won't ever accept that someone else, or my performance when compared with someone else, determines whether or not I feel substantial. For example, I might be a running champion when racing 5km (3 miles) against my 75-year-old father, but an embarrassment to the family name when racing my teenage son. That "achievement" is relative. It's very destabilizing if we look at self-worth through this lens. If we're motivated only by the egoic certainty that we will reign victorious, there's a danger that we'll hold back in life, never risking new abilities or efforts that may yield low performance and thus run the risk of triggering low self-worth. We would end up in a place where we won't chance being invalidated because our ego thwarts us from entering the arena in the first place, or at least it will try.

What if self-worth comes from living with integrity, from honouring heartfelt values and from a grounded knowing that "I am enough"? I believe that in trying out new abilities and applying new levels of effort, we effect change on an inner level, which consequently positively impacts the outer. Stepping into ownership of self-worth through inner power, never extrinsic dependencies, is where true lasting expansion occurs.

Melinda was now on the cusp of testing her ability and effort, consequent performance and thus self-worth. She was finally ready to halt her ego's debilitating fear of failure and judgement and step into a place of courage as the only (and best) way forward.

Stepping into Courage

Did you know that fear and curiosity cannot coexist? Really think about this. They are both mind states. I can look at the dog growling in front of me and either be fearful or curious. I can go into the boardroom to negotiate my severance package and be either fearful or curious. I can publish my first YouTube video and await the likes, dislikes and comments with either fear or curiosity. In every instance, curiosity is the healthier state to be in. Within curiosity lies an endearing innocence to the moment that swells into courage.

When women lean into life with curiosity, courage and positive intention, magic happens. There are numerous examples of inspiring women who embody this, of women who followed their curiosity, seized their pluckiness and forged onward with positive intention. Marie Curie pioneered female contribution to physics and chemistry, winning Nobel prizes in both fields,

making history. The goddess Oprah Winfrey has rocked media mogul-
dom, creating and using her platform to inspire millions for good. Eleanor
Roosevelt, beyond her duties as First Lady of the United States, was a hardcore
civil rights activist. Then there's Jane Goodall and her mesmerizing work with
chimpanzees. Such bravery present always. And such impact, oh, such impact.

Malala Yousafzai, born on 12 July 1997 in Mingora, Pakistan, was journeying
home from a school exam on the bus with her friends beside her, as buddies
do, when the teenagers were shot at by the Taliban. Malala received a bullet
to the head, but she and her friends survived the assassination attempt. She
now devotes her life to advocating for women's rights. She has rightfully
earned the status as a global symbol for girls' education, and her story serves
as a powerful testament to the impact that one individual, even at a young
age, can have in the fight for education and human rights. Her courage and
resilience have inspired millions around the world and if you haven't read her
memoir, *I am Malala: The Girl Who Stood Up for Education and Was Shot
By the Taliban,* I recommend you do. She puts the fear of asking for a pay
rise into stark perspective. On finding courage to risk her activism, she states,
"I told myself, Malala, you have already faced death. This is your second life.
Don't be afraid — if you are afraid, you can't move forward."[47]

Alas, unlike Malala, too many women I meet believe they can't move
forward. They are held back by fear, by limiting beliefs, playing small, wasting
their talents and the "one life" opportunity. My workshops are overflowing
with clients impassioned with wishes and wants, should-haves and could-
haves, voices that aren't being heard. There's so much talent and desire buried
beneath a lack of self-worth. To beat this and get into a zone of your biggest
impact, there are four focus areas of self I invite you to now manage as you
expand into your Mindset Strategy for Big Impact. They are:

- Self-Awareness
- Self-Compassion
- Self-Direction
- Self-Worth

Mastering Self-Awareness

"People need to know that they have all the tools within themselves. Self-awareness, which means awareness of their body, awareness of their mental space, awareness of their relationships – not only with each other, but with life and the ecosystem."

— Deepak Chopra

Deep self-awareness is a prerequisite to growth, always. In coaching, we learn a practice of self-management that focuses on what the client is saying and listening without judgement, without our own stories, without assumptions. We listen and observe the client without getting caught up in their story and if we do become derailed by empathy, or frustration, or want to give advice, we become self-aware of what is occurring in our own minds and self-manage. This skill keeps us performing with the client's agenda as the priority and able to deliver our work optimally.

And so it is in life. If we bring the skill of self-awareness to each moment (or as many moments as we can muster), we avert the risk of becoming unconscious. If we live unconsciously, we create habits, perspectives and thoughts that may not serve us; they may in fact be limiting us and hindering our expansion into a shinier tomorrow. Becoming self-aware and raising our understanding of ourselves and what is driving our habits, perspectives and thoughts, is the road to positive change and, to a certain extent, liberty. Core to this are two important factors – our belief system and our ego.

Belief System

Your adorable, squidgy little baby face emerged into this world as a blank canvas, ready to be imprinted by life. Then life very busily went about training you in what to think. Depending on your family, community, education, location, home and demography, your training will have varied from the baby's in the crib next door. As well as all the mentors flitting around you as you grew, sharing their wisdom with you, you'll have been busy amassing your own experiences, sharpening or deadening some of what you were told. You'll have had bucketloads of fascination encouraging you to explore the world and make sense of it all, as you intuitively sought out what felt right and wrong.

Along the way, your instincts probably got squashed by some of what the well-intended mentors taught you, so, rather than being innate, those imprints were created. You started to realize if you suppressed some of what you felt and thought, or if you said what made the people around you smile and nod approvingly, better things happened, i.e. you got the extra rusk. So, gradually, the buoyant spark of you learned to conform. You may have forayed through childhood gradually believing it was no longer okay to twirl on the dance floor despite how amazing it felt spinning in that skirt with all your might, abandoned to the moment. Then you hit those turbulent teenage years when fitting in was all that mattered, so you absolutely conformed. Then eventually you emerged into adulthood when it felt like you knew it all by then. You learned to navigate the world through a set of beliefs partially passed down to you, partially mandated, partially experienced. You may have rebelled sometimes, and built your own independent beliefs based on your own learning, but for the main part, your belief system was set.

The breadth and diversity of belief systems is what keeps relationships interesting. It's also the cause of a lot of wars and societal fragmentation. There's so much polarization, totalitarianism and dogma to contend with. Modern media, big tech and big corporate profit agendas only cause further confusion. It's hard to know what to believe. But that's not for us to solve here. What we will focus on, and solve for the better, is the role your belief system is playing in your impact.

Limiting beliefs can be as innocuous as, "Oh, I can't slice onions!" or "I'm always late" to the more catastrophizing, "I will never succeed" or "I'll never find a partner". Whatever their gravity, they will inevitably come to pass. If you believe you can't slice onions, you'll never pick up the knife and start chopping. If you operate your life under the apparent inner truth that you are always late, then my lovely flustered one, you will indeed always be late. And if you absolutely, emphatically believe you'll be single, poor, a business failure, destitute, lonely and ill, my doomy gloomy one, so you shall be. As the saying goes, "If you believe you can or you can't, you're right."

What all these negative beliefs do is keep us apparently safe. We don't risk holding the knife, we don't bother going to the networking event, we don't launch the business and we don't register on the dating app because we're too afraid of rejection, failure, shame and all the other awkward emotions we might trigger. We prefer to sit in our limiting belief because we're afraid to try. Trying might cause a momentary tension and hurt us, and we're not sure we're ready to risk that tension, there's too much uncertainty. But oh, the potential beyond that uncertainty!

The first step to flipping limiting beliefs from contraction to expansion is to identify that you have them (and we all do). So, I invite you to complete the following exercise to expand your mind once again and this time note the stories you tell yourself that could be dragging you down muddy holes you're obliviously sliding into.

BIG IMPACT REFLECTION: BLOWING THE CLOUDS OF LIMITING BELIEFS AWAY

Step 1: Create Your Wheel of Big Impact

Take an A4 sheet of paper – on both sides, draw a circle and divide them into eight segments, labelling them with the Big Impact strategy areas of your life: Energy, Mindset, Purpose, Time, Work, Connection, Wealth and Fulfilment. Title one circle "Today" and the one on the reverse "Tomorrow".

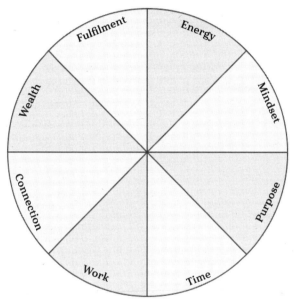

Step 2: Rate Today

Now, starting with the Limiting Wheel, reflect on your current satisfaction level in each area, rating yourself from 1 (very dissatisfied) to 10 (fully satisfied) – 1 is the centre of the wheel, 10 is the outer periphery. Mark a curved line across each respective wedge denoting your score. Then, in your journal, write your thoughts and attitudes to each of the slices of the wheel. Spend ten minutes freewriting in this way.

Step 3: Identify Limiting Beliefs

Take a look at what you have written. Are any of the statements negative? Acknowledge where belief systems are negatively impacting your progress. These are your limiting beliefs. Now, for each area, identify the most dominant and inhibiting limiting belief that might be holding you back and write it in the relevant wedge e.g. **Purpose**: "I don't have a clear purpose in life."

Step 4: Flip Limiting Beliefs into Empowering Ones

Now we start to make the magic happen. Here begins the very simple reframe, where you simply rewrite the negative statement as a positive one. This is how you transform each limiting belief into an empowering belief. Flip your sheet over to the side titled "Tomorrow" and now write these new beliefs in the relevant wedge, e.g. **Purpose**: "I can explore my passions and find a meaningful purpose."

Step 5: Liberating and Reinforcing Action

For each empowering belief, brainstorm all the potential actions you could take to support your new belief and strategize what you can do most immediately to move closer to satisfaction in this realm. Also consider ways you can reinforce these new beliefs with ideas like Post-it notes on your dashboard, affirmations on your makeup mirror and so on. Take responsibility right now in this moment for deciding to shift from limiting into empowering beliefs. Write these action steps in your journal, e.g. **Purpose**: "Spend time exploring different hobbies and volunteering activities to discover what resonates with me."

Step 6: Reflect and Commit

Reflect on how these new beliefs and actions will positively impact your life. Commit to revisiting your Wheel of Big Impact regularly to reassess and adjust your beliefs and actions as needed. Most immediately, pledge to honour your integrity by taking daily action to own your new positive beliefs and become ultra-conscious of decisions or choices made from a self-limiting or preferably self-empowering stance. Reimagine yourself fully as this limitless being ready for your biggest impact.

Let's return to Melinda's story. Her core limiting belief was that "the man would always be the provider". Trapped in this mental container, there was no room for her to seriously step out into the work arena and provide for her children herself. It didn't fit with the model she had lived her life within to this point. The enormity of flipping this belief was crushing to her. It felt too big to overcome. We spent time deconstructing it across a series of sessions, and piece by piece, metaphorical brick by brick, started to build a new model of a home with Melinda and her two tots safely together, with her as the proud, sole income source.

The process had begun with a self-awareness, an acknowledgement that her thoughts were keeping her locked in a narrow view of how the world could look, function and be, and then evolved into a flipped belief of positivity. We spent time expanding the fulfilling and inspiring new potential of "Melinda as the provider" and her imagination soared as she gained confidence in the vision, easing into her newfound permission to perceive and operate in the world anew. She very quickly moved from tentatively owning the ideal of herself as bread winner into surges of training, job-hunting, home-sorting and party-hosting, and began to relish her newfound confidence. Once the action accompanied her flipped, positive statement, her fortunes began to change as provenance aligned, as it so often does once we take bold steps, and the harrowing past withered from dominating her thoughts. She had also awoken to the role of her ego ...

The Ego

According to Eckhart Tolle, soothing spiritual master and famed author of *The Power of Now* and *A New Earth*, "Ego is the part of your mind that comments, doubts and speculates on everything. The ego is driven by fear of being nothing, which it tries to alleviate through identification with material, thought, and emotional elements, giving rise to what you think of as your 'self'."[48]

Tolle is basically saying there's a You inside that is a pure, spiritual consciousness, and then there's the Ego You, chattering away in the mind, giving you your illusory sense of self, driven by superiority kicks – "I earn more than you" – and protective self-direction – "Don't get up on stage, you'll embarrass yourself". We need our ego to navigate the physical world. It can be propelling and motivate us onward and upward to work harder and be better. But it can be destructive in its pursuits of extrinsic accolades and success metrics, as well as its tirades of negative thinking. Our good ego operates with fact, our bad ego with judgement. The ego can wildly distort perspective and actions – "I'm the only one competent enough to complete this project so I'll have to do it myself. You're all fired!" – and thus it's wise to learn to become aware of when our ego (as separate from our pure Self) is responsible for arising emotions.

Your ego is tripping you up when you don't listen to others, when you behave in an impulsive, knee-jerk way, making rash decisions that suit you but not necessarily others, when you talk at people. When you hear yourself saying I, I, I, and when your voice dominates conversations and meetings, you've brought your ego out to play (and it's exhausting for everyone around you). In the professional world, where strong leaders are prerequisites for high-performing organizations with stable cultures, effective leadership requires humility and the ability to listen and empathize (more on this in the Connection chapter), so if you want to soar in your company, be acutely aware of how much of you and how much of your ego is present in the boardroom and dial down the ego before the board dials down you.

There is a delicate line between ego and ambition. Without ego, progressive action may not be taken as the ego does indeed provide drive, but if the drive is to simply inflate self-worth without diligently pursuing ambitions – for example, buying a gym membership and telling everyone about it but never going – you're locked in an empty egoic state. At the opposite end of the scale, where you take frenzied action, driven by unrelenting perfectionism to soothe the ego's endless self-critical barrages, you run the risk of frenetic over-doing and crashing into burnout. The ego needs careful management between Motivator and Enemy.

Here are twelve signs the Enemy Ego is inflated:

1.   You need to always be right (and everyone else is wrong).
2.   You're judging everyone else (and they're not as good as you).
3.   You obsess about your looks.
4.   You ignore advice and feedback (but love the attention so may seek it anyway).
5.   You always want more (this can creep into hedonistic self-soothing and self-sabotaging behaviours).
6.   You endlessly seek praise and reassurance from others that you're marvellous, promotion-worthy, a fabulous human and so on.
7.   You always have to be the winner, be the best, earn the most, have the perfect relationship, highest achieving children, etc., and constantly tell everyone how great you and everything in your life are.
8.   You never admit your mistakes, and over-glorify your successes.
9.   You take everything personally and live in "What about me?" perpetuity.
10. It's always everyone else's fault (and you quite like a snappy confrontation).
11. You don't let others get a word in and you barely listen.
12. You act impulsively, making self-serving decisions while disregarding others.

None of these traits will support a life of Big Impact. Conversely, you will exhaust yourself with your own thought cycles and run the risk of alienating loved ones, colleagues and your network. The key to combatting unhealthy egocentricity like the above starts with self-awareness.

BIG IMPACT REFLECTION: IS YOUR EGO YOUR ENEMY?

To understand if your ego is in check, reflect on a recent conflict or challenging situation you faced. Write about what happened; how you responded, the words you said, the tone you used, your body posture, gesticulations and thoughts throughout. Notice whether you or your "false" ego-self presided. Consider if your response was influenced by an urge to defend your pride, prove your superiority or avoid admitting fault. Were you kind, empathic and self-aware in the moment? Ask yourself if your actions served the best interest of the situation or were more about protecting your ego. Whatever you observe, don't self-chastise but think of your ego as a protective mask that, with courage, can be removed. There will be work to do. Try to examine what you're afraid of and need protection from i.e., why you're wearing such a tight and garish mask. Think about how you may approach a similar situation differently in the future to ensure your ego doesn't hinder your growth or relationships. We'll learn how to manage any egoic negativity throughout the rest of this book, including how to distinguish healthy guiding voices in our heads – our intuition – from detrimentally egoistic ones, and how to silence any unwelcome talk. For now, be aware and wary.

The Thrill of Expansion

"Look closely. The beautiful may be small."

— Immanuel Kant

Go and stand at the window and look outside. If you're outside, look up from the page and see what's around you. At first glance, you'll see a garden, a street, another office block perhaps. You'll see a scene with a horizon in it; trees or concrete or people or whatever you're gazing upon. Now look harder. You'll start to see dogs, maybe squirrels or umbrellas and buses and lampposts. Now look harder still. You may see the splashes of rain droplets rippling in the pond, and the little girl in the fingerless gloves holding her mother's hand, and the poster for the latest blockbuster. Look harder again and see if you can spot the bored kebab shop owner reading his paper through the storefront glass, or the spiderweb on your window ledge with the tiny white feather trapped in it. Suddenly, there are five different varieties of bird flitting around and so many different styles of boots – a wealth of detail zooms into focus. All at once, you are fully aware and absorbing a much fuller scene than first presented itself.

And so it is with the exquisite complexity of you. Look harder and riches will be revealed. Be curious and new possibilities emerge. Within a mindset of curiosity lies the magic of a beginner's mind; and when we lean into situations as nascent explorers, there is consistent opportunity for growth. This is how we expand.

In *Mindset: The New Psychology of Success*, Carol S Dweck teaches how effort above ability is the ultimate stimulus for growth, and that a growth mindset rather than a fixed one is essential for success. A growth mindset is one where we lean into learning, hungrily absorbing information pertaining to the new. A fixed mindset is one that assumes no progress is possible and the status quo is locked, à la "I can't slice onions" belief. In numerous studies over decades with children, university scholars, professionals, musicians, athletes and more, Dweck shares evidence demonstrating that applying effort and a dogged intent "to try" is how personal evolution and advancement occur; "Most often people believe that the 'gift' is the ability itself. Yet what feeds it is that constant, endless curiosity and challenge seeking."[49] In other words, when innate potential is nurtured properly – by our environment, thoughts and effort – it flourishes. When an attitude to life is one of leaning into new challenges positively instead of negatively, fearful, reluctant, or otherwise, then growth occurs. We expand beyond the seeds of the skill exponentially.

It makes sense; a fixed mindset keeps us small and life the same. Think Einstein and his insanity portrayal – doing the same thing over and over again while expecting different results. It just won't ever happen. If we're fixed and repetitive, each day immersed in the same rhythms and routines, we're doolally to expect to feel different, or indeed for life to be different. We need to lean into growth, through both mindset and action, and relish the unknown, unseen and un-experienced as potential paths to better.

BIG IMPACT REFLECTION: GLORIOUS GROWTH

Think about a recent failure or setback you experienced. It can be anything from missing a train, to a row with your partner, to losing your favourite handbag. Write about what happened and how you operated in that moment or throughout the event/interaction. Now, look at that experience through the lens of whether or not you held a fixed or growth mindset as you approached that moment? Could that challenge have been an opportunity? Reflect how it could have been a moment for growth or zone in on how it already was. Moving forward, consider how you can expand your general way of thinking into becoming more growth-oriented consistently and journal for ten minutes on what you can introduce into your life to be in a growth mindset continually. Here are some ideas:

- Identify certain areas where you may have a fixed mindset
- Seek feedback and learn from criticism
- Embrace failure
- Pursue challenges
- Persist through obstacles
- Cultivate curiosity by asking questions always
- Take pride in the journey
- Set learning goals
- Celebrate effort not just abilities
- Surround yourself with growth-oriented people
- Stay adaptable
- Affirm your belief in your abilities to improve and grow through effort and perseverance

End your reflection with a voracious trip into Growth Mindset Oriented You *all the time*!!! Absorb how fantastic this will feel and what life will look like when you are constantly in the expansive state of growth-orientation.

Nobody Likes a Victim

"Successful people don't make demands of others but set the scene so that Human in others can respond, rather than their Chimp."

— Professor Steve Peters

Sometimes the ego suppresses curiosity, thwarting wide perspective and suffocating us into victimhood. Now, I'm all for a little private pity party here and there; there's a delight in the refreshing cleanse of a good cry (and salted caramel Häagen-Dazs, pyjama days and binge-watching rom coms), but to wallow in the trenches of suffering self-indulgently to the detriment of our glorious lives is, well, a tad pathetic. Bad stuff happens, 100 per cent. We will be let down, dreams will be dashed, people will disappoint, situations won't materialize as we visualized, we will fail, things will go wrong, but it is for us to manage our attitudes. Yes, the pain will be momentarily all-consuming, with hurt, rage, abandonment, disbelief, sadness, grief and so on enveloping us, but it's how we respond to adversity that ensures we bloom or wither. I'm definitely in the bloom camp. Coming?

In *Man's Search for Meaning*, the brave Holocaust survivor, psychotherapist and author Viktor Frankl teaches us that once you understand that attitude is a conscious choice, once you harness the power of your mind and learn how to direct it, mentally attaching to meaning, purpose and wisps of positivity, you can remove limitations and withstand whatever conditions or circumstances occur. His wise enlightenment arose from being imprisoned in Auschwitz during World War II. He was one of the rare few who survived. He attributes this to his attitude: "Everything can be taken from a man but one thing: the last of the human freedoms – to choose one's attitude in any given set of circumstances, to choose one's own way."[50] Maya Angelou, majestic woman of words, similarly tells us, "If you don't like something, change it. If you can't change it, change your attitude."

What's the attitude of a victim then? Well, a victim presents themselves as weak, put upon, tormented by their own suffering and revels in blame. Oh, the blame game. It is always everyone else's fault and the victim takes zero accountability for what's going on. Sweetheart, if you plan to have Big Impact and really unleash yourself out into the world, there is no room for passivity nor "Woe is me" laments. You will not succeed if you feel a warped sense of power and comfort in victimhood.

And let's face it, it can feel snuggly in there, cocooned in the ego's reassuring whispers that this wasn't anything to do with us, and it's so tough and sad that the world makes our plight so arduous, how could they treat me like this, blah, blah, blah. But when you confront your circumstances with a big girl acknowledgement of your role in them, serious expansion occurs and finally good change can come.

For example, even when you've been fired, or your partner doesn't propose, or the kids refuse to eat their vegetables, there is always an opportunity to ask, "Okay, so what can I learn here?" In the case of leaving your company, perhaps the writing was on the wall for some time. Maybe you weren't enjoying the graft anymore and management have simply accelerated what you were too afraid to bring to a head yourself. If you were anticipating a proposal that never materialized, perhaps you might realize that you'd never truly communicated your expectations with your partner. And as for naughty, nutritionally rebellious children, you could weep over your wasted labours trying to feed your ungrateful rabble, or you could make note to purée the vegetables into the sauce next time. There is always a way to reframe the situation and regain an empowered perspective. Always.

When we blame others, we are rocking away from our own essence and instead being subsumed by the ego's shadow. It's a self-defense mechanism triggered most prevalently when people who struggle with their own emotional regulation are hit with a negative feeling. As their own shame, fear, guilt, panic or whatever dark feeling worsens, they start to project accusations out onto others (often mirroring the very emotion they are experiencing). The projection manifests as their own shortcomings, mistakes or misfortunes pushed onto (ironically) the people nearest and dearest, and at its base is simply their stirred-up ego, desperately seeking protection. Most extreme in the case of narcissists, blamers tend to have deep wounds in need of healing, and it can be wildly frustrating to observe their blame games erupt (and agonizing to be on the receiving end). But we're all human and, as we know, that ego is a powerful little tyrant, so we're all subject to elements of blame-throwing here and there, to varying degrees, especially when stressed. Watch a TV show like *The Apprentice* to see how apparently collaborative comrades scathingly throw each other under the metaphorical bus once the pressure intensifies. Blame, whether a subtle voice niggling away in your head, or an outlandish public accusation, has no integrity and won't get you any closer to succeeding in your ambitions. It's just misdirected, wasteful energy.

Where I invite you to expand your own self-awareness now is around how you dance into victimhood and blame, or not. A narcissist simply cannot shift from her locked beliefs that she is right, the world is wrong, everyone else is to blame and she is doomed to suffer solitarily. Only a therapist can help her, if at all. But you, my ambitious, aware one, understand the benefits and grace of a curious, growth-oriented, information-gathering, expansive perspective where you hold the lead role in your life experience and there is no blame to lay anywhere except humbly at your own door. You are not a victim.

BIG IMPACT REFLECTION: EXPANDED HORIZONS

Reflect on one area in your life where you're aware you're in suffering mode. You feel hard done by and the circumstances are unfair. Journal for ten minutes on fresh perspectives through which you can look at this situation. Consider a perspective of gratitude, one of hilarity, one of empowerment, one of a student, one of a teacher ... conjure up different perspective stances you can play with and freewrite to see what comes up for you. For example, "I've been overlooked for a promotion, but ... by embracing gratitude, I appreciate the skills and supportive colleagues I've gained, humour helps me see the absurdity in comparing myself to others, empowerment reminds me to take control and seek new opportunities, as a student I keep growing, as a teacher I have even more to share.

Recognize that sitting in a victim camp is limiting your glorious life and chances of Big Impact, so have fun indulging in wild and varied alternative views until the victim stance becomes an unappealing one.

Mastering Self-Compassion

The inspiring, courageous and beautiful-inside-and-out Nicola Mendelsohn CBE, Head of the Global Business Group for Meta and mother of four, was diagnosed with incurable cancer, follicular lymphoma, in 2016. As Meta's, previously known as Facebook, most senior woman in the world outside of Silicon Valley, she described the jolt of adjusting from a full diary of meetings to a schedule of doctor's appointments and treatment. She went through a grave and urgent reset of priorities, figuring out what mattered most: health, family and work. When we met, Nicola told me life came into stark focus as she made various adjustments to ensure she could keep all that she cherished in life still flowing; "The journey through chemotherapy was at times physically challenging and lasted six months. I had fourteen sessions of chemotherapy, all while working remotely. My commitment to work was a conscious choice. It kept my mind from dwelling on the illness, and I felt a sense of normalcy in the midst of treatment." She also overhauled her diet, dropping sugar, and ensured she took gentle daily exercise, just half an hour of strolling. Returning to work and in remission, Nicola cut back on international travel and, when essential, would fly the night before to avoid early morning flights and interrupted sleep. "Given the kids were all older and technology is amazing, I could keep in touch in different ways."

Nicola also founded the Follicular Lymphoma Foundation, a support group now with over 10,000 members, plus Meta's She Means Business initiative, encouraging female entrepreneurs to step into their ambitions with financial readiness and digital marketing training. Nicola is a woman resilient in the face of adversity. She is a model of how to thrive, and quite literally survive. She never wavered in her impact, in spite of a devastating diagnosis; in fact, her impact expanded in multiple dimensions.

The self-compassion required in moments of extreme stress doesn't always come naturally. Often, when our thoughts are cloudy with stress hormones, creating rushes and flushes of anxiety, we unconsciously default to self-soothing, but not necessarily compassionate soothing. The mollifying can take the form of alcohol, comfort eating or procrastination, like mindlessly scrolling through social media. We can run away from who or what we need to address, or, in extremes, turn to recreational drugs, hardcore gym sessions, sex, frenetic productivity, shopping, shoplifting, whatever makes us feel better. If we're not careful, the soft soothing can veer into hard self-sabotage as a coping mechanism. It's the ego luring us down a path of least resistance, but also least substance. It's essential we learn to distinguish what type of soothing we're canoodling into, and that we can stop those that are harmful to us.

In *The Mountain Is You: Transforming Self-Sabotage into Self-Mastery*, the author and spiritual nymph Brianna Wiest states, "Self-sabotage is what happens when we refuse to consciously meet our innermost needs, often because we do not believe we are capable of handling them."[51] She asserts that we default into sabotaging behaviour because we fear what might happen if we actually overcome the blocker that's stressing us out, that there's an underlying terror paralysing us from moving forward healthily in the right direction and that these fears are rooted in childhood experiences, micro-traumas or stuck beliefs. As an example of this (exaggerated for creative emphasis), if someone is addicted to spending instead of saving, dangerously plundering funds and risking the very roof over their heads, perhaps it is because they grew up believing that rich people are bad, and that, in turn, money management was evil, and having a big bank balance made you a part of the cruel, manipulative wealthy elite. If we learn to dissect why we behave hurtfully toward ourselves and create a new coping method, then we prime ourselves for a whole new realm of personal development. Wiest declares, "To put an end to your self-sabotaging behaviour absolutely means that change is on the horizon. Your new life is going to cost you your old one. It's going to cost you your comfort zone and your sense of direction."[52] This is an exciting perspective.

I believe we self-sabotage when a belief system conflicts with an inner truth. For example, "I need to work myself into the ground" is a culturally accepted norm we may have internalized to people-please, satisfy our perfectionism, to silence our ego and so on. So, when we're exhausted and need a break, we don't stop; we dishonour the inner truth that we need to rest, and we push ourselves. As we tumble into push mode, a defiant form of resentment of self may petulantly swell: "Oh well, I'll do this to myself too, ha!" Enter more fake energy, more work, more hedonism, more whatever form of "I know it's bad for me, but I'll do it anyway" that you surrender to.

If you acknowledge that you're actually outside of your integrity and unintentionally causing a conflict between your heart and your mind, you open yourself up to examining a limiting belief, then are able to drop down into a more instinctive truth, softening toward yourself and breaking the self-sabotaging pattern by inviting more benevolent thinking and choices.

Healthy self-compassion immediately reduces stress. We collaborate with our body to halt the rush, and to gain mental clarity as we observe our thoughts kindly. We thwart the amygdala hijack and allow the prefrontal cortex, our brain's CEO, to rationalize the situation. We step away from the stressor, person or event to recalibrate. We make a choice to become aware of what created the shift inside from harmonious to reckless. We examine why disharmony surfaced. Why are you triggered? When did it arise? Who said what? What's the real issue here? How are you being compromised and what values are being squashed?

How you recalibrate from moments of potential self-sabotage depends on the time you have available to you. When you recognize that you're in a heightened negative emotional state, which could be a precursor to sabotaging behaviour, harming yourself and/or others, step away from the fire and cool down by going within. As quickly as you can. Find a moment to be alone and sit with the raw emotion and breathe. Feel into your body and shift from self-sabotage to self-compassion. If you're at work, go to the restroom an take five deep belly breaths to steady your nerves and get present, right now. If you have ten minutes, get outside, be in nature, sit under a tree and journal. Get your thoughts out on paper, write, flow, be. Again, get present, right now. If you have ten hours, go and take a lavender aromatherapy bath and sleep, in the dark, ideally alone, and without pharmacological aid. If you have ten weeks, practice daily meditations, hours and hours of them. De-stress your distress through inner calmness and breath. Get creative, do crafts, spend time gardening. Get present, every day, as often as you can, starting right now. In all instances, go within, to positively affect the outer. (And please get professional help to support any extreme self-sabotage.)

BIG IMPACT REFLECTION: MELTING SELF-SABOTAGE, RISING SELF-COMPASSION

Coming back to our master Big Impact strategies of Energy, Mindset, Purpose, Time, Work, Connection, Wealth and Fulfilment, in your journal, draw three large columns. Title column two "Self-Sabotage", column three "Self-Compassion". In column one, write down each of the Big Impact strategy titles, so you have a list of eight running down the left of the page.

Now, set a timer for five minutes and start freewriting into your grid, working through each life realm on the left and filling in the Self-Sabotage column. What do you do that is self-sabotaging in your Energy realm? Your Time realm? Your Work realm? And so on. No judgement, no exploration, just freewrite and list everything in a rapid brain dump.

If you don't have any bad habits in one realm, great, move on to the next. Five minutes max. Go!

After five minutes, stop and analyse what you've written. Now explore the moments that trigger these reactions. What leads up to the sabotage? Why does it create the response it does?

Now you have clarity of where you're going awry, let's pay attention to the Self-Compassion column. Just as you flipped your limiting beliefs earlier into empowering ones, now consider how you can shift away from self-criticism and all you detailed in the sabotage column into a space of kindness toward yourself. Match each negative entry with a new compassionate, soothing method you could introduce into your life in those particular circumstances. Conclude your reflection with a total overview of your Big Impact life through the lens of self-compassion. Get carried away with how good this new state will feel and be, and how much more able to step into your Big Impact dreams you will be.

But What About if We're Really, Really Triggered?

I love getting triggered. Yup, seriously. Defined as an "intense and usually negative emotional reaction in someone",[53] in the spiritual sense, a trigger is your soul's invitation to grow. When you burn with an inflamed response to something with unusual ferocity, something interesting is going on, and if you embrace the presence of mind to detach from the surging emotions, there's an opportunity for expansion. This won't be easy, but growth never is.

Elise works hard. I mean impressively hard. Not only does she work hard, she cares hard and loves her remit. She's one of those clients whose sheer effectiveness and joy for life I choose to channel in my own moments of floundering. She contacted me between sessions via a string of WhatsApp messages and screenshots. She was distraught. A recently fired employee had posted slanderous accusations about her on Glassdoor.com. It was a very personal attack – untrue, unfair, cruel and deliberately hurtful. I immediately called Elise. I explained we were going to ground her into her body to control her sobs and safely let the intensity of the emotion flow out. With me on loudspeaker, I guided her to put her feet flat on the floor, close her eyes, hold her back erect and gently push her fingertips together in pulsing movements while taking deep diaphragmatic breaths. We stayed like this together for ten breaths. Once her energy was less frantic, we could move into exploring the wound opened by this trigger and how to move through it and out.

Elise, like most of us, is sensitive to rejection. The sting of this type of rejection was especially brutal because it was public and potentially damaging to her business. It was an assault of pain and worry. Her surging thoughts bolted from rage to disgust to sadness to fury to panic to an overwhelming sense of being crushed. This situation did not require dramatic external action (like calling the police and preparing litigation on the grounds of slander), but required immediate internal focus on mental, physical and emotional self-care, a state of acceptance and a macro-perspective.

We started with self-care, which involved a plan to come offline immediately and stop looking at the review, spend the evening with loved ones, talking and exorcising the upset out into the open. Acceptance involved Elise acknowledging that this bad thing had happened, and it was unfair, but that the strong emotions would pass in time and she needed to focus on preserving as much homeostatic equilibrium in both her body and mind as possible while the emotions diminished gradually. The macro-perspective is where change began to occur. Elise could see that if she was tormented by the poisoned text, the bad witch would have won –that if she lifted up into the broader context of the situation, she would emerge unscathed. We explored the facts, further grounding Elise, this time intellectually, which all evidenced the toxic words were nonsense, that she is a well-regarded boss constantly praised by staff, that the defamatory woman rarely crossed paths with her. She then shifted into curiosity about what could have provoked the woman and became interested in her troll's state of mind. With compassion, Elise eventually realized how sorry she felt for the nefarious woman, because, as she put it, "Surely hate only stems from pain". In her innate loveliness, she decided she would focus on sending positive vibes of healing and happiness to the disruptive woman and not let it affect her any more.

In the entirety of this experience, Elise self-managed. She didn't take reflexive action, which is so often a threat in a triggered scenario. She didn't lash out, didn't self-sabotage, didn't do anything to exacerbate a negative situation but worked through it to a place of ever-increasing peace. And that is key: when sparked, not taking action nor being dragged down into judgemental, revengeful action, but leaning open-eyed into the stimulus with self-care, acceptance and a grander perspective.

This works with all triggers. Whether it's the annoying woman in the office who says black every time you say white, the driver bumper-to-bumper behind you, the late food delivery, the friend who didn't show up for your birthday dinner – when the sting stings, there's always a clue you have something to learn. So, detach from the stab and observe it from every angle until you have a management plan and tingle with expansion.

BIG IMPACT REFLECTION: MANAGING TRIGGERS

Reflect on a recent situation when you felt triggered. In your journal, describe the event and the emotions it brought up for you. Identify how this trigger might be connected to an old wound or past experience. With empathy and kindness, explore the underlying needs or fears that were activated. Write about constructive ways to address these needs, such as self-care, setting healthy boundaries or seeking support from others. Consider how this trigger is not just a source of discomfort, but a calling from your soul to heal. Focus on transforming this triggering experience into an opportunity for growth, ensuring your actions align with your values and integrity. Try to reaffirm your commitment to self-compassion and personal development, recognizing that facing and learning from triggers is a courageous and essential part of your life journey – they are a good way to expand into your greatest self. But, do acknowledge the pain you are in and please self-soothe. Finally, conclude with a visualization where you step into yourself in that recent situation without getting triggered. Flow into a place of calm nonchalance where the event occurs and you remain empowered. How good does that feel?

Ten Things to Remember When Triggered

1. Focus on your own self-care as the number one priority.
2. Surrender to a place of acceptance, knowing "this too shall pass".
3. Take a macro-perspective and examine the broader context by playing with multiple lenses.
4. Be gentle with yourself as you have an open wound. Understand that wound and the needs and fears it stimulates. How can you best heal it?
5. Consider healthy boundaries that may support your wellbeing and how to communicate them effectively to others.
6. Seek support – a problem shared is truly a problem halved.
7. Stay in your integrity. Don't react or lash out, breathe.
8. Commit to self-compassion when triggers arise.
9. Remember triggers are an essential part of your healing journey, so work out how you can best grow from this situation.
10. Despite all the coping mechanisms here, acknowledge this hurts, it's difficult, there is pain and be so, so, so kind to yourself, please.

The Sting of Rejection

Rejection is an aspect of life that will rear up repeatedly. Whether romantic rejection, a "no" to a job application, or our own children rebuffing our political or religious beliefs, rejection is inevitable. So too is the fact that, as we just saw with Elise, it will more than likely stimulate a strong response. The response is going to be all the more painful if we've got any lingering rejection wounds from childhood, stemming from any primary caregiver micro-traumas, i.e. if an emotional need wasn't met. Rejection will affect us emotionally, mentally and potentially behaviourally. The sudden sting may violently lower self-esteem, both short- and long-term, and provoke anger and aggressive behaviour, or retreat and cower mode. Often rejection reactions are unconscious, bodily impulses from old wounds stored in our bodies. We will feel the hurt viscerally. If we have an intention of Big Impact, we will be exposing ourselves and our work to the threat of rejection, and no matter how much we chant, "Not everyone will like us and that's okay", we are better equipped having built a rejection resilience plan in advance.

Neuroscientists have identified that the area of the brain activated when we experience rejection is the same area that lights up in scans when we experience a physical wound, which explains why the pain shudders and judders through us so deeply. That first date hunk we're starting to fall for saying he's not up for taking things further may as well have chopped our left leg off. It's raw. It's excruciating.

Two contrasting things tend to happen when we're spurned. We blame others or we blame ourselves. Neither are healthy. And generally, neither reaction is conscious. As children, we learned to cope with rejection one way or the other. Now, as adults, becoming aware of your response is how you'll build your rejection resilience muscle. You can start to flex the muscle and build up an immunity to a certain type of rejection, allowing it to become redirection.

I interviewed an 18-year-old rapper; let's call him Beau Grills. Freshly signed to an international label, he's a viral phenomenon, racking up 32 million views on his first, starburst TikTok post. What comes with these 32 million views, as well as an abundance of gushing fandom, is a never-ending stream of online hate. Beau is attacked for everything from his lyrics, his looks, his race, his style, the lot. I'm in awe of how he, young and new to life, never mind the music scene, can self-manage. He explains that while initially he was riddled with upset at the piercing words, he's now numb to them. He's close with his family, and he and his parents laugh at the lunacy of some of the comments together, deconstructing the words as simply silly, letting them glide over Beau instead of through. So, rather than harden his innocent heart, Beau has practised building immunity to the relentless rejection assaults. Bravo, Beau.

What is most impressive about Beau is that he is not retreating from the arena. He will not let rejection shrink him. He is making music and his mission shall continue. Brené Brown, likewise, in her Netflix documentary *The Call to Courage*, describes the insults she received after her TED Talk on vulnerability went viral, and how she eventually learned that anyone can shout from the sidelines, but it takes a true hero to enter the arena and risk that rejection. Bravo, Brené.

So, Beau and Brené have taken to their respective global stages to anesthetize themselves from the sting of rejection. But what about you? How can you stay brave and avert angry, resentful outbursts or retraction into the safe zone? As with triggers, it comes down to pausing, taking deep breaths and strategizing self-compassion (not sabotage), acceptance and an elevated perspective. As Eckhart Tolle teaches, "Whatever the present moment contains, accept it as if you had chosen it." Indeed, there are always lessons to be learned – I fervently believe that there is always something better in the grand design anyway, so a little trust in the order of the universe helps soothe any rejection sting too.

BIG IMPACT REFLECTION:
BUILDING REJECTION RESILIENCE

Rejection can take many forms, from an angry driver gesticulating obscenities from across the road (a weird, random personal hurt of mine!) to social media spite, to a business partnership not working out. Boundless varieties of rejection occur each day, so practise building up your rejection resilience muscle with the smaller moments of rejection so you are better prepared for the bigger, more life-impacting ones.

Use the following steps to build your resilience muscle

Step 1: As the sting arises in you, you will be reopening a rejection wound from childhood. Observe it, feel it and go back through your earliest memories to see if you can pinpoint the first moment this pain arose.

Step 2: With the perspective of your younger self, examine each time, situation or person that has triggered this pain, drawing it all out on a timeline. Write the details of each hurt you experienced then.

Step 3: Compare the pain then to the pain now and acknowledge the pattern and the old wound that has been opened.

Step 4: Sit with the emotions and physicality of this current pain and examine them. Where do you feel it in your body? How does it flow through you? Where is it blocked? Where is it virulent? What colour is it? Just observe it.

Step 5: Ground yourself into the Earth, feet flat on the floor, back straight. Hold your fingertips together, close your eyes and take five deep belly breaths.

Step 6: Observe the instinctive reactions that arose when the sting first stung. Did you want to lash out or retreat? Hurt yourself or others in some way? Want to punch a pillow, down a whisky, have sex, scream, attack? What is your learned reaction to the pain of rejection?

Step 7: Observe this coping mechanism as a clever, brave and inventive way younger you learned to cope. Wish this part of you well and invite it to settle now and make space for a new, grown-up way of coping with rejection.

Step 8: Design your new, self-compassionate way of soothing yourself when the pain stings. How can you lovingly, maturely work through this pain from now on? Design a conscious plan to combat feelings of rejection that is loving, easy to implement and effective.

Step 9: Build up your self-worth in this very raw moment, reconnecting to your self-acceptance and self-authority by focusing in on a recent achievement, be it a successful work project or as fleeting as a stranger responding to your smile.

Step 10: Take action to remind the body and mind that you are safe and this rejection is not you, it is something happening to you.

Please take your time with this exercise, be gentle with yourself and steadily design your rejection resilience strategy. Once designed, practise using it and recognize your empowerment as rejection loses its ability to floor you. You're becoming stronger every time.

Mastering Self-Direction

"You gain strength, courage and confidence by every experience in which you really stop to look fear in the face. You are able to say to yourself, 'I have lived through this horror. I can take the next thing that comes along.' You must do the thing you think you cannot do."

— Eleanor Roosevelt

Stepping into the arena of Big Impact means overcoming fear. In overcoming fear, we boost our self-esteem, confidence and courage, continuing to grow. The hurdle is putting our stage clothes on in the first place and not freezing when the curtain goes up.

As we learned with the wound of rejection, areas of our brains are illuminated identically in scans whether pain is physical or mental. Fear too sparks us to suffer pain viscerally. But just as fear is created in the mind, it can be managed by the mind. As Susan Jeffers says in *Feel the Fear and Do It Anyway*: "The only way to get rid of the fear of doing something is to go out and do it."

Here are six ways to self-direct to overcome any fear that may be holding you back.

1. **Repeated exposure to the fear.** In phobia therapy, repeated exposure to the imagined threat numbs it until it evaporates entirely. Because illogical fear is often a fantasy scenario looping endlessly in our imaginations, once we usurp the vision with a reality, the fear disappears. We realize it was just an illusion all along.

   Cheeky life prompter and psychologist Harriet Lerner describes in *Fear and Uninvited Guests: Tackling the Anxiety, Fear and Shame that Keep Us From Optimal Living and Loving* how she tasked a client with healthy ways to overcome his fear of amorous rejection. The client was too nervous to ask a colleague out on a date so she instructed him to get 100 date rejections. He had to stand at the foot of an escalator in a busy shopping centre and politely (not creepily, we hope!) ask women on dates until he achieved 100 refusals. By the time he had twelve no's, he had accrued five yes's. And so his confidence started to build. Once he got to 34 requests, he stopped the experiment, feeling a newfound confidence and optimism. The fear was extinguished. Repeated exposure had built immunity.

   I used to be an abominable public speaker, quivery-voiced and shaky-legged. I was once asked if I was ill after a presentation because of my visible hand jitters. So, I made it my mission to leap wholeheartedly into this fear and overcome the heck out of it. I joined speaker groups, hosted my own Speaker Mastery lunchtime group at work, put my hand up for every keynote, hosted workshops for my local community and got on stage after stage after stage until I was anesthetized, and it became fun not fear. Yes, it took years, endless stamina and graft, and my god, I shook in my stilettos those first few times. But I knew I needed to crush this out of me to be the communicator I wanted to be, and so I did.

Exposing yourself to fear doesn't need to be as epic as addressing an audience of 2,000 from a spotlit conference stage, it can be a small micro-step of relevant risk-taking that builds your confidence gradually. Task yourself with doing one brave thing toward your dream every single day. Just one. Track it and watch your confidence bloom and the fear fade.

2. **Play with, then silence, the inner critic.** The way we speak to ourselves is rarely how we would address someone we know or love. Tara Mohr, author of *Playing Big*, warns, "The inner critic will show up whenever we're on the edge of playing bigger and whenever we're taking a new risk and stretching ourselves. And so we just need tools to deal with it."[54]

We'll go deeper into meeting and managing your pathological critic later, but for now, try this: Give your critic a nickname. Acknowledge the noise it's making in your head and talk back to it. "Come on, Mrs Trunchball, not today." "Oh Patrick, trying to play with my insecurities, are you? Not helpful. Now please, back in your box!" Replace the sabotaging voice with positive rationalizations – "I am enough", "I know what I know", "I am here with love and curiosity", etc. If you stabilize yourself in rational fact and say it repeatedly to yourself with enough conviction, you'll come to believe the thought, your nervous system will react positively accordingly and you'll quickly overshadow the nagging critic.

3. **Visualize success scenarios and shrink the fear.** In NLP, the art of neuro linguistic programming, where psychological techniques influence cognition and thus behaviour, there's a tool where we take our clients into a meditative state in which they visualize a positive outcome as shinier, brighter, larger and more dominant than the imagined fear scenario. We guide the client through the worst-case image versus the best-case image, and we shrink the image of fear into black and white, inversed, upside-down, rippled, distorted, smaller and smaller until it's gone and there is only the vibrant, positive outcome left.

If you aren't currently working with a coach or NLP practitioner, you can still practice your own positive visualization daily. Write down every tiny, inspiring detail of what a good outcome looks like in the scenario in which your fear is vanquished, from what you're wearing, to the environment, the conversation, the mood, the sounds, the smells and so on. Then relish quiet time deeply immersed in the vision and enjoy the rich sensations within your body, mind and soul.

I do this nightly if I have a big milestone life moment ahead. Neuroscience again proves that centres in our brain light up identically, whether or not we are experiencing a visualization or a real-life event. A stunning study showed that music students were able to perfectly play a piece of complex music on the piano after having solely visualized playing it in their imaginations for weeks beforehand. The mind is truly your most powerful tool. As Oprah says, "Anything you can imagine, you can create."[55]

4. **Breathe, and flip fear into excitement.** As I said earlier, fear and curiosity cannot exist simultaneously. Fact. So, take a deep belly breath and flip that fear into a bodily sensation of curiosity and fresh potential. Consciously connect your body with your mind. When things become an experiment, we're motivated by interest and perhaps excitement to explore the outcome. So, walk into your next meeting treating yourself as an experiment. How adeptly will you influence the group to make the decision you desire? How effectively will you make eye contact and establish respect from your most vociferous detractor? How will you relay your numbers insightfully and energetically? Play a game with the situation to make it one of exploration and motivating possibilities.

5. **Get perspective; people are thinking about themselves.** Our brain's default state is to think about ourselves. Studies have shown that the majority of our conversation (78 per cent) is about ourselves[56]. We use our own experiences to make assumptions about other people (known as unconscious bias). Our wiring also prompts us to think about ourselves when not engaged in other external demands. The research is clear: we're mostly thinking about ourselves.

You may be painfully nervous about publishing that article on your work intranet, exposing your POV to a vast network of peers, but the reality is it will get milliseconds of attention, if any at all. You may agonize over a point missed when delivering a presentation, but no one will ever know. You may be frozen with nervousness over raising your hand to ask a question at a conference, but you'll be forgotten by the time the next question is asked.

When you feel judged, ask yourself, "Whose feedback actually matters?". Reflect on any fear-eliciting judgement scenario and write down a list of those people whose feedback actually does matter to you. Your mum, your partner, your boss, your teacher? If they're the ones that count, any other feedback is mere noise you can choose not to listen to.

Also, work hard to frame the situation in a macro-context. It probably really doesn't matter in the grand scheme of things. Will I be forever remembered as the woman who did a reading at a christening who shook so much she couldn't hold the paper still? I hope not. Life moves on and everyone focuses back in on their own universes.

6. **Sit at the table and lean in.** In my experience, imposter syndrome is an affliction men and women suffer at every stage of the career journey. It doesn't seem to matter how senior you are, or how many years of

service you've rocked; unless you're one of the rare un-imposter-riddled ones, the little creepy gremlin of "I bet everyone else has more right to be here than me" never seems to recede. I suppose we could view imposter syndrome as humility – those who believe everyone else is entitled to be there and that they are privileged to be among them; it's an endearing trait. But only when you actually show up. If imposter syndrome stops you playing the game or enshrouds you with nerves so great your performance wobbles, then it needs to be stamped out. You are not an imposter. You have every right to play. You, and all your vibrant uniqueness, is what will create something fresh and new. By stepping into the arena you are contributing, you are creating, you are not consuming. You are fantabulously . great, and thank god for you overcoming fears, muzzling your inner critic, shooting this imposter syndrome niggle down and getting out there and giving it your all. We all want to see what you have to share, I promise. As the Roman philosopher Marcus Aurelius said, "It is not death that a man should fear, but he should fear never beginning to live." Let's live.

BIG IMPACT REFLECTION: ANESTHETIZING FEAR AS EMBOLDENED YOU EMERGES

What would you do if you weren't afraid? That's the big question to reflect on here. The answer tells you what matters (and actually being scared of something is always a clue that it matters). So, how can you get closer to doing this thing today? What can you deliberately, safely expose yourself to in order to grow into the version of you who does this thing you would do if you weren't afraid? Reflect on a role model who's already doing it and detail everything they do that you want to do. Now brainstorm strategies that could become experiments for you to start trialling. Think big then teeny tiny microscopic. So, if your dream is a TED Talk, don't start there, start giving a little talk at the family dinner table tonight, then offer to lead the team meeting, then join a speaker club and so on. Just start small so the big dream inches closer day by day. This is another marginal gains strategy as you find your fear starts to shrink and so the tasks can get riskier. Visualize yourself as this Big Impact woman who is not held back by fear. What does she look like? What does she wear? What does she do? Where is she? Who is she with? Go technicolour and vibrant and paint this fearless, gorgeous, luminous picture of magnificent you!

Mastering Self-Worth

With all this self-awareness, self-compassion and self-direction, we are closer to mastering the Mindset Strategy for Big Impact. Ultimately, though, confidence stems from our self-worth – both building it up and maintaining it through myriad ways. You'll get a little inner "Well done, Girl" kick from feeding the neighbour's cat while they're on holiday, or from mentoring a colleague into a promotion, or from producing work that is well received or well graded, winning the race, losing the weight or gaining the muscle. These micro and macro achievements can bolster how we feel about ourselves, enable us to courageously be ourselves and daringly allow a spotlight to shine on us.

As much as we can do these things to give more of our authentic selves positive self-worth, sometimes our self-worthiness is hampered by our past, and despite our brightest dreams, we become locked in a version of ourselves from yesteryear where progress feels impossible. In this space, it's imperative we forgive ourselves for what has played out apparently "imperfectly" and embrace the gift of failure then, now and in the future.

The Magnificent Gift of Failure

Mistakes are deliciously interesting. They represent those decisions we made, either unconsciously or consciously, which propelled us in a surprise direction. They are the choices we made that took us down a retrospectively identified "wrong" path. Hindsight is always a beautiful thing, but what if we embrace a bold reframe and acknowledge there's no such thing as a wrong path, that it's all learning? That, in fact, failure is a blessing. Failure proves that we leaned into life and tried. It gives us the clue about what not to do next time – think Edison and his 1,000 ways not to build a lightbulb.

The ghastly side of failure is its power to shrink us. Because, let's be honest, who hasn't shrivelled and felt their self-esteem melting down into a puddle when they've done something blatantly wrong. It's painful and the most difficult of pills to swallow. But let's experiment with shifting this. Let's move failure from pain to power.

BIG IMPACT REFLECTION: DARE TO FAIL

Here are four steps to begin positively reacting to failure:

1. **Take full accountability for the mistake.** You made the decision that caused the consequences you're now labelling a mistake. Now own it, and reflect hard on it. Take the time to create a growth moment. What were the circumstances? Prior to deciding, did you consider alternate outcomes? Were you mentally present/awake when you made the call? What were the drivers motivating you to decide the way you did? Is there any pattern to observe: for example, have you done this before?

2. **Embrace the gift of "What Not To Do Again".** Choose to change course and try anew. In *How To Fail*, loveable literary celebrity Elizabeth Day cites failure as "a necessary staging post on a journey towards greater success". View it this way and progress onward, differently.

3. **Persevere.** Commit fully to this new relationship with failure and calmly glide over any inevitable bumps along the way. Lean in wholeheartedly to your new tack-changing efforts. Have the resilience and foresight to acknowledge that it's okay if the new path doesn't lead directly to Nirvana and kinks inevitably form. Even a technologically advanced, satellite-oriented flight path needs repeated course correction. Reorientation is an acceptable part of the process. Don't give up.

4. **Relax.** After you've seized the learnings, laugh it off with a "So what?", "Who cares?", "Oh well" laissez-faire nonchalance. Because once more, it really doesn't matter in the grand scheme of things, and no one except your own monster is judging you harshly. If fear of judgement is strangling your confidence to try again, commit to pushing your boundaries daily – send company-wide emails, post more on social media, address your pathological critic as Bob and chastise him for sabotaging your good thoughts, then eventually you'll become non-plussed by what others may think and can focus on the task at hand, creating you and your brilliant work.

When failure becomes exciting and triggers become interesting, life itself expands. Once the blasts of adversity glimmer as fresh opportunity, resilience leads us into ever more powerful experiences and impact. When shocked 67-year-old Thomas Edison witnessed his entire life's work and factory burning to the ground, he cried, "Hey son, get your mother. This is one unbelievable sight! Look at that fire!"[57] In disaster, he marvelled at the spectacle, then after the dramatic melee, pragmatically embraced the thrust to rebuild. At 5.30 the next morning, when the fire was barely yet under control, he called his employees together and announced, "We're rebuilding!" He philosophized, "You can always make capital out of disaster. We've just cleared out a bunch of old rubbish! We'll build bigger and better on these ruins."[58] Amen, and here's to bigger and better You.

Hushing the Pathological Critic

When we are faced with a moment of uplevelling of some sort and about to enter the arena, step up and out, be brave and bold and share our work with the world, often the pesky sabotaging voice tries to derail us. We must remember any devil on our shoulder is simply there to protect us as part of our primeval wiring; it's up to us to rationalize it into healthier chatter and cajole it down off its boycotting branch.

The 'pathological critic' is a phrase used to describe this negative inner voice attacking and judging us in our moments of pushing beyond our comfort zones. Named by psychologist Eugen Sagan, he recognized that everyone has one to a varying degree. The path to peace resides in forming a relationship with it and learning to silence it, not with brute force but with understanding and loving acceptance. The voice exists only to protect us. People with low self-esteem or self-worth tend to have more nasty and noisy pathological critics, so this work is even more essential if you recognize this within you.

Our negative ninny loves to control the narrative. And when they've got hold of the reins, boy do they love the game of undermining us; they will scream insults, exaggerate weaknesses, lay blame at your door for anything going awry, set ludicrous standards and really get giddy-upping when they can unkindly compare you to others. The internal noise can be vicious and violent, and yet the self-attacks feel so much a part of us and our daily inner monologue, we often fail to even notice the voice as separate from our positive, self-fuelling ones. We inadvertently accept the critic's words as truth, as us. We trust it and thus grant it power to break down good feelings we have about ourselves. If we have one, our voluble critic will be loud, toxic and never go away. Forming a relationship with it is the only way to hush it, disempower it and break free from the poison it spits.

While there aren't official, study-backed stats as to the percentage of us that have garrulous inner monologues, those of us that do, according to psychologists Matthew McKay and Patrick Fanning, can blame the origin of our critic on five "Oh, so I'm not okay then?" factors from childhood:

1. **The degree to which issues of taste, personal needs, safety or good judgement were mislabelled as moral imperatives.** So, if you liked running up the stairs but your dad called you an oaf, or you loved long, flowy locks but your mum enforced a pixie cut, or the family banned you from singing in your bedroom because your melodies grated, in each case you would have started to feel a sense of "wrongness".

2. **The degree to which parents failed to differentiate between behaviour and identity.** This relates to you having been negatively labelled instead of your behaviour, i.e. "You're stupid!", rather than, "That was dangerous running into the road." The insult becomes ingrained as a dominant internalized label, "I'm stupid" ... hangs head in shame.

3. **The frequency of the forbidding gestures.** If you keep hearing something, eventually it morphs into a truth, so if your parents endlessly chastised you for being the "naughty one", eventually you believe it (and act to form, the naughty little pickle you believe you are).

4. **The consistency of the forbidden gestures.** If rules at home changed inconsistently and you were confused by actions that were sometimes allowed, then at other times banned, i.e. using swear words – funny in front of family friends but absolutely intolerable with the grandparents – any arising confusion hops away from the action itself into an internalized belief that it was you who was wrong, not the action, nor the situations. "I don't get it. Can I swear or can't I? Oh, forget it, I give up, I'm just a baddie always. I can't win. It's all my fault."

5. **The frequency with which forbidding gestures were tied to parental anger or withdrawal.** Children are fairly tolerant of criticism, but when accompanied by a parent's anger or withdrawal (threatened or actual), all poor little us would have heard was "You're bad and I'm rejecting you", which is the most terrifying thing Young Us could have heard. McKay and Fanning state, "The child retains the strong impression of his or her wrongness. And the critic will use that sense of wrongness to psychologically beat and kick you as an adult."[59]

Parents rarely intend to create hurts deliberately and it's important to remember no baby is born with a manual. Your parents did their best, just as you are also instinctively, simply, faithfully trying your best. So, don't go and bop your pop on the head for telling you off for chewing too noisily as a kid because, actually, he was operating from good intentions. He thought his perpetual naggy correcting, "Darling, for goodness' sake, stop chomping so disgustingly" would grant you more finesse as your lovely lady-self lunched later in London, not that he'd skewer you with a screaming internal demon beseeching you to never to accept meal invitations because "You sound disgusting, you eat like a pig, you cannot be seen in public, blah blah blah". He meant it lovingly. And so does your little Tasmanian devil, interestingly. The reason the critic does hold so much power over us is because it has a use. It actually serves a shielding function. We all need and want to feel:

- Secure and unafraid
- Effective and competent in the world
- Accepted by parents and significant others
- A sense of worth and okay-ness in most situations

The critic is thus protective and working faithfully to ensure we don't jeopardize any of the above. But, left untended, it limits our expansion, keeping us small and safe, shrinking dreams, shrivelling potential success. Becoming aware of its manipulations is essential to stabilize both self-worth and self-esteem to ensure we experiment out in the arena.

So, what's it up to? Well, your critic uses tricks known as cognitive distortions that bend the truth, warping your sense of reality. The good news is that each sly piece of sorcery can be magicked away from nonsensical, manipulative attack statements into guiding, nurturing ones grounded in fact through an exercise of rebuttals. Let's examine the nine most common distortions[60] here first, then work with your personal ones.

1. **Overgeneralization.** Something happens once, but you make a general universal rule. If you were late once, you'll always be late.
2. **Global labelling.** Rather than factually describing your qualities, you default to the derogatory. "I'm fat, ugly, inexperienced, no good," etc.
3. **Filtering.** Your spectacles are grey-tinted, never rose-coloured, and you selectively spot the negative and disregard the positive. The glass is half empty.
4. **Polarized thinking.** Your brain organizes the world into extremes of this or that, black or white, right or wrong, left or right, with no middle ground. You have to win or you're a failure.
5. **Self-blame.** You are overly self-accountable, taking responsibility for things that actually aren't necessarily your fault. "He left me because I'm not a good enough wife," etc.
6. **Personalization.** All roads lead to your ego and every sensitive situation, comment or event centres around you. From this central vantage point you negatively compare yourself to everyone else. "Oh woe is me."
7. **Mind reading, also known as Projection.** You make sweeping assumptions that others are upset with you, don't like you, don't care about you, don't

want to be with you and so on, without any facts to support your beliefs. It's always everyone else's fault.

8. **Control fallacies.** You either sit in desperate and hopeless victimhood or extreme and total responsibility for everybody and everything.

9. **Emotional reasoning.** The way you feel becomes your version of the way things are. "I'm upset therefore the world is against me."

BIG IMPACT REFLECTION: SILENCING YOUR SABOTEUR

This exercise will find your "rebuttal voice" to silence your critic and state kinder inner messages. Give your critic a name, shape and form to personify its voice. Now, take this further and start a discussion with him, her or it to combat what it's saying. Create three large columns on a sheet of paper headed: Self-Statements, Distortions and Rebuttal. In the Self-Statements column, write down everything your critic says across a 24-hour period. In the Distortion column label the statement per the cognitive distortion used. Then, in the final column, write your Rebuttal using your kind and nurturing inner voice, your "Leader Within", emanating from your powerful, progressive, integrated source of self-energy. For example, "I'm always late" is an overgeneralization, so your rebuttal could be, "I plan well to ensure I arrive on time. This is my positive intention." Now use these rebuttals all the time!

Examine the Encouraging Voices in Our Heads Too

While our pathological critic has the ability to stunt our progress, keep us small and away from our Big Impact dreams, there are other voices cajoling us along when we're motivated into action too. But, and alas, there are so many buts within the complexities of our beautiful brains, the encouraging words may also not be best serving us. We may inadvertently be hearing advice ingrained into our psyches that also may need a little analysing and updating. What do I mean? Let's say you had one parent or teacher whose approach to work was go, go, go, at any cost, get the work done. You've adopted this work mode your whole life and subconsciously slip into patterns to honour this encouragement instead of honouring yourself. You may hear this advice in your head and propel yourself through work tasks, pushing on and on, avoiding sleep, working long hours, artificially stimulating energy levels, doing stuff you know on an intellectual level risks pushing you closer to burnout, but subconsciously, you're unaware you're even doing this as you're on autopilot and the voices reverberate deeply. Let's say you also had another parent or teacher whose approach to suffering was to soothe stress with comforting food and drink – "Oh have a frothy warm something", "Eat some cookies then you'll feel better", "Eat another bowl of something as a little pick-me-up". This voice surreptitiously leads you to the kitchen for snack after meal after cappuccino after Deliveroo as your stress levels rise and work challenges increase, again erroneously leading you away from your harmonic energy state, into physical disruption and closer to burnout.

So, become aware. When you're ready to throw yourself into action, watch out for how the action materializes and is supported. What do you do to maintain action? Remember to honour yourself so success in all its multifaceted, ever-evolving forms is never self-sabotaging. Yours is the voice to listen to, so pay attention to who is driving you, and stay in control!

Knowledge Is Empowering

"The more that you read, the more things you will know. The more that you learn, the more places you'll go."

— Dr Seuss

When I am informed, I am confident. If I am ill-prepared or lacking knowledge, my inner critic runs wild and fear, anxiety, imposter syndrome, self-doubt and the rest of the negative-ninny gang dominate. I'm sure you're the same. We feel more self-assured when we've got the info we need. So, to bolster self-worth and thus confidence, conscientious knowledge gathering is essential.

Steve Jobs, pioneer of the most familiar technological innovation in history, heavily restricted his own children's device time. Interesting. We should pay attention to this. The inventor of the iPad himself was protective of both the volume and quality of information beaming through those devices into his cherubs' minds. He wanted to fully direct his children's attention and thus learning and not leave it to random media spontaneity, so controlled this.

Today, as well as so much media noise vying for our attention, the algorithmic echo chambers big tech solicits mean that what we are exposed to as "news" comprises a narrower and much-filtered bubble. This means we now need to work harder to expand our consumption universes, learn the two sides to every story, gain multiple perspectives and so on simply to be fully and fairly informed. Editorial is rarely journalistically neutral. And the advent of online worlds, social media and smart phones mean accessibility of this abundant information is rapid and vast. Good for immediately answering why the sky is blue, and

"Do ducks sleep, Mummy?", but bad for our ability to concentrate and process long-form content. With so much going on extrinsically, we need to work harder to proactively select what we learn and what we expose ourselves to.

If knowledge is power and we seek empowerment for confidence and self-worth, let's understand learning based on our neurology. There are three factors impacting our optimal learning state.

1. Our cognitive function peaks when hormones and neurotransmitters are in harmony. So serotonin, norepinephrine and dopamine levels should be steady and regular for the right emotional and physiological state to receive new information.
2. Protecting the homeostatic chemical state of the body, as we know, is achieved through a healthy lifestyle, which means a nutritious diet restricted in or devoid of processed foods, alcohol and nicotine and regular physical activity. And, yes, a caffeine surge may increase alertness initially, but it's not a sustainable state purely by dint of the fact it's artificially altering your body's equilibrium. Whenever we adjust a state synthetically, our body and brain work harder to compensate in other ways and thus nervous system fatigue eventually ensues.
3. Leading us to the final point that we need plenty of rest to learn, maintain concentration and retain information. This manifests in two ways – rest between bursts of productivity, and decent, quality sleep each night.

Assuming we maintain neurological solidity and are self-optimized to learn, it's now about selecting exactly what knowledge we seek. What knowledge will empower us as we expand into Big Impact and achieve the life, work, relationship, vitality and success we want. As ever, it comes down to self-accountability and devising a plan.

BIG IMPACT REFLECTION: KNOWLEDGE IS POWER

1. Write a list of every topic you want to learn about. This list should tumble out abundantly, with things you're interested in for pure interest's sake, subjects for professional growth and career development, and items for necessity e.g. health, parenting, etc. What do you want to learn and why?
2. Now consider where you can get this information and in what form? My children rely on YouTube as their "magical universe of learning" (actual phrase my eight-year-old son once used). Which industry newsletters can you subscribe to?

Which editorial can you unsubscribe from? Does the BBC serve impartial news or propaganda? Ask yourself which voices you trust or which new voices you fancy pushing yourself to listen to? Expand and modify your feed.

3. Organize your time to allow for learning with dedicated mental space to consume. An hour every morning reading the paper? A podcast while you run? An audiobook as you clean? What works for you to fit learning in each day, week, month? Can you go even further and build in devoted study weeks across the year, as Bill Gates does, for example? He shuts himself in a cabin with numerous tomes and reads and thinks undisturbed for two weeks every year religiously.

4. Observe your physical state and assess any lifestyle improvements you could make that would be more conducive to peak cognitive function. Remember we are all bio-individual so if a friend is sluggish and can't concentrate after a heavy bread-fest, it doesn't mean grains necessarily slow down your brain's processing power too. Observe and play with your own learning optimization.

Building a Mindset Practice

Mastering your mind will take daily rigour and forever be a work in progress. You can't do the exercises and reflections in this chapter and assume you're cooked. Nope, you are an emerging work of art in need of constant creation and course correction. I write more about the habit of self-awareness and journalling as a spiritual practice in one of my previous books, *Flourish: Redefine Success & Create More Time, Energy, Impact and Happiness.*

Core activities I recommend there, with more added here, are:

- Make space for yourself – alone time is a prerequisite for growth (if you're not comfortable in quiet stillness, this is a red flag).
- Practice mindfulness – find presence in as many moments across the day as you can. Simply slow down and be aware of the details in front of you using every sense.
- Keep a journal – reflect, reflect, reflect and try to physically write rather than type, but even an iPhone-tapped musing on the commute home is better than nothing.
- Practise being a good listener and observe how you self-manage in conversations and meetings to honour the speaker.

- Gain different perspectives and don't shun those different to yours: all are valid.
- Meditate – the more stressed out and busy you are, the more you should prioritize chunks of time in meditation.
- Seek feedback from loved ones and colleagues.
- Direct your learning to fuel growth in the directions you choose.
- Restrict reactivity and only consume media you choose proactively.
- Be grateful, gracious and giving to yourself and others.
- Honour your body as well as your mind with regular exercise, fresh air and nutrition.
- Step into your fears, gently or boldly, and observe your progress.
- Architect your learning to support your ambitions, avoiding attention stealers.
- Live life embracing the mantra, "I take complete responsibility for everything in my life. I am fully accountable for who I am."

Wayne W Dyer, a spiritual and pragmatic guru of positive mindset, taught the core notion of living a meaningful life; "With everything that has happened to you, you can either feel sorry for yourself or treat what has happened as a gift. Everything is either an opportunity to grow or an obstacle to keep you from growing. You get to choose." His, as yours can now be, is a principle of autonomy, accountability and positivity.

Your Big Impact Mindset Expansion Grid

Now you understand the key components to creating your bespoke Mindset Strategy for Big Impact – self-awareness, self-compassion, self-direction and self-worth – it's time to take stock and evaluate what you recognize in yourself, what work you need to do, what you'd like to research further and what pledges you will make to embrace deliberate self-awareness in your life.

In the grid below is what you now know how to manage.

It's time to translate this into solid action to make your expansion a reality.

Grab your journal and review the statements below, focusing on the "Expanding To" column. Now spend 30 minutes freewriting on everything that comes up for you when you read the expansion statements. Elaborate on them where you see fit and make them entirely yours. As well as writing the "what", dive into the "how" and "why". Really explore the statements, applying your newfound knowledge, and have fun exploring all the life-altering ways you're going to feel and how you're going to get there. Let the inspiration pour forth and capture everything that comes to mind.

FROM	EXPANDING TO ...
I am a victim of life, blaming others for circumstances or feelings.	I am self-accountable and responsive, examining triggers for growth.
I am self-sabotaging, especially in moments of stress.	I am self-compassionate and aware of my negative tendencies and how to manage them.
I am afraid, living in fear with a loud and dominant inner critic.	I am brave and curious with management strategies to silence the saboteur within.
I am rife with imposter syndrome and fear failure.	I am confident and resilient, embracing the unknown and excited by new adventures.
I am narrow-minded, locked in fixed beliefs.	I am growth-oriented and open-minded.
I am driven by egocentricity.	I am self-aware and heart-centred.
I am self-serving in pursuit of what makes me feel superior.	I am conscious of others and aware when ego is making me behave negatively.
I am paralysed by limiting beliefs.	I know how to reverse mind patterns to create empowering beliefs.
I never spend time alone or in self-reflection.	I prioritize inner work to expand outwardly.
My mind is bombarded with random, scattered information.	I have a clear learning plan with time to gain the knowledge I seek.
Rejection and the fear of rejection can paralyse me.	I have built a resilience to rejection and will not be thwarted from my dreams by fear.

Your Big Impact Decision Pledges

It's decision time. You're now clear on focus areas to prioritize as you expand into becoming more conscious of how you show up in the world. You've explored lots around belief systems, fear and your ego in your journal reflection exercises.

Now, harnessing the power of decision, write down three Mindset Pledges you will make to ensure your expansion unfurls.

I pledge to work on my mindset to create my biggest impact without ever burning out by ...

_____

_____

_____

YOUR BIG IMPACT STRATEGY NO. 3: PURPOSE

"Do whatever brings you to life, then. Follow your own fascinations, obsessions, and compulsions. Trust them. Create whatever causes a revolution in your heart."

— Elizabeth Gilbert

When I think of a woman living a purpose-driven life, I think of Kate Groch. Kate is the fearless, giant-hearted founder and CEO of Good Work Foundation (GWF), an education non-profit bringing "wonder-filled" learning to rural communities in South Africa. Kate started GWF from the back of her red Citi Golf in 2010, impassioned by the plight of so many deserving, yet deprived children in the country. With a zoology degree, Kate fell into her "calling" after being invited to travel with the entrepreneurial Varty family to teach their children on the road (the Vartys built one of South Africa's original private game reserves, Londolozi, now a magical luxury safari destination). She quickly realized that trying to maintain links with a curriculum back home was less impactful than noting what inspired the children most on the family's adventures, then linking that back to history, biology, literature, etc. to engage them in knowledge expansion. As she leaned into celebrating the innate curiosity and passions within the children, their learning exponentially accelerated and her teaching simultaneously became more powerful. She began to see the connection between self-belief and self-development and acknowledged her unique ability to see the potential in others before they see it in themselves. So, Kate started creating community learning initiatives, building schools and inspiring rural children to love learning. Having initiated her transformational work in the small town of Philippolis, South Africa, Kate now leads a team of 150, stretching border to border across Sabi Sands and Kruger National Park.

Kate has already positively impacted tens of thousands of children, helping to bring a quality of education to their lives that sets foundations for further education, elevated employment opportunities and thus income potential. Kate lives every day in honour of the children she serves and her business mission, waking to the daily thought, "How can I best be of service to this organization today?" She bursts with passion, enthusiasm and joy; she literally radiates pure love. (I actually cried during our interview I was so moved by her kind purposefulness.) She talks about "How good it feels when you fit in your skin" and this is what she teaches her employees and the thousands of children whose lives she touches, encouraging, "Be yourself, then you have something to give" and "Take the first step, as long as it's yours." Her whole company beams with the South African mantra *Ubuntu* – "I am because of you". Authenticity, determination, dogged intention and pride for her work and her mission make her one of the most inspiring exemplars of Purpose I've had the privilege to meet.

Kate exemplifies wonder-filled living. And wonder truly does abound when, like Kate, we live and work with purpose. In a state of purpose we are fulfilled, motivated, alive and invigorated. Each day sees us eagerly springing out of bed, not groggily slamming the snooze button. Within purpose, energy is created. Work becomes play. Life is exhilarating. As Confucius, the robed and dangly-eyebrowed, fervently selfless Chinese sage, advised: "Choose a job you love, and you will never have to work a day in your life."

In this chapter, you will learn the principles of leading a meaningful life through the lenses of Greek philosophers to modern day "dopamine distraction" experts, understanding why identifying and honouring your innate value set is key to a life fulfilled, and indeed a life of motivation. You'll design your purpose statement and create a multimedia vision of who you will be to deliver it. You'll understand the role of habits in shaping your reality and how inspiration is a guiding beacon to pay attention to.

What Is Purpose?

The Cambridge Dictionary defines purpose as "why you do something or why something exists", and it's that word "why" that's integral to you flourishing. When we feel a deep connection to a why, there's a propelling reason to work toward a task *beyond* the task itself. Think about popping the woolly hat on your toddler daughter's head before you go out in the snow. The task was to put her hat on, the why is because you love her like no feeling you've ever felt before and every protective cell in your body wants to ensure she's snuggly, warm and safe. The knitted hat is a symbol of how unequivocally, unconditionally and immortally your love embalms her. There is a meaningful intention behind the obvious functionality. And where there's meaningful intention, there's a rainbow cascade of happiness.

Over 2,300 years ago, Aristotle posed one of the big philosophical questions: "What is the ultimate purpose of human activity?" He concluded it was happiness. He went further to dissect happiness, and the pursuit thereof, into two distinct types – eudaimonia and hedonia. The "daimon" in eudaimonia refers to our "true self" and "most divine", thus eudaimonia represents glowy, self-transcending happiness emanating from within. Hedonia, by contrast, relates to (less radiant) hedonism, the indulging in pleasures for short-term gratification (from external sources). He warned against excess of the latter, stating, "The many, the most vulgar, would seem to conceive the good and happiness as pleasure. ... Here they appear completely slavish, since the life they decide on is a life for grazing animals."[61]

Now, grazing animals we may not consider ourselves to be, but it is certain most of us do like to graze: on food, drink, sex, beauty and anything that gives us the buzz of pleasure. The buzzes are all the more prevalent and accessible today with our dopamine-rich lives abundant with likes, followers, DMs, dating apps, song streaming, knowledge at the click of a button, online shopping and so on. As Aristotle alludes, hedonism is slavish. If he saw my four teens on their phones right now, he'd certainly think there was some tech slavery apparent in this room. Modern society is distracted and distractable. Are we any happier? No, it seems. And in fact, according to self-actualization ethics examined by modern philosopher David Norton, "it is every person's primary responsibility first to discover the daimon within him and thereafter to live in accordance with it".[62]

Why Does Purpose Make You Happier?

In *Dopamine Nation*, psychiatrist Dr Anna Lembke, connoisseur of translating the scientifically complex into digestible information for the layperson, teaches that the pleasure and pain seesaw in the brain should ideally rest in a state of equilibrium, that a little bit of a happy high and a little bit of pain (the come down) here and there are normal, well tolerated and the body can cope with automatically restabilizing back into our unconscious utopia, homeostasis. However, what scientists have recently learned is that as tolerance builds (we need more wine to feel mellow, more sex to feel satiated, more coffee to bounce, more lamas in our sanctuary, more hair extensions on our head and so on), the more violently the pendulum swings with oscillations of extreme highs, then consequential punishing lows, and the less we're able to readily return to our harmonious, steady state. In addition, the more extreme highs diminish the functionality of our dopamine receptors. We literally decrease our own reward circuitry through overstimulation, until we eventually trigger anhedonia, "which is the inability to enjoy pleasure of any kind".[63] Thus, addictive patterns to substances, habits, and other methods simply get us back to base, to our equilibrium. You may have heard about dopamine fasting – abstinence for a set period from anything pleasurable, which is a deliberate attempt to force a momentary recalibration before we eventually get back on the crack, so to speak. It's a fine tightrope we teeter on, this dopamine malarky, and today's technological explosion is jiggling the rope all the more wildly.

Our brains last evolved 200,000 years ago. This was when they stopped growing in size, but, according to the *New Scientist*, in the past 10,000 to 15,000 years, the average size of the human brain compared with our bodies has actually shrunk by around 4 per cent.[64] So, not only has the brain not adapted in any way to keep pace with technological changes, but it's smaller. Now, size may not yet apparently matter (science is estimated to understand only a fraction of what the brain can do), but the problematic lack of adaption lies in what Dr Lembke refers to as the "phylogenetically uber-ancient neurological machinery for processing pleasure and pain" that "has remained largely intact throughout evolution and across species."[65] So, where pleasure used to spark us to eat and reproduce, and pain to avert injury and death, we now have stratospherically raised our neural set point for pleasure and therefore seek lots of it.

The reason this is a problem for us modern, happy seeking, gratification addicts is that, unlike the cave-dwelling early humans with a few berries to binge on each spring, today there is perpetual abundance; particularly in most of the Western world where we live in The Land of Plenty. Today, we can fill our knee-high patent boots with good stuff over and over while the sociological ecosystem furnishes us with our every desire endlessly and immediately, but as Dr Lembke warns, "Our brains are not evolved for this world of plenty"[66] and we're drowning in dopamine.

But why does any of this matter to your grand life of Big Impact? Well, we want to avoid burnout and there are some eerie implications looming in our worlds of overstimulation. Neuroscientist Samuel McClure and his team examined which areas of the brain activated when a subject received immediate gratification as opposed to a delayed reward[67]. The immediate thrill triggered the emotion and reward-processing parts of the brain, whereas the delayed treat activated the prefrontal cortex – the part of the brain involved in planning and abstract thinking. The implication here is that we are all now potentially "vulnerable to prefrontal cortical atrophy as our reward pathway has become the dominant driver of our lives".[68] In other words, our ever-greatening reliance on immediate pleasure and dopamine hits is quite literally shrinking our grey matter and diminishing our ability to plan and CEO our lives. Think about this through our "avoiding burnout" lens. Catastrophic! No way do we want to lose any ability to plan and organize as that's fundamental to our successful and peaceful futures!

Short-term hedonism may feel like the simplest route to happiness, but beyond the buzz and ensuing crash, there's a little soul empty of substantial joy. Which takes us back to the Greeks and eudaimonia. If producing happiness through meaning and a purpose-driven life delivers sustainable utopia, deeper and way more enriching than any hedonistic forays, then surely that's the path to follow. But it's not the path of least resistance, and therein lies our challenge. It's quicker to teeter into the cocktail bar with the girls and order a dirty martini than get on our meditation mat or commit to our noble cause. The quick fix is more convenient. And we've kind of redefined happiness into the shallow glamour of those martinis resplendent with their plump olives and iridescent ice cubes. As David Norton cautions, "Most of us today have no sense of an oracle within. ... Turning our backs to the void, we become infinitely distractible by outward things, prizing those that 'demand' our attention." He goes on to say we even love the sensationalism of news crises, from political dramas to global conflict to climate disasters in what he terms "mental ambulance-chasing".[69]

Evidently, it's easy to ooh and aah at news and gossip about the nerd in the office or the neighbour's new car, and prattle merrily on, deriving a lot of fun from all of this. And don't get me wrong, I'm the first to organize a Big Night Out, but ultimately, a hedonistic skew toward self-indulgent play as a life mainstay (and perhaps escapism from something or things), doesn't build the inner robustness to expand into either our greatest selves, nor our greatest lives, and actually risks total mental ineptitude if something goes wrong (which inevitably it will). A short-term, vacuous approach to life not only skips building a foundation for expansion, but actually distracts from what matters most – you living in your integrity, honouring your values and connecting wholly into your purpose. Because, you won't want your headstone shaped like a martini glass, I promise you (and there's way more abundance awaiting you than anything you'll find in the bottom of that glass anyway).

There are plenty of supporting health stats too. Multiple studies have proven that people living in accordance with eudaimonia as opposed to hedonistically have less propensity toward stress and anxiety, and are healthier, with a "stark contrast at the level of molecular physiology"[70] i.e., immune response and general vitality markers all score significantly higher. They are able to learn better, are less prone to any depressive feelings, experience greater life satisfaction and have higher self-esteem. Heart-disease afflicted patients are 22 per cent less likely to suffer a stroke when living on purpose.[71]

So, what does matter most?

Bronnie Ware was a palliative nurse who cared for hospice patients before their death. Her tender bedside conversations revealed common regrets of the dying as they faced their own mortality. "I learnt never to underestimate someone's capacity for growth. Some changes were phenomenal. Each experienced a variety of emotions, as expected, denial, fear, anger, remorse, more denial and eventually acceptance. Every single patient found their peace before they departed though, every one of them."[72] What can we learn from their final reflections to infuse our lives with peace now, without the need for deathbed regrets? These were the top five regrets of the dying, as reported by Bronnie Ware:

1. I wish I'd had the courage to live a life true to myself, not the life others expected of me.
2. I wish I hadn't worked so hard.
3. I wish I'd had the courage to express my feelings.
4. I wish I'd stayed in touch with my friends.
5. I wish that I had let myself be happier.

Absorbing these musings, it's impossible not to be stirred, to envision the anguish of faces etched with crinkles of time, ruefully mourning lives lived inauthentically and devoid of vulnerability, intimate friendships and overall happiness. It's a touching guidepost toward roads less travelled.

The Value of Values

Clarifying a purpose in life and weaving everything we do with meaningful intention requires articulation of our values. According to the Co-Active Training Institute, the global body that certified my coaching credentials, "Our values are the lighted signposts on the fulfilment path, the arrows that tell a client which journey will hold the most fulfilment". This intertwining of values and fulfilment is absolutely core to how we live purposefully. Values guide and motivate us, they excite and invigorate us, they are the certainties we take forward with us each day.

When we feel those trigger pangs we explored earlier (page 81), it's generally because a value has been compromised in some way. You observe someone at work gaining preferential treatment, being fast-tracked to promotion without merit, when one of your values is fairness, this triggers you because it compromises your value. Your son forgets to walk the dog and you arrive home to soiled sofas and a distressed dog – when one of your values is responsibility, this represents a compromised value. You find out your friend's husband is having an affair, when one of your values is loyalty, this is a compromised value. In each triggering scenario, your personal sense of integrity is incensed, outraged and furiously keen to act.

In the reverse case, when we feel sublimely content, it's because values are being honoured. Your boss invites you to independently lead a new innovation project, when one of your values is autonomy – tick. Your partner starts saying "we" instead of "I" in public, when one of your values is togetherness – tick. Your renovation project is finally complete, when one of your values is progress – tick. Each scenario presents life flowing in congruence with your value set.

Values represent our fundamental beliefs and guiding principles. We tend to build our lives, where we live, what we do, what we learn, friendship groups, habits and more around our values. They are the things that matter most to you, and they help dictate your behaviour and actions. Understanding your values is essential work as part of your self-awareness and ability to effect Impact. Impact won't be possible if values are not being honoured, as your foundations won't be strong enough. Whenever there is dissatisfaction in an area of life, it always comes back to incongruence with a value set.

BIG IMPACT REFLECTION: IDENTIFY YOUR VALUES

Think about a peak experience in your life — a moment when you felt truly fulfilled, alive and engaged. Close your eyes and reenact it. Be there. Smell the smells, feel the feels. Who were you with? Where were you? What were you doing? Now, in your journal, describe this beautiful experience in detail, focusing on what made it so special and memorable. Reflect on the emotions, actions and interactions. As you immerse into this gorgeous memory, think about which aspects of this moment resonate deeply with your sense of purpose and fulfilment and let some core values bubble up.

Now, list your top ten values, mentally noting how each one contributes to your overall sense of wellbeing and authenticity. Don't overthink or overanalyse, just jot them down as these are your prevalent life values.

Next, build out word strings from each word. Each of us will have different, personal meanings associated with each value, so expand through your word string to deepen the value.

Here are some examples:

- Love/connection/intimacy
- Harmony/collaboration/peace
- Progress/creation/expansion

Now, score each value from 1 to 10 in terms of whether it is currently being satisfied in your life, 10 being "super duper, life is zinging with this juiciness right now", and 1 being "damn, we have a serious hole here".

Generally, you want 10s throughout, so anything less needs work. Continue with your journalling and now spend a few minutes on each <10 result. Why did you score it that way? What could you do to improve it so you are living with the value being honoured? What changes are needed in your life? What can you do now/tomorrow/next week? How important is it to fix this chasm and get it up to a 10?

This is a powerful exercise in assessing your general level of happiness right now and spotlights where progressive thought, planning and eventual (or immediate) action is required.

Simon Sinek, bespectacled TED Talker extraordinaire, recommends expanding values into verbs, so this is something interesting to play with too: "For values or guiding principles to be truly effective they have to be verbs. It's not 'integrity', it's 'always do the right thing'. It's not 'innovation', it's 'look at the problem from a different angle'. Articulating our values as verbs gives us a clear idea – we have a clear idea of how to act in any situation."[73]

Values-Empowered Decision-Making

Being clear about what matters most to us can be extremely helpful when we're at a tricky choice juncture. Our values are innate. They represent what our heart feels and wants. They bubble within the essence of us. So, when faced with hard decisions, leaning into the answer by honouring our values makes deciding all the easier.

Should I take the new job? How many of my values does it honour?

Should I get divorced? How many of my values does staying married dishonour? How many would divorce honour?

Should I eat another bowl of ice cream? Which values am I honouring or dishonouring if I do that?

Should we try for a baby? How does parenting fit into my value set?

BIG IMPACT REFLECTION: VIBRATING VALUES

One way to deeply zone in on a value you may inadvertently be compromising is to do a value elaboration exercise where we get your value to vibrationally expand. In this, you explode the value into a technicolour, animated representation, adding more instinctual detail to what it means and feels like to you.

- Take one value. Close your eyes and breathe into it. Really immerse yourself in what this value means to you. Why is it important? How do you want it to be present in your life? Which areas of your life does it touch? How, where, when and who, if relevant? Build out the picture of this value so it starts to feel more tangible. Add colours, smells, feelings to it. Start to experience the value viscerally.
- Picture a scene where the value is being honoured most magnificently. Who's there? How do you feel? What is everyone doing? Where are you? Build, visualize, fantasize, expand, explore and have fun really elaborating on the gorgeous essence of what this value means to you.
- Now give it a memorable name with a descriptive adjective e.g. Vibrant Vitality, Pacey Progress, Lacey Love, whatever adds more imaginative texture to the value.

Having clarity around exactly what a value represents and why it's so pivotal to your world keeps you grounded in who you are. You know exactly what you need to honour them consistently and indeed see them honoured consistently around you. Therefore, it can also be useful to share with your loved ones as you step more resolutely into it. It can also be hugely valuable at sweeping away bad habits, which we secretly know don't serve us, such as smoking, drinking, mindless snacking, mindless scrolling, mindless anything ... you get the picture.

Derailing Any Derailing Habits (Through Values)

Perfect doesn't always have to be the goal, but perfectionism can be wonderfully invigorating. Perfectionists do attain fabulous things, and I am all for setting high standards, which I know you are too. In *The Perfectionist's Guide to Losing Control*, Katherine Morgan Schafler, who we met earlier, blows up all negativity around perfectionism, teaching us it's a superpower and for us to reframe our relationship with it, embracing it as a gift. She writes, "A restored perfectionist understands that it's not that you long for some external thing or for yourself to be perfect, it's that you long to feel whole and to help others feel whole."[74] So, when the moment strikes that we feel conflicted with whether to be perfect or perfectly imperfect, and do or not do the imperfect thing like smoke, drink, slob out, veg out, take a look through the lens of your values to help you decide. Is having two glasses of wine on a Monday night too much of a derail from our perfect plan, or should we decide to treat ourselves and know that, tonight, imperfect is okay too? How about we just check in with our value set? What actually matters most right now? If your value were Vibrant Vitality, the dedication to prioritizing health in order to sleep well, work well and be well, the wine doesn't honour that value, and the decision is made. Sparkling water with a dash of lime; perfect it is. Equally, if your value were Celebrate Family and you celebrate best with wine, and it's your cousin's birthday, go and honour that value and let your hair down – perfect it still is!

As you evolve into your Big Impact self, you will inevitably outgrow certain habits and discover automatic patterns in your daily routine that are no longer relevant, nor necessarily serving you well, especially through the lens of your values. This could be anything from the calorie-laden latte you buy on autopilot on your way into the office, to the supplements you started taking in your teens and never thought to stop or reexamine, to doing the same abstoning exercise for twenty years (yes, that's me!). Habits become unconscious and so it takes conscious awareness and effort to reevaluate and assess them; the good, the bad and the ugly. It's wise to conduct a habit stocktake as you create your Big Impact self, and then design a deliberate habit strategy aligned with your shiniest vision of you – a programme to eliminate the habits that no longer serve you and reprogramme new, self-developing ones. I run all-day workshops addressing habit formation and maintenance, as habits are a complicated, multi-tendrilled dimension of life, but for now I invite you to focus on one desired new habit per life realm below and master the method.

BIG IMPACT REFLECTION: BIG IMPACT SHINY HABITS

Step 1: What – Draw the table opposite in your journal and, reflecting on each of the Big Impact areas on the left, write down one new habit you would like to introduce to embrace a shiny version of You in that realm. Pick one you identify as most important to your ambitions, one that you know will be most transformational.

Step 2: Why – Next, enhance these listed habits by elaborating on why each habit matters. What about this habit will be beneficial to you? Why is it important? How will it enhance your Big Impact plans? Ensure you include which Value this habit honours too.

Step 3: Prompt – We now get into the detail of what's known in behavioural science as a habit formation loop where a prompt stimulates an action, which stimulates a reward and thus is repeated, eventually being repeated so often it becomes an automatic behaviour and thus the habit is formed. Tip: tiny habits and easy prompts are the most powerful starting points for ingraining new habits. For example, if you have a Big Impact ambition to get healthier, a good start could be the tiny habit of drinking more lemon-infused water, with an easy prompt of keeping a bowl of lemons by the tap. The habit starts small, the prompt is impossible to miss and you're more likely to do it.

Step 4: Action – Describe the behaviour to occur after the prompt is initiated. For example, you see the lemons, you know to pour yourself a glass of water, slice a wedge of lemon into it, and drink.

Step 5: Celebrate – Now, associate an emotional reward with that action by deciding how you'll celebrate it. Repeatedly taking the new action and experiencing this satisfying, celebratory, fist-pump, high-five rush of emotions will more rapidly establish new neural networks in your brain and invite repetition – the more satisfying the reward, the more likely repetition is, so lock in how you'll acknowledge your feat positively. This can be anything from a smile, a "Get me!" cheer out loud, or a private wink to yourself. It's a super important step in habit formation, so allow yourself to buzz with a mini pat on the back of some form.

Step 6: Pledge – Write a pledge to yourself to commit to this new habit. What will you do in moments of weakness? How will you retain the vibrancy of your values and Big Impact goals at the forefront of upholding the new, better habit?

Step 7: Depth – Spend time writing about how good the new, positive habit will feel and how these feelings contribute to your Big Impact dreams.

	Habit to introduce	Why? Include which value is being honoured	Prompt	Action	Celebrate	Pledge	How good will this habit make you feel?
Energy							
Mindset							
Purpose							
Time							
Work							
Connection							
Wealth							
Fulfilment							

Inspiration and Imagination

"There is one quality which one must possess to win, and that is definiteness of purpose, the knowledge of what one wants, and a burning desire to possess it."
— Napoleon Hill

Esteemed wealth master, Napoleon Hill, talks of "definiteness of purpose". I think of this every time an errant driver dawdles in front of me on the school run when a clear manoeuvre would ensure we all get through the traffic efficiently and thus children in classrooms on time. "Drive with definiteness of purpose, Nut Nut!" the children often hear me chant. Beyond my frustrated steering wheel and within Napoleon's firm definiteness, within the pulsing intentionality of purpose lie power, energy and motivation. Now, motivation is an elixir of life, pure medicinal electricity! Waking up motivated and charging into the day is a superb feeling.

Inspiration is essential to motivation. When we are inspired by a person, a role, a target, a purpose, we are electrified. Coming from the Latin *inspirare*, meaning "to breathe into", the word "inspiration" was originally used in a divine context to mean a mystical animating force, a profound idea or truth revealed to an unsuspecting person. It meant sleeping souls were awoken by a lightning bolt from heaven: a magical calling, a purpose, an imagination stirred to create.

When we embrace inspiration and make space for that celestial intervention to enter our psyches, creativity surges and the golden shimmer of imagination births idea after idea. It may appear as a dream, a flash of knowing. However it shows up, when we grab it and roll with it, it grows and so does our output, and in turn, our impact. The impact grows because we're inspired to act on the idea. Motivation ensues.

So, trust your imagination. Have you noticed how sometimes problems get solved in your sleep? You go to bed pondering a perplexing challenge, then wake with the solution. You daydream during the lecture and in your disconnected trance you see a vision of what needs to happen next. You're out on a walk and suddenly know what to do to solve the percolating niggle. Flash!

BIG IMPACT REFLECTION: CAPTURING THE MAGIC OF YOUR IMAGINATION

Keep a journal by your bed to capture the symbolism within your dreams, scrawling notes in your semi-sleepy state before your conscious mind suppresses these potentially potent subconscious whispers. Have you woken with a prevalent feeling, thought of someone or a solution to a problem, the words of a song, a vision of a place, or anything that's hovering between the land of your subliminal bubblings and your conscious mind? Don't let it melt back into dreamland, grab it before it floats away.

In your waking hours, have a notebook with you always to capture your ideas as they pepper your mind throughout the day. Notice what piques your interest and jot it down. Add any flashes of inspiration that strike. Capture the crazy, the fun, the logical, the lot. The more you train yourself to revere your ideas, the more they'll abound.

The next time you observe a painting, listen to a song, admire a sculpture or get lost in a Netflix series, ponder the creative genius behind the work and what ignited their mind to create such memorable output. They were inspired by a spark, which unleashed their imagination, and magic occurred.

Throughout history, artists, writers, composers and musicians through to modern-day ad agency creatives and more have attributed their masterpieces to their "muse". And once the muse arrives, it seems flow is inevitable.

Steven Pressfield, powerful author and creative guide, teaches us in *The War of Art* that the muse is the source of all creative expansion; "The Muse takes note of our dedication. She approves. We have earned favour in her sight. When we sit down and work, we become like a magnetized rod that attracts iron filings."[75] So, not only does productivity abound but provenance aligns to open up further ideas and opportunities. Once we are inspired, the muse arrives, flow begins and we feel innately plugged in. As Maya Angelou put it, "When I'm writing, I write. And then it's as if the muse is convinced that I'm serious and says, 'Okay. Okay. I'll come.'"

It's what Joseph Campbell refers to as "following our bliss". In *The Power of Myth*, Campbell states, "You put yourself on a kind of track that has been there all the while waiting for you, and the life that you ought to be living is the one you're living. When you can see that, you begin to meet people who are in your field of your bliss, and they open the doors to you. I say, follow your bliss and don't be afraid, and doors will open where you didn't know they were going to be".[76]

I'm sure you've noticed that before. Those "coincidences" that spring up, which quickly start effusively gushing; the people you meet, the opportunities that arise, the abundance of ideas, the ease of materialization, the effortless productivity that feels like fun, the stars aligning, the "right place, right time" nature of everything. You're following your bliss, your "personal legend" as Paulo Coelho describes it, you're on purpose. So, where's your muse? Where's your bliss? Your legend? If there isn't fizz in your daily output right now, you need to explore where the bubbles have gone and find them.

BIG IMPACT REFLECTION: YOUR INSPIRATIONAL WELL

Inspiration is the clue to motivation. When you are inspired, you are called to act. This exercise invites you to reflect on who and what inspires you and when moments of inspiration have struck in the past.

Firstly, think of people in your orbit, real world or imaginary: celebrities, historical figures, family, friends, colleagues, anyone who strikes you as inspiring. What is about them that stirs you? What are their attributes? How do they conduct themselves? How do they work? What do they do? How do they dress, speak, move, behave? What is their lifestyle like? Identify everything about them that resonates with you as worthy of note.

Their noteworthy bits are the bits you want too, and you absolutely can emulate anything and everything you admire with the right energy, focus and attention.

When you follow your inspiration, you are tuning into where your heart is intuitively guiding you (so ideally you should always be inspired). Allow role models to become your masters, the guides tickling your soul to follow an exciting new path, inviting the muse to appear.

Next, consider what else inspires you – nature, art, places, events. Write about times you've felt most inspired in the past. Where were you and what was happening to cause your flush of inspiration?

Finally, think about times in your life when funny coincidences kept occurring, helping you progress toward an ambition. Were you in a state of inspiration then? How? What were you doing? What did it feel like?

Embrace this journal entry as a moment to get clear on the what and how of these inspirational role models and/or moments and places, and freewrite on what this means for you, and what potential action this can stimulate today as you step into your Big Impact dreams. "I admire xxx because xxx and so I will xxx."

Remember, inspiration can strike anywhere, anytime, so always be ready with your notebook to capture the flash!

The Power of Vision

"It is only you that can harness the power within yourself. And that is the real magic."

— Dr James R Doty

Sara Blakely never set out to be one of *Forbes'* most influential women in the world, in her words, she "just wanted to make impact at a party". But way beyond that party, she had big Big Impact dreams and was virulently intent on making a success of herself and always honouring her personal vision. The glamorous and unwaveringly humble founder of Spanx, Sara became the world's youngest self-made female billionaire at only 41. Impassioned, personable and straight-talking, she went from door-to-door fax machine sales to creating and running the world's largest underwear empire. It wasn't overnight success, of course, but rather took years and years of isolated (and isolating) graft coupled with wily, incessant and unbreakable determination. As witty as she is hard-working (she did stints as a stand-up comedienne in her 20s), she attributes her success to a clear and inspiring vision that she relentlessly worked toward, achieving goal after goal, ambition unfurling majestically each year. She famously even "manifested" her appearance on *Oprah*!

When we intrinsically connect with a vision as a propelling force, like Sara, we find a power to produce that is as liberating as it is motivating. And when we start producing, the universe aligns to cocreate even more propelling energy so we, and simultaneously our impact, expand. Defining a vision we wholeheartedly believe in is crucial.

Throughout his career, Edison obtained 1,093 patents. And while many of these inventions — such as the light bulb, stock printer, phonograph and alkaline battery — were ground-breaking, even more of them were unsuccessful. On and on he persevered, trying and trying. Edison is renowned in fact for saying that genius is "1 per cent inspiration and 99 per cent perspiration." Indeed, there are endless inspiring tales of entrepreneurs persevering fervently to reach their eventual heady heights – think of Walt Disney's repeated rejections and poverty so extreme he ate dog food for a period, and JK Rowling's rock bottom before her $15bn empire burgeoned. A Wharton study examining "Age and High Growth Entrepreneurship"[77] resoundingly proved that the most successful founders are in their mid-40s. Experience pays off ultimately.

In Angela Duckworth's bestseller *Grit: The Power and Passion of Perseverance*, she introduces a "grit scale", which proves that talent and luck won't suffice alone but need determined action to breed success. As she states, "As much as talent counts, effort counts twice."[78] Malcolm Gladwell similarly teaches in *Outliers,* "Ten thousand hours is the magic number of greatness."[79] We can't just dream and hope we'll drift into magnificence, because we won't. Accountability for effort is essential too.

When I set up my first business, The Bespoke Gift Company, I had two key demonstrative moments where perseverance catapulted the business forward after numerous doors had been slammed in my face. Firstly, I needed to quickly increase production capability to meet ever-booming demand, so I had to source a print production unit to partner with me. I trawled multiple grungy industrial estate printworks spanning southeast England, ladened with my canvas and acrylic product samples, double buggy and small people in tow. After repeated rejection on the grounds that I was too "cottage industry", I eventually secured a "Yes!", meaning production and global expansion finally scaled rapidly. The second was negotiating a national contract with WHSmith, a major British high street retailer. Over several months, I hounded the head of buying, a gracious and kind man, with calls, emails and letters, until eventually, I was in the Berkshire headquarters signing the legalities for my full suite of personalized products to join the WHSmith gift range. I was only 27 years old, bold, determined and fastidious in my belief that my vision was a good one. I was also learning the truth that if you don't ask, indeed, you don't get! So, never forget – persistence pays off.

The funny thing is that persistence doesn't feel like effort when you're clear on your why and impassioned by the what. A passion by its very nature stimulates natural effort. It invigorates both our physicality and our spirit. We feel more alive. We long to do the work. We are less burdened by failure as passion thrusts us onward. We have so much fresh and yielding energy. However, there is a difference between passion and purpose. Purpose grounds us in the why, passion is the what. So, by all means explore your passion, lean into your passion, love your passion and indulge it, but evolve passion into clear purpose, because on the other side of purpose sparkles impact.

For example, you may be a singer whose passion is crooning and whose purpose is to lift others up and brighten moods with your voice. You may sing all day, every day, in the shower, in the car, in the garden, but only the birds, your children and tolerant neighbours hear you. When you take your passion out of your home and garden onto the public stage, you lift others up and brighten moods with your gift because you are working on purpose. Impassioned action delivered on purpose stimulates magic.

Just Mercy author and humble activist Bryan Stevenson has devoted his life's work to eradicating injustice of the undeservingly punished. What started as a passion to study law quickly became a purpose of protection and slowly saw him move into the public arena to further his cause. Over the past 30 years, since founding the Equal Justice Initiative in Montgomery, Alabama, Stevenson has freed over 100 unjustly convicted prisoners. His work revealed black Americans are disproportionately penalised at every stage of the criminal justice system. "For years I was one of these people – I just wanted to put my head down and do my work. I didn't even have a sign on the door."[80] But as his purpose strengthened, Stevenson went from his book to a TED Talk to a museum and monument to an HBO documentary, feature film and, perhaps most glossy of all, an interview on Oprah's *Super Soul Special*. The limelight became a mechanic for even more purposeful work, to have more impact. "Things I would have said 'absolutely not' to ten years ago, I'm now much more open to – mostly as a medium for getting people to see the system and the way it functions more clearly."[81] Today, Stevenson is aiming for nothing less than "an American era of truth and reconciliation on race, especially as it relates to inequality in the criminal justice system".[82] He's come to recognize that to have impact he needs to be heard. And so, with passion and purpose, now he most definitely is.

My sister, Melissa, runs multiple businesses. She's smart, entrepreneurial and creative, harnessing both her skills and experience. She's a makeup artist, a hair stylist, she's a garden designer, she sells beauty products and, most recently, wedding hair accessories, tiaras and diamanté pins. My sis is always evolving her wares, her time focus and, by consequence, her primary income streams. When I tell you that Melissa was obsessed, and I mean sometimes creepily, by Girl's Worlds, pay attention to the clue. Remember those 1980s rubber heads with large eyes, perfect noses and synthetic hair that girls shared their dressing tables with, ensuring Sally was preened first before we attacked our own heads, complete with blue eye shadow, French plaits, glitter lashes, the lot? My sister took the term "head management" to the next level. Seriously. I mean, she had around eight of these haunting heads on various stands, tables, window ledges and the floor of her room, which meant popping in to ask my little sis how school was today had the potential to freeze time and petrify me with a paranoid realization that adjacent to my bedroom sanctuary existed a world run by latex loonies.

My sister dabbled in photography, waitressing, motherhood (she's still dabbling in this one), interiors, being a film extra (*Love, Actually,* no less), and always hair and makeup. Despite all the other distractions, bridal hair, makeup and hair accessories are her thang. They were always her thang. She started draping those creepy dolls with crystal embellishments when she was eight. It's no wonder that, at 48, despite meandering into many another fields, she is always lured right back to where she began and it's where her big bucks roll in. She is booked years in advance and it's not just her services beautifying the wedding entourage, but making and selling jewel-encrusted tiaras, bobby pins and sparkly combs. She's right back where she started and her bridal business is booming. She's learned that sticking with her passions pays more.

So, look out for the clues in your interests. What did you do for fun as a kid that should probably be how you make money as an adult? I'm not talking nose-picking and spider racing of course, but maybe there's potential in the bath potions you used to make, your love of sketching or how many hedgehogs you rescued. Follow your passions with purpose and charge a premium (per your experience). Simple.

Finding Your Purpose

Purpose sits at the intersection between what you're passionate about (everything you love), what you're good at (your skills and innate talents), what others need (who is asking you for what) and what you value most (your values). It is taking your love and your brilliance to those who need it most while honouring your values. Picture it as a Venn diagram with that resplendent sweet spot representing You. If you feel you are drifting in life, ambling without direction and nervous you haven't found your purpose yet, this exercise will reveal your gold. Equally, if you feel clear on your purpose, complete this exercise to elaborate or polish your treasure.

BIG IMPACT REFLECTION: FINDING YOUR PURPOSE

Finding and honouring your purpose is transformative. It stimulates a joyful life journey that aligns your innermost values, passions, strengths and desired impact. By using a four-circle Venn diagram, you can visually and thoughtfully explore these key aspects of your life, leading to a clear and meaningful purpose statement. Follow these steps to discover where these elements intersect and guide you into your most fulfilling and purposeful life.

Step 1: Draw the four circles below in your journal.

Step 2: In each circle, write down key elements that define each of the four categories for you:

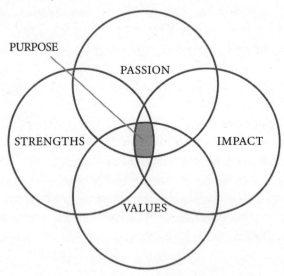

- **Values:** the principles and beliefs identified as most important to you earlier (see the Big Impact Reflection on page 108) e.g. honesty, compassion, creativity.

- **Passions:** what activities or subjects excite and energize you (and you find yourself researching in bed on an idle Saturday morning)? e.g. teaching, writing, helping others
- **Strengths:** what are your natural talents and skills (what do you find effortlessly easy compared to others)? e.g. problem-solving, communication, empathy
- **Desired Impact:** what difference do you want to make in the world or in the lives of others? e.g. improving education, promoting health, fostering community, kind leadership (a big one of mine!)

Step 3: Next, look at the sections where the circles overlap and reflect on your observations of the overlaps:

- **Values + Passions:** Activities or causes that align with both your values and passions.
- **Passions + Strengths:** What you are both passionate about and skilled at.
- **Strengths + Desired Impact:** How you can use your skills to make an impact.
- **Values + Desired Impact:** Impacts that align with your core values.

I suggest freewriting in your journal for a few minutes per overlap, as the insights will connect you more deeply to what authentically matters to you.

Step 4: The central intersection where all four circles overlap is your magic! This is your purpose. Now, spend five minutes reflecting on the assortment of realizations this exercise has revealed, assimilating them into your purpose and really tune into it. It should inspire you, bringing a rush of energy, and stimulate ideas instantly. Remember, purpose should not feel like effort; it should be naturally invigorating. It's who you are as well as what you do and what drives you.

Step 5: Create a purpose statement that resonates deeply with you. Make it specific, personal, and authentic. Here's mine: "To vibrantly illuminate and energize others to excitedly expand into their greatest potential and stimulate their highest, most invigorating, fun, impactful and rewarding contribution to the world." Share it with loved ones. Print it out. Use it as your phone screensaver. Write it inside your work notebook. Refer back to it whenever you feel wobbled, lost, afraid, hurt, nervous … to ground yourself back into the positive energy, radiant spirit and divine intention that is wonderful You!

Creating Yourself

Living on purpose goes beyond the intentional action that you're going to take and includes creating yourself anew. Who do you want to be? And how is she different from how you show up today? When you did your values exercise, what did you learn about yourself, and where there is dissonance between what matters most to you and how you are living your life today? As George Bernard Shaw stated, "Life isn't about finding yourself. Life is about creating yourself." So, who do you want to create?

Sara Blakely, Malala Yousafzai, Nicola Mendelsohn and Kate Groch all had clarity around who they would need to be to deliver their purposes. They recognized the need to shape themselves as a priority to be able to honour their purpose. So, when you say your purpose out loud, who do you need to become to be that impactful, intentional woman?

BIG IMPACT REFLECTION: THE VISION OF YOU

This is my multimedia modern day version of a vision board that you can create using any apps you choose. The intention is to create an audio and visual stimulation to magnify your vision of who you want to be (and who you know you really are). Personally, I use Pinterest and Spotify, but there are an abundance of similar tools.

Step 1: Freewrite for ten minutes about how you want to feel over the next year. Write in the present tense. Construct your prose as though this is your reality already, today, now. Really focus in on the feelings that will come from being the very best version of yourself. Try to prioritize your emotions first in your reflections, as how you want to feel holds more power than a goal about looks or lifestyle, for example. Once you've captured all those tantalizing feelings, then you can have fun visualizing the other aspects, like where you want to spend time, what you want to look like, how you want your career to evolve and how you want to be showing up across all realms of your life 12 months from now. We're now going to capture these strong emotions and wishes visually and aurally to create a readily accessible tool to remind yourself of your Vision of You.

Step 2: Choose a keyword that sums up that You intention for the year. Make it expressive and meaningful enough that it will strike an inner chord connecting you back into that vision of you. For example, Peace, Wealth, Sparkle, Radiant, Butterfly ... whatever is your soul focus for this new phase of your life.

Step 3: Next, create an image library or board and name it with your keyword and year and the important label "Me", so 2025 Radiant Me, 2026 Wealthy Me, 2027 Unstoppable Me, 2028 In Love Me, etc. Within this board, save as many inspiring images as you are drawn to, which represent who you want to be this year. For example, if your focus is on feeling more present as a mother, select images of mothers attentively nurturing children. If you choose to feel stronger and more relaxed when presenting, select images of seemingly powerful speakers addressing large audiences. If feeling fit is your priority, find images of runners in stunning landscapes or looking strong on treadmills. If you want to bring more creativity into your life, use representations of creativity like gorgeous flowerbed creations, arty meals, interior spaces and so on. Focus fully on *who* you want to be, with images that vibrantly depict how good that version of you will *feel*. So, it's not a woman on a treadmill if you hate running indoors; it has to be images that inspire the sensation of how good you will feel when fit and invigorated i.e., outside and freely running into the sunset. Whatever your thing is, those emotions you want to fill your life with, your soul's goals, capture them expressively in your visual board.

Step 4: Create a playlist with songs that inspire all of these amazing feelings. Choose songs that uplift you and resonate with that vision you designed in your freewriting. Keep adding to it every time you hear a song that makes you feel good. I have an "Unstoppable" playlist, a "Flourish" playlist and a "Zing" playlist created per each of my year's keywords.

Step 5: Apply your year's keyword to as many aspects of your life as makes sense. From wall art to your screensaver, fill your life with this keyword so you're constantly reminded of the You you're stepping into. You'll also find bizarre synchronicities start to appear the more you evolve into this word. It will appear everywhere, as part of the universal alignment. Suddenly, you'll be surrounded by your keyword. This means, as Mr Joseph Campbell would say, you're plugged in to your bliss.

Step 6: Review your board, listen to your music and connect to your keyword at regular intervals that suit you and your intention. Initially, I recommend two daily ten-minute sessions to immerse both your conscious and subconscious into this new realm of creation. The more your conscious mind absorbs the delicious ways you're going to feel, the more your subconscious will start to align too and support new neural programming, which will encourage more nonresistant action.

I've also created a New You visualization you can download at my website, biancabest.com.

Breaking Up With the Old You

This new programming may necessitate dismissing old habits and old patterns of thinking that no longer serve you, especially when those old habits have been born out of a stress response. For example, comfort eating when upset, drinking alcohol when stressed, shouting when angry, judging when insecure, etc. Becoming conscious of when old negative patterns are being invoked is how they can be intercepted and broken. Having a richer, crystal-clear impression of the new, positive patterns and the more desirable version of you in multimedia, in repeatable, readily accessible proximity, means you can transition from unconscious to conscious more adeptly. You can remind yourself who you are becoming and who you no longer want to be. Remember, your old ways of being have been enforced by years and years of habit and behaviour, so rewiring yourself will take effort, but it is absolutely possible. Posh Spice created Victoria Beckham – same woman, different impact (different body mass index, voice, fashion, work and more). Madonna created ... well, different executions of herself every year (and still does). It's never too late! Have a quick google of "women who (re)invented themselves" and explore the millions of articles for a plethora of examples.

Grounding Yourself Into Your Purpose With Your Why

Let's go back to how we opened this strategy chapter. With why. Where there is a will there is a way, and where there is a way, I firmly believe there needs to be a why. Yes, a why is now there in terms of your sweet spot – because I'm good at this, passionate about this, my values are this and the world needs this – and yes, a why is there in terms of how you will show up and feel (the gorgeous new conscious version of yourself), but there also needs to be a gigantic macro. This will be a fulfilling, "I want it written on my gravestone" why. Your ultimate Why.

As an example, let's take my own purpose statement included in the exercise earlier, and let's evolve it by asking the question "Why?" Why do I want to illuminate and energize others? Why does it matter that they expand into their greatest potential?

You know what? Because my heart says this is what I'm meant to do. That is why. How and what I'm going to do is figured out through all the behaviours, actions, mindset, values, rewired neural pathways, vision board and playlists, etc., but the why is simply because it feels right. Instinctively, when I step into this purpose, I feel aligned, happy, motivated and spurred into creativity and manifesting. My intuition, my gut, my soul, my spirit, my consciousness and unconsciousness all vibe resonantly in a way that reassures me I'm on the right path. This is where I'm meant to be and what I'm meant to be doing and I am plugged in. This is integrity.

When our actions synchronize with our heart's calling, dissonance is removed, congruence abounds and in congruence lies peace. So, if your why is anything other than "because it feels right in my body, mind and soul" check and double check your raison d'etre. The ego is going to want you to have it all to satisfy its (selfish, protective and fear-based) cravings, but if there's a pure, heartful, altruistic sense of purpose that feels good on every level, then you're in true inner and outer harmony and you've found it. You're ensuring you have the courage to live a life true to yourself, not the life others expected of you. No regrets upon your deathbed.

Once you're in this beautiful place where you are clear on what matters most to you and why, you become empowered to ruthlessly say no to everything else. You become more diligent in solely pursuing euthymia, what one of the great stoic philosophers, Seneca, defined as the tranquillity of knowing what you seek without being distracted by others. So, in our dopamine-overloaded modern lives, when highly focused on our purpose, we maintain commitment to that which matters most, and we reject the rest with ease and grace. We elegantly master how to say no, staying effortlessly grounded in our Purpose, which we rightfully revere as sacred, and as Nietzsche immortally hums, "One who has a why can bear almost any how." This is the truest path to Big Impact Without Burnout.

A Word on Purpose, Passion and Balance

Recall the reference to "I wish I hadn't worked so hard" in the regrets of the dying list – let's explore this momentarily. This is a book about avoiding burnout. In avoiding burnout, there is a need for inner balance to stimulate the outer shine. However, the quest for balance can become mythological when it comes to passion and purpose. When we are utterly absorbed in the pursuit of a calling, in love with a project, person or thing, we can veer very much off balance, becoming all consumed by the Thing. Passion generally, by its very nature, is disruptive. So, when we're in the grips of budding inspiration blooming into impact, we should maintain awareness of what else needs to give to allow this particular Thing to flourish.

Taking my own life as a case study, at the time of writing this book, I had three big workstreams coalesce to mean my life would be primarily work-focused for three months. A new corporate promotion (my biggest gig yet), the conclusion of two years of coaching study to certify and gain international accreditation, plus writing this book. I consciously and responsibly looked at ways to preserve some inner balance, aware that my outer focus would be imbalanced and prioritized on work for a while. I took proactive steps to manage honouring my purpose in a way that would enable me to have impact and stay healthily productive, as this overemphasis on work for 12 weeks would require. It was a way of acknowledging disproportionate attention on the work arena of life temporarily and organizing other aspects of life to accommodate strategically.

I decided to prioritize work, children, love and my health, with an overarching objective of preserving and maximizing my own energy. I made space for these aspects as the absolute essentials for me to stay inwardly balanced, never tipping down the negative side of the Stress Productivity scale (see page 53). I decided to meditate daily and nightly, upping my mindfulness practice as a way to minimize my risk of stress. I sat my children down and explained what the next three months would entail and we cocreated a plan of shared domestic responsibilities. This alleviated my burden while respecting theirs, with each of them contributing to my purpose, generously understanding the give and take of life's ebbs and flows. I shut down social media apps and hung up my "I'm writing, back soon" digital signage for my followers. I hosted a mini temporary farewell party with my friends and extended family before I went into a three-month hibernation. I eliminated caffeine and alcohol to enable maximum natural energy and deep sleep. I made space for outdoor runs as often as possible throughout the week and eliminated nonessential meetings. I organized everything to allow me to focus where attention was needed most during this time. So, I remain in inner balance, despite the outer imbalance of necessary work.

Where figures like Gandhi and Warren Buffett notoriously diminished the quality of their family lives through work obsession by their own admission (Gandhi even disowned his son!), you could herald them as examples that balance is impossible when impassioned, but I don't believe it is so. They were balanced toward what mattered most to them, just as I am balance-based today, focusing my attention on what matters most to me. Gandhi, Buffett and I (now, there's one sentence I never thought I'd write!) are each living on/lived on purpose and are maintaining/maintained balance in ways unique to us. We have all chosen our euthymia – we know what we seek and won't be distracted. For me, being dedicated to my iridescent Why inspires the energy, grace and ease of prioritizing my purpose at this work-biased time.

My invitation to you here is to always be mindful of the zing of attention different areas of life require, so you can remain stable, homeostatic, grounded and organized in such a way that honours the equilibrium you need. If your child is in hospital, stop work and focus attention on him. If your partner just divorced you, focus on healing your heart-basking in love from friendships. If you're being made redundant, stop ironing sheets and diminish domesticity until your income is secure again. Own your blend in honour of what matters most to you now, next week and next month. Stay intentional. Always.

Your Big Impact Purpose Expansion Grid

You now understand the key components to create your bespoke Purpose Strategy for Big Impact; you know how to find and honour your values, tune into intuitive thought, clarify and illuminate your vision, and to create yourself and ground yourself in what matters most. It's time to take stock and evaluate what you need to practise or research further and what pledges you will make to expand intentional living more vigorously into your daily life.

In the grid below is what you now know how to manage.

It's time to translate this into solid action to make your expansion a reality.

Grab your journal and review the statements below, focusing on the "Expanding To" column. Now spend 30 minutes freewriting on everything that comes up for you as you read the expansion statements. Elaborate on them where you see fit and make them entirely yours. As well as writing the "what", dive into the "how" and "why". Really explore the statements, applying your newfound knowledge, and have fun exploring all the life-altering ways you're going to feel and how you're going to get there. Let the inspiration pour forth and capture everything that comes to mind.

FROM	EXPANDING TO ...
I have total lack of direction.	I am purposeful, clear on what matters most, why it matters and am targeted in my actions.
I am unmotivated and feel lost.	I am excited and energized, feeling directional.
I am passive. Life happens to me.	I am decisive and action-oriented.

(Continued)

FROM	EXPANDING TO ...
I am one of life's drifters/horizon holders.	I am infectiously inspiring and magnetic.
I feel stuck.	I am progressive.
I make decisions tentatively.	I am decisive.
I say yes to everything. I find it hard to say no.	I say no with ease and grace.
I find it hard to break bad habits.	I am clear which habits need breaking and how to break them.
I feel uninspired.	I feel inspired and know how to awaken my imagination.
I worry life will be wasted.	I know I won't have regrets on my deathbed because I am honouring what matters most to me always.
I'm not sure who I am or who I am becoming.	I have an inspiring Vision of Me which propels and excites me every day!

Your Big Impact Decision Pledges

It's decision time. You're now clear on focus areas to prioritize as you expand into becoming more conscious of how you show up in the world as your most intentional self. You've explored lots around values, meaning and motive in your journal reflection exercises.

Now, harnessing the power of decision, write down three Purpose Pledges you will make to ensure your expansion unfurls.

I pledge to work with my purpose to create my biggest impact without ever burning out by ...

_____

_____

_____

YOUR BIG IMPACT STRATEGY NO. 4: TIME

"Busy is the new stupid."

— Warren Buffett

This is not a chapter about mastering time management, introducing life hacks or doing more in less time. No, this chapter is about focus and prioritizing attention so time no longer feels scarce. Your reality today is a reflection of your attention so far in life. If there's change you desire, like bigger impact without burnout, your attention needs to be directed toward that change. In this chapter we will explore how allocating your time based on what matters most, aligned with that purpose you just clarified, is how you'll unlock a sense of reclaiming time.

"Joyless urgency" is a term coined by Pulitzer prize-winning author Marilynne Robinson to emphasize the headless-chicken style of busyness too many of us are ensconced in today. "We are less interested in the exploration of the glorious mind, more engrossed in the drama of staying ahead of whatever it is we think is pursuing us,"[83] she says. This is evident when a friendly daily enquiry of "How are you doing?" provokes a trickle of predictable replies along the lines of "Manic", "Stacked", "Slammed", "Ridiculously busy", and so on.

Industrialization made society more productive and, in turn, changed our relationship with time. No longer was time a simple guide – start work now the sun is up, stop work now it's dark – but instead, time was filled with hours measured by output; as work mechanized so time's value altered too. It wasn't how long you toiled for, but what you produced while you grafted. As time became more fervently about productivity, the concept of time thus shifted from being part of nature's elegance, to be respected and revered, our days rolling with the sun, the moon and the rhythmic seasons, to becoming something we race against. Productivity became a thing obsessed over and the "Time and Productivity" combo became our third-millennium nemesis with "I wish I had more time" now the mantra of young and old.

This ever-engulfing sense that time is evaporating dominates modern life. As soon as babies are born, we're racing to hit milestones, from where they sit on a growth-percentile graph to the momentous (and unnecessarily competitive) date of first steps, to academic capability assessments, from handwriting up to bachelor's degrees. At each life stage, we ask ourselves if we are doing enough. When we enter into the world of work, the pressure to be productive slams into us, warping self-esteem and convincing us to do more to get promoted quicker and earn more faster. Quick, quick, hurry, hurry, the clock of life is ticking. "HURRY UP PLEASE ITS [*sic*] TIME!"[84] as T S Elliot instructs.

Not only are we in perpetual race mode but we're psychologically obsessed with where we'll be tomorrow. We're so incessant about arriving somewhere, we're missing where we are already. We unconsciously mythologize an ethereal tomorrow where life will feel more stable, manageable and glossy. We'll have more money, love, work we enjoy, holidays, houses, any manner of tantalizing wish-list wants shimmering on our heart-conjured horizons, and of course – more time. We imagine a tomorrow abundant in time to do and have all the things we dream of, but we're missing the point that if happiness comes in our being-ness, not doing-ness or having-ness or "givenness"[85] as Marilynne Robinson calls it, then we need a shift in approach today. We don't need to wait for tomorrow to feel good when we have the autonomy to craft how we feel today. We can reclaim time today.

The Scourge of Over-Productivity

Have you heard the Mexican fisherman fable? A wealthy businessman on holiday, let's call him Peter, strolls down to the harbourside and gets into conversation with a local fisherman, let's call him Pedro. Pedro tells Peter his life is one of fishing peacefully in the morning, revelling in the ocean's stillness at sunrise, lunching with friends and family, snoozing in the afternoon and whiling away the evening hours strumming guitar, drinking wine and relishing in contentment. Peter asks Pedro why he hasn't considered industrializing his fishing endeavours. Pedro asks why he should. "Why? Well, once you invest in motorized equipment, staff, systems and logistics, the business can rapidly expand, enabling voluminous hauls, voluminous profits and a voluminous life," smug, all-knowing Peter replies, smoothing the lapels of his white blazer with one hand while fanning himself with his hat with the other. "And then what would I do?" asks Pedro, stroking the stray cat sleepily purring atop the crumbling stone wall the two men are chatting beside. "Why, then you'll have time for mornings revelling in the ocean's stillness at sunrise, lunching with friends and family, snoozing in the afternoon, and whiling away the evening hours strumming guitar, drinking wine, and relishing in contentment ..." And therein lies the parable's irony. Pedro already has everything his heart desires without frantically having expended time, effort and exhausting energy to get there. Pedro thinks Peter is utterly crackers, for the record.

So, why is it that we feel an obligation to pack so much more into our time here on this planet? Why is Peter's approach so ingrained in our modern lives? Why has aiming for maximum productivity become the status quo, especially for the average ambitious woman? There's that link between productivity and self-worth, of course, that we have already discussed. But there's also a more shadowy side: addiction. An addiction to productivity, to the act of working incessantly, may self-soothe as a form of quelling anxiety. It feels safe and comfortable, despite the unnatural energy it takes. While it may ironically feel safe (hello ego, my old friend), there's a fine line between well-managed devotion to output and frenzied *doing* because we can't face *being*. Because if we're not doing, we have to confront the being, and that risks exposing all sorts of emotional disquiet.

Now, I'm not saying those of us who enjoy high standards, strong output and getting stuff done are emotionally disregulated and only working hard because we're scared to confront what lies outside of work – nope, not at all. Working hard is a good thing. We grow, we create, we generate, we give. But I am heeding the advice of Marcus Aurelius: an unexamined life is not worth living. If you do notice a tendency within yourself to seek distraction and self-soothing through more work, more people, and more busyness, then perhaps – unconsciously – you may be avoiding some kind of inner unrest, and addiction may be afoot. You could be using busyness as a coping mechanism, surreptitiously channelling emotional pain or discomfort away. The work you then need to do is to ask yourself: what are you busy for? What are you avoiding? And are you avoiding doing, being, or both?

BIG IMPACT REFLECTION: ARE YOU ADDICTED TO WORK?

Take some time to honestly reflect on your relationship with work and answer the following questions in your journal.

- **Work Habits:** How many hours per week do you typically work (including at home)? Do you regularly work overtime, nights and weekends? Do you have trouble disconnecting from work and check emails constantly? Do you skip breaks and/or eat meals at your desk while working?

- **Motivations:** What drives you to work so many hours (e.g. passion, financial pressure, praise)? Do you get an adrenaline rush or sense of excitement from heavy workloads? Do you feel guilty or anxious when not working?

- **Impact on life:** How does your work schedule impact your personal relationships and social life? Do you have difficulty relaxing or enjoying hobbies/leisure time? Have you neglected self-care to prioritize work? Do you rely on caffeine, alcohol or other substances to sustain your work pace?

- **Emotions:** How do you feel after an intense, exceptionally long work period – accomplished, drained, numb? Do you often feel stressed, irritable, or depressed related to your workload? Do coworkers, friends or family ever express concern about how much you work?

Reflect deeply and write freely. Identifying compulsive or unhealthy patterns with work is the first step to restoring inner balance. Please conclude your exercise with a visualization of what your life would look like without so much work and pay attention to what emotions this stirs in you. Be delicate in your exploration here and try to enjoy this concluding creation.

Regardless of its root cause, over-productivity leads to imbalance and burnout. Doing too much, for too long, as we have learned repeatedly, hurts us. What I call graceful productivity is what in fact we should be striving for. This is how we'll flourish.

Graceful Productivity

In a world of graceful productivity, we get stuff done, we make impact, we do our glorious thing, but marvellously, without burning ourselves into the ground doing so. When productivity flows elegantly aligned with priorities, hitting deadlines that matter most, with output that matters most, the work stops feeling like pressure, we feel less burdened and time doesn't feel like the enemy. We fall in love with time, learning to orchestrate focus and deliver our highest contribution to be consistently and sustainably impactful. There are three pitfalls to be wary of before the romance can begin: the shallows of "busywork", the myth of multitasking and the misdirection of the 20 per cent.

The Shallows of Busywork

I first came across the term "busywork" in discussion with the charismatic Nishma Patel Robb, President of WACL, ex CMO Google UK (and one of my favourite fellow industry twin mums). Busywork, Nishma informed me, refers to work that keeps a person busy but has little value in itself. It's also known as "shallow work" and comprises tasks that give the appearance of productivity but are just activity that is not necessarily progressive or useful. Think of scheduling trips, replying to nonessential, wide-distribution email threads, lengthy discussions without decisions being made or actions taken, for example. Google, along with many organizations then and since, introduced healthy productivity training to eliminate busywork and stimulate consistently efficient productivity.

This type of training generally takes the form of categorizing tasks by urgent and important, not urgent and not important, and prioritizing time to the former. In *The 7 Habits of Highly Effective People*, Stephen Covey teaches us to Put First Things First. "Putting first things first means organizing and executing around your most important priorities. It is living and being driven by the principles you value most, not by the agendas and forces surrounding you."[86] In this approach, we create and focus on tasks that are non-urgent but importantly oriented toward our own learning, recharging and growth. We deprioritize the cluttery life-stuttery stuff through delegation and re-prioritization, categorizing to-do lists with a progressive flavour of time allocation that both complements and goes beyond the business agenda into our personal impact agenda.

Silicon Valley has long embraced the Pomodoro Technique, named after a quirky Italian kitchen timer shaped like a tomato, where work is chunked into 25-minute increments with the tomato set to ensure full immersion in the given task until it buzzes. After a five-minute break, another tomato-supervised 25-minute work stint follows. Repeat four times, then take a longer 30-minute break, then go again. Similar to the strategy of "timeboxing", this short, sharp burst approach is much lauded. It assumes we can't focus without the discipline of a timer, though, and I know very productive people capable of great work who don't need a vegetable with a bell to facilitate their greatest output.

There are, of course, many time management tools around. The quicker the pace accelerates, the more society grapples with efficiency and effectiveness, bouncing from one solution to the next, desperately trying to discover utopian time control. By all means, play with time management to experiment with your own efficiency but don't expect time to feel abundant because of a cool app – sorry, but there's deeper work to do.

The Myth of Multitasking

Beyond the realms of time management, there's multitasking. Oh Madame Multitask, you are not our friend. Show me a girlfriend who hasn't got an oven burn scar from attempting to complete a myriad of domestic, intellectual and familial tasks simultaneously. Show me a colleague who successfully caught the most important aspect of the meeting while she was noisily tapping out emails during the discussion (infuriating everyone else trying to hear the conversation over her irritating acrylic nail clatter). And show me a child doing their best homework with cartoons on and music blaring.

Multitasking does not work. Worse, it creates an ever-spiralling dopamine-addiction feedback loop rewarding the brain for finding another stimulus, and another and another, where the very act of losing focus then buzzing elsewhere gives us a merry hit. The irony here for those of us who are trying to focus amid competing activities is clear: the brain region we need to rely on for staying on task is alas easily distracted. It's why while prepping dinner we check our email, respond to a text, chat to the kids, order a food shop, schedule a Brazilian, and each of these actions tweaks the novelty-seeking, reward-hungry centres of the brain with a visceral rush. As these centres illuminate, we zing with endogenous opiods, which feel amazing – "I'm on fire, I'm Superwoman, get me!" – but derail us from staying on task. As Dr Lembke writes illustratively, "It's the ultimate empty-caloried brain candy. Instead of reaping the big rewards that come from sustained, focused effort, we reap empty rewards from completing a thousand little sugar-coated tasks."[87]

The addictive nature of multitasking not only detrimentally affects our overall performance, meaning we're more likely to make mistakes and produce lower quality work, but studies prove we hinder our wider ability to filter out irrelevant information, neurologically becoming more inept the more we multitask! Even the mere opportunity of being able to multitask hampers cognitive performance. Glenn Wilson, former visiting professor of psychology at Gresham College, London, calls it "infomania". His research found that being in a situation whereby you are trying to concentrate on a task, but there is an email sitting unread in your inbox, can reduce your effective IQ by ten points.[88] There's truly nothing positive about mutlitasking, so for Big Impact, don't!

The Misdirection of the 20 Per Cent

Don't get caught up doing low impact work. The Pareto Rule encourages us to focus on the 20 per cent of tasks that will contribute to 80 per cent of our objectives, and this does indeed yield. My sales strategy building up The Bespoke Gift Company targeted the largest 20 per cent of national online retail accounts, those with the highest volume of daily site visitors, highest value basket spends and biggest loyal customer base for direct marketing promotions. The maths made sense – the 20 per cent could generate more revenue for me than the smaller retailers, and they did – 80/20 worked.

In your own work, be cautious that you are embracing the magic of the 20 per cent instead of misdirecting effort. Don't allow the allure, fun or ease of a task lower down on the to-do list to divert you from that which can drive more success more immediately. Always ask yourself how aligned the task is with the overall objective of the project, day, business, etc. before you begin. Evaluate the task's impact. Always.

Back to the important question here: is our busyness because we're generally inefficient, seeking validation or running from ourselves? Why are we diluting our time and, by default, our impact with futile busywork, multitasking or low-yield diversions? Henry David Thoreau provocatively put it: "It is not enough to be busy. So are the ants. The question is: What are we busy about?" When we consider that activity is not necessarily productivity, indeed, what are you busy about?

How Conscious Is Your Calendar?

One of my corporate clients, Chrissy, tells me she's a writer at heart. She works as a marketing executive in her organization but is destined to be a full-time writer. It is wonderful that she's found her purpose, but when I ask in our session how much writing she's done that day, the answer disappoints. None. How about yesterday? Nope, no time yesterday either. The day before? Week? Month? Come on, the year before? No, no, no, alas, no ... "Sorry, writer, did you say? Shouldn't a writer write?"

How we spend our time has to corroborate with what matters most. If Chrissy sees herself as a writer, no amount of visioning, wishing and blustering to the world about her writing career holds any substance if there's no congruence with how she's spending her time. She is not a writer if she's not writing. She will never be a writer unless she starts writing. Time has to be invested in creating the version of ourselves and the impact we dream of making by actually doing something, anything, relevant.

How much time we allocate to something is based on its importance to us. Even if Chrissy's writing is not urgent, per Covey's model, it is absolutely important. It's her calling, her passion, her Thing, but until the Thing gets its TLC, it's ethereal. When I explain this to Chrissy, she brims with excuses and reasons why she's not a writer "yet", and that once this and that is sorted and the kids have grown up and the day job deadlines are met and the house renovation completed and the fitness goals achieved, once there's room in her life, then the writing will begin. When I point out that the imaginary tomorrow where time is mastered and the stars align for her work to begin will never arrive, she looks crestfallen, confused and annoyed. Defensively she asserts she simply doesn't have time and she's too drained by everything else to start.

Like Chrissy, lack of time and energy are the most consistent problems my clients feel in their lives. But here's a tickly thought for you: when someone is falling in love, they suddenly discover a newfound abundance of time for their intoxicating new situation. Suddenly, time expands and hours (and hours!) are found for indulging in the relationship.

It seems that when passion, true passion, takes hold, time itself feels different; our relationship with it is different. When we're engrossed in what matters most, right now, time cocoons us in expansive abundance. We are fully present and able to focus completely. The Greeks even had a term for this type of time as different from chronological time. They called it *kairos*, this slidey, glidey, nebulous, ballooning type of flow time. By contrast, *chronos* is the steady, regularly progressing time of tick tock, tick tock, clockwork time.

In our work worlds, we inevitably experience elements of both. *Chronos* is embodied by the clock-watching tedium of factory workers willing the monotonous working day to end. *Kairos* is embodied by the inventor, hair askew, wildly bolting contraptions together, potions a' bubbling, machinery whirring, creations manifesting. The latter is invigoration at play, a mind inspired, intent and alive. In this state, our wizardesque inventor has no sense of time. She is absorbed wholly in the task at hand, in love with what she's doing, emblazoned by commitment and focus. In this state, work is pure pleasure and no interruption is even conceivable, let alone welcome.

We're generally not going to be in that bliss state most of the time, and nor should we be. Our kids would go hungry, the dog would soil himself and we wouldn't have any friends through sheer lack of hygiene. If we forever lived in a state of impassioned productivity, that would simply be too imbalanced. However, creating space for ideas, prioritizing energy-giving work and enjoying frequent blasts of work exultations like our giddy inventor is the Time-Energy-Work nirvana available to us all. It's there for us to seize once we reclaim time, focus in on what creates most energy and do work we love. So, when Chrissy tells me she doesn't have the time, I question if writing is truly her passion, because, as I tell her, if she really was committed to being a writer, she would write.

BIG IMPACT REFLECTION: A CONSCIOUS CALENDAR

This exercise is always popular with my clients as it is easy and evocative! Let's explore what your time allocation reveals is most important to you by seeing what you're committing to in actuality. Try this one-week exercise. You can use Outlook, Excel, a whiteboard, good old paper or a traditional scheduling diary if you have one.

Label and colour-code all your activities in a grid across the next week, starting from today, including exercise, sleep, family time, domesticity, work work, passion work, leisure, etc. in the following colours – **green** for working toward productive goals (e.g. gym), **yellow** for necessities (e.g. sleep), **blue** for rejuvenations and relaxation (e.g. hobbies), and **red** for distractions/timewasters. Go as far as allocating work meetings a relevant colour. If they were pointless and didn't contribute to a longer-term personal objective, they should not be green.

Review each day's time investment, noting energy levels too. At the end of the week, dive into the colour revelations, observing patterns. List out the green activities that moved you toward fulfilment and achievement. Identify the red time drains – distractions, procrastination or unproductive habits. Brainstorm adjustments to minimize wasted time and reallocate it meaningfully. Use these insights to make intentional choices aligned with your priorities. Become conscious of where your time investment is well directed versus misspent on distractions. To make this exercise easy and something you can do immediately, I've created a template for you to download at biancabest.com. This is definitely worth doing regularly, especially if you feel a niggling time pressure bubbling up.

Falling in Love With Time

There are four powers that will enable you to achieve graceful, fulfilling productivity. These are Attention, Focus, Flow and Prioritization.

1. The Power of Attention

"There is an enormous difference between attention directed objectively and attention directed subjectively, and the capacity to change your future depends on the latter."

— Neville Goddard

Where our attention goes, our energy flows. James Redfield, world-renowned spiritual author of *The Celestine Prophecy* (23 million copies sold), teaches us this. Tony Robbins, self-help author, philanthropist, Netflix superstar, teaches us this. And I'm teaching you this. Where your attention goes is absolutely, unwaveringly, categorically where your energy flows. So, if you're happy letting your energy flow into TikTok, BBC4, the lunch hour tittle-tattle, *Suits* Season 7, scrubbing the shower tiles daily, or whatever whiles away your hours, then continue merrily away, my sweet. If, however, you hold a longing for bigger and better impact, sustainable impact, without any burnout, then you need to pay significant attention to where you're directing your attention.

Let's keep things simple – there is objective attention and subjective attention. Objective attention arises from extraneous inputs. We hear the news, the gossip, we watch the reels, the drama, the perhaps inadvertent entertainment, and our minds absorb the content, either consciously or unconsciously. Subjective attention is where we choose what we consume, what we hear and watch, and thus what we focus on. In both realms our attention affects our thoughts, which affect our feelings, which affect our behaviour and ultimately our lives. As Goddard states in the quote above, your future depends on how you direct your attention subjectively.

Creating space in our minds for what matters most, and making the time for what is truly most important to you, comes down to this subjective attention. There will always be noise around you. The cacophony is louder today than ever in our explosive attention economy (we are confronted by up to 5,000 adverts a day, according to some studies).[89] And let's not forget that novelty bias of our prefrontal cortex meaning its attention can be easily hijacked by something new. We simply have to become masterful at screening out that which doesn't interest or serve us. If we don't concentrate on the inputs we want, we'll drown in inputs we don't.

There may be habits, people, places, work, situations, even material objects which are dragging us down and cluttering our lives unhelpfully. Just because we feel stuck within habitual ways of being, or comfy in our familiar environment, it doesn't mean we can't start anew. It's okay to reassess your life and do a reorg. In fact it's more than okay; it's essential.

When it comes to people, we are influenced by others, whether those closest to us or a fleeting interaction with a stranger. What they say to us echoes through us, whether we like it or not. Sometimes their words may bring joy, sometimes they may sting, make us laugh, cry, raise an eyebrow, but they always pierce. How others "feel" energetically also reverberates through us. Subliminally, we absorb their vibe – at extremes, being either repulsed or magnetized by them. Those we gravitate toward form our tight circle of besties and tend to be those who lift us up, make us laugh and radiate the good feelings we desire. The mentors we seek are those we respect, finding their work inspiring and credible. The tribes we join bolster a sense of belonging through shared interest. The organizations we work for should ooze with a culture that motivates us to thrive.

We need to be careful to protect ourselves from negative people who drain our energy, time and spirit, and be aware enough to detach when necessary. It's imperative to cull the psychic vampires from our lives (and feel integrity, not guilt, for doing so). I call this cleansing the energy-zappers.

In *The Four Agreements*, Don Miguel Ruiz describes the end of a toxic relationship as a gift; "If someone is not treating you with love and respect, it is a gift if they walk away from you. If that person doesn't walk away, you will surely endure many years of suffering with him or her." He encourages you to responsibly sever your ties, from person, tribe or company, reassuring that "Walking away may hurt for a while, but your heart will eventually heal. Then you can choose what you really want. You will find that you don't need to trust others as much as you need to trust yourself to make the right choices."[90] It comes down to empowered choice. Who do you choose to be around and who do you choose to have around you?

What about the media, habits and situations that take your attention and energy into objective as opposed to subjective realms? Are there opportunities to adjust and improve?

Media noise is easy. Turn off apps and notifications, don't read the news if it bothers you, and limit background intake to carefully architected consumption with a purpose. Self-manage in alignment with goals and curated selection.

Habits, likewise, require a simple review, and building on the work you undertook in the last strategy to design a new habit per Big Impact life realm (see page 113), there are excellent books like James Clear's *Atomic Habits*, Charles Duhigg's *The Power of Habit* and BJ Fogg's *Tiny Habits* examining the psychology of habit formation to empower you to ditch those you don't want any more and encourage newer, better ones. Self-manage and constantly update habits to suit your evolved self.

Negative attention-stealing situations take more work to change, but it all starts with analysing where there is misalignment. If a situation triggers an emotional sigh and doesn't feel quite right anymore, maybe it is draining your energy and wearying your spirit. So, go within and examine why, peeling the layers away with why upon why until you reach the core. If a decision needs to be made, get the information you need to make it, decide and move on. If circumstances steal your time unexpectedly, like a traffic jam, flat tyre, tantrumming toddler, sick friend, drunken lech etc., getting angry and frustrated won't help the situation improve, so accept what is and try to divert your attention in a positive way. Embrace your blessings outside of this moment, watch the clouds to calm your mind, finding shapes in the white puffs, count to ten, meditate, philosophize it could be worse, but whatever you do, let your attention dwell on good rather than bad (except the lech, skidaddle fast away from that one!). This is enlivening time through choice, what Robert Greene describes as "Alive" time instead of "Dead" time.[91] Let situations invigorate and expand you. Remember, anything you give your attention to, positively or negatively, is influencing your destiny, so stay subjective and turn down the noise.

2. The Power of Focus

"Whenever you squander attention on something that doesn't put your brain through its paces and stimulate change, your mind stagnates a little and life feels dull."

— Winifred Gallagher

As technology accelerates everything around us and impatience, immediacy and automation pervade, those of us who cultivate an ability to deeply focus and deliver consistent, prolific output without burning the midnight oil will thrive. "The ability to perform deep work is becoming increasingly rare at exactly the same time it is becoming increasingly valuable in our economy", writes Cal Newport in *Deep Work,* his study of what makes modern-day expert performers exceptional. It comes down to "a life-long period of deliberate effort to improve performance in a specific domain."[92] He prides himself on never working beyond 5pm on weekdays and always having weekends off while producing ferocious output through his daily blocks of at least four to five hours of concentrated, uninterruptible work time.

While I'm not there yet with that idealistic volume of leisure time, I do agree that rewiring our minds to embrace and master focus is essential. Fabulously, as with all neuroplastic springiness, the more we flex the focus muscle, the easier focus becomes.

Okay, so how do we do this? Let's learn from an expert in this field. In his book *Focus: The Hidden Driver of Excellence*, Daniel Goleman teaches us about three kinds of focus leaders need to get results:

- **Inner focus:** the way we tap into our intuition, honour our values and decide with integrity.
- **Other focus:** the way we sensitively and respectfully nourish relationships positively with awareness.
- **Outer focus:** remembering the context of the macro environment within which we operate.

He says, "A leader tuned out of his internal world will be rudderless; one blind to the world of others will be clueless; those indifferent to the larger systems within which they operate will be blindsided."[93]

So, while Newport and Goleman are both fervent focus fans, Newport guides us to chunk time to enable single-minded thought for concentrated periods, whereas Goleman encourages a tripartite attention-oriented approach to focus. Both are relevant for Big Impact productivity. Without the inner, other and outer attention, we're not going to focus on the right things in the right way. Without the discipline of sitting down to work without interruption, we'll never get decent chunks of work done. Deliberate, organized concentration, one task at a time for dedicated periods, is essential to productivity. So, triangulate and concentrate. Easy.

Where and how we focus also matters for peak performance. Let's start with environment. An Olympic swimmer has a neurological association with a pool as her "productivity zone". It's the place where she (quite literally) flows. She sees the pool and automatically unleashes every skill she's learned, every move she's practised, and importantly, every mindset she's ever conditioned herself to associate with swimming a race. She sees the pool and her body and mind spark innately into peak action because of mental associations formed over hours and years of repetition.

This is called ecological psychology, a blooming branch of neuroscience linking behaviour with environment. The premise can be encapsulated by a chair; you see a chair and you interpret such an assembly of legs, seat and back as something to sit on. When a baby sees a chair, however, there's no instinctive association with sitting; it is just a strange assembly of objects. The chair becoming a seat is learned through the behaviour of sitting on many chairs. And so we can build the associations of primed focus in the places we work.

Stephen King must write at the same time, at the same desk, listening to the same music (hardcore heavy mental) as his cue for creativity. He vociferously denounces waiting for the muse, citing in his memoir *On Writing*, "Don't wait for the muse. ... Your job is to make sure the muse knows where you are going to be every day from nine 'til noon or seven 'til three. If he does know, I assure you he'll start showing up."[94] Similarly, devout meditators always have a zen corner ready and waiting for immediate inner transportation the moment they settle lotus-legged onto their trusty cushion.

Priming ourselves to get into the zone is essential when modern work entails hopping around so much from office to train, bus, subway, plane to coffee shop to guest bedroom to kitchen to hotel, so as well as having optimal environments for our best focus, we can be further empowered when we introduce ritual. Think of world-class performers before they go on stage, holding hands with their crew, saying prayers or mantras together. Or the pre-match talk from sports coaches, guiding bodies and minds into their winning states.

Of course, there are different types of work, requiring different types of focus and thus potentially distinctive rituals. We probably flit across several task types each day. Each category of work may require a different mindset. Analytical work needs an alert, engrossed state; creative work a loose, expansive state; collaborative work a more extrovert, communicative state perhaps. You will know what mood you need to be in to deliver your best for each type of work. What's exciting here is the power in creating a trigger ritual, or series of rituals, bespoke to you to stimulate the focus state you need, when and where you need it.

For me, grounding myself in creative work, like writing this book for example, comprises a slow, "present" walk around the garden with my dalmatian, four slow, deep belly breaths once seated, my slippers on, a herbal tea with fresh lemon, ginger and mint in my Big Impact mug (yes, I'm a sucker for a personalized manifestation prop here and there) and a vanilla candle flickering. My ritual complete, I enter my intellectual sanctuary, focused to write peacefully and industriously. By contrast, to get into my pumped-up exercise mood, it's the process of scraping my hair up high into a ponytail, putting on my trainers and my "Unstoppable" playlist on max as I psyche myself up. To adjust to the office environment, I bring high energy (and heels – a psychological power cue for me) for physical meetings, so I like to have exercised before the working day begins. I deliberately cluster back-to-back, face-to-face meetings into office time, so knowing I'll need to unwaveringly keep focus and motivation up for hours (my choice), I ensure nuts, fruit and snacks keep me upbeat and consistently "on", after having had a big veg juice en route as part of my vitality ritual.

Our ability to focus varies based on our bio-individuality, from circadian rhythms to hormone fluctuations to stress responses. According to the

Oxford Dictionary, a chronotype is "a person's natural inclination with regard to the times of day when they prefer to sleep or when they are most alert or energetic." For example, I may be an early morning lark; you may be a night owl. As you know, we have natural cycles of hormone surges and depletions, and varying reactions to daylight, blue light and stimulants that are unique to each of us. A cortisol awakening response (CAR) gives us a rush of energy generally around one hour after waking (this does not apply to caffeine users as prolonged caffeine use disrupts the body's natural cycles), so many high performers and business leaders maximize their work schedules to ensure they are doing their most important work to coincide with this natural peak state. Easier said than done when you have a million dependents and a school run to do, but worth being aware of as you start monitoring your best work moods and modes to design your days better.

3. The Power of Flow

Mihály Csíkszentmihályi was a Hungarian-American "positive psychologist" who was excited by all things happiness-related. He contributed pioneering work to our understanding of human fulfilment, especially the notion of a state of consciousness called flow. He discovered that people reach a state of heightened focus and find deep and genuine satisfaction during the bewitching magnificence of flow. In this semi-magical state, we become completely absorbed in an activity (especially one that involves creative abilities like art, play and work) and, like the love affairs we mentioned earlier, time becomes elastic and expansive, perhaps even irrelevant. During the optimal experience of a flow state, people feel "strong, alert, in effortless control, unselfconscious, and at the peak of their abilities."[95]

Proven to stimulate higher productivity, increased life satisfaction and improved emotional regulation, not only do flow states de-stress us, releasing us from the intensity of life's onslaught of stressors, but they are accessible to us all as often as we choose to create them. As children, we naturally gravitate to activities that interest us and if the interest deepens, we become absorbed and locked into the activity in flow; think of a little child building her Lego set; she wouldn't flinch if a gorilla ran across the room. As adults, we have to work harder to carve out flow states especially, as Csíkszentmihályi acknowledged, "Distraction is the enemy of flow". But these moments can become plentiful once we expand our awareness of them. We can find ourselves serenely cascading into flow while we're designing a new business plan. Or sublimely while we're building sandcastles with our cherubs. Or innocently while peeling carrots for the casserole. We can serendipitously trip into flow, but the benefits are more when we deliberately invite this enticing state into our lives more permanently, when we organize our lives to stimulate flow daily.

Eight enticing qualities of the flow zone are:

1. **Challenge and skill blend.** Is the challenge a healthy stretch or too easy? If a task is too demanding we can become anxious and rapidly overwhelmed, disheartened by the uphill battle. Conversely, if a task is too easy, we quickly lose interest and get bored. A flow state arises when we're healthily stimulated and have a base level of competence and confidence already – skiing or composing music are good examples.

2. **Progress towards prowess.** When there is a clear goal and we are able to continuously tweak our inputs to meet the required demands of the task, we flow onwards, unfettered. For example, a skier is adjusting posture, technique and speed per the undulations and conditions of the piste, continuously fine-tuning skill and competence.

3. **Immersion in Action.** Where action and awareness merge, an activity becomes totally absorbing and second nature; control and self-agency dominate and any self-rumination disappears. Picture an athlete striking gold.

4. **Melty concentration.** In this state, wholly focused attention makes external and internal distractions dissolve. There is only this moment. Think rapturous passion, like making love.

5. **Proud, accelerating control.** There's a sense of being unstoppable and that there are no limits, that anything can be achieved. Think Jerry Maguire and his nocturnal "change sports sponsorship forever" proposal creation. He very much had us beyond "hello" with his excited work frenzy.

6. **Freedom from self-consciousness.** When we experience a total loss of paranoia and release from self-monitoring, we're able to progress onwards with intuitive engagement and a touch of zeal.

7. **Time transformation.** Like the *chairos* "flow time" the Greeks revered, and we learned about in the Time Strategy, when utterly absorbed in the moment the passage of time bends. It may speed up, slow down or become deliciously irrelevant.

8. **Self-directed experiences.** When we are intrinsically motivated we enter what Csíkszentmihályi called an "autotelic" experience. From the ancient Greek *autós*, meaning "self", and *télos*, meaning "result/outcome/end", this is when a task is performed for pure want alone. And it's satisfying. Nobody made us do this; we just did it because we wanted to. Bliss.

When the conditions are right, you have the motivation, a base level of competence, interest, desire, passion and you apply single-minded attention, the dream flow state is yours to savour. The eighth, intrinsic motivation factor needs underlining in bold. The interest, ability and desire to immerse yourself in the task has to come from within for flow to be achieved. My daughter won't achieve a flow state when I command her to tidy her room, but when she feels inspired to organize those nail varnishes and colour-code her wardrobe, she reaches her private inner sanctum of blissfulness because she was intrinsically motivated to conduct the task.

So, doing more of what you want to do and letting yourself rip wildly into it, without interruption, will elevate you into an almost spiritual state of presence and boundless energy. Your life will feel happier all round just by introducing more pockets of flow into each day. Through this lens, we seem a bit silly letting ourselves be so easily distracted when there's paradise on the other side of bouncing around from task to task. Give yourself the gift of flow and both productivity and life enjoyment will soar.

4. The Power of Prioritization

Many religions and personal development trainings teach the importance of respecting death, thereby building a greater respect for life. The Buddhists recommend living "mindful, clear-eyed lives",[96] accepting that death can arrive at any time and thus time is not to be wasted. The focus is not on death as an enemy to be feared but simply a reminder of the impermanence of all things (situations, relationships, emotions and life itself). Being realistic about mortality is thus a strong motivator to live a fuller, more meaningful life, bereft of time wasting and rich in presence. Similarly, Hindus believe in karma and that how we live in this life establishes our quality of life in the next, thus encouraging us to do good now for the sake of the heavenly tomorrow.

There's a powerful impetus stimulated when we acknowledge that life is temporary. This is our only ride after all. This is not a rehearsal. This realization prompts more reverence for how we spend our short lives. Oliver Burkeman warns us that the average lifespan lasts only 4,000 weeks and, in his brilliant dissection of modern time and the sheer futility of our busyness, *Four Thousand Weeks: Time Management for Mortals,* he encourages us to embrace the Joy of Missing Out; JOMO instead of FOMO. "Convenience culture seduces us into imagining that we might find room for everything important by eliminating only life's tedious tasks. But it's a lie. You have to choose a few things, sacrifice everything else, and deal with the inevitable sense of loss that results."[97]

So, you can't "have it all" as the shoulder-padded women of yesteryear demanded. Time is, in fact, absolutely limited. It's not just the inevitability of death that smacks us with that, it's the immovable fact that days last 24 hours; we need to sleep and eat and there's a sheer finitude to life. Thus, power lies in prioritizing how we spend our time, not how much we pack in nor how productively we believe we're racing through more, but in devoting time to what matters most and relishing time itself.

Saying "no" artfully is a talent every Big Impact woman should finesse. It's not rude. It's not lazy. It's not shirking. It's simply empowered. Too much of our people-pleasing, good-girl, *"yes* mode" culture has fostered real toe-curling awkwardness around saying no for way too many of us. My burnt-out client, Emma, a senior client services director in a large global media agency, asked me how she could start saying no to business dinners. Not only did she work (before the rise in flexible working hours) long 40-hour weeks in the office, running huge teams to hit client satisfaction targets, but several nights per week she was obligated to attend work dinners, or so she felt. When we explored where this sense of obligation came from, Emma told me that she had grown up as an only child in a family where her parents ran a successful manufacturing business devoting most weeknight evenings to entertaining clients. Emma had subconsciously assumed that was what everyone who worked did, that adults worked day and night; that's how it was. She'd unconsciously fallen into this pattern, without questioning her belief system, nor what felt true to her. While her parents loved the nightly wining and dining, Emma was an introvert, happier at home unwinding alone after her intensely people-centric workdays. We worked on tuning her more overtly back into her value of "contentment" until she felt empowered to claim back her time as an essential way to move back into the very essence of herself. Saying no to four out of every five invitations made not one single negative dent in her career, and actually gave her team more opportunities to start expanding their own client dinner skills themselves as they went in her place.

It's important to reframe "no" as empowering, not anything to be ashamed of. The skill of "no" becomes easier as we clarify "yes". When we, like Emma, tune in to what we want and keep our values in charge of our decision-making, it becomes joyful to miss out, not fearful. Embracing JOMO is simply strategic prioritization.

BIG IMPACT REFLECTION: DESIGN YOUR DREAM DAY

Seizing the four powers available to you – Attention, Focus, Flow and Prioritization – now let's design your Dream Day. Imagine it's perfect, free of obligations or constraints, wholly directed by you and your grand intentions. In your journal, map out what your dream day would look like from start to finish. When would you wake up and what morning routine would energize you? What activities, adventures or pursuits would you fill your day with to feel fully alive and joyful? Who would you spend time with? Where would you go? What environments or settings would you immerse yourself in? What creative, productive or meaningful endeavours would you devote time to? How would you nourish your mind, body and soul? Design every delicious detail of your ultimate day, letting your imagination create without limits. Then, let this ideal blueprint inspire you to fall in love with time and start weaving more pockets of peace, purpose and presence into your daily life. You can also download a Dream Day audio visualization created with love from me to you at biancabest.com.

If you're feeling overwhelmed, consider prioritizing "the next right thing". Atop my dusty attic shelf stands a well-leafed, well-loved storybook about a teddy bear separated from his owner, working out how to stop feeling so lost. His little furry self is overwhelmed by the magnitude of the world and its apparent lack of signposting. But then, *eureka!* He spots a path, and knows to walk along it. He spots a boat, and knows to climb aboard it. He spots a hand, and knows to hold it. Each charmingly illustrated page ends with the sentence "... and then Bear knew what to do next."[98]

When meeting one of my clients recently, a female CEO of an international design group, we discussed the undulations of the past few years with its perpetual disruptions, volatility, technological advancement, and so on. She told me that during the pandemic, "I would wake each morning and think 'what is the next right thing to do today?'". She was fastidious about being very deliberate with what she did next, her number one priority, to stave off overwhelm.

In Alcoholics Anonymous, the programme participants take one day at a time and are encouraged to do the next right thing, minute by minute if necessary. It's a powerful intention in all walks of life – "Do the next right thing."

Carl Jung advised a woeful, anxiety-ridden and directionless client: "There is no pit you cannot climb out of provided you make the right effort at the right place. ... do the next thing with diligence and devotion." There's no need for panic. As Jung advises, we hold the power to stop our laments and overwhelm (and all too prevalent indecisive inertia) simply by seizing diligence and devotion and, indeed, doing that next right thing.

Zoning intentionally in on the next right thing strips actions back to what will have most impact most immediately. It forces decision-making and the most progressive steps being identified and taken. It also stops any mental swirling. Go macro or micro, but the key is always identifying the next right thing to a clear end objective.

For example, if there is a macro objective of, let's say, an annual KPI of "demonstrate solid team unity and effectiveness", the next right thing will inevitably vary day by day, but perhaps today's next right thing is to book that offsite team bonding day, then perhaps tomorrow's next right thing is to host a cross-unit status meeting, and the day after simply to spontaneously embrace an unscheduled watercooler chat with a new colleague.

If we are talking about a micro goal of perhaps eliminating refined sugar from your life, the next right thing may be to eat your breakfast porridge without the twinkly stuff sprinkled on top. There's something pleasingly simple about the purity of the question. What indeed, my dear Watson, is the right thing to do next? This question halts confusion when there are myriad options, routes and tasks whirling ominously all at once. It becomes an efficiency mechanism, keeping us focused on what matters most.

Another small-business owner I interviewed told me she has ingrained this mentality into every member of staff. Each day, they prioritize their task list by identifying the next right thing to "make us the most money". Logical. From administrative staff to product designers to the sales team, the entire culture is infused with this streamlined decisiveness.

It's not only efficient but soothing on the mind, as it lessens the cognitive burden. Remember those 35,000 decisions we make on average per day, 90 per cent being unconscious (page 12)? Well, the other 10 per cent is ideally not too taxing, but requires significant thought. Framing the decision with "the next right thing" becomes reassuringly neat. We settle into tight immediacy, thus avoiding the daunting complexity of a wieldy long-term plan.

It's also as spiritual as it is productive. On a soul level, what truly is the next right thing? Listen to your gut and all that. Even sages like Winston Churchill agreed: "The chain of destiny can only be grasped one link at a time."

Here are six ways to ensure you always do the Next Right Thing:

1. Upon waking, do not look at your phone, listen to the news, or even talk to your children before you have pondered this question for the day ahead, "What is the next right thing?" Your subliminal mind hasn't receded fully yet, and intuitive guidance is generally to be trusted. It will lead you to the next right thing.

2. When dissecting your to-do list, prioritize tasks by those that will have the highest impact on your organization or team's purpose, and do this first (the important and urgent or also important and non-urgent).
3. When overwhelmed in a situation with constant moving parts, examine the status right here, right now, and honour the perspective of the next right thing as it relates to right now.
4. When you are struggling to self-manage and hedonistic, self-sabotaging temptation is swarming, take deep breaths and do the next right thing moment by moment until the craving passes.
5. When your brain is overloaded with the enormity of an uncertain future and how to navigate toward that new horizon, stop overthinking, overanalysing and over-designing and just do the next right thing in the moment.

There's a mental and emotional liberation in the simplicity of the next right thing. That teddy bear is definitely one of my heroes.

If you do the next right thing, focus your attention deliberately and strategically prioritize, you will discover there's a comforting deliciousness in time that makes it something to snuggle into and caress. Time is not to be feared or dominated. Productivity is not to be frenetic or relentless. Gently surrendering to time as finite and acknowledging ourselves as limited humans leaning heartfully into these 4,000 weeks with delicacy and grace is the way to hop off the treadmill and relax. As Oliver Burkeman says, "If you can step more fully into the condition of being a limited human – you will reach the greatest heights of productivity, accomplishment, service and fulfilment that were ever in the cards for you to begin with." I find as you relax into and fall in love with time, it loses its scarcity and truly abounds.

BIG IMPACT REFLECTION: BUILDING YOUR GRACEFUL PEAK PRODUCTIVITY PLAN (PPP)

Let's bring all of this chapter's learnings together to build your peak productivity plan based on environment, ritual, rhythms, focus, flow, prioritization, alertness and more. We're going to start by analysing the different types of work you do across any given week, then detail the locations where you work, correlate energy to the type of work, factor in your individual rhythms and build a bespoke plan 100 per cent optimized to you to deliver your best and biggest impact work.

Step 1: Analyse Work Patterns (including domestic)

1. List the different types of work you do across a week, e.g. creative, admin, financial analysis, laundry, food shopping, etc.
2. List the locations where you work, e.g. home, office, train, Starbucks, kitchen, etc.
3. Create three Mindset Categories for how you work. For example, I use: 1. Introvert Energy = focused/alert, 2. Low Energy/Low Mood = mundane tasks, 3. Extrovert Energy = expansive/communicative.
4. Reflect on your chronotype, natural daily energy rhythms and conditions for flow states to identify your peaks and troughs across the day and week.

Step 2: Optimize Strategically

Now, create a grid like the one below and complete each field per category with your mindset, preferred location and preferred time of day/week. I've entered some example entries for demonstration purposes but be inspired to create your own as relevant.

Category of work	Mindset	Preferred Location	Preferred Time of Day/Week
Creative	Introvert Energy	Home	AM
Admin	Low Energy	Anywhere	PM
Emails	Low Energy	Anywhere	Commuting
Financial Analysis	Introvert Energy	Home	AM
F2F comms	Extrovert Energy	Office	AM/PM (3 days per week ideally)
Strategic Planning	Introvert Energy	Home	AM

Step 3: Design Your Schedule

You are now empowered to map out your ideal work and domestic schedule each week and then build grounding rituals to support yourself entering the relevant "zones" most immediately.

Take time to review your calendar for next week and beyond and adjust as much as you can to optimize You. Do you need Fridays with zero meetings to recover from a high-energy eight hours on Thursday? Can you cluster admin to an hour every day post-lunch? Can you block three mornings each week for "focus time" where you tackle your most challenging tasks? Where and how do exercise and family time fit in ideally? If you're most alert upon waking, can you work immediately before the school run? Are there rituals you can introduce to instantly orient to a new task, environment and necessary work mode?

This is an important step in falling in love with time. This Graceful PPP is optimized to maximize you and your rhythms, so this will encourage more grace in your productivity and reduce the cognitive jolts bustling from one task and place to the next. Keep playing with your plan, implementing it and honing it week by week and tell your colleagues and loved ones this is how you're rolling now and why. I've made a video tutorial with more detailed instructions for you, plus a template at biancabest.com.

Your Big Impact Time Expansion Grid

You now understand the key components to create your bespoke Time Strategy for Big Impact; you know how to fall back in love with time and stop feeling beholden to it, and instead how to expand and honour it to suit What Matters Most.

In the grid below is what you now know how to manage.

It's time to translate this into solid action to make your expansion a reality.

Grab your journal and review the statements below, focusing on the "Expanding To" column. Now spend 30 minutes freewriting on everything that comes up for you when you read the the expansion statements. Elaborate on them where you see fit and make them entirely yours. As well as writing the "what", dive into the "how" and "why". Really explore the statements, applying your newfound knowledge, and have fun exploring all the life-altering ways you're going to feel and how you're going to get there. Let the inspiration pour forth and capture everything that comes to mind.

(Continued)

FROM	EXPANDING TO...
I don't have enough time for everything or space for what matters most to me.	I have a fulfilling schedule with planning that optimizes how time is spent on what.
Time is evaporating too quickly.	Time feels abundant and expansive.
I am chronologically following life in sequence, ticking off task lists.	I have heightened focus and ability to get into and maintain flow.
Life feels like an exhausting race.	I feel life moves at the right pace for me.
I don't have time to learn what I want.	I have the time to learn and pursue interests that help me grow.
I can't concentrate where and when I work.	I have solid plans and rituals in place to stimulate my best work consistently.
I bounce from task to task, never feeling that I deliver my best quality.	I focus on one task at a time, delivering excellence as my average.
I never know where to start.	I have learned that when I'm overwhelmed, I start with the next right thing.
I don't know how to manage time.	I experiment with time management techniques to suit my personality.
I am desperately trying to master time.	I have learned it is not about mastering time but being fully present in the time that I have here and now.

Your Big Impact Decision Pledges

It's decision time. You're now clear on which focus areas to prioritize as you expand into becoming more conscious of time.

Harnessing the power of decision, write down three Time Pledges you will make to ensure your expansion unfurls.

I pledge to work with my time to create my biggest impact without ever burning out by ...

_____

_____

_____

PART TWO

THE EXPANSION PHENOMENON

NOW, GO AND GIVE YOUR ALL

"I knew that if I allowed fear to overtake me, my journey was doomed. Fear, to a great extent, is born of a story we tell ourselves, and so I chose to tell myself a different story from the one women are told. I decided I was safe. I was strong. I was brave. Nothing could vanquish me."

—Cheryl Strayed

You've covered a lot of ground now to ward off any risk of burnout and imbue yourself with more courage and confidence. So far, you've made 12 decision pledges as you've worked through the previous four Big Impact strategies. You have gone within and cemented your footings to flourish. It's now time to go beyond the self and into the realm of others. Who will you serve and how? Who will your impact affect?

In this part, we enter the arenas of the practical and actual. It's time to focus on what strategies are necessary to get your work out into the world and how this varies if you're an entrepreneur, a corporate employee, a creator, or a blend of all three. We will work through aspects of creation and management to hone your highest contribution of work volume and quality (gracefully and from an inspired place).

We will explore why relationships and how you connect with others are important to your work's impact. We will ask: who are your tribes? How do you serve your networks? What Positive Relational Energy do you exude?

How do you communicate your brand value? And more. You'll build plans around all of this, mastering the art of conversation, public speaking and branding.

Then there's wealth. Oh, wealth. Who doesn't want to be rich? But we'll go beyond income, looking more broadly at the multidimensional aspects of wealth, exploring self-esteem's connection to self-identity, as well as money mastery. You'll learn how to personally redefine success and design a wealth map bespoke to you.

And finally, fulfilment, your rightly deserved sense of contentment and joy. How to maintain your peace as you walk your path of integrity, honouring values, everything you cherish and most importantly, your authentic self.

In establishing your Foundation Imperatives, you made decisions. Now, in your Expansion Phenomenon phase, you're going to shift into designing solid actions at the end of each strategy, with timings set to implement these actions as part of a 12-month Big Impact Without Burnout master plan. Follow the instructions as you work through the chapters, step by step, reflection by reflection, transposing ideas into solid plans, capturing the commitments in your journal (or in spreadsheets) as you go, rigorously giving yourself deadlines. This is your moment to take the accountability you've practised so far onward, proceeding into tangible, empowered and no doubt up-levelled output. I'm so privileged we're sharing this journey together. Let's continue.

YOUR BIG IMPACT STRATEGY NO. 5: WORK

"The meaning of life is to find your gift. The purpose of life is to give it away."
— Pablo Picasso

It's a gift to be able to contribute to the world in our unique, however small but important ways. There is only one you, and your talents, ideas, inspiration and creations are so special, it's simply wasteful if you don't unleash them. As my old NLP master used to teach me, "Make the best of the resources available to you". Okay, so when we factor in your skills, your knowledge, your inner gold, your divine resources, what indeed is your best?

In my wellbeing practice, I hear a lot of excuses about why best wasn't or isn't possible. I hear a lot of wistful "what ifs" taking the form of unrealized dreams, wonky prioritizations, lots of playing small and omnipresent overwhelm. What if I had reached for the stars and had pursued my ambitions? What if I'd played bigger, bolder, better? What if I hadn't been so exhausted or pulled in so many directions? What if?

These frustrations regularly dominate the complaints of female business peers. They lie beneath the proliferation of wellbeing courses, workshops, female empowerment retreats and more, all attempting to soothe our perplexed soul-searching. We need to overcome these frustrations that are barriers to our best, because, my darling, if not now, when; and if not you, for goodness' sake, who? It is never too late, as I coach and mentor woman after woman at every stage of her life and career (and men for that matter), and I do believe you're reading this book because right now, finally, is your time.

So, let's focus in on the resources you have available to you and build your ultimate Big Impact Work Strategy. We've optimized your energy, cleansed your mindset, defined your purpose and organized your time, so you're primed and ready to shine your sparkle. In this chapter we're going to explore how to lean into ambition, embrace work with confidence and manage overwhelm, binning excuses along the way. We're shifting into the "output" phase of the book now, where your strategies yield concrete one-year plans. As Rumi pondered, "You were born with wings, why prefer to crawl through life?"

Your Big Impact Without Burnout One-Year Master Plan

There are two aspects to any one-, three-, five-, ten- (or however long) year plan – the overarching strategy and the tactical components to be implemented. Think of "strategy" as the big fat objective – the what and the why; "tactics" are the steps to get there – the how. Your one-year master plan, which you're about to design across the next four strategies, will firstly comprise two work aspects, Creation and Management. Creation centres on how you'll launch yourself and your work into the Big Impact arena, while Management centres on keeping yourself and your work there. Creation takes bravery, courage and focus. Management takes commitment and resilience. Both are equally important for success.

In my experience, and why I now teach this, catapulting work outward and upward in grander and ever-expanding scale over the years has always involved the blend of Creation and Management principles I share here. These principles apply whether you are an entrepreneur running your own enterprise, an employee in an organization or a creator independently producing your art. If you follow these steps to the wire, adapting tactics to your bespoke strategy, I promise Big Impact Without Burnout will follow.

Step 1: Creation

The output phase of your work strategy, where you maximize your contribution to the world, comes down to four simple Big Impact Work Principles:

1. **Know Thyself.** What are your innate strengths, gifts, talents, interests? How can you bolster them, along with your self-worth, and how can you sprinkle this formula into each day and to what effect?
2. **Know Thine Context.** Where does this brilliance create most value, i.e., what happens when you map your skills to the organization/sector/world's needs?
3. **Do the Work.** Get on with getting on, squashing resistance and procrastination, embracing failure and focusing on the outcome.

4. **Get It Out There.** Showcase your wares and watch ripples become waves become tsunamis ...

As logical as these principles sound, as we learned earlier, unconscious limits often thwart women from following them, as the dazzling reality of impending exposure blinds us into inertia. The terror of judgement strikes and that most crippling doubt of all halts us in our tracks: What If I'm Not Good Enough? Too many brilliant women's lights are dimly hiding under bushels, at grave risk of flickering out entirely, and that is not what your spectacular life is about.

Creation Principle 1: Know Thyself

Here are nine ways to optimize yourself in your work arena:

1. **Strengthen Your Strengths.** Please don't waste time trying to improve any of your below-average skills (unless there are abilities you intuitively, excitedly feel impelled to learn) because all that effort will wearily bring you up to average, and Big Impact doesn't tolerate average. Ambitions aren't realized with mediocre abilities, but with excellence. Excellence comes from strengthening your strengths and honing your superpowers, the things you already notice you do more easily than most. Become an expert where your talents are guiding you and don't dilute your power. Any time spent learning and practicing nonessential and uninteresting business skills is time wasted.

2. **Find Your Masters.** Where gaps do exist in your business or team, strategically surround yourself with experts who have already mastered their craft in that area. Know your weaknesses and gaps? Surround yourself with gifted people who are way better than you at those things, and you won't need to master them. These teachers don't need to be in your physical environment either. Read books, watch TED Talks, go online and find the individuals who are broadcasting what you need to learn and devour their content. Richard Branson, famously dyslexic, proudly only learned the difference between net and gross income aged 55 when he hesitated in a billion-dollar deal roundtable, deferring to his CFO, who later took him aside and privately tutored him on P&L intricacies (for interest, not necessity). Branson learned early on to rely on experts around him and focus on bettering his best. Reflect on what you'd like to learn, where the sources are and how to prioritize this within your schedule. Remember, too, that this extends beyond

the work arena into soul teachers as well, those who you perceive as spiritual masters who can contribute to your personal growth as well as the professional guides affecting your work prowess.

3. **Chase Work That Energizes You.** Bend your daily remit to comprise as much work you love as you can. There will always be elements within any role, be it corporate employee or business founder, that don't float your boat. But when you maximize your time plugged into work that you find invigorating, stimulating and that puts you in your flow state, you will be contributing with higher productivity and quality. In turn, the mundane tasks won't drag you down as much as they would if they took up the majority of your day.

4. **Commoditize Your Interests.** There are clues in your passions. Gold lies in your ideas. Pay attention to where your imagination and instincts lead you. One day I wrote a poem that became a personalized gift empire. Another day, one January in my living room, I hosted a free workshop for neighbours on "Maximizing Impact Without Burnout", which became this book and an entire global wellbeing enterprise. What do you do that could be commercialized? Pay attention to that which others ask you for advice on. Where you are perceived as an expert is often a gem that can yield income treasure once polished. Examine it.

5. **Ensure Your Outer Reflects Your Inner.** I coached a client who in our weekly sessions repeatedly bemoaned not being taken seriously by colleagues, her peer set or her boss. She didn't feel her ideas were heard. She didn't know how to make people listen, and so on. Session after session, she lamented the world's lack of notice. And, as she lamented, I inwardly lamented her cosy, creased hoodies, her slumped demeanour, her unkempt hair, scuffed DMs and her chewed biro caps. Gradually, as we worked on her self-authority, her inner power and how to bring gravitas forth from within, her confidence and courage grew and she naturally started to stand taller and straighter, wearing striking, vibrant colours and almost unconsciously began presenting herself as a woman wanting to step up. Sure enough, promotion and job satisfaction soon followed. How you show up every day is how the world receives you. Dress and look like the bright and best image you hold of yourself.

6. **Embrace Ecological Psychology**. Don't waver from honouring and constantly reassessing and adjusting your Peak Productivity Plan (page 149); when you quickly get into the zone (geographically and mentally), and the zones have been designed for the task, you will be consistently working at your best (your muse may even already be there, ready and waiting!).

7. **Shrink the Tedium.** Tedious work tasks should be clustered or delegated. To cluster, pre-allocate designated time each week for this work, so it doesn't interrupt or distract from more important productivity, and plough through it stoically. Be smart with clustering same types of work into categories, as per your systematic creation of your Graceful PPP (page 149). Then, if you know you're great at clearing your inbox with the TV on or while at the ball pit with the kids, do so at that time (remembering of course that I discourage multitasking). If you strategically save your "thinking emails" to be dealt with on a Friday morning, get up at 6am and address them fully focused, before the day has taken hold, knowing that task will be complete ahead of the weekend. If you need to finesse your PowerPoint designs, can you do this with ease while listening to a podcast? Work out the tasks you can blast through at times that make it more tolerable for you, ensuring that any blast does not diminish your core focus of growing your business, or shining at work. It goes without saying that you should delegate strategically, always when it makes sense – bookkeepers, admins, domestic support, whatever you need to eliminate chores so you can focus on your priorities and strengths and build an army around you. You'll learn more on the art of shrinking or delegating tasks through process in the Wealth Strategy.

8. **Make Space for Ideation.** Ensure in your weekly time chunking that you allocate time blocks with holy, empty space for creativity and intuition to rain forth. This could be walking around your garden, taking a bath, typing thoughts into a blank document, doodling, journalling, napping ... whatever invites lightning bolts of inspiration to strike you.

9. **Have a One-, Three-, Five- or Ten-Year Plan** (like the one you're building here). Please. And always know how you're pacing within it, in case strategies or actions need tweaking. I've created a Five-Year Planner template for you at biancabest.com.

BIG IMPACT REFLECTION: KNOW THYSELF

Now, take your journal and reflect on each of these Creation Principles, following the layout below. Start reflecting on where you currently sit in terms of that principle through the lens of your work output and expand your visioning to where you'd like to be. Then add any actions and time frames to bring you closer to this vision in the subsequent columns or lines in your journal.

ONE-YEAR BIG IMPACT WITHOUT BURNOUT MASTER PLAN			
PRINCIPLE 1: KNOW THYSELF	REFLECTIONS	ACTIONS	DEADLINE
I play to my strengths.			
I have identified my masters.			
I know what work energizes me.			
I commoditize my skills.			
I present myself as my future vision.			
I optimize ritual, environment and rhythms.			
I shrink tedious tasks.			
I make space for ideas.			
I have a five-year plan.			

Creation Principle 2: Know Thine Context

It's up to you to get clear on where your unique contribution will have greatest impact, be it in an industry, based on reaching a certain type of consumer, or within your organization, a country, customer segment and so on.

Value is Subjective

Demand creates value. Value fluctuates based on myriad factors. Look at Uber's surge pricing where the cost of your ride home as much as trebles in peak Christmas party season because the market places a higher value on a December journey. An interior designer refurbishing an apartment on Pall Mall in front of Buckingham Palace can charge £100k per room as opposed to her equally-as-qualified counterpart charging £150 per room just 2 miles away in a Tower Bridge block. Your value is always relative.

When I was 19 and foraying into journalism. I took a first job at a cool magazine, *Girl About Town*, a free weekly publication in London, as an admin assistant. My editor wouldn't let me officially write for the magazine on account of me being too "green", so I set up my first limited company, used my mother's name as a pseudonym, provided sample content to the editor via a discreet cheerleading colleague, got the gig and was appointed as a freelance advertorial writer. It all happened via snail mail then. The real kick – I was earning double my official starter salary each month in freelance writing income, without the editor ever knowing their star advertorial writer was little ol' green me. My value doubled in the context of being presumed an experienced freelance copywriter whose work the editor and clients loved, despite being told by the *same* editor that I was too inexperienced to write. The contribution was identical, the value totally subjective. I learned early on in life the paramount importance of framing and context. And so should you.

- **Advice for the Entrepreneur: Your Value Within Your Industry**

Daniel Priestley, friend and global authority on entrepreneurialism, in his book *Key Person of Influence* and DENT Global programme, teaches that until you know your niche, you can't truly know your price point.

Finding your niche is about trusting your gut and then trialling market engagement. When I launched my personalized poem gift range, I had the intention of selling directly to gift shoppers online. I would use Google paid search ads to reach customers one advert, and one large bill, at a time. I realized a far larger, quicker and more accessible market existed if I targeted online shops that were already busy doing the work of finding customers. I modified my product pricing to allow for retailer margins, pivoted into a trade model, and business skyrocketed exponentially as each retailer showered me with multiple orders daily. I had found my niche in gift retailers. (Equally, I'd nailed the 80/20 rule of graceful productivity you'll recall from the Time chapter; page 135)

Today, the internet offers a level playing field for anyone wanting to sell anything or reach anyone. From gamers making millions while they babble and play on Twitch, to ecommerce child prodigies drop-shipping Star Wars collectibles after school from their bedrooms, to bloggers evolving to found media empires, to Shopify personalized T-shirt vendors – those who persevere, offer quality and stand out first and fastest in their niche can and will succeed.

There are simple, easily accessible tools to appraise your potential market and target segment before you set about building your business. Use Google's free Keyword Tool to analyse the highest trending search terms in your business area to learn who's thinking about what. Access social monitoring tools to listen to the conversations being had in your sector. Study behavioural statistics published online on statista.com to track the size of your prize. Then test, test and test what lands. Build a web page, launch social profiles, run some ads, track who responds to what. Learn in real-time who values what and where, which creative messaging works, which demographic responds to which price points, and more. It's all literally at your fingertips. So, get the data, hone your niche and know your market value. As digital guru Brendan Kane guides in his book, *One Million Followers*, "Hypothesize, test, learn and pivot".[99] I highly recommend this book if you're building an online brand.

- **Advice for Employees: Your Value Within Your Organization**

You've been hired for a reason. Your employer sees value in you and wants you; you're in. Now it's up to you to soar in this role, make a strong mark and carry on toward your longer-term personal goals. Whenever you start any new gig, even if just rising through the ranks within your current business, read *The First 90 Days: Critical Success Strategies for New Leaders at All Levels* by leadership and negotiation expert, Michael Watkins. This is a bible for professional impact, guiding you to assess the current state of business play, design your strategy and take immediate action to get noticed as a serious player within those early weeks. It's a well-mapped pathway to respect and job security, or at least passing the three-month probation goal we have as standard in the UK workplace.

Your employer has brought you into your role believing that you can fulfil the needs of the organization, so focus on applying your strengths to hit your remit overtly, and I mean smashing your goals, and demonstrating to the organization how adeptly you deliver in your remit. If you've been hired because you have good leadership skills, lead. If core to the role is product development, develop. If it's to affect culture, affect culture. A very simple rule of thumb is to be razor sharp at delivering the KPIs your manager sets. If you're not clear, get clear. (And if KPIs don't yet exist in your organization, suggest the introduction of them.) Get crystal-clear on what the organization's expectations are, how quickly you need to deliver what, how to work together throughout your delivery and what matters most to them. Every manager wants you to succeed, and implicitly make them look good, so learn how to do this from day one.

Plan what you will share in your one-on-one meetings with your manager, so that you immediately get to the point. Share what work you have done that satisfies the business agenda. Focus on the commercial aspects – how your work is impacting revenue positively (that's what everyone in corporate is always being assessed on. Never forget: no matter how much you love your company and they love you, you are simply a line item on a P&L, as harsh as that sounds). Please don't cloud the brilliant work you've been doing in your manager discussions with irrelevant, tangential sidenotes that interfere with the progressive conversation you should be having. Try to anticipate your manager's needs too, as there's nothing more pleasing than someone having done some thinking for you (from picking up a favourite sandwich to solving a working-through-lunch stress, to compiling a new prospect list unbriefed). If you can surprise and delight managers and colleagues, your reputational credibility will ascend from strength to strength.

One final piece of advice on asserting your value in your work environment, especially if you want to get noticed and promoted (and rightfully so), is to create the role you want to hold. If you spot a niche in your organization, or a way of doing something better, prove there's opportunity there, unlock the value, do the work, then package it up and tell everyone all about it, building trust. When ready, ask the business for recognition: be it in title, salary or both. My client, Annabel, managed this expertly when she wanted to transcend out of a technical role into a broader managerial role, straddling multiple pillars across the company. We worked together on identifying which people were responsible for any decisions around budgets, promotions, organizational structure and work output. We built a strategy for Annabel to start building relationships with these leaders and colleagues, proffering support, useful information and ideas. We built a learning plan to elevate Annabel's knowledge of parallel technical teams, the other pillars, enough for her to have a broad understanding of the synergies, symbiosis and impact of the combined business areas on the company revenue. She became more skilful at making progressive suggestions, until she became the go-to person to solve business challenges. It became a logical and mutual business decision to promote her into the cross-functional leadership role. Don't ask, don't get. (And if, after all the proof and packaging, there's no promotion, it is time to move on to pastures new.)

- **Advice for Creators: Your Value in the World**

The remarkable era we're living and working through gives rise to new products, new sectors, new experiences and new economies continuously. Think about subscription razors, audiobooks, online member communities, not to mention book launches in the metaverse, live music gigs of holograms (ABBA Voyage grossed more than $150 million[100] in the first 15 months of trading alone ... and these are dancing images!) and toilet roll delivered to your front door ten minutes after you realize you've run out. These are unprecedented and exhilarating times where the brightest minds can quickly reach mass audiences and get instant feedback.

What these businesses do is map their offering to the world until they find the sweet spot. Lana Del Rey hit global fame through seeding her music videos on YouTube after record labels turned her away. Steven Bartlett fine-tuned his *Diary of a CEO* podcast digital promotional activity down to the finest detail; he tailored episode titles, creative copy and placements for each audience segment to maximize reach and engagement to become the world's most downloaded podcast. He's still optimizing data this way every day to keep growing and honing according to audience responses. Viral social media beasts, whether you love or hate them, play algorithmic games asking fellow creators to "tag me here and I'll give you this there" so they dupe the system to rise to the top of the feature pages.

You can play this game too. Create your art. Release it and test its value out in the big wide world. If you choose to step into the arena right now, today, go upload it and you're out there ...

Tap into Gems Within Your Environment

You have resources, probably more than you realize. These include your own body, mind and spirit, and access to learning. Perhaps your organization has an L&D programme you've never explored. Perhaps your old childminder has already sold a business like yours and can guide you now as you sell yours. Perhaps your kids have useful perspectives on your latest blog post. Perhaps your old school friend lives in the town you're about to travel to. Open your mind to all the resources available to you and realize how abundantly you're blessed.

Critical Thinking

In school we are rewarded for learning by rote and being compliant with what the institution demands. In work, this doesn't work. (Neither does it in school for that matter. If you haven't yet watched Sir Ken Robinson's TED Talk, "Do Schools Kill Creativity?", watch it; it's worthy of its 78 million views.) To get ahead, we need to build a habit of critical thinking, of observing what could be improved, what can be fixed and how, and never to accept no, nor blindly say yes. Mechanical plodding and people-pleasing have no place in Big Impact Work Strategies. By all means be generous, but never at your own expense. And when you spot a problem, never, ever – please promise me – take it to a manager before you've thought through potential solutions. Managers appreciate critical thought, presented with optional actions, risks, benefits and costs if needs be, so their role is simple decision-making. There's little more disheartening to a manager than receiving flag after flag without requisite analysis to warrant a path forward.

Learn Constantly

Organize your time to allow for learning with dedicated mental space to consume. Refer back to your Knowledge Is Power reflection, on page 98 in the Mindset Strategy, to orient your learning based on current work goals and optimize your neurological state for absorbing and retaining new information.

BIG IMPACT REFLECTION: KNOW THINE CONTEXT

Now, take your journal and reflect on each of these Creation Principles, following the layout below. Start reflecting on where you currently sit in terms of that principle through the lens of your work output, and expand your visioning to where you'd like to be. Then add any actions and time frames to bring you closer to this vision in the subsequent columns or in your journal.

PRINCIPLE 2: KNOW THINE CONTEXT	REFLECTIONS	ACTIONS	DEADLINE
I am clear on my niche.			
I am aware of the abundant resources around me.			
I think critically and exploratorily.			
I learn constantly.			

Creation Principle 3: Do the Work

There's no shortcut here, sorry. You'll need to graft. Effort will always yield results. Just start.

Pay Attention to the Wisdom Within Resistance

Truly. Know this: where you feel resistance to an important pending task and getting to it feels a little repulsive, this is where the growth you need lies. Observe how procrastination presents itself: do you suddenly decide to prep a meal, do some filing, walk the dog or do other low-priority tasks when there is something big you should be doing? If the top priority in your life right now, for example, is certifying in clinical psychology and your Open University course is paid for and waiting to be downloaded, as soon as you're back from the school run, download it, then study for one hour every day. You are responsible for hacking away consistently at your Big Thing with big intention. Do not let the laundry, kitchen, mowing the lawn, dusting the china or washing and drying your makeup brushes distract you from The Most Important Thing.

When we delay important work, it is due to either laziness or fear. These two states can tell you something valuable. Laziness indicates that you don't actually care about the task and therefore it has been incorrectly categorized as high priority. Fear shows you are worried about your work being viewed negatively and avoiding the work feels safer than the terror of judgement. The former needs addressing by either delegating the task or dropping it entirely. The latter is simply a state of mind. Remember what we learned about limiting beliefs and flipping them (page 69)? Now is the time to take deep breaths, remember that nothing ever grows in our safe, dull comfort zone, wiggle one brave little toe into the water, and remember that you are enough. Just start ...

Failure is Never a Reason to Stop

Astro Teller, co-founder and CEO of X at Alphabet, Google's innovation division famed for self-driving cars and eyewear technology, radically taught, "Fail fast, fail often, fail forward."[101] His philosophy is now much adopted in startup culture and corporate behemoths, with phrases such as, "How many things can you break today?" Failure is encouraged as a means to accelerate learning in today's rapidly evolving and competitive world, where risks and experimentation are essential for growth. So, if organizations recognize the power in failure, what happens when you apply this to yourself and your career? If something isn't working and you're not achieving the success you desire, then change strategy – whether it's the social media content strategy you've been slogging over for months that yields low conversion rates, the apprenticeship you don't want to finish or the business you launched but now despise; just stop doing what you're doing, right now. It didn't work. It failed; that's okay. Try anew. This is still progress.

Power On With the "Just Five Minutes" Discipline

Sometimes you just don't feel like working. At those times, this discipline is essential to progressing into Big Impact; a funny thing happens when you sit down regularly and just start. Rather like when you cannot face going for a run on a winter's night and you tell yourself, "I'll just put the running gear on and do five minutes," but you end up getting into your groove and doing a full 10k, then fancy doing it again the next night too, and before you know it, you've gone from couch potato to a competitive runner, so it is with work. Sit down, set that tomato timer, perform your getting-into-the-zone ritual and just start. As Steven Pressfield, who we met in the Purpose Strategy, effuses, it's about the consistent effort, repeated day after day, when all at once, "something mysterious starts to happen. A process is set into motion by which, inevitably and infallibly, heaven comes to our aid. Unseen forces enlist in our cause; serendipity reinforces our purpose."[102] All just by taking that first step of beginning, ensuring we begin again and again and again.

Get Feedback

Unsure of the salience of your efforts? Actively seek feedback at regular intervals. This is not a practice in approval-seeking and ego-stroking, but an opportunity to ask, "Is this useful?" and "How valuable is this to you?" Ask your mentors, social media followers, parents, friends, boss, peers or network if you need a check-in before you go deeper. Have the confidence to share your work and ask. By our very nature, humans are generous, and as the wonderfully plentiful offers to proofread this very manuscript have taught me, there are a lot of kind-hearted souls prepared to sacrifice their time to support a fellow grafter. So, select your confidants and ask for their input. Promise something of equal value in return, something even more valuable if you're a giver, and if you're a taker – well, you know who you are and how you roll!

BIG IMPACT REFLECTION: DO THE WORK

Now, take your journal and reflect on each of these Creation Principles following the layout below. Start reflecting on where you currently sit in terms of that principle through the lens of your work output and expand your visioning to where you'd like to be. Then add any actions and time frames to bring you closer to this vision in the subsequent columns or in your journal.

PRINCIPLE 3: DO THE WORK	REFLECTIONS	ACTIONS	DEADLINE
I see the wisdom in resistance.			
I recognize failure as opportunity.			
I always start... just for five minutes...			
I gain feedback.			

Creation Principle 4: Get Out There!

Only you can shine your brilliance, no one else will, can or should do it for you. Deep breaths and go ...!

Preparation is Everything

When taking your work out into the public arena, preparation is the most certain way to quell nerves and know you're presenting your best. So, don't wing it, please, as that won't be your best. Schedule in preparation time, respecting and revering it. Rehearse before a big speech. Allow for editing before the final document deadline. Run through the numbers once, or twice more. Check the biographies of the people you're about to pitch to. Factor in the additional time to make your big reveal as outstanding as it deserves to be.

Embrace Confidence as You Showcase Your Wares

Now is your time to own your confidence, not with superficial swagger and empty bluster, but with the humble reassurance that you and your work are of absolute substance and worthy of attention. Every moment so far in your life has led you here to share your creations with the world. It is simply not an option to hide anymore, because you are grounded in the knowledge that your work needs to be seen for maximum impact to ripple outward. You have worked through all the foundational imperatives, so trust yourself, trust your work and trust that now is your time. Play big!

Be Reflective

Reflect often on how far you've come, acknowledging the progress you've made from the seeds of an idea to ever-swelling impact and ever-expanding knowledge. Observe how much stronger you and your work are, how much more expansive the fruits of your labour are now, how your audience has broadened, your sales have increased, your income has risen, your dreams enlarged and how so many more of those twinkling stars are now within reach. This also applies to those just starting out. The bravery of deciding to even go after Big Impact and pick up this book is a valuable victory. It all counts. Always in life, moments of retrospective appreciation for the magnitude of ground you've covered – from where you were five years ago, one year ago, six months ago, even one week ago – strengthen self-belief, which by default encourage more perseverance, progress and motivation.

Magnificently Tell Your Story (Lots!)

Crucially now, it's time to enter the arena with a bang. Whether you're selling a product, a service, a brand or yourself (and remember we're all selling all the time, "sales" is not a dirty word, just business), successfully impacting an industry with your work takes excellent storytelling. Understanding who the stakeholders are in your organization or industry and how to match your wares with their needs with artful positioning is your golden ticket to Big Impact (more on brand communication in the next chapter). This is how you elevate your respectability and credibility across your network and one way you establish a growing reputation for delivering excellence. The best storytellers know how to frame their work, their value and their impact, managing upward and outward with dexterous influence. It's your turn to master this. It's a Big Impact Imperative. Here's how.

Storytelling is a powerful tool to captivate your audience, listener, colleague, boss, whoever, and leave a lasting impression. To perfect this art so it becomes a natural aspect of how you work, be clear on the core message or lesson you want to convey, in any and every interaction, and craft a narrative arc with a compelling beginning, engaging middle and thought-provoking conclusion. Easier in a 20-minute keynote on a big stage, but also wholly possible in your weekly one-to-one with your boss, describing your progress against your annual strategy. For the big stage moments, incorporate vivid sensory details, relatable characters and emotional hooks that resonate with your listeners. In your one-to-one, describe a problem, the solution and the positive impact (even if it was a negative result, end your "story" with the proactive actions you've taken to rise from the failure).

Practise delivering your stories with confidence, using vocal variety and expressive body language to emphasize key points (big gesticulators are apparently cleverer than most!). Most importantly, infuse your storytelling with authenticity, vulnerability, and a genuine desire to inspire and connect with others. By harnessing your unique power of storytelling, you effortlessly leave an indelible mark on those around you, igniting positive change.

You will learn more on public speaking in the Connection Strategy as you hone your skills around "communicating to inspire", but I want you to incorporate storytelling here as part of your Work Strategy. Every interaction is a moment to tell your story and create impact. Once you articulate clearly where you stand and what you stand for, you become a magnet for opportunity. People love stories, and your story deserves to be told. Your action is to tell it.

BIG IMPACT REFLECTION: GET OUT THERE!

Now, take your journal and reflect on each of these Creation Principles, following the layout below. Start reflecting on where you currently sit in terms of that principle through the lens of your work output and expand your visioning to where you'd like to be. Then add any actions and time frames to bring you closer to this vision in the subsequent columns or in your journal.

PRINCIPLE 4: GET OUT THERE	REFLECTIONS	ACTIONS	DEADLINE
I am prepared.			
I am confident.			
I reflect on my progress.			
I always tell magnificent stories.			

ONE-YEAR BIG IMPACT WITHOUT BURNOUT MASTER PLAN

I invite you now to bring all these reflections together into priority areas of focus you've now identified as integral to your master plan according to the Creation Principles (we'll be using these at the end of the chapter). Distil what you've captured so far, lifting out highlights, always tuning into your values and overarching impact goals as you ponder. Complete the grid below.

ONE-YEAR BIG IMPACT WITHOUT BURNOUT MASTER PLAN	
PRINCIPLE 1: KNOW THYSELF	
PRINCIPLE 2: KNOW THINE CONTEXT	My priorities are...
PRINCIPLE 3: DO THE WORK	
PRINCIPLE 4: GET OUT THERE	

Step 2: Management

Creation feels great. Motivating, propelling, inspiring. Once every idea is cultivated, multiple workstreams borne, action plans in a Gantt chart, deadlines set, enthusiasm and energy abound. There's a thrill to each progressive tick on the Master Plan to-do list, healthy adrenaline surges and leads to gushes of output. But, as we learned in our burnout dissection at the start of this book, there's a precarious tipping point on that Stress Performance Curve, and it's unsustainable to maintain a perpetual flurry of activity without rest and careful management. In a state of hyperactivity, we are in a semipermanent danger zone. When overworked and overworking, there are ominous threats of:

1. Diluting the quality of our output by stretching ourselves too thin = lessened impact
2. Prolonged stress taking its evil short- and long-term toll = risk of burnout

So, let's examine and deal with each of these, because you deserve to thrive.

Management Principle 1:
Maintaining Quality of Output to Preserve Impact

Harvard scientists have confirmed that small amounts of visible, tangible progress each day increase workers' motivation[103]. So, whether working on our career, ourselves or domestic work, we can start a snowball of enthusiasm and self-esteem rolling through task completion. Mini is fine. Start small. Just drink a glass of water upon waking daily to get a little burst of pride for doing something virtuous. That one sip of water helps our confidence tingle, intention take shape, and bigger things suddenly feel achievable and alluring. Introduce me to a woman who isn't secretly satisfied when the kitchen is sparkling, the laundry summer-meadow scented and crisply folded away, with a Le Creuset hot-pot, swimming with home-grown herbs, simmering in the oven. There is a reassuring satisfaction when the kids look box-fresh, groomed with neat trims and ironed attire. And, oh, the bliss of walking back into the house after the school run to smell the cleanliness of a pristine home. We get micro-dosed kicks and soul-satisfied glee from domestic order. That's a woman thing. According to some philosophers at the University of Cambridge, men seek the order too, but they don't necessarily experience the satisfaction of ploughing through the tasks to achieve it, nor hold the same efficiency standards.[104] (No disrespect intended, lads, it's something to do with a brain state called "affordance theory"; according to a study, women are wired to notice the crumbs that need wiping away, whereas you don't see them[105] – we're all good though, no nagging afoot!).

Generally, traditionally employed or entrepreneurial women manage the home to create space to be able to get to our work (that has certainly been my experience). Comparatively, our male partners seem more able to less cumbersomely get directly to their work. Over 90 per cent of women with children in Europe spend at least one hour per day on housework, compared with 30 per cent of men with children,[106] with over 60 per cent of the domestic load generally still resting on our shoulders.[107] None of this is exactly the "fair play" Eve Rodsky is striving for with her well-intentioned, and clearly much needed, equitable solutions card game and book, to encourage sharing the domestic load. As she warns women in *Fair Play*, "If you're not careful, domestic encroachment will trap you every time. The net result is that you spend less time on your career and social outlets, and likely deny yourself mental breathers and important self-care."[108] Fair point.

However, this is not a book about solving gender inequality but is around how we manage such imbalance at home, as it poses several risks. Firstly, there's the risk of energy depletion. If childcare and domesticity require energy and so does work, how should we prioritize? Secondly, there's the sheer dilution of focus as time and attention is so broadly diversified that excelling at the one big work goal becomes nigh impossible. Both scenarios jeopardize our most magnificent impact potential.

Investing in Big Impact

You analysed your Conscious Calendar (page 137) in the last chapter to appraise where your time was being spent. This may have given you surprising clarity around how much time is currently allocated to domesticity, or not, compared with work focus. You may already have organized your life so the domestic burden is balanced. Great if so. Balancing investment of time, energy and money is a core part of your Work Strategy for Big Impact. It takes conscious design. I'll share here how I do it with the caveat that I recognize I am not representative of the norm, with four children, no partner and blessed to currently have financial means. However, I am epitomizing how I have made space for work as one of my top priorities and encourage you to do the same, in whatever unique ways make sense and are possible for you.

While I don't have a partner here to share the load, I do have all these boisterous, loveable (and capable with a lot of cajoling) dependents as well as my significant workload, so I have made it my priority to organize efficient domestic management to ensure I make the Big Impact where I want it most. I choose to spend my time on the things I enjoy with the people I love, and that includes work and kids. Domestically, it does include cooking soups, salads and my veggie juices, but that is it. My soul shrinks when I iron, food shop, make beds, fold laundry, wash floors or cook for children who don't like it, grrrrr. Don't get me wrong, sometimes a Saturday morning cleaning blitz gives me all sorts of self-satisfied hormonal kicks, but generally, I get those more often from producing good work. I'm up for creation more than restoration, and creating impactful, valuable work output as opposed to restoring boys' bedrooms back to less smelly states. So, I've delegated responsibilities to the children where appropriate and outsourced my main domestic load. Mrs Mop is my once-a-week fairy godmother, keeping our home orderly and my time free to focus on work, the kids and leisure. Tom is my gardener, Karina my dog walker, and I have a digital Rolodex of other trusty helpers on hand as and when I need them. The kids cook their own meals themselves now – teaching them to cook was an absolute priority in our household (because they'd starve, not because I'm a supermum!). Laundry lessons will come next. This is all part of my business strategy. To deliver my Biggest Impact, I direct investment toward delegation, not as a luxury but an imperative.

I used to have a partner and no financial means for any of this, so the juggle used to look different, but I still prioritized work and the children as they have always been my strongest motivators. Then, I deprioritized ironing bed linen (never!) and hoovering (twice monthly), and instead clustered housework and laundry into weekly blitzes, making it fun time with the kids, sharing tasks with my ex (agreeing up front who was responsible for what), but always preserved my time and energy for where I wanted biggest impact aligned with long-term goals.

As we have covered at length throughout this book, time and energy are our most precious and limited resources. So, as I matured, my life evolved, and since my burnout chapter ended, I have very carefully prioritized my budgets to factor in domestic help the moment I could afford it as a nonnegotiable essential to enable my world to spin in my way, and for it to grow in the way I intended it. I needed the space to manifest the bigger and bigger impact I intended and intend. This has been my way of doing it for me and my life vision and I invite you to design your way of doing it.

I have clients who savour aspects of running their homes as their personal blast of therapy, feeling energized by the physicality of cleaning and the mindfulness found when polishing the silver. Contrastingly, I have clients who choose to plop children into clubs throughout the holidays, eat only ready-meals and don't even remember how to change a hoover bag, which is how they stay energized.

Design your plan based on how you want your life to look, as opposed to what you can comfortably afford. This stepping out of your comfort zone with a financial stretch may need to become a core part of your strategy for success to avert burnout. As you would invest in a bookkeeper if that's a part of your business you don't enjoy managing or aren't qualified to manage, so invest in support around you in the home. Your kingdoms are not separate, they are one. Address the imbalances of your time and attention, calculate where investment financially or energetically should flow and incorporate this into your business and career plan. Run your empire with your biggest impact in mind.

Committing to Big Impact (Without Dilution)

When we stretch ourselves too thin, domestically or taking on too much work, it's very hard to maintain excellence in any one area. Remember the fogginess that starts to descend as burnout cloaks overworked individuals? Working too hard, too late and too long seriously risks errors being made and retrograde career progress. It's not worth the risk taking on more and then more again. Know your limits. Time management tools measure capacity for a reason; identify your maximum capacity and respect it.

I'm often asked why I sold my first business and am not on a yacht right now in a wide-brimmed sunhat, basking in the caress of a Caribbean breeze. Well, aside from the twin pregnancy news, I recognized the business had had its day. I had seized the opportunity to launch The Bespoke Gift Company within a burgeoning consumer market rapidly expanding the business in the early years, but a decade later, after the early boom, I had been distracted from the core essence of the business, repeatedly diversifying to chase new product lines, new markets, new sales mechanics, always new, new, shiny and new. Eventually, I reflect, because I deviated from the core thrust consistently, year after year, I missed my moment. Markets changed, the business model evolved, profitability shifted. I'd been looking in the wrong direction, trying to stay ahead of the market, but no longer shaping the market as I had been initially. No regrets, but I share this tale with clients and in my workshops as a lesson to stay focused on the core goal – do not be distracted, do not waiver, do not diminish the power in that original idea (until it's either expanded or usurped). Don't let dilution be a factor demeaning your Big Impact Strategy.

How you concentrate best on your Big Impact goal is for you to strategize personally. Consider undiluted commitment as follows:

The Entrepreneur: remember your niche, know your market, know your customers, know your strategy, know your next most important thing, which is ot necessarily the most interesting, tantalizing, trending thing, and protect core revenue generation.

The Employee: remember your remit, review your job description, learn your KPIs off by heart, track them, report where you are in relation to them in your weekly/monthly review meetings with your boss, always be commercially minded, stay on task and deliver.

The Creator: create what you set out to create, bind yourself to the original vision and hold it firm while embracing imaginative expansion. Don't be disheartened or distracted, stay committed.

BIG IMPACT REFLECTION: MAINTAINING QUALITY OF OUTPUT TO PRESERVE IMPACT

Now, take your journal and reflect on each of these Management Principles, following the layout below. Start reflecting on where you currently sit in terms of that principle through the lens of your work output and expand your visioning to where you'd like to be. Then add any actions and time frames to bring you closer to this vision in the subsequent columns or in your journal. If there are no actions to take, great, leave the row blank.

ONE-YEAR BIG IMPACT WITHOUT BURNOUT MASTER PLAN			
PRINCIPLE 1: MAINTAINING QUALITY OF OUTPUT TO PRESERVE IMPACT	REFLECTIONS	ACTIONS	DEADLINE
I invest in my Big Impact by carefully allocating time, energy and money optimally.			
I commit to concentrating on my Big Impact goals without diluting my focus.			

Management Principle 2:
Big Impact Stress Tactics to Avoid Burnout

"I'm taking the summer off," Ella announcedm settling into our video call, the sixth in a series of "emergency" weekly sessions she'd booked with me to support her during what she described as the most "brutal, soul-burning period of her career". Within her sector, Ella is an esteemed industry veteran with 30 years of experience, spanning roles in operations, strategy and product. Well-liked, warm and affable, Ella laughs a lot. She presents as happy and vivacious, pretty, willowy, always impeccably dressed. Her professional reputation is one of resilience, proactivity and always pushing to achieve excellence. Well-qualified from the off, she has been promoted, head-hunted, promoted, then head-hunted cyclically. She's one of those women with the perfect LinkedIn profile, an A-star chronology of ever-impressive work experience. But for the first time in Ella's career, at almost 50 years old, in her most recent role, right at the top of powerful industry boards, things have gone awry. She's clashed with irate clients, then finger-pointing colleagues, head-butting in negotiations, which became contentious and then slanderous. She has been removed from accounts, then received threats, crippling feedback, ostracization, blocks, politics, dirty words and dirty work everywhere. Her career star was rapidly catapulting downward.

At no point during this six-month period of battle had Ella minimized her efforts. Consistently, evermore wearily, she had tried to honour her goals, protect the client objectives, work harmoniously with colleagues, push the agendas forward, but with intensifying hostilities, she recognized urgent change was necessary before she broke. We were working together on maintaining Ella's resilience, protecting her self-esteem and keeping her in her power during this fraught time. Wed to her pride and personal standards, we needed to ensure these were honoured, despite the intense, unrelenting stress.

Stress assaults us in many ways. As with Ella's experience, and too many of my seemingly successful clients, it may be caused by the politics of an uncomfortable work environment we're inhabiting. It may be the volume of work, the type of work, the people we're working with, disengagement from the work, change in management, change of heart, or so on. Outside of work, it may be the pressure of a death, a breakup, a dementia-afflicted parent or errant adolescents wobbling our inner foundations. It may be a pandemic, economic volatility, redundancy halving household income, a burst pipe. It can originate externally and be utterly beyond our control, or internally with anxiety and panic seemingly also beyond our control. Whatever form it takes, emotional stress is catastrophic if not managed, triggering fear, anxiety and anger, and, when prolonged, leading to depression and apathy.

However, adversity builds resilience. Fact. Study after scientific study proves it.[109] Stress that you can control or master seems to have an inoculation effect, making you stronger and better able to cope next time stress hits. The key is in that sense of control. The hijacked amygdala can't distinguish between good or bad stress, so it is ready for fight, flight or freeze every time until we train ourselves to respond differently. Easy when we've come across the situation before and know we've got this; harder when it's entirely new, foreign, frightening and we feel extremely vulnerable. When we have no point of reference, we need to take steps to acknowledge we're out of our depth and implement management strategies. In Ella's case, this was to urgently and immediately remove herself from the situation to get back a sense of control while working through my Stress Success System.

The Stress Success System

To ensure you continue bravely and confidently propelling your work out into the world, having your biggest impact while averting burnout, here are nine ways I recommend tactically gaining a sense of control in stressful situations:

1. Ground yourself in the present moment
2. Process your emotions
3. Practice self-compassion
4. Recognize which part of the stressor you can control
5. Learn ways to rewire your responses
6. Acknowledge when stress is sabotaging decision-making
7. Minimise stress exposure
8. Proactively balance stress and rest for sustainable productivity
9. Weave impact into every work situation

1. Ground Yourself in the Present Moment

When we concentrate on grounding ourselves, we focus our attention on a nonthreatening aspect of our current and immediate environment. We use our mind to bring us back to safety, connecting with our surroundings to soothe us into feeling more solid, firmly centred and stabilized. With my one-to-one clients, and at the beginning of workshops, I invite clients and audiences to place their feet firmly on the floor, kick heels off if necessary, and truly feel a connection with the Earth, close their eyes and breathe deeply, feeling their energy flowing into the floor and vice versa. Visualizing a strong, flourishing tree with deep roots is also powerful here. The physicality of lung-expanding belly-inflating breaths and hyperawareness of our bodies bring us back into a sense of calm. You can use this technique before any meeting, pitch, work task, event ... to ground yourself in the here and now before taking your work and impact forth.

Presence is always powerful and I believe integral to a life of Big Impact, so we will go deeper in the final strategy, Fulfilment, into honing this delicious way to embrace life.

2. Process Your Emotions

I have spent many, many hours honing one of the Co-Active Training Institute's core coaching principles, Process. The essence of Process coaching is about being with clients wherever they are in their lives by allowing them to fully feel whatever it is that they are feeling. We are trained to help clients be with what is. When individuals become connected to themselves, to what is truly going on within their body, mind and soul, that simplicity alone becomes transformative. "This enhances their aliveness. They expand into the fullness, the roundness and richness of being human."[110] As I have witnessed many times, when clients do indeed experience their very aliveness by acknowledging the dominant emotion and how it is swirling through them, however uncomfortable the emotion, energy starts to shift. They regrasp the ability to move forward and relax into the naturally resourceful, creative and whole range of themselves and their lives, simply by becoming aware of the emotion.

Biologically, some scientists believe emotions last only for around 60 to 90 seconds before they float off, replete with having triggered whatever chemical reaction they induced.[111] It's thoughts that linger around, keeping us locked in the pain or joy of the moment. But when you recognize that any emotion is only here momentarily, that this too shall pass, that these sensations are fleeting, and when you accept how you feel, there's a temporary liberation from your suffering. The more comfortable and adept we are at processing emotions this way, the better equipped we are to manage anger, overwhelm, fear and other stress-related feelings. (We'll learn more on detachment from negative emotions and thoughts in the Fulfilment Strategy.)

3. Practice Self-Compassion

As situations intensify, often we react with a subconscious striving to do more, hardening to our needs, failing to gain control, so it feels counterintuitive to break and soften toward ourselves. The more stressed we feel, the more guilty we feel that we're not doing enough, and perfectionism stops being a healthy intrinsic motivator (yes, I see it as a positive trait when not extreme), and instead becomes a whip for self-flagellation; "You should be perfect. You should be on top of this. You are so off-kilter right now."

In fact, nurturing ourselves in these times and moments of stress is the best and most loving response. What makes this especially hard to remember is that the stress triggers old wounds to open, with old coping mechanisms trotting out, and we risk self-sabotaging by default. So, we automatically start to push harder, hurt deeper, do more, produce more, use substances, lash out, "boss it", brag, lie, pity ourselves ... whichever way our protective armour shows up, because that petulant inner critic is screaming at our ineptitude, demanding more action.

Here's what you need to do: elevate up out of the physical and mental state you're in, become astutely aware, pause, breathe, drop intellectually and emotionally into your heart, hold a hand physically over your heart, stop the swirling and consider what is more loving to yourself right now, what is aligned with your values, what will bring you closer to your Big Impact work goals. Then implement the loving self-compassion practices you learned in the Mindset Strategy.

4. Recognize Which Part of the Stressor You Can Control

A prevalent constituent of burnout is the feeling of loss of control. It's this feeling that's the problem, as the feeling can override fact. We may feel totally out of control when in actuality there are elements which do indeed remain within our control. Once we are faced with stressful situations, it's important to understand where control lies.

Control itself can be wildly damaging when excessive – think of narcissists trying to control people through manipulation and distortion of facts, perfectionists obsessed with controlling every tiny aspect of their lives, psychopathic micromanagers, etc. But a healthy sense of self-reliance and ability to control what is indeed controllable helps us to live life accountably. The more you trust yourself to manage what is manageable, the more your confidence grows and the stressor loses power over you.

5. Learn Ways to Rewire Your Responses

"Your personality creates your personal reality"[112] is a mantra espoused by Dr Joe Dispenza, charismatic, progressive author of *Evolve Your Brain*. As a (self-claimed) leading scientist on neuro-psychopathy, Dr Dispenza believes that we are not hardwired to be a certain way (which neuroplasticity proves) and that the brain is capable of change despite so much prior unconscious programming. He believes we can change anytime we want to if we repeatedly practise new ways of thinking, behaving and "being" . He runs vast lab experiments observing brain activity, documenting how altered inner states create lasting outer change. His theory is that through inner work, subliminal reprogramming, we can change our outer reality per the opening statement of this paragraph: your personality creates your personal reality.

I wholeheartedly believe and know from experience that this concept is 100 per cent true for Big Impact lives and we can and should apply these principles to effective stress management. You can absolutely reprogramme a stress response. For example, if you retreated when your father scolded you as a child, and your default state since the age of five has been to quietly recoil from the room, sit alone, and disengage until you feel better, your body and mind have learned that "this is what happens when an authoritative male chastises me". While this may have been effective for Little Girl you, it doesn't serve you when your male boss gives you negative feedback at age 35. This is where rewiring comes in and you need to design a new modus operandi for a new response to authoritative male guidance – instead of cowering and retreating, maturely digesting and responding constructively.

Do this in three ways. Firstly, **gather self-knowledge** – find out all the information and facts related to what you believe and deconstruct the false from truth, layer in more, learn, learn, learn, rather like disproving one of your limiting beliefs identified earlier. So if, for example, you're tired of feeling and thinking a certain way about that male boss, weary of feeling afraid, subservient and disempowered, unpick fact from fiction, examining what your actual experience with this boss is, who are they, how they treat you, what their tone means, what words they say ... and understand your entire situation and relationship from every angle more fully. Secondly, **seek instruction** – get a mentor, coach, psychotherapist, whoever can help you ingrain new, better ways of thinking about this issue, trialling new perspectives. I often invite clients to go directly to the source and ask the "very intimidating male", for example, for feedback on your relationship and work. Working more closely with the apparent threat is a fantastic way to gain new insight to stimulate different responses. Finally, gain **broader life feedback** – from yourself and others as you start implementing the new less stress-inflamed version of yourself you're testing out. Are the new responses working better for you? You'll know what feels good and right the more you do it. As more neural pathways fire, they wire together, and a new, calmer, further-from-burnout you will be born.

6. Acknowledge when Stress is Sabotaging Decision-Making

Don't make decisions in haste. Ever. If we're stressed, we are also reactive and agitated, and decisions made in this state risk being knee-jerk and putting events in motion that we may regret later. So, however heated you feel, flushed with anger, impatience, nervousness, desire, whatever intensity is bubbling within you, do not decide in this state. Even the stoics preached this. As Marcus Aurelius wrote in *Meditations*: "The nearer a man comes to a calm mind, the closer he is to strength," and Epictetus, Aurelius's mentor (and some say primary influence) wrote: "When we are frustrated, angry or unhappy, never hold anyone except ourselves – that is, our judgements – accountable."

Give yourself the time to calm down before you decide. Walk away, even if just to lock yourself in the bathroom, close your eyes and breathe. If this isn't an option, and your child is about to run into the road, for example, trust your gut and act instinctively, of course. Business decisions rarely save lives but need reverence, as they will always reflect you and your impact very publicly.

7. Minimize Stress Exposure
Where you have the option to avoid stress, do. If certain people, programmes, situations, foods, sights or whatever make your blood pressure rise, do what you can to protect yourself by ignoring them, putting space between you and them, avoiding them or just minimizing exposure to them.

Studies prove that hospital patients heal faster when all they see is nature outside of their window instead of high-rise concrete offices and city bustle. Different views stimulate different psychological responses in our bodies. Beyond hospital views and across the arena of your life, look at your stressors and become aware of how they stimulate your senses and what action you can take to control your environments to optimize your zen. As Melanie Greenberg writes in *The Stress-Proof Brain*, "How you view your stressor is just as important as your actual circumstances when it comes to long-term effects on your health and happiness."[113] So, don't just remain victim to it; adjust what you can to minimize it.

In my case, to my family's annoyance, I avoid watching horror movies, action thrillers, anything with death, crime, life's dark side. It's just not somewhere I want to go. The images would invade my dreams, mood and hormones, so I consciously choose to preserve myself and avoid them. Likewise, with the news. I choose not to digest what I cannot control. For years now, current affairs reach me through others, and only anecdotally, never as a primary something for me to deal with. Has it impacted my life detrimentally? Nope, the opposite, my subconscious isn't clouded by processing darkness unnecessarily and my thoughts and dreams stay where I prefer them to. I believe this enables me to concentrate better on showing up as my best, biggest impact self. My choice, but I do invite you to explore if for yourself.

8. Proactively Balance Stress and Rest for Sustainable Productivity
Give yourself the thrill of that stimulating stress, like the rush of a shark dive or pitching your business proposal, frequently. It not only builds resilience to be regularly exposed to good stress, but it expands our competence and capabilities, so seek it out. Take one little risk toward a goal each day. Buzz,

buzz. Then, also be mindful of how you recover after that kick. Factor in time to rest. Remember the equation of Brad Stulberg and Steve Magness (page 48), the mathematical path to peak performance: Stress + Rest = Growth. Never forget to plan in rejuvenation time after intense surges of work progress, be they mega pitches, stage presentations or project completion. Plan for the post-surge recovery as a Big Impact tactic.

9. Weave Impact into Every Work Situation

When we feel "trapped" in a work environment we no longer enjoy, but are obligated to stay in it because of financial demands, limited employment options, etc., we can make peace with our cage by tapping into our dharma: our eternal purpose, our spiritual essence, our blend of passion, compassion and expertise. There will always be ways you can weave more of what matters most to you into every work situation, in how you speak, behave, the strengths you deploy and the example you are. Focus on "giving" as an antidote to burnout.

Adam Grant, psychologist and Wharton professor, describes how the arduous shifts of doctors and nurses are palatable, as well as survivable, because a "sense of lasting impact protects against stress, preventing exhaustion,"[114] and he encourages people in high-stress jobs to actively seek out opportunities to give back in intimate ways. You don't have to work in a people-oriented, charitable job to apply this. If you're an accountant with a yearning to be a life coach, ensure every meeting you lead inspires your team, colleagues and clients to contribute their highest inputs by listening, encouraging and gently probing with powerful questions to make their work better. You're still hitting the business agenda and your role remit but simultaneously working more deliberately in your dharma. As monk, management consultant and spiritual podcaster and author Jay Shetty advises in *Think Like a Monk*, "We live with intention in our dharma", and "Life is more meaningful when we define ourselves by our intentions rather than our achievements."[115]

Much of the success of this 9-step Stress Success System is founded on what psychologists refer to as an enhanced state of "interoception". This is the ability to be aware of internal sensations arising in the body, as well as noticing emotional sensations. Once we practise heightening our self-awareness of both body and mind in stressful moments, we are better able to intercept our reactions through conscious, positive self-management. We create our own intervention to protect our homeostatic, healthier state with body and mind delicately harmonized. Mastering this is burnout resilience nailed.

BIG IMPACT REFLECTION:
STRESS TACTICS TO AVOID BURNOUT

Now, take your journal and reflect on each of these Management Principles following the layout below. Start reflecting on where you currently sit in terms of that principle through the lens of your work output and expand your visioning to where you'd like to be. Then add any actions and time frames to bring you closer to this vision in the subsequent columns or in your journal. If there are no actions to take, great, leave the row blank.

PRINCIPLE 2: BIG IMPACT STRESS TACTICS TO AVOID BURNOUT	REFLECTIONS	ACTIONS	DEADLINE
I know how to ground myself.			
I can healthily process my emotions.			
I practice self-compassion.			
I identify which stressors I can control and relax about those I can't.			
I practise rewiring negative stress responses.			
I avoid decision-making when stressed.			
I minimize unnecessary stress exposure.			
I ensure I blend stress and rest to preserve my growth and consistent impact.			
I weave impact into every work situation.			

Your Big Impact Work Expansion Grid

You now understand the key components to create your bespoke Work Strategy for Big Impact. You know yourself, your context, how to combat resistance, get cracking and get out there with gusto. You know how to maintain your output levels healthily and consistently, building resilience as you go, always protecting yourself and your work.

In the grid below is what you now know how to manage.

It's time to translate this into solid action to make your expansion a reality.

Grab your journal and review the statements below, focusing on the "Expanding To" column. Now spend 30 minutes freewriting on everything that comes up for you when you read the expansion statements. Elaborate on them where you see fit and make them entirely yours. As well as writing the "what", dive into the "how" and "why". Really explore the statements, applying your newfound knowledge, and have fun exploring all the life-altering ways you're going to feel and how you're going to get there. Let the inspiration pour forth and capture everything that comes to mind.

FROM	EXPANDING TO...
I have diluted focus.	I apply my strengths to achieve excellence consistently with focused commitment to my biggest impact goals.
I deliver frenetic, exhausting output.	I have graceful, abundant productivity and spend much of my working life in flow.
I produce average work and suffer from low motivation.	I am bursting with innovation, creativity, and boundary-pushing ideas bubble up bountifully.
I have low recognition throughout my organization and in my industry.	I am always top of mind for promotion, regularly win awards and magnetize plentiful opportunities.
I feel boxed in, stuck where I am, often swirling with imposter syndrome.	I feel confident not accepting when someone tells me no and asking again or for more, playing big and enjoying positive self-esteem.
Mainly, I plough through my tasks logically, with little passion in my work world.	I always follow my heart, indulge my passions and bloom with ideas – and a lot of fun!
I am resistant to doing my work and procrastinate often.	I am leaned in and doing the work, an expert at delegating or eliminating when necessary.
I am afraid of failure and limited by shame.	I am experimental and bold, confident doing things anyway and doing them my way!

Work Strategy Priority Actions

It's time for serious action. Now bring your reflections together and organize them into priority areas of focus that you identify as integral to your master Work Strategy toward Big Impact Without Burnout across the next 12 months.

Drawing the grid below in your notebook or in a spreadsheet, list as many reflections and actions with deadlines per principle as you can, based on all you've learned. Then distil all of these action ideas into **three Work Strategy Priority Actions**, which we'll incorporate into your master plan at the end of the book. Remember to always tune into your values and overarching impact goals as you create your plans. Make the three action priorities realistic, achievable and inspiring, and rigorously tied to firm deadlines.

ONE-YEAR BIG IMPACT WITHOUT BURNOUT MASTER PLAN				
		REFLECTIONS	ACTIONS	DEADLINE
Principle 1	Maintaining quality of output to preserve impact			
Principle 2	Big Impact stress tactics to avoid burnout			
		My three Work Strategy Priority Actions are: 1....2....3....		

YOUR BIG IMPACT STRATEGY NO. 6: CONNECTION

"When you meet someone who embraces their own spirit and the spirit of others in a loving way it engenders connection."

— Marianne Williamson

Astronauts realizing their dreams at NASA HQ undergo rigorous cultural competency training before they can, quite literally, reach their stars. A core NASA principle teaches students to go "beyond your own beliefs and understand, appreciate and value the beliefs of others. Only in creating paths that allow the team to work together can you move forward in your expeditions". [116]That's bigger than infinity and beyond; that's universal connection in every sense. Without working together, there is no moving forward.

If NASA, with their galactic mission to "expand the frontiers of knowledge, capability and opportunity in space",[117] emphasize connection as important, then your life of big dreams and Big Impact also needs a Connection Strategy. You'll need to design a plan determining how you'll manage your relationships – intimate, professional, familial, online, IRL (in real life) ... and IRS (in real space) if you're an astronaut!

Relationships are funny old things. We're born into the hands of caregivers who do, or don't do, a good job; we pick up mates along the way who we click with; we avoid repugnant others; at school we get stuck with all sorts; we later get jobs with all sorts; over time we pick faves and build gangs, forming several tribes as we go, sometimes overlapping, sometimes very separate. We find life partners, then maybe divorce them, then maybe repeat twice or thrice more. We pick besties, we later pick new besties to suit the times, we vary levels of intimacy, who we share what with and when. We move onward, sometimes creating our own little people, sometimes lonely, sometimes too popular, sometimes social butterflies, sometimes hibernators. Our relationships are always expanding, contracting, changing and bending as we evolve.

Relationships are dynamic. Absolutely. The relationships we cherish and savour are those that bring us joy, energy and a sense of "home". We're magnetically drawn to each other, and our tribe vibe tends to resonate at a consistent "energetic frequency", with shared interests, humour, age, demography and all that. When you're with your crew, you feel able to be absolutely 100 per cent yourself, no falsehoods required. You also feel it at work when there's an electrifying synergy amid the team. You fuse symbiotically, gelling through shared purpose, combined progressive value, soaring as you work together creating ideas and quality work, which the organization or world needs. You're in flow together, working in unison for the greater good. It feels amazing, moving your expeditions forward in this way.

But relationships aren't guaranteed to always be effortlessly harmonious. Conversely, at times we'll need to work, and perhaps play, with people vibrating very differently from us, and this may create inner tension, the ego reacting defensively. And this is where bad behaviour can emerge, where conversations become battles, progress is stunted and everyone feels out of flow and a bit tired. So, having a strategy around how we connect, and awareness of how others connect, is important, because not to have one is naive and potentially self-limiting.

I believe building a positive personal plan around how you communicate and with whom is critical to Big Impact. Networking is not being calculating and negatively political, it's expansive and exciting. Saying no and negotiating assertively is powerful and directional. Being influential is not manipulative or shameful, it's simply fundamental to having impact. So, in this chapter we're going to build your competencies in making and sustaining relationships. You're going to learn the 101 of communication skills and how to increase your emotional intelligence to connect powerfully. When you conscientiously build a Connection Strategy centered around harmony, oriented toward respectful "win-win for all" situations, and healthy, empathic "listen and be heard" communication, then business, self-esteem and partnerships all flourish. Your time working together, as a happy byproduct, also becomes a lot more fun.

The real benefit of implementing this strategy is that as your confidence to connect increases, you radiate a new magnetism that becomes infectious to others. Your newfound self-belief – that inner balance that was established in part one of this book – and new-found connection clarity (this strategy), contagiously ripple outward, projecting an outer shine, and abundant new and existing connections deepen.

When you hone this strategy, you will find:

1. New interesting friends and peers with fresh perspectives
2. Expanded professional networks yielding stimulating opportunities
3. The ability to consistently create new value with new connections
4. A sense of belonging in different "tribes"
5. Romantic love may also bloom
6. Existing relationships will deepen
7. Impact increases at an accelerated pace
8. A sense of calm around connection eases stress
9. Communication itself becomes an art to be enjoyed

This strategy will contribute to your Big Impact Without Burnout One-Year Master Plan through tactics we'll identify as you complete your reflections, bringing you ever closer to your ambitions through connection genius.

The 101 of Big Impact Communication

We're going to build your connection expertise through four cornerstones of excellent communication:

1. The Art of Communicating to Inspire
2. The Art of Listening and Nurturing
3. The Art of Leadership
4. The Art of Building Your Brand

1. The Art of Communicating to Inspire

Effective communication is essential to impact. All relationships flow and grow, falter and end, depending on how well we communicate. From listening to understand to speaking to inspire, if we don't take the time to consider how we communicate and how we make people feel through our communication, the Big Impact we desire will take longer or may never unfurl. From marriages to colleagues to children to the girl at the checkout, respect the power of positive communication. Let's start with two absolute fundamentals. How do you speak and how do you make people feel?

How Do You Speak?
The way you speak can build authority and trust, has the ability to immediately foster credibility or alter the entire dynamic of an interaction or even a room.

Here are some foundational tips for speaking well:

- Hold eye contact
- Speak clearly and confidently
- Be aware of volume, pace and tone
- Do not shout
- Do not mumble
- Do not interrupt
- Do not swear
- Smile often
- Gesticulate
- Pronounce your vowels and consonants phonetically (slang won't help your career and is unprofessional)
- Own your accent with pride, authenticity is everything
- Hold an open posture with shoulders back, spine erect and neck long (this primes the soft tissue of the pharynx and muscles that elevate the larynx to improve voice control and resonance, thus actually makes speech easier,[118] honestly)
- Breathe steadily to avoid speaking too hastily

How Do You Make People Feel?

The biggest-hearted people leave a warm glow in their wake. Their kind, expansive energy embalms those they encounter with uplifting ripples that linger. We remember their positive essence and forever think fondly of them. As Maya Angelou famously said, "People will forget what you said, people will forget what you did, but people will never forget how you made them feel." I revere this wholeheartedly and live by it.

Beyond the feel-good factor, people who are authentically energizing prove to be the most impactful and desirable souls in business. Their natural disposition infectiously uplifts others, stimulating improved performance, not just in individuals but, by virtuosity, the entire organization.

A 2022 *Harvard Business Review* study found that the greatest predictor of success for leaders is "not their charisma, influence, or power. It is not personality, attractiveness, or innovative genius. The one thing that supersedes all these factors is positive relational energy: the energy exchanged between people that helps uplift, enthuse, and renew them."[119]

In Positive Relational Energy, we're not talking about fluffy, superficial "smile and the world smiles with you" types, but leaders honouring their own values, working with integrity, nurturing the workforce with sincerity, demonstrating emotional intelligence and kind authority. This, the researchers conclude, is the "most underutilized yet powerful predictor of leadership and organizational success."

In our global burnout crisis, employee wellbeing remains at the top of every corporate and personal agenda; hence this very book and important conversation you and I are having right now. There's an acknowledgement that good mental health is a priority for high performance and that positive culture is a core determinant of a flourishing organization. Key to that culture is the necessity for a high proportion of Positive Relational Energy. That energy which uplifts, enthuses and renews.

Think about how you feel at work when you are blanketed with psychological safety. When you are inspired by a colleague or boss exuding a present, giving and invigorating energy, you can't help but brighten and feel more motivated. You want to share an idea, take action, build something, contribute to the big agenda. You come to life and feel infused within their safety and by any excitement they share, as their enthusiasm sparkles contagiously.

Interestingly, the impact of this positive energy stimulates a physical surge as well as a mental boost. Your body responds hormonally with oxytocin release, and at a cellular level, inflammation is reduced, increasing immunity longer term. Extrinsically, the company benefits too, with stats linking a higher proportion of positive energy ambassadors with superior shareholder returns, and outcomes over four times the industry averages in productivity and profitability.

On the flip side, research by UC Irvine professor Sarah Pressman reveals that feeling disconnected relationally, alone and lonely, at work or home, leads to a higher risk of death than smoking or obesity.[120] Seriously.

Unequivocally, we need more Positive Energizers (again, to reiterate, we are not talking about tap-dancing clowns, but values-based, empathetic people). We need more Positive Relational Energy consistently in our lives and businesses. We need to play well together at work to make the work better (and fun). Fundamentally, we need to become aware of how we make others feel by embracing our own inherent ability to skip into the Positive Energizer category. If you're not already there, but want your career, organization and personal happiness to thrive, it's essential you take accountability for the unseen energetic frequency you're radiating, because when you think about it: how do you want to be remembered?

BIG IMPACT REFLECTION: HOW POSITIVE IS YOUR RELATIONAL ENERGY?

Take five minutes immediately after each meeting or significant interaction over the next week to reflect on how your energy and presence impacted the room. Use the following prompts to guide your reflections:

1. Rate your energy level at the start, middle and end of the meeting on a scale of 1–10.
2. What was your language like – positive/negative, inclusive/exclusive?
3. How was your posture and eye contact – engaged or disconnected?
4. What was the quality of your intellectual and emotional contributions?
5. How did your mindset/attitude evolve over the course of the interaction?
6. Did you play a role in setting, changing or improving the mood?
7. How would you rate your overall productivity and the value added?

At the end of the week, review your reflections to identify any patterns. Where did you consistently uplift, enthuse and renew those around you through your energy and presence? Where did you potentially de-energize or disconnect from others? Get specific on one or two areas to improve. Commit to actively working on those areas during all your engagements.

Once you step into consciously playing the role of a Positive Energizer, you'll find more pleasure in your day to day. Just remember, it needs to be 100 per cent from the heart, not fake, or manipulative. Zone into your true self, honouring your value-set and be you. Be your most positive, energizing you. Goal: uplift, enthuse and renew.

2. The Art of Listening and Nurturing

"No one is as deaf as the man who will not listen."

— Jewish proverb

I'll cut straight to it. If you don't listen, you won't succeed. If you don't listen, you won't learn. If you don't listen, you won't connect. If you don't listen, you won't understand. If you don't listen, you will limit yourself, your work, your potential and your team's potential, just by naively thinking it's all about what you want to say. It is not. This is categorically not the case. Deeply listening is the most important skill I advise you to learn to manifest your Big Impact wishes. Listeners get ahead (and go far, in fact).

If you enter a conversation and fill the moment with only your thoughts and your perspectives, what do you imagine will grow in that moment? What will flourish between you and your listener? What are the two of you co-creating? Nothing. A conversation is not a one-way broadcast, it's a two-way interaction. *Co* is the Latin root for "together" and *versare* means "to turn", so the word "conversation" literally means "turning together".

If you are simply using another human to absorb your thoughts, your experiences, opinions, worries, fears, excitements, *yawn, yawn, yawn*, you are exhuming your inner ramblings and not in a conversation. You will quickly lose that person's respect, patience and eventual connection (however interesting you believe your tales and perspectives are).

However, when you actively listen and allow a conversation to flow respectfully in balance, the gold you can turn together can be dazzling. Active listening is the art of listening with the intent to understand. It can be loving, it can be expansive, it can be healing, it can help the other "empty his heart" as Buddhist sage, Thich Nhat Hanh, says of earnest listening. Without a doubt, compassionate, empathic, other-centred listening engenders friendship and respect, and when such authenticity and trust percolate in the business arena colleagues develop meaningful and productive relationships, which facilitate higher quality work.

In habit number five of Stephen Covey's timeless bible, *The 7 Habits of Highly Effective People*, Covey teaches, "Seek first to Understand, then be Understood".[121] Hear, hear (quite literally)! I have doused my children in this lesson since their first utterances. In highlighting listening's importance, Covey outlines, "Most people do not listen with the intent to understand; they listen with the intent to reply." Watch an excited group of teenagers prattle away together to see this in full effect, eagerly-emerging innocent ego selves vying to dominate the babble and launching straight into their oratory, without acknowledgement of the last speaker. As adults, if we fall into this trap of tuning out while we formulate our own response, we will never be fully present with the person sitting in front of us and we limit our chance of fully understanding them. This limitation not only means we jeopardize their sense of feeling heard and valued, and risk the likelihood of a long-term breakdown in connection, but more ominously in business, we will not have the information we need to effectively lead our teams, make informed decisions and collaboratively surge ahead with the work opportunity.

Of course, there are times we need to vent and times we need to patiently listen. Talking therapy is effective and a gift – so often the core gain from a counsellor is simply being heard, and hooray for the beauty of deep friendships, being able to talk and talk and talk without judgement or interruption, then to reciprocate patiently as the listener when crises require. But in general, everyday interactions, too, it's important to herald the sacredness of all conversations. Even the briefest moments of connection – when chatting to your Uber driver, the insurance salesperson running through your options, or your weekly team catchups – are all opportunities to notice another, to open your heart and mind and connect.

A tremendous amount of research has demonstrated the impact and power of listening. From meditative awareness of the other, to organizational benefits like stronger relationships, greater trust, more effective team collaborations, enhanced decision-making, more prolific creativity and innovation, and ultimately, more consistent, greater productivity.[122] It unequivocally makes sense to listen and train listening as core to that sense of psychological safety employees need to feel better able to express themselves at work.

Psychological safety is "broadly defined as a climate in which people are comfortable expressing and being themselves",[123] according to author Amy C Edmondson in *The Fearless Organization: Creating Psychological Safety in the Worplace for Learning, Innovation, and Growth*. Once people feel safe, they are comfortable sharing mistakes or flagging concerns without fear of embarrassment or retribution. There's a confidence to ask questions, be braver, speak up and work harder.

Séverine Charbon, International Chief Talent Officer for Publicis Groupe, which includes over 85,000 employees across 100 countries, has devoted over two decades to building up a culture consistently infused with such safety. She says, "Active listening by managers has been one of my favourite cornerstones for creating an environment of psychological safety for many years now, decades even! We meticulously track the impact it has and consistently validate how it unlocks super performance and talent retention." If listening is proven effective as a strategy across a vast global workforce, it can most certainly be effective for us individually. It's all logical; when we feel heard, validated and valued we want to contribute more, so we should take strides to exemplify this in our efforts toward Big Impact.

When we listen primarily to understand, to fully intone what is being shared with us, we open up new levels of insight potential. When we concentrate fully on the person speaking before us, we learn more than just the words being spoken. In Mehrabian's Rule, psychology professor Albert Mehrabian observed that only 7 per cent of meaning is communicated through spoken word, with 38 per cent through tone of voice, and 55 per cent through body language. It's why you can understand the gist of what a foreigner is saying, despite the language being entirely unfamiliar. Mehrabian's studies evidenced that no matter what a person is saying, if their expressions, tone and body language don't match up, the person listening instinctively won't trust them as credible. So, when we're actively listening, the visual cues – the posture, the eye movements, the gesticulations, the "vibe" – all convey rich clues to what is truly being said. This applies to video interactions as well as those in real life. Becoming attuned to reading the entirety of what the other person is sharing truly expands the moment.

In 2010, Marina Abramović showcased her deeply engaging exhibition, "The Artist is Present", at New York's Museum of Modern Art. Exploring themes of presence, endurance, the power of the gaze and silence itself, Abramović sat, regal and still, for 75 days, inviting visitors to sit opposite her, be with her and simply stare into her eyes, without words, movement or physical contact. She sat for 736 hours and 30 minutes. In this beautiful and touching modern art, invisible chords crackled between the artist and voyeur and, watching the numerous recordings online, whether young or old, emotional or stony, the connections are visceral and powerful. Her lost love from 20 years prior turned up unexpectedly and their tears and raw emotion captured on film remain one of the most intimate scenes I've ever witnessed. Google "Abramović and Ulay" and try not to cry.

The point is that by gaze and presence alone, communication is possible. Connection is possible. Words aren't necessary to create connection. Words are of course pretty useful in cutting to the chase and for relationships generally, but there's a grace to sensing the entirety of a person beyond their words. It's also rather effortless when communicating with body and soul, devoid of aural language. There's no pushing against anything, nor resorting to any complexity of rhetoric. In a silent state, body and soul can still be communicating organically and easily, no stress, far from burnout, simply sharing energy. Ethereal and yet powerful. So, experiment in conversation, try listening with your eyes and ears, as the children's rainbow song goes.

When I met former Chief Inclusion, Culture & Wellbeing Officer at PwC Sarah Churchman OBE, we discussed the importance of listening throughout her career and she described it as an "underutilized superpower", telling me, "I'm a firm believer in making our own luck and creating our own opportunities. Something I wish I'd learned way earlier on in my career is that by listening hard, respectfully and intently, you can identify what matters most to whom and thus work out how you can have more personal impact quickest. It's such a simple way to accelerate your value to an organization or team."

When you establish your reputation as one of a listener, more people want to spend time with you. Listeners are attractive because human nature is such that we feel validated when we are heard. We don't necessarily want everyone to agree with us always, but when we express how we feel, especially when experiencing suffering or anxiety, another's acknowledgement legitimizes our sentiments.

Validation is essential to rapport. The minute we feel substantiated and truly seen by another, we feel connection and trust builds. Trust is further strengthened by a sense of mutual interest and credible competence i.e., I won't just scratch your back and you scratch mine, but I'll show you how I scratch and you can show me your way and together we'll work out how to scratch better and be the best back scratchers around. Add a blend of consistency, showing up the same way, doing the same thing repeatedly – "My speciality is the upper left shoulder section", and transparency – "Yikes, I'm nervous about scratching too hard", and there's a solid relationship base afoot. From this solidity, where respect, empathy, trust and validation predominate, a relationship can cement, and two become three – you, them and The Relationship.

BIG IMPACT REFLECTION: BUILDING RAPPORT

In your next conversation, consciously practise rapport-building techniques. Before speaking, observe the other person's body language, tone, and energy level. As they talk, mirror their posture, gestures, and volume while maintaining positive eye contact. Instead of planning what to say next, focus intently on listening and allowing them to fully express themselves without judgement. Occasionally paraphrase their points to confirm understanding. Ask follow-up questions that demonstrate empathy and a desire to see their perspective. Notice if you feel a connection developing through matched energy levels and a conversational flow. After the interaction, journal about what rapport-building techniques came naturally versus which ones required more conscious effort. Reflect on how prioritizing active listening and seeking to understand the other person impacted the quality of your connection. Identify areas for continued practice in an authentic, respectful way that facilitates trust and mutual engagement.

Nurturing Relationships

I came home from school one afternoon to find my mother ushering me toward the phone to talk to my father. This was an unusual situation. I was nine years old and my generation was most definitely not phone savvy.

I held the receiver and tentatively said, "Hello, Daddy", aghast at the sheer awkwardness of the moment. My father asked how my day was and I probably mumbled for a few moments, monosyllabic and shy; then he asked a question that has loomed over me ever since: "Aren't you going to ask me how I am?" I blushed with shame, then indeed asked him, and he explained he'd been in a near-fatal car accident and was calling from his hospital bed (having survived with concussion and a few scrapes, hence the provocative joviality). From that moment on, I have never, ever answered the phone nor called anyone without earnestly asking, "How are you?", and deeply, intensely meaning it.

Now, I may have micro-traumatic reasons for embracing this, but think about how you feel when someone calls you to monologue at you and doesn't get round to asking you about you? Or when you call them to check in and they don't check back? Or when you're in the office on Monday morning, bursting with news of your weekend, and nobody asks how it was? Or when a "friend" sends a "Hope you are well" message, hurtfully missing the compassion of a question mark. The basic human etiquette of reciprocally checking in on one another is one of the easiest, loveliest way to share that you care. It's decent human kindness, and whether personal or professional, it's super important. So, in honour of my father or indeed general decorum, ask people how they are, please. And mean it.

EXPANSION EXERCISE: HOW ARE YOU?

Play the HAY game for two weeks. Start *every* conversation – phone, text or email –with HAY: How Are You. You ask, then listen. Every meeting, every video call, every quick chat with your partner, or your kids, or the gang, or your mum – HAY – ask, listen, repeat. Even if it's a stranger in a call centre, or the colleague who irritates you, or the teacher who just gave your child a detention unfairly, stick with the game. At the end of the two weeks, grab your journal and reflect on how relationships have evolved through the lens of your Positive Relational Energy – did you uplift, enthuse and renew? What happened to the energy in that conversation and the relationship across the weeks? How did you feel? How did they respond? Do you feel a shift in your overall positivity after this experiment? Will this be your de facto start to interactions henceforth? NB: If you have colleagues, even a manager, friends, or whomever, who don't make space for this and launch directly into conversation, interrupt and say, "First things first, how are you?" Reflect on what happens to relationships and work after this two-week period.

Beyond greetings, generally there's a purpose to an interaction and a reason this person is in our lives, however fleetingly. The people orbiting you usually satisfy a personal, professional, social or developmental function, ranging from emotional support to community belonging, to career progress, to life practicalities, to knowledge sharing, innovation and value creation, to mentoring and more. There are limitless potentials to the different individuals and groups we intermingle with. What scientists do tell us, whether our networks comprise happy-makers or otherwise, is that we are influenced by these groups, and up to three degrees of separation. In other words, friends of friends of friends can influence us.

"Network effects" refers to how influenced we are by our networks in an unconscious way and their impact has exploded since technology made social connections instantaneous and prolific. Our networks supposedly shape our behaviours, from how we dress to rates of divorce, contentment levels, obesity levels or likelihood of smoking.[124] More and more studies demonstrate an unseen power of interconnectivity whereby as personal a choice as a friend's health habits might shape ours (or their friend's friend even), and a collective emotional pulse may subtly cascade throughout a group. Whether we're aware of it or not, we're being influenced.

This also means that we have the option to choose how we're influenced by choosing which networks we're part of. When we acknowledge that our tribes can bring us down or lift us up, hold us back or encourage us to soar, we can choose to reorient our groups in accordance with our aspirations i.e., surround ourselves with people conscientiously. Many of my clients have this epiphany when they hit milestone life moments. They suddenly find confidence to veer away from people and networks they no longer feel fit them. You began an element of this energy-zapper, people-draining cleansing as part of your Time Strategy, now let's expand this through the lens of our impact.

The impact of our work, and by default our very essence, will ideally ripple positively, our substance recognized. We want our impact to course outward because we've got value to share with the world. We've established that the people who are most valuable in business uplift, enthuse and renew. We've established that networks influence up or down. So, looking at the map of network effects, we simply need to identify who we wish to influence, who we're happy being influenced by, and begin our two-way up-levelling. When we begin this cascade of positivity, it's not about influence without substance but about spreading value. What can you bring that is of benefit?

A Focus on Giving

At work, the most successful business leaders are what Adam Grant calls givers. In his book, *Give and Take: Why Helping Others Drives Our Success*, he categorizes people into givers, takers and matchers. He explains: "Whereas takers strive to get as much as possible from others and matchers aim to trade evenly, givers are the rare breed of people who contribute to others without expecting anything in return."[125]

- **Takers** think about themselves primarily and always, choosing only to help others when the effort of the personal cost (financial or energetic) will be of strategic benefit.
- However, **givers** naturally help others, and especially whenever the impact for the other extends beyond their own personal cost. They are innately all heart.
- Then we have the **matchers**, who desire balance and an equality between what's given and received. Mutual reciprocity is their mantra.

None of us are ever fixed in one behavioural default and, in fact, giving, taking and matching are standard ways we interact. Our dominant style may alter as we traverse different life situations, tasks and relationships. For instance, you may be a giver when coaching a colleague into negotiating her promotion salary, in more of a taker mode when settling a redundancy package, and a matcher when sharing teatime cooking tips with a friend.

What's especially compelling about Grant's work, and relevant to this book's theme, is that while givers are the most prosperous, highest impact people, they sit at the low end of the success scale as well as at the top. The low-end givers trip themselves up by being too selfless, giving away too much of themselves, thus eventually forsaking their own achievement through burnout. Meanwhile, the top-end givers win at work and life, surrounded by well-earned cheerleaders propelling them further upward still. The gold-star, top-end givers may appear less altruistic than selfless low-end givers on the surface, but they have better propensity to be consistently productive and their resilience against burnout enables them to contribute more.

So, when thinking about how we engage with others, it's far healthier to behave generously with the stance of a giver, for our own benefit as much as for the recipient and potentially the organization. We can influence our own destiny and impact this way. As Grant explains: "Every time we interact with another person at work, we have a choice to make: do we try to claim as much value as we can, or contribute value without worrying about what we receive in return?"

Maintaining your network and building your own reputational credibility comes down to how consistently and usefully you serve others. Instead of focusing purely on sales and getting what you want, lean into a mindset shift of building long-term relationships rich in integrity and authenticity based on giving. Indeed, as the fun and pragmatic *Squiggly Careers* authors and podcasters, Helen Tupper and Sarah Ellis, describe networking, it's simply "people helping people"!

So, give generously with these key principles:

- Be reliable – prove your trustworthiness by always honouring your word.
- Share useful knowledge – inspire the relationship with your experience and expertise.
- Exchange ideas – be innovative and don't covet your own ideas.
- Suggest proactively – generosity of time and effort is always gratefully received.
- Surprise and delight – someone who stands out as being thoughtful is rarely forgotten.
- Connect people – make useful introductions.
- Have substance – ensure you contribute meaningfully.

When you consistently add value to people and groups, a natural symbiosis occurs where the value pings back to you and newer levels of collaborative value are created. You all start to elevate each other. The work gets better, you get better and the impact potential swells; the ripple becomes a wave.

My dear colleague, co-workshop host, best-selling author and podcaster, Rishad Tobaccowala, writes about the power of community in his book *Restoring the Soul of Business*, inviting us to "think about community as a forum for storytelling in the broadest definition of that term".[126] He speaks of the "multiple stories of an organizational community providing people with common language, ideas and personalities, offering a narrative of which they are part." He's right. We need our tribes, our networks, to feel a sense of belonging and shared meaning.

No matter how powerful the belonging though, giving doesn't always feel easy, especially in our modern world of distributed workplaces. Although we yearn for community – shared gyms, workspaces, and so on – a significant detrimental impact of such a high proportion of working society living in constant stress states is that stress generally makes people more insular, suspicious and uninteresting. I met neuroscientist Hannah Critchlow, author of *Joined-Up Thinking*, to discuss the impact of stress on our sense of belonging, and she told me, "Numerous studies have shown that fearful people struggle to empathize with others and plan for the future," reiterating her point with the fact that war tactics similarly deliberately demoralize and exhaust people.

She explained that when bodies and brains are trapped in survival mode, they are so focused on immediate threat that "they've no chance of contributing to any project beyond that". She's suggesting a collective push to legislate boundaries around the toxic pull of digital media as part of her important work on technology's impact on society. Her work also emphasizes to me once again the necessity for us, individually as well as collectively, to minimize our stress responses, avert the threat of burnout, and stay in our optimal, homeostatic state, but this time to be able to connect well, if at all!

Bonnie Marcus advises in her book, *The Politics of Promotion*, that relationships with colleagues, mentors, sponsors and allies aren't just for fun times, but are crucial components of career success. Developing and massaging strong professional networks is not dirty politics but smart business sense as our connections provide us with support, guidance and opportunities. All of this escalates potential advancement and our all-important impact. So, yes, while we focus on the giving, we inadvertently (well, okay, perhaps tactically) receive too. "Political skills are essential career competencies to get ahead and stay ahead", Marcus says. See, not dirty! Political mastery also includes your level of pride and self-awareness, so that you're comfortable sharing your value and confident you are being additive when you distribute your wares. Marcus states that, "When you feel good about the value you offer ... communicating and demonstrating your value to others is much easier."[127] Basically, believe in your own substance and shout about it strategically.

Learning from my tripart career experience, operating within the corporate realm, and as an entrepreneur and a creator, I advise a blend of self-advocacy and visibility – observe workplace or industry dynamics, be clear who is making decisions relevant to you and your work, who you need on side or whose attention you seek to attract, and ensure they know categorically what you're achieving and how. We'll work on your personal brand building later in this chapter. In terms of any office or industry in-fighting (dirty), stay out, remain in your integrity and focus unwaveringly on the business agenda (never forgetting that saving your energy by investing attention in what matters most, i.e. your Big Impact goals, is the top priority in avoiding burnout).

In general, find your tribes, enjoy your network, lean into relevant circles, nurture them and be buoyed as they nurture you right back. There are abundant industry WhatsApp groups, networking events, work initiatives and ways to connect like never before, so strategize your "Who's" and get giving. Once within your circle, respect and revere it. Don't gossip, don't blame, don't make it all about you. And never forget the adage, "We're the average of the five people we spend the most time with." What does your best average look like? Let's strategize through a Big Impact Reflection ...

BIG IMPACT REFLECTION:
CULTIVATING YOUR UPLIFTING CIRCLES

Step 1: Mapping your current networks

1. Make a list of the different groups, communities and circles you are currently part of (work, friends, family, hobbies, online, etc.).
2. For each group, reflect on how the group/network makes you feel – uplifted or drained? What value are you giving and receiving from this circle? Is this an environment that aligns with your values and aspirations?
3. Identify one or two groups that energize you the most and have the most positive impact.

Step 2: Envision your ideal circles

1. Write a description of what your "best average" circle would look like. What values, mindsets and behaviours would the people embody?
2. Are there any existing groups that come close to this ideal? If not, what type of new circle could you join or create?
3. Make a plan for how you can spend more time engaging with and contributing value to your current uplifting circles.
4. Brainstorm three ways you can be a positive force who uplifts others in these groups through your actions.

Step 3: Uplevel your commitment

1. Within your ideal circles, what guidelines will you follow to respect the community e.g. no gossip, blame, self-centredness, etc.?
2. Write an affirmation, stating your commitment to being a source of positive energy who gives generously to your circles.
3. Set a calendar reminder to review this exercise regularly (ideally monthly) and readjust as needed to cultivate circles aligned with your "Big Impact Without Burnout" self.

Remember, the company we keep has a profound impact on our mindset, motivation and momentum. By cultivating circles that inspire you to grow while allowing you to contribute your work (and gifts!), you amplify your ability to create positive ripples of influence for even greater impact. Visualize yourself in these circles, happy, gracefully productive and ever-expanding.

3. The Art of Leadership

As your confidence in your abilities, your work and the robustness of your relationships grows, you step into a place of effortless leadership. In this role of a leader (of your life and your work), you hold huge sway, able to influence many things around you, from who buys your product, to who works with you, to where you'll raise your family, to which holiday you book, to if you get promoted, to how high a pay rise you negotiate and more. You start to significantly determine your destiny. Influence matters.

Let's distinguish influence from manipulation. Influence is effective persuasion. While manipulation is underhand, influence is ethical, authentic and empowering. Quirkily, the word has heavenly origins relating to "celestial fluid", which apparently flowed down from the stars, influencing the behaviour of Earth's inhabitants. Today defined as the "power to change or affect someone or something",[128] influence connotes the power to effect change but not command it. When harnessed well, influence should be positive, contributory and another one of your core foundations for impact. If you can't sweep others along with your divine celestial fluid, then your ideas and your potential will stagnate. When you spend time honing your skills as an influencer, as every YouTuber, Insta star and TikTok sensation evidence, you hold another golden key to success.

Once people trust you because you have given value to them and rapport is established, influence becomes easier. Influence further expands when what and how we communicate satisfies a need in our listener (perhaps as yet unidentified by themselves), factoring in the nuances of desire and lack that underpin much of human behaviour. Working in the advertising industry, as I do, we are acutely aware of the privilege and delicacy of the latter. There are rigorous safety standards in place to protect audiences from misinformation or offensive content. When compliant and working optimally, advertising can be world-alteringly powerful.

Effective advertising appeals to psychological principles and biases, artfully creating lack to stimulate desire. For example, "Oh you've had a rubbish day? You need a bubble bath and some of our smooth, melty chocolate." It works. We do start to associate a tough workday with luxuriating in the bath, gobbling chocolate. Subliminally or overtly, we become programmed by the messaging and trust the brand doing the advertising to meet our needs.

This extends into your business strategy. Ensure your product, service, or you as an individual, meets a highlighted (or even created) need. Call out the problem you solve, the gap you fill (even if that gap wasn't obvious to others in the first place) and then list the features and benefits, spotlighting why you're the only one who can do this, your product the leading one on the market, your method uniquely suited, etc. Your knowledge of the questions your potential customers, audience, boss, colleagues or clients are asking themselves – what is keeping them up at night – means you can tailor your messaging aligned with their interests and values to penetrate their hearts as well as minds. Blend the emotional with the rational and you're well on your way to effective influence. This is called framing.

Clever Framing

Don't just limit this artistry to pitching products or services, really think about the optimal framing of every message you convey. Think of framing as the "magical stuff" that determines people's experiences and how they think. Zoe Chance, author of *Influence is Your Superpower*, believes in its mysticism explaining: "Framing is how spellcasting works in the real world. Just by describing something or giving it a name, you called it into being. A well-chosen frame can determine what's relevant, what's important, or what's good. When you frame someone's experience in a compelling way, you shape their expectations as well as their interpretation of events."[129]

This can manifest through words, as simply as adding an adjective to provide nuance – my "excellent" end of year review, your "fascinating" research or the "slow" project –to more exponentially in singular words – a "movement" as opposed to a campaign, "team" versus group, "leader" versus manager and so on. Setting scenes and context, describing problems evocatively with emotional embellishment means that when you suggest your product/service/you as the solution, it's a no-brainer and your spell has indeed been cast.

You need to do the work to know your frame down to the miniscule details. You must know your product, your customers, your value, your solutions, why you matter, why you're valuable, and organize your framing to reflect this, inside and out. Only once you radiate this with clarity and power do you become a magnet for opportunity. You must be proactive about positioning your work and yourself.

When You Hear "No", Opportunity Beckons ...

If, despite your witchy wonder-spell being cast, you don't hear "yes", but instead a disappointing "no", stay in your zone of self-belief and persist. Ask again. Ask: why not? Ask, what Chance calls the magic question: "What would it take?" Asking this invites collusion to create a way of moving forward together (indeed, "turning together", as we've already learned, that's how the best conversations flow). Or as Karren Brady told me defiantly, "I'm the sort of person who doesn't hear the word 'no'. I hear 'find another way to get what you want."

A "no" can be an invitation for creativity and fresh thinking, a moment to pursue different paths. My client Charlie is a mid-level manager who is single, coolly nomadic in her friendship groups and eclectic in style. She and I had been addressing her challenge of "finding more enjoyment at work". She had come to me for professional coaching, apparently open to improving things in her current role or moving up and out in the pursuit of enjoyable work. Over many weeks, we had explored her values, her skills, her strengths, her peak experiences, strategized her own reframes, peacefully surrendered to what she couldn't change, made adjustments where she could, worked on deepening self-awareness, designing life purpose and connecting to an inspiring vision, but still Charlie felt stuck. And so did I.

In one of our last sessions together, we worked through yet another live scenario where Charlie bemoaned the team, the unfair workload, the manager, the structure, the time it would take for her organizational strategies to take effect and so on. I asked her to consider the unknown: the potential of other roles, other industries, other countries, and she defensively slammed me down. She couldn't risk job hunting as that was too painful, too terrifying and she was not prepared to even discuss it conceptually. I held out my palms, upturned like a scale, weighing her current job on the left against her world of opportunity on the right. I invited her to use her heart to consider the emotions and energy seesawing on either side of the scales and to choose which side felt lighter and more appealing. She shook her head and said, "Neither. They're both horrendous."

I realized in that moment that Charlie was in a deep, melancholic, long-term depression and didn't require career coaching but professional psychotherapy or psychiatry. I suspected she had childhood wounds around a fear of rejection and starkly absent self-worth. We started discussing the roots of her self-dislike, born from a tough upbringing with dysfunctional caregivers, and met one final time to discuss her inner work required before we could continue her professional coaching. She then found a therapist. We remain in contact and I'm proud of her bravery. For me, it was one of those moments when two options – both "no" and "no" – signalled that an entirely new approach was needed.

Becoming comfortable with "no" as a route to opportunity makes "no" empowering. As you release any fear of hearing "no", you gain the freedom to ask for things. You can probably recall lots of times in your life a door was shut in your face and you were devastated at the time, but in hindsight it was the right thing. Somehow, a "no" generally does always work out for the best. We grow from every "no".

Influencing Win-Win

When a "no" needs to be "yes" for the success of your business, middle-ground has to be negotiated. The most adept leaders recognize that it doesn't have to always be a zero-sum game with one winner and one loser; it is possible to create a win-win, and that denotes what I call success with integrity. You do not need to, nor should you, crush others for your own gain. Conversely, making inroads toward your own gain will feel all the more satisfying when you bring others along with you as part of a mutually supportive and progressive system. Back to our old buddy Mr Stephen Covey who emphasizes win-win as a cornerstone of high-trust relationships stating, "Win/Win is not a personality technique. It's a total paradigm of human interaction. It comes from a character of integrity, maturity and the Abundance Mentality."[130] Win-win quite literally wins the day because it arises from respect for each other's viewpoints. Refusing to consider another's position or perspective narrows your ability as a leader. If you rigidly say "no" with a "my way or the highway" stance, you will rapidly lose respect, hamper your influence and diminish your authority. Remember that a negotiation should be a conversation where you listen, understand and progress. Negotiate well by clarifying beliefs and expectations on both sides, without refuting either stance, but rather respecting each other's bearing and seeking to achieve mutual accomplishment.

It's also worth exploring what negotiation consultants call the BATNA, your Best Alternative to a Negotiated Agreement. This is a strong alternative route that enables you to walk away from a deal that doesn't meet your needs or that would compromise your vision or ethics into something that wasn't even on the table originally. This could definitely be worth considering having up your sleeve if you're ever in a stalemate situation. My recommendation for Charlie to seek therapy was my BATNA when the scales just wouldn't balance and I needed a new option entirely. To practise this alternative negotiation strategy, clearly define the "walk away" conditions where you would pursue your BATNA instead of settling. Strengthen your BATNA by lining up other opportunities or fallback plans. This gives you more leverage and confidence in negotiations. When faced with an unsatisfactory proposal, calmly restate your requirements. If they cannot be met, be prepared to respectfully walk away toward your BATNA rather than accept something that diminishes your ability to create maximum impact. Having a strong alternative path prevents you from feeling forced into an agreement that doesn't align with your goals. Stay in your Big Impact power!

Emotionally Aware Leadership

Influence through effective leadership, with all its subsets of trust, framing, negotiation and so on, comes down to emotional intelligence (known as EQ, for Emotional Quotient). Successful leaders have both self-awareness and social awareness. They know how to manage relationships and themselves. The four skills shared below constitute EQ and are the most sought-after interpersonal skills in the workplace. In fact, "71 per cent of employers value emotional intelligence more than technical skills when evaluating candidates".[131] High EQ is the strongest predictor of performance, and according to the good old *Harvard Business Review*, "Employees with high emotional intelligence are more likely to stay calm under pressure, resolve conflict effectively, and respond to co-workers with empathy." When delicately intertwined, these EQ skills affect leadership prowess.

1. Self-awareness
2. Self-management
3. Social awareness
4. Relationship management

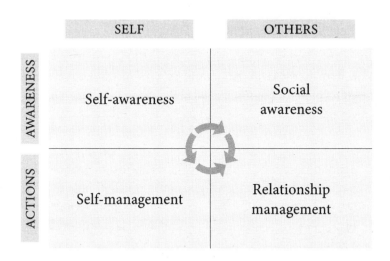

BIG IMPACT REFLECTION: EMOTIONAL INTELLIGENCE SKILLS FOR BIG IMPACT CONNECTION

Reflect on how you perceive your current level of EQ. Consider your self-awareness, self-regulation, motivation, empathy and relationships management skills and how they have manifested at work over the past week. Reflect on when you've demonstrated high EQ and the impact of those moments, then think of examples where you could have been more effective leveraging skillful EQ. Hone your reflections into a specific skill you choose to work on over the coming week and specify how you'll practise it. Envisage yourself operating with high EQ, being the best leader you know yourself to be.

Knowing your strengths and skills and when to build a support network around you to empower improved delivery is essential to scaling your impact. Even a lone artist will eventually need a broad team to enable maximum exposure of her art if she seeks to commercialize her talents, be it via artwork sales, teaching or similar. However much you may prefer not to manage people, if you run your own business, are a freelancer or a cog in a corporate wheel, at some point, you can't do it all alone and nor should you. Being adept at working with your assistant or direct report requires social awareness and relationship management. As a general rule, "Do unto others as you would have done unto you" and foster Positive Relational Energy, embracing EQ as much as feels natural.

It is helpful to regularly invite feedback to learn how your leadership can be improved. Trust that feedback is a gift to both receive and give generously. Too many people confuse feedback with criticism and withhold it. My advice: share feedback immediately, kindly, openly and, if negative, address the mismatch of expectations and what could be remedied next time. If positive, frame the praise with specific examples. When seeking feedback, send out surveys, ask your coworkers, manager, team. Talk to your manager as a peer, respectfully asking for feedback while sharing self-reflections. Don't complain, ever, but share your ideas, excitement and any hesitations. This vulnerability builds huge respect and connection. I've never seen it fail.

My client Kitty is a hard-working, delightful soul. She is always over-delivering and super ambitious. She lacked self-confidence, however, and was extremely nervous of senior business leaders. Our success strategizing focused on establishing her inner sense of capability and credibility, reaffirming her well-evidenced business impact within her organization, to prepare her for promotion. She was locked in a self-created need to be perfect, never wanting to disappoint, and she never felt quite good enough. We worked on facts not emotions, listing out her large budget allocation to build a bigger team, senior management invitation to lead a global workstream, her fantastic 360 review scores and more. We then explored Kitty's fear scenarios – examining all the potentials that could happen if she had an honest, expansive conversation with her manager. Eventually, she felt courageous and prepared enough to discuss her future with her boss. In this conversation, she opened up enthusiastically about her ideas for business expansion, her contribution, which she observed had already proved powerful and why, the ways she recognized the organization was flourishing in her division, and bravely expressed where she felt perhaps she could have led a pillar better than a colleague. She leaned in, elbows on the table, thoughts professionally shared, all with an agenda of growth. And you know what? Her boss leaned right back into the conversation, sharing her own career highs and lows, responding to Kitty's ideas with intrigue and elaboration, and best of all, she shared exactly why she saw Kitty as a rising star. Kitty expressed her nervousness at her inadequacy, lacking certain skills a colleague held, and her boss explained that was by design, two complementary skill sets, and that Kitty held exactly the talents the business needed and to focus on strengthening those instead. Within weeks of that conversation, Kitty had been promoted. Bravery combined with vulnerability creates positive progress.

Kitty demonstrated genuine humility here. She was self-aware, self-reflective and self-confident while still being humble. This is a noble, emotionally intelligent skill and what is often referred to as values-based leadership. Balancing confidence with genuine humility is a surefire way to lead organizations and teams effectively. It's also a beautiful recipe for impact grounded in authenticity.

4. The Art of Building Your Brand

When I consider CVs, the first thing I do is click on the candidate's LinkedIn profile, and if it doesn't engage me instantly, I'm out. Without a clear photo and intriguing profile description, I move on. You are your own brand, and as we know in today's rapid-fire attention economy, you only have mere seconds to attract attention and keep it. The best CV I received recently had a large headline across the top and also cleverly down the side, stating, "I'M A STORYTELLER". A good story she told, and she now works for me. I was hooked from the get-go.

That's the premise of brand-building – hook your audience. Once they're hooked, then you hit them with your USP. In marketing, we use hooks for every campaign, tailoring the message to the audience, feeling for the mood and moment that matters. Precision targeting and dynamic creative optimization means that in digital advertising we can test and learn exactly who responds to what best. And so it is with the brand of You; you can experiment with what resonates with your target audience, be they online shoppers, the board in your organization or a wider industry cohort.

Let's look at the ways to build your brand and establish your reputational credibility:

- **In your company**

Within a corporate environment, networking effectively to raise your profile means ensuring your latest accomplishments are known by everyone who needs to be aware of them (i.e. internal decision makers and influencers). Don't be shy to share your progress, learnings, successes, challenges and outcomes. Senior leaders are always interested in business intel, good or bad, and rely on staff to share the ins and outs of what's going on. If you have the privilege of someone senior's ear, share constructive information, especially if it relates to your proactive, impactful work. Do not assume anyone else will be informing them on your behalf; take the helm yourself. Promote yourself, usefully not boastfully.

- **In your industry**

Within an industry, turn your work into insights for the sector and create useful content from your products, services, experiences and so on. There is gold in your every day and when you package it up with a flourish, creating interesting, entertaining and high-quality digital content, online media audiences lap it up. Practise varying types of content from video to graphic, long form to short, TikTok to Facebook, LinkedIn to X, experiment again and again. And remember once again, please, to always be useful not boastful.

- **In the wider world**

As a personal brand is becoming an evermore effective way to gain opportunities and achieve far-reaching impact, don't limit yourself to your immediate networks or industries. Strategize ways to break into new sectors. There is more cross-pollination of sectors today where "old" news in one sector lands as "fresh" in another. So, seek novel ways to bring You and Your Work, your brand, into new landscapes. For example, while my professional industries are advertising, writing and coaching, I will break into management consultancy, finance and legal sectors to penetrate areas with highest burnout cases as I trust my skills as relevant. I've also struck partnerships with venues like Soho House, moving into hospitality, to do book readings, with catering businesses like The Best Ever Brownie Company to cocreate bespoke Big Impact goodies, and so on. There are always creative ways to take your brand into new, invigorating spaces.

BIG IMPACT REFLECTION: 10 STEPS TO BUILD YOUR BRAND

Here are ten steps to building and promoting the brand of You like a precision-targeted ad campaign hooking people in, considering both yourself *and* your work.

Step 1: Know your audience and key decision-makers – who they are, what their problems are and how you are solving them, where they are (in the organization or industry), what they currently think, what they want to think, what they currently feel, what they want to feel, what values they respect, what media they consume or who they listen to, what interests them or keeps them up at night, what they need, their demographics, etc.

Step 2: Define your brand (do this for You and Your Work) – your mission, values, passions, strengths, expertise, USP (unique selling proposition), distinguishing factors from the competition or your peers, experience, awards, client logos, testimonials, etc.

Step 3: Analyse the competition – who else is playing in your field or organization or going for the same interview, etc.? How do they show up, what are they doing well/not so well, what could be done better, etc.?

Step 4: Create your unique brand identity (again, for You and Your Work) – develop a style, colour palette, mood board, social profiles, website, marketing collateral, events programme, etc., using cohesive visual elements to reinforce your bespoke essence. If you're building an internal corporate reputation, be clear on the strengths, projects and impact you want to be known for (it's okay to include your sphere of influence; networking ability is valuable too!).

Step 5: Build your promotional plan – what messages to share with whom, how and when, including online presence and in-person events, speaking gigs, workshops, writing a book, etc. Internally, be strategic with "catchups" and how and when you share useful and relevant information.

Step 6: Allocate budget (and/or time) – invest in design and build of website, social assets, marketing material, exhibitions, travel, networking and for paid advertising and/or marketing support. Internally, allocate time to execute your Connection Strategy for Big Impact.

Step 7: Launch with a bang across all platforms and networks simultaneously with online and offline promotion plus verbal communication.

Step 8: Maintain visibility with your chosen audiences – updating social feeds and/or intranets with thought pieces, points of view, useful content, client testimonials, videos, blogs, reminders of your unique take on the world, as well as raising your profile by speaking on panels, at conferences, hosting workshops in corporates, schools, etc.

Step 9: Stay authentically you in tone of voice and always be current – audiences are cynical and discerning so be yourself. Keep updating your profiles and online presence with latest awards, service offerings, etc.

Step 10: Keep testing audience reactions and adjust types of content, style of content and advertising platforms.

For more templates and collateral to build your digital marketing funnel, from "acquisition" of new customers to "conversion" through organic or paid advertising, download some examples I've created from my own strategies at biancabest.com.

Tips for Online Brand Building

Brand voice: Don't try to be funny if you're not. Don't try too hard as it will come across as inauthentic. Always try to ground yourself in the service of others. What is the intention of your content? It should be to serve in some way, whether informative or entertaining. If you're really uncomfortable, hire an agency or freelancer to manage your social feeds for you and depersonalize your content away from you as the star of your brand, focusing solely on your branded products and services or your work itself.

Measurement: Ensure analytics and a rigorous measurement strategy are part of your brand building plans. As Peter Drucker's wisdom (apparently the most widely used business quote ever) goes, "If you can't measure it, you can't manage it."[132] Be clear on what you want to measure and set your own KPIs, targeting precisely what success means for you. For example, how many newsletter sign ups, daily website visitors, book sales, etc. Track your conversion funnel from paid media through to customers landing on your website, to how they navigate through your website (even analyse what they type into your site search bar if you have one) and work out what influences a higher "conversion" per whatever you have defined as a conversion, such as an online membership sale or Facebook video ad full view (watching the full 30 seconds).

Optimization: Optimize your strategy toward your goals and consistently deliver per your schedule daily, weekly, monthly, constantly monitoring what is or isn't working and adjusting creative designs, reallocating budgets to other media or digital platforms, flowing your messaging to different target audiences to suit your marketing objectives. Never stop improving your performance. It's one of the blessings of our modern marketing age that we can indeed measure and accelerate goal conversion in real time.

Build demand: Creating scarcity is a powerful tactic for driving conversion – 80 per cent sold out, limited time offer, and so on. So, when promoting your event, or online course, or your availability, the less accessible, the more appealing. Scarcity increasing value upward is not only an economic principle, but also a powerful behavioural bias, where our brains allocate a premium to the value of an item based on its level of rarity or unavailability. Crazy consumers that we are! There's also a funky decision trio you can leverage – offer three price points, from low to high. Psychology dictates that people will generally take the mid-point (so make this your desired sale price, the other two are tactical only). Too many options drive customers away, only one option is too starkly a "take it or leave it" decision, but three truly is the magic number; it seems to not overwhelm, gives consumers a sense of control and the majority will opt for the mid-point.

Nudge: You can also play with nudging tactics like the all too familiar online check-out basket reminder "Did you forget Pringles?" when you do a supermarket shop. Or by leveraging social proof, "32 sold in the last hour", or authoritative endorsements by leading experts, celebrities or effusive customers. Keep trialling to see what builds trust and encourages a relationship with a customer.

As any entrepreneur or creator knows, running your own show is time-consuming and you're "always on", so anything that alleviates the intensity of it all will reduce the threat of burnout. Approaching all of the above essential yet laborious marketing tactics will feel easier and more energizing when being yourself. Authentic content, created from the heart, aligned with your aims and grounded in your work's purpose will be more exciting to deliver and more engaging and impactful, without necessarily zapping your energy!

Brand Building as Procrastination
A word of caution on brand building. It can be fun – sharing your mission statement, printing out your expressively typefaced business values, gazing at

colour wheels, experimenting with WordPress themes and naming your social profiles. It can be energizing to remodel the corner of your bedroom into a green room, spotlights, tripod and all. It can feel like progress, plotting out your content calendar for the year in a gazillion-tabbed Excel spreadsheet, detailing themes, social platforms, objectives and 52 Motivational Monday quotes. However, as entertaining (and yes, essential) as thinking about and working on your business is, be cautious that it's not distracting you from the core work you actually need to prioritize. That it doesn't become what you do all day, all week, instead of actually building products, seeing clients or delivering your service. Marketing yourself and your business is integral to your success, absolutely, but not at the expense of having a business to market in the first place.

So, as part of your strategizing, allocate set time frames for building the brand, launching the brand, then maintaining the brand and stop yourself indulging above and beyond the vital. For contexet, websites tend to need refreshing every one to two years. There will always be brand design work to do so don't labour over it disproportionately from the crux of what will generate income and enable you to unleash your services into the world.

A Corporate Connection Catapult

"Do the job you seek to hold" is a strong strategy for promotion. This advice hinges on visualizing yourself in a higher-level role with more responsibility and more of what you want, the future state you most desire in your organization. But instead of just daydreams and subliminal nightly programming, actually stepping up and doing it now, ensuring your organization sees you in all your blatant, reinvented, uplevelled glory. Don't just think you could do it, do it, and do it now. It's a bit like (supposedly) Gandhi's "Be the change you want to see", but less lofty and world-changing, unless your service will indeed change our dear planet. I pass this advice on to clients and team members repeatedly. It was given to me early on in my forays into corporate land and, seriously, if you behave like you already have the responsibility of the job you seek to hold, and proactively carve out space to do it, what do you know? Suddenly you are the one responsible for that remit. And now you've proved yourself highly competent at it and are already generating results, so "hello, organization, please can I now have the title and commensurate salary?" It's a smarter way to get where you want to go than whining about not ascending quickly enough (or worse, complaining about not being given opportunities when you're so brilliant and why isn't the company paying attention. Show us what you're capable of and then you will have our rapt attention).

Mastering the Art of Public Speaking

When it comes to public speaking, I encourage two lines of Big Impact thought. One, think of yourself as a vessel conveying a message, with no overanalysis nor overthinking, you're just a messenger, and two, communicate to inspire. It's that simple. At least it should be ...

As is well-documented, public speaking is the number one cited fear in every survey ever, even ahead of death.[133] At the prospect of speaking up, our amygdala wails like a siren, urging us into our internal bomb shelter. Whether presenting to two people in the boardroom, asking a question at a conference or addressing a large audience from a stage, fear can ruin this really quite luxurious experience. Because, let's face it, you're being given airtime and people are inviting you to speak so they can listen. It's architected active listening and you're the one that gets to do the talking and exclusively be heard.

In most other situations, you want to be heard. Think of therapy: you pay for that person to listen to you. But take away the intimacy and suddenly terror kicks in and you don't want to be heard any more. Well, you do, actually, you've got a point to make, but you're suddenly not quite sure how much you want to make it. The mental invasion here? That pesky fear of judgement has reared its ugly head. Once again, the only way you will overcome this fear is through repeated exposure. So, it's time to get up on stage and talk and talk until the fear is gone.

Put yourself up for every talk going. Tell your manager you're growing your public speaking muscle. Join a local public speaking group like Toastmasters. Start a group at work or with friends and practise together. Expose yourself to opportunities to become more comfortable under the spotlight. Try stand-up comedy, local amateur dramatics, volunteering as entertainment at your local theme park or school fundraiser. Just play in the space of addressing crowds until the spotlight is not scary and you can shift focus to honing how you deliver your message, create audience connection and get that inspirational communication flowing.

10 Steps to Delivering a Phenomenal Talk

- **Step 1:** Know your audience – find out as much as possible about your crowd so you can tailor your message to their needs, world views, etc.
- **Step 2:** Know your venue – visit the venue beforehand so you can plan your "choreography" – can you pace across the stage or not (warning – once one of my stiletto heels slipped down between two stage blocks, leaving me

stuck mid-stride at a client TED Talk session, so beware of pushed-together stage blocks!). Also, fanatically check the tech set-up so you can plan your digital material accordingly – no warped slides from Mac to laptop, plus speaker notes visibility, clock counter, space for camera crew, microphone setup and so on.

- **Step 3:** Tell a story to engage hearts and minds – ensure your script conveys your message in the form of a story, taking your audience on a journey with a beginning, middle and end, establishing a problem, introducing the solution and ending with a punchy conclusion that inspires action because it moves people (even just to buy your product, but maybe to join a movement, donate, whatever). Ensure there are three key points threading the entire content together (we are more likely to remember three things) and keep recapping, orienting your audience to follow you. Brain MRI scans show that when we follow a story, our brain areas light up in synchronicity with the storyteller's, hence story being key to enhancing your message and keeping a connected flow between you and your listeners.
- **Step 4:** Create a visually stunning presentation (if you're using slides) – avoid words on screen unless essential. Keep headlines as the main, most interesting takeaway from the slide, so not "2024 Results" but "The Way XXX Made History in One Week". The slide contains the same stats, but in the latter framing they are more memorable. Ensure consistent design formatting throughout so the viewer stays in the flow, with section dividers clearly distinguished as such.
- **Step 5:** Check grammar, check spelling, read it out loud (to practise those phrases we don't yet realise are harder to say than read), then check it all again.
- **Step 6:** Rehearse as many times as you can – ideally five times for a full run-through. For my stuck-stiletto presentation, I wasn't allowed slides or memory cards, so I had rehearsed that 18-minute talk for around 12 hours prior. (For the record, I released my heel from between the stage blocks, made a joke about "my power props not usually being so unreliable" and got back into my (heeled) stride!)
- **Step 7:** Practise delivering your content – rehearse in front of a trusted friend or colleague for feedback well in advance so you can tweak and learn content. Play with interactivity by presenting live to a test audience prior to the main event to trial tactics for use when on stage for real.
- **Step 8:** If it's a big gig, book time with a speaker coach and rehearse with them. Watch TED Talks, study public speaking resources, devour content and principles for effective speeches and pick the strategies that work for you, based on your unique self. Authenticity always wins, so be true to yourself, ensuring you speak from your heart (even if parroting a company

line, personalize it so you truly own the message in that moment). Ensure your voice conveys your message optimally. Don't rise up at the end of sentences if it's not a question, lubricate your throat (lemon tea is good, coffee and mucous-forming milky drinks bad), use varying intonation and volume, and practise, practise, practise.

- **Step 9:** Know what relaxation techniques you will use on the big day. Social psychologist Amy Cuddy suggests in her TED Talk, "Your Body Language May Shape Who You Are", the power pose – legs hip-width apart, shoulders back, three deep breaths – to get testosterone free-flowing around your body, thus stimulating physiological assertiveness. There are also simple breathing techniques and soothing thumb and forefinger rubbing tactics you can try. Experiment and know how you will ground your energy as the spotlight shines on you. If you've practised it beforehand you can trust it to work once the cortisol starts surging.
- **Step 10:** Focus on your act of service as a privilege. Once you have prepared to the nth degree, try to relax into the moment as a gift where you get to share your message in the service of others to inspire, entertain, inform, educate or whatever the core reason you are speaking to them is. Count your blessings. And enjoy your moment! It's truly a gift!

How Connection Locks into Your Big Impact Without Burnout One-Year Master Plan

Tony Robbins' now endlessly "pinned" quote rings true here as we fold your lessons in building connection into your master plan: "The quality of your life is the quality of your relationships".[134] And I believe this applies to your impact. People will be drawn to you and your work when you show up to give and serve, inspire intimacy and share excitedly and authentically. Do it right and you'll magnetize everything you give right back to you.

After the 1969 space mission when the Apollo 11 astronauts landed on the moon, they drifted into gloomy depression upon their return to boring old Earth. They missed their purpose, they missed their work, but most importantly, they missed each other. The collaboration of that unfathomably interconnected, intergalactic teamwork where they were intertwined with each other, wholly interdependent on each other in space, in such intensity, for so long, left them grieving for the experience after it was gone. We each have the opportunity to create our own multidimensional connections and infuse them with as much meaning and positive interrelatedness down here on Earth, every single day. So, let's shoot for the moon and weave connection into your one-year plan ...

Your Big Impact Connection Expansion Grid

You now understand the key components to create your bespoke Connection Strategy for Big Impact; you know how to honour the 101 of communication, build and maintain a network supporting your sphere of influence, with a focus on empathic leadership. You also know how to build your own brand and master the art of public speaking.

In the grid below is what you now know how to manage.

It's time to translate this into solid action to make your expansion a reality.

Grab your journal and review the statements below, focusing on the "Expanding To" column. Now spend 30 minutes freewriting on everything that comes up for you when you read the expansion statements. Elaborate on them where you see fit and make them entirely yours. As well as writing the "what", dive into the "how" and "why". Really explore the statements, applying your newfound knowledge, and have fun exploring all the life-altering ways you're going to feel and how you're going to get there. Let the inspiration pour forth and capture everything that comes to mind.

FROM	EXPANDING TO...
I have uninspiring relationships.	I have a powerful network – work, friends, partner – all elevating my thinking and simultaneously my contribution to the world and my life.
I sadly lack influence.	I am proud to embody effective leadership, strong negotiation skills and the honed ability to sell my ideas more confidently.
I have low credibility and little reputation.	I am a key ambassador for my industry/self/product.
I have no voice and am timid in my sphere.	I am a confident public speaker, boardroom contributor, voice of my brand/business internally and externally.
I don't feel part of any networks or know who my tribes are.	I have a deep-rooted sense of belonging.
I am insular, lacking depth in my connections.	I know how to nurture relationships, listen deeply and demonstrate empathy.
I find it hard to get people to trust me.	I have rewarding relationships built on trust.

FROM	EXPANDING TO...
I find it difficult to lift a room.	I radiate Positive Relational Energy and know I competently communicate to inspire.
I have doors constantly shut in my face.	I see "no" as an opportunity to seek another way.
I am limited by how to share my worth.	I am clear on my brand-building strategy for maximum impact.

Connection Strategy Priority Actions

It's time for serious action. Now bring your reflections together and organize them into priority areas of focus that you identify as integral to your master Connection Strategy for Big Impact Without Burnout across the next 12 months.

Drawing the grid below in your notebook or in a spreadsheet, list as many reflections and actions with deadlines per connection theme as you can based on all you've learned. Then distil all of these action ideas into **three Connection Strategy Priority Actions**, which we'll incorporate into your master plan at the end of the book. Remember to always tune into your values and overarching impact goals as you create your plans. Make the three action priorities realistic, achievable and inspiring, and rigorously tied to firm deadlines.

ONE-YEAR BIG IMPACT WITHOUT BURNOUT MASTER PLAN			
CONNECTION STRATEGY	REFLECTIONS	ACTIONS	DEADLINE
The Art of Communicating to Inspire			
The Art of Listening and Nurturing			
The Art of Leadership			
The Art of Building Your Brand			
	My three Work Strategy Priority Actions are: 1....2....3....		

YOUR BIG IMPACT STRATEGY NO. 7: WEALTH

"The law of work seems unfair, but nothing can change it; the more enjoyment you get out of your work, the more money you will make."

— Mark Twain

If I ask what wealth means to you, do you think of yachts, fast cars and glamour? Diamonds, nannies and wardrobes overflowing with designer garb? Or do you think of wealth in terms of happiness and fulfilment? Or a bit of both? Wealth, by its very definition means profusion, which applies to materialistic abundance like blingy stuff and staff, but also soulful riches like serenity and joy.

Indeed, wealth is multidimensional and not just about money. Health is often cited as the first wealth in fact. Whichever way we construe it, hear this: Big Impact Without Burnout creates wealth in all the dimensions that matter to you – physical, intellectual, emotional, spiritual, and, yes, financial too. When you operate with integrity, honouring those foundations we established in Part One, then do the work and connect as we've covered in Part Two, the wheels of fate glide into the version of wealth you wish for.

Wealth is wholly personal. It will mean something different to each one of us. In a discovery session with one client, when we got to the wealth wedge of her Big Impact wheel and I asked how happy she felt regarding whatever interpretation of "wealth" she held, she burst into tears. Gently enquiring about where the tears came from, she gushed with gratitude for her children, husband, employer, home and beyond. She was bathed in her version of wealth, harmoniously synergized with her life values.

Another client, Suzanne, who you'll meet in a moment, has tied wealth so tautly together with income, status and achievement that her self-identity is being wildly destabilized as bankruptcy looms. For her, wealth is solely financial.

Our sense of security and safety is absolutely influenced by our bank balance, but our relationship with money, how we respect and relate to that number, influences so much more than what we spend the cash on. In this chapter we will explore the psychology of wealth from all angles, understanding how it shows up for you as connected to your identity and self-worth, revealing opportunities for some updating or perhaps radical readjustment here and there. We'll examine powerful money management methods to build in healthy control, confronting your money beliefs and habits head on. Finally, we'll address satisfaction and when enough is enough, so you get closer to your bespoke redefinition of success. By the end of this chapter, you will have designed your Wealth Strategy to incorporate into your Big Impact Without Burnout One-Year Master Plan. You will have a positive relationship with wealth. You will become wealthier.

The Psychology of Wealth

In today's fast culture where immediacy dominates every desire, "get rich" is often heralded over building wealth. However, it is a short-term attitude, in a do-it-quickly kind of way, and is fuelled by the media's celebrations of "overnight successes", lottery winners and Silicon Valley tech kids who seemingly emerged from their student bedrooms into the top 1 per cent of global earners. By contrast, building wealth, slowly, steadily and gradually, is firstly more realistic and secondly mentally healthier. Embracing this more responsible approach involves having a conscientious relationship with money.

Having money can certainly reduce anxiety related to financial uncertainties, improving access to essential services like healthcare and education, not to mention an elevated quality of life, comfort and freedom. However, a lot of it can bring all sorts of psychological pressures, especially if high standards of living need to be maintained, for both yourself and any dependents. Our financial status can affect our behaviour, emotions and social interactions. It can boost self-esteem and confidence, but just as readily wreck it. Our financial ambitions can be hugely propelling but can route us wonkily toward material success perhaps at the expense of overall life satisfaction. Socially, wealth can increase opportunities for networking and influence, but may also result in social isolation due to envy or distrust from others. If self-worth is closely tied to financial success, it's fragile, being too dependent on external validation, possessions and ultimately the uncontrollable. Unquestionably, wealth is complex.

Understanding Your Relationship with Money

Suzanne had run her own successful marketing agency for over a decade. With an "alpha" personality, she was used to leading every aspect of her life, from running her organization, driving expansion through hires, business initiatives, making bold decisions and all the intense graft that comes with entrepreneurialism, to being the primary bread winner in her household, funding her three children through education, and always leading the major family decisions. Now, economic volatility meant her thriving business was no longer booming and monthly income was receding rapidly. She was on the brink of bankruptcy with a lot of dependents, both staff and family. Although adept at dealing with stress after years of The Juggle, as she now risked losing the entirety of her life's work, she began to unravel emotionally, which was when we met. Her husband had suggested she seek help.

Defiant and defensive, Suzanne presented herself as strong and "together". A blunt fringe, peroxide bob and black leather jacket, she was slim and taut, her heavily made-up eyes holding my gaze across the table in our plush London meeting venue, a grand atrium awash with large-fronded plants and clinking teacups. She was a stark contrast against the elegance of the setting with her aura of palpable brittleness. Her smile felt false. Our conversation juddered along, me asking, Suzanne answering, as we slowly uncloaked the bravado to reveal the woman beneath.

With self-identity tightly tied to her status and achievements, and most acutely her fiscal wealth, Suzanne's very essence was flailing as her accomplishments simultaneously flailed. "Secret" habits were becoming more dominant as she found herself surreptitiously sugar-snacking in the larder while the kids ate supper, binge-drinking at home most of the weekend and sometimes mid-week, mainlining coffee all day and prescription sleeping tablets at night. She was retreating from her friendship groups, snapping at her children and alienating her husband, always on her phone, behind her laptop or working out. She was aware she was sliding but unaware of how to get her sense of self back. Beneath the "make lots of money and you'll be happy" life philosophy, she'd forgotten who "Suzanne Before The Business" was, and was unconsciously seeking fixes to stabilize her now slippery foundations. Suzanne's outer confidence was waning. Beneath it, there was little self-esteem left.

Self-esteem is essential for psychological survival. One of the main factors differentiating humans from other animals is our awareness of self; the ability to form an identity and then attach a value to it – "I am a kind person, therefore I do kind things and thus my self-esteem is strong and I have a right to exist in this world as my kind self." Suzanne is an example of having formed an identity of a successful businesswoman and attached an over-indexed proportion of her self-esteem to it. Now, as her actual and symbolic wealth evaporated – income, business solidity, children's schooling, home, cars, holidays, luxury lifestyle – she was frantically trying to drown out her fear and pathological self-loathing with numbing tactics. The work we needed to do was shift her sense of self from the outer (increasingly out of her control) to the inner (where she could begin anew to cement terra firma), effectively to separate her self-esteem from her current identity and ground her back into her innate, brilliant self beneath the blonde bob and leather.

Rooting our identity in things we have (the house, the car, the business), and what we achieve (the job title, the awards, the letters after our name), and what others say (the praise, the public recognition, the gushy fawning) only works to boost our self-esteem temporarily. We will never feel satiated by this long-term because the outer world is way too volatile. Our inner world is where we can maintain more certainty, as it's where self-worth resides.

Self-esteem is different from self-worth. We create our self-esteem, whereas self-worth originates more deeply from within as more of a vibrating feeling state. Self-esteem can be ratcheted up based on external factors, like Suzanne's tick list of life impact and financial gain. It builds confidence and the drive to go again and try harder. As we learned in the Mindset Strategy, by comparison, self-worth goes many levels deeper and is more connected to how much we value ourselves, what we truly feel and believe we deserve, as in "I am worthy."

But despite worthiness being our birthright, life happens and we don't always feel worthy, notwithstanding all those Post-it notes on our bathroom mirror reminding us, "I am enough". Insecurity may dominate our internal self-worth system, no matter how confident (and/or rich) we appear to the outside world. Think of Robbie Williams standing in front of 100,000 enthusiastic fans, apparently petrified with stage fright as his sense of unworthiness enshrouded him (watch his Netflix documentary to view his life through the lens of a man unjustifiably, yet so belligerently, riddled with self-doubt).

While both are important as we strategize for wealth, psychologists believe it's self-worth that has a more essential role in life because "unlike self-esteem, self-worth provides a stable sense of mental and emotional armour that external forces can't sway easily".[135] If Suzanne had a more robust sense of self-worth, she wouldn't be so destabilized by her business collapse and her survival props wouldn't be so necessary. Her "wealth" would remain in spite of her financial loss.

History is awash with inspiring tales of bankruptcy then boomerang success. From Walt Disney to Will Smith to Abraham Lincoln to Lady Gaga to

Simon Cowell to Donald Trump, financial demise hasn't necessarily broken the person. Self-worth pervaded, resilience burned and from their business ashes these phoenixes rose to build again, inspired by their aspirations. Equally, history shines with numerous role models rich in life's abundance, who would describe themselves as wealthy emotionally, creatively or however else, despite abject poverty. Think of all the spiritual gurus, blessed and happy living bare-foot and threadbare atop dusty earth, oft found beneath the Bodhi Tree. Wealth is as much a state of mind as it is complex and personal.

So, Who Are You Anyway?

Establishing how your self-identity is linked to your wealth – how you define it, what it means to you and your bank balance – is significant. One of the first questions I ask my clients in their discovery questionnaire is this – "Who are you?" The answers are revelatory. For all of us, this question detaches from "what we do" and the identity we've created as our outer shell – that public face we present to the world, the job title we hold, the 9-to-5 remit – and instead provokes deeper contemplation. Who indeed are you? There's that You who pops on the perhaps literal, perhaps metaphorical, mask each morning before you step outside the front door or turn on your camera for the first video call of the day, made up, hair groomed, jewellery a' sparkling, the You who everyone expects to see, and then there's the inner rumbling of your spirit, whispering who you actually feel and know you are really, deep inside. This is the gold I work with my clients to reveal and buff. To listen to the whispers.

"Who are you?" is a big question. If you don't contemplate this, you risk getting stuck in an outer version of self, dependent on status and how others perceive you, which is ultimately beyond your control and only ever temporary. You are not your job title. You are not the letters on your certificate. You are not the family name you adopted through marriage. You are not even the face and body you present today. You may be fired, your work may be criticized, you will age so your looks will inevitably change ... There is transience in everything. Rooting your sense of self in your inner core and what you value provides more foundational solidity from which to go forth and experience life. Reflecting on the inner to better, more authentically evolve the outer is what I believe it's all about, especially in the pursuit of consistent impact, and certainly to build wealth in all its senses, including financial, across our lifetimes. Now, let's listen to those whispers of yours.

BIG IMPACT REFLECTION: WHO ARE YOU?

Spend five minutes answering this question, remembering your job title is not the answer – Who Are You? Next, devote a few minutes to describing the identity you generally present to the world today. Then freewrite for several minutes, imagining the uncompromised version of You, living life authentically in all realms, without any hidden aspects of Self, fully aligned within and out. Where do you work? What do you do? Who are you with? How do you feel? What impact do you make? How do you dress? Where do you live, and so on. Finally, reflect on any disconnect you observed between today's reality and the uncompromised You dream. Consider how you can close any gaps to allow the inner You to present explicitly outwardly and actions to take with timelines.

Powerful Money Management

Whether you want to "get rich quick" (inadvisable) or build wealth over time (preferable), you need a money management plan. It starts by becoming aware of your attitude toward money, that overarching relationship you have with financial wealth, dissecting and adjusting your money beliefs to become more positive and action-oriented in alignment with your Big Impact intentions, then finally, ensuring your income reflects your worth and that you master how to "premium-ize" your value and optimize your delivery. So, we're going to address:

1. Your ego: Are you driven by scarcity or abundance?
2. Your money beliefs: Are you limiting your own wealth potential?
3. Premiumizing yourself: Are you undervaluing and under-delivering your market potential?

1. Your Ego: Are You Driven by Scarcity or Abundance?

Remember the saboteur side of the ego we learned about back in the Mindset chapter (page 93)? Let's go back to her and consider the influence she plays on our money mindset. Our sense of self is going to influence whether or not we have an attitude of abundance or scarcity. An abundance mindset flows out of a deep inner sense of personal worth, self-compassion and security. It's a framework based on the ever-expansive belief that there is more than enough for everyone, plenty more fish in the sea, the Land of Plenty. It's sweet and altruistic by its very nature. Alternatively, a scarcity mindset is the feeling that there will never be enough, resulting in fear, stress and anxiety. It can trigger greed, self-aggrandizement and malpractice when we fight to win, never mind who is squashed in the process. It means ruthlessly putting yourself before anyone else whether than means ignoring others, hurting yourself or limiting your perspective on the world.

An abundance-focused woman is one who embraces experiences, others and opportunities, and is generous, giving, optimistic and energetically magnetic. Conversely, a scarcity-focused woman lives in an apprehensive, self-oriented state, terrified that for self-preservation she has to ensure she gets the last cookie, or trips up the coworker to guarantee she gets the promotion, or makes her round the penny-pinching one at the end of the night once everyone is cocktail-ed out and ready for sparkling water, despite having taken advantage of others' generosity all night!

It's exhausting living in The World of Scarcity. Threat is around every corner. Life isn't as much fun as it could be because the cost of the mortgage, the car maintenance, the holiday, the new kettle. Everything is too expensive, superfluous, with "Ugh, I need to replace that?" sighs and begrudging eye rolls. Supermarket own-brands and 2-for-1 offers proffer secret hallelujah tingles. Don't get me wrong, I'm all for smart spending and love a supermarket own-brand soap (decanted into my beautiful silver-speckled dispenser, why not?), but when you are limiting your joie de vivre because you're enshrouded in miserly misery and alienating others through your decision-making – "No, we can't afford to eat there", "No, don't opt for the thickest pile rug", "No, let's not upgrade" – you're keeping yourself, your business and your life small.

As ever, it's all connected to self-esteem and self-assuredness. Abundant beliefs stem from inner confidence and a foundation of security. When you know there's enough to go round, and absolutely believe it with every cell in your body, you feel complete as you are and as the world is. If, however, you're doubting your own abilities, riddled with survival issues, lacking trust and paranoid everyone is out to get you and take the little you have, it's a frightening space to exist in, and you're trapped in your own doom.

So, observe yourself in your day-to-day and look at whether you're thinking and behaving abundantly or not. If there's scarcity shadowing choices you're making and limiting your progress, experiment with abundant thinking instead. For example, give a sandwich to the homeless man, make the phone call to the relative you've been putting off, send a "You Make Me Smile" card to your bestie, buy the luxurious balsam tissues, have the dessert! Catch yourself in moments of scarcity-based decision-making, like not letting the kids upgrade to the supersize meal, not booking the trip spontaneously, not hosting the gathering, not going for the promotion and so on. The more abundant you are and the more abundantly you think, coincidentally the more abundance you attract. It's far more fun to be in The World of Abundance and its Land of Plenty!

BIG IMPACT REFLECTION: LIVING IN ABUNDANCE

Journal for five minutes about your observations on the role your ego is playing in driving which world you live in most – Scarcity or Abundance, and steps you can take to embrace more abundance in your daily life. Visualize yourself operating happily in The World of Abundance, honouring an abundance mindset most prevalently.

---

2. Your Money Beliefs: Are You Limiting Your Own Wealth Potential?

Denise Duffield-Thomas is one of the world's most renowned "money manifestors". Not Warren Buffett, no, but an affable, down-to-earth Aussie millionairess, she teaches women to own their money dreams by shifting them from wishes and wants into hardcore, *simple* (her emphasis) daily actions. Her tens of thousands of global money boot camp participants and her bestselling book *Get Rich, Lucky Bitch!* prove she's onto something. Warren isn't a man many of us can relate to; Denise is a woman I assume we all can. Her advice and personal multi-million-dollar success centres on releasing money blocks and honouring an abundance mindset. The power in this is as transformational as it is straightforward.

Releasing Money Blocks

Money blocks are your limiting beliefs about money. When you identify and address your money blocks, you make space for wealth in your life. As ironic as this may sound, despite it being a rare woman who doesn't seek financial abundance, many a woman is subconsciously thwarting her own wealth. Money blocks could be thoughts like "money is hard to come by", or "the wealthy got there through ill-gotten gains", or simply, "I need to save not spend, ever". Exploring and releasing your own negative money beliefs begins with reflection.

BIG IMPACT REFLECTION: RELEASING MONEY BLOCKS

Brainstorm your beliefs and look for patterns of negativity or scarcity thinking. Deconstruct why you believe you need to save obsessively. What were your family-entrenched money attitudes that you've unconsciously inherited? Do they work for you today? Do you agree with them? When have you rowed about money with your partner? Or family? Why? Light a candle, journal on this and go deep. Reflect until you uncover anything seemingly negative, then work on reframing these beliefs into more positive and abundant ones, following the principles you learned in your Mindset Strategy (page 69) on how to flip beliefs from limiting to empowering. Example financial flips could look like – "Investing is careless and too risky" to "I invest with consideration and extensive expert consultation", or "I never earn enough to make ends meet" to "I am capable of paying all my bills and saving each month", or "The man should provide" to "We all contribute to the household income". End with a visusalization freewriting about your life without money blocks and money resentment.

I encourage you to be sure to release any money resentment that may surface as you realize which familial money attitudes you have unconsciously adopted. A key step once blocks are revealed is entering a state of forgiveness and gratitude to the people or circumstances who may have influenced some of those barriers that have kept you from a healthy wealth mindset so far. Accept, forgive and release. Get excited about prosperity.

Honouring an Abundance Mindset

Denise teaches that when you behave like a millionairess, you'll attract more money into your world. So, when you know you can afford it, indulge in luxurious fripperies to ensure you feel special. I love this little bit of advice! Treats can be anything from chamomile teabags from Fortnum & Mason (my favourite) to fresh flowers, to a silver frame for your favourite pet photograph, just indulge in the unnecessary for a moment or two.

Expanding this, she also trains her students to cultivate a daily positive money mindset practice to reinforce an upgraded approach to money. Consistency and focus are key as apparently billionaires write their money goals down several times a day! For myself and my clients, I recommend clarifying financial targets and having the big, ambitious number for the year written down as a reminder.

My Non-Negotiable Rules for Big Impact Money Management

Be scrupulous. Know exactly how much money you have right now and are owed, in your personal account and in your business account, what interest rates you are paying, and what percentage of income you are saving. Never lose a grip on exactly how your money is flowing in and out. Know all the details, examine them scrupulously and often. Check your banking apps repeatedly across each day (obviously ensure they are all downloaded and accessible on your phone). Know how much tax you are paying and why. Use the purchase categorization your bank app offers (or if your bank doesn't, download an integrated app) to know what proportion of your income goes on entertainment, household bills, food, travel, etc. – assess and refine spending habits wherever and however is logical. Know exactly where your money is going.

Be efficient. Invest in finance professionals. Get an accountant, get a bookkeeper, befriend your payroll officer at work. Know your local tax office and tax number. Have separate personal and business bank accounts with separate bank cards if you're a business owner or sole trader. Set up automatic monthly saving deposits at a fixed percentage of income. Establish standing orders for repetitive payments, direct debits for household bills – anything that can be automated, automate. Use loyalty schemes. Get free money where you can by using reward points. Make your money work for you.

Set tantalizing goals. Create financial targets that inspire and energize you. Expand into the prospect of prosperity. Be specific about how much you want by when. Write the number down. Jim Carrey is all over the internet with his "I wrote myself a ten million dollar cheque" tale of manifestation. I can shyly admit similar tactics have worked for me and I still gulp when I find a tatty Post-it with a big number on it that later arrived that same year, or a wish list salary that became a reality within 12 months. The how never seems to matter as much as the what. Write it down. And underline it. Three times.

Be brave. Take inspired actions toward your money goals, following through on ideas that excite you and intuitively feel right, even if they seem a bit kooky, like contacting someone you haven't spoken to for a decade to suggest a business idea or investing in a tangential course or host an event and invite a new audience. Trust your instincts and take calculated risks.

Be okay with spreadsheets. Excel does not titillate me, but it's a secret wonder-woman weapon you need only a basic level of competence to use. Once you master key formula functions, make yourself design financial models and play with forecasts and pipelines. Understand the mechanics of a P&L (watch tutorials, buy a book, decipher the acronyms – P&L is Profit and Loss, btw), obsess over your company's commercial dashboards, and run your life and/or business with the rigour of a haughty Victorian bean counter. At any point, know where you stand and what you're working toward, the size of any risk and so on.

Don't spend what you don't have. Aside from the big-ticket items like a house or car, my advice is not to borrow. If and when you do, ensure you are fully aware of the debt magnitude, any asset depreciation forecast if relevant, and have a plan of repayment. I endured my father, like many of his friends, going bankrupt in the early 90s, bombing from an extravagant, lavish lifestyle with multiple homes, cars and first-class holidays, to the juxtaposed austerity of moving back into my ever-welcoming retired grandparents' guest room.

Be careful when sharing. When you have joint money management plans to honour. such as with a business partner or shareholders, a divorce settlement or a will to probate, ensure any contract you sign protects you today and tomorrow. Don't find yourself sharing a business with someone happy spending from the overdraft if you're not comfortable with debt. Don't agree to fixed child-maintenance payment terms based on the children's ages today, think about ten years from now. And where siblings and wills are concerned, never assume all parties will have the same intentions. Be clear before you ink the paper on all the long-term implications of what you're signing up for to avoid risk of frustration and conflict later. Protect your preferred money management strategies always.

BIG IMPACT REFLECTION: MONEY GOALS

Please spend time on this one and use a spreadsheet if available as well as your journal once the numbers start coming into focus. Define your financial goals clearly. Determine how much money you want to earn, save and invest. Elaborate with the how and by when. Break down the big financial goals into smaller, actionable steps. Visualize your goals as already achieved to help manifest them into reality. Maybe even write yourself a fake cheque à la Jim Carrey!

---

3. "Premiumizing" Yourself: Are You Undervaluing and Under-Delivering Your Market Worth?

As part of your Wealth Strategy, I invite you to "premium-ize" yourself. You and your work are valuable. Too many women undervalue themselves.

Too many of my clients are afraid to pitch themselves out at a premium, but then feel disappointed when the bank balance isn't fattening. The gender pay gap is a hot topic. It's a globally acknowledged fact, and you probably have first-hand experience of the stark reality of it.

Valuing Your Value

What is your current market value? What would you like that value to be? Why? How unique is your USP? How premium do you want to be? If you're setting price points for your services, decide based on a set of criteria you pre-determine. Is your positioning mass market or niche? Are you about volume, or less is more? Don't crowdsource to get a sense of your value either. I used to include a question in my post-event feedback survey after my one-day retreats asking, "What would you pay for a three-day retreat?" I wanted to know if there would be an appetite for a residential Balearic Island version. I had an unfathomably broad band of responses from £50 to £5,000. It gave me more insight into the respondent's money beliefs than into an appropriate price point for the envisaged retreat.

Bring all of your money block journalling into your financial worth decision. Was there a family belief that you had to work really hard to earn money, and so, if you find your work easy (if you're doing what you love, it should be, by the way), you feel you don't deserve to earn more? If you think with an abundance mindset, like your most revered role model, what would you charge then?

I have several clients who openly admit how nervous they feel discussing money. Asking for a pay rise induces palpitations rather than healthy conversations. We have to change this. It's the most important negotiation of the year. Equally, when setting price points to sell their personal service, instead of stopping at, say, £25 per hour, the end, they continue on justifying why. This is unnecessary. Too often, I also see women shy away from getting actual paying clients, preferring to do the work for free in order to "gain more experience". Any transaction has a value. All experience has a value. You have value. Do not undermine this. I recommend sales and negotiation training for every woman intent on premiumizing her worth.

When you know your work is good, you can feel it. Muse on this now for a moment. Think of a peak work moment when you were rocking your impact. Perhaps you led a team to complete a complex project over many months and were praised for your stoic, progressive management throughout. You pitched to a tough client and were on fire, palms dutifully eaten from, licked even. You got yourself into a flow state and produced an award-winning industry POV. What made you so excellent in those moments? No, go deeper, what was your impact in those moments and why? How did you excel? Okay, list these reflections down. That's your gold. That's your value. That's your special. No one else could have produced that effect or done it your way. You have a Unique Sales Proposition. You are a Uniquely Special Person. You! And you know what? You peaked then, you've probably done it again since, you'll definitely do it again in the future, and again, and again. The more you do it, the more competent you become and the more valuable you are because your experience and expertise grows, and thus your value increases. Do not diminish this. You do not plateau in value just because it becomes easier. That skill gained through the struggle is why you premiumize. It's what distinguishes you from someone starting out. You have a right to charge for your worth.

BIG IMPACT REFLECTION: PREMIUMIZING YOU

Taking those reflections you just captured, identify three key strengths that contributed to your success and consider the broader impact of your work, including both tangible results (like revenue growth) and intangible benefits (like team morale). Next, research industry standards for your role and compare them with your unique contributions to determine a fair and competitive price point for your services or salary. Next, plot actions you can take to activate your new premiumized self, today, next week and within the next month. Conclude by writing an affirmation of your value, such as, "I am a highly skilled professional whose unique strengths and impactful contributions justify my premium value, and I confidently negotiate and set prices that reflect my worth." Use this reflection to confidently approach salary negotiations or set service prices, knowing the unique value you bring. Now, visualize yourself as that person, charging those rates, negotiating that salary – immerse into your premiumized self, owning your USP.

Marianne Williamson, wise woman-cum-ferocious-politician, teaches that we subconsciously fear and shun the sheer enormity and potential within the very strength of ourselves. In *A Return to Love*, she writes, "Our deepest fear is not that we are inadequate. Our deepest fear is that we are powerful beyond measure. It is our light, not our darkness that most frightens us."[136] This is poignant. I agree. I admit, I've done this! Under our rational decision-making radar, we may limit ourselves through a subliminal, neurotic nervousness that unleashing our greatest potential might just make a dent in the world, and, if we're truthful, scare the heck out of us actually. We're afraid to do what we're good at because, yes, we risk failing or being criticized, but perhaps most intimidatingly, we might just realize something about ourselves that necessitates a change in our self-perception. A big decision and commitment to a new reality would need to be made.

And that's just it. When we lean into what excites us, what we're good at, what we feel with every heart-fluttery beat will be majestic, it feels knee-knockingly outrageous. It's as terrifying as it is tantalizing. This very act of doing what we do well repeatedly, honing our brilliance, putting more of ourselves and our work out there while increasing our rates or salary in accordance with our experience, means we risk changing our destiny. To our cosy ego minds, safe, secure and snuggly, that's treacherous. We're leaving the realm of the known and stepping into the unknown, way beyond our private nightly visualizations, where hopes and dreams shimmer. The potential of our strengthened strengths and seizing our ambitions means venturing into a new arena, exposing a raw and untested uplevelling, challenging the stamina of even our most courageous selves, and thus it's often way more tempting to circle around in the comfy shallows with the rest of the shoal and give it all a miss.

Please don't! Recognize the more you lean into what feels good, the more your worth increases. The more you work in "your zone", the more impact you will have, and thus the more you deserve to charge.

Process as a Premiumizing Tactic

I am a huge fan of process. As I single-parent four children, work full time for a large communication group, write, coach, study and run my wellbeing business, the only way I can flourish, and happily flourish at that, is through process. I have to run a tight ship, sailing through every aspect of my life to ensure my time and energy are abundant and maximized. As you now know, without carefully crafted awareness and plans, time and energy deplete, productivity becomes a struggle, overwhelm and burnout hit and ships sink. But I don't sink, and neither do you. Because we manage ourselves and our lives accordingly. You're now going to become an expert in adding process to your plans and processing the heck out of your beautiful life to ensure wealth is your every day – in time, energy and subsequently money – because you make space for more graceful productivity where it matters most.

The processes I put in place focus on Delegating – anything and everything that is not my forte nor passion – and Optimizing – maximizing my own strengths to make space for what and who matter. These processes are constantly evolving and adapting based on circumstances and priorities. Let me share what I do so you can create the same style of process plan for yourself.

The Process of Delegation

Delegation Step 1 – Clarity: I am good at my job, at writing, at parenting, at organizing and planning generally, etc. I enjoy dog walking, exercising, photography, juicing, snuggling and so on. I am not good at, and generally do not enjoy, DIY, shopping, cooking, changing beds, etc. The things I am good at and the things that I enjoy are the things I choose to fill my life with in abundance.

Delegation Step 2 – Action: The things I am not good at and don't enjoy I **shrink** or **reframe** or **delegate** entirely. For example:

- I'm blessed with sons who happily help with DIY (for a cheeky fee obvs). Delegate.
- Modern times mean I can automate the food shop and even get the school uniform via Amazon's one-click. Shrink.
- I've taught the children to cook so my kitchen remit has dwindled to simply stocking the fridge. Shrink.
- Next on my household efficiency mission is training the twins to do their own laundry. Delegate.
- Of course, occasionally I come home from business trips abroad to find the kids have forgotten we own a dishwasher and that we need clean utensils now and then and maybe we don't want rats to move in, so have the odd 11pm kitchen battle. But after the entitled rant, instead of enduring laments, I pop my headphones on and immerse myself in an audiobook to listen and learn while reclaiming kitchen order. Reframe.

What all this process means is that I have space to focus on the aspects of life that chime with my values: creative time, family together time and work time. The work time is thus not stressful, my output is higher calibre and higher volume, and thus my income increases.

The Process of Optimizing Myself

Optimizing Step 1 – Clarity: To perform at a healthy and consistent level of productive output, I need and choose good sleep, daily exercise, time in nature, excellent nutrition and to ground myself regularly. (These are, in fact, some of my No Room For Compromise Life Mandatories, hence interwoven into the entirety of this book and these eight strategies, which I have automated into my life via process.)

Optimizing Step 2 – Action: Implementing my No Room For Compromise Life Mandatories as easily, cleverly and simply as I can integrate into my life. For example:

- I need and choose fast nutrition, so I have a Nutribullet and our food orders include all the blendable ingredients. Weekends are for the messy, more complex juices using the annoying-to-clean juicer.
- I need and choose my almost daily 5k runs, so have had a treadmill in my garage since I could first afford a rudimentary secondhand one in my first home a million years ago. When I wake up I automatically walk downstairs and run on autopilot.
- I need and choose quality sleep, so have optimized my bedroom and habits accordingly. No more caffeine after 10am, the finest sheets, topper and duvet I could afford in the January sales one year and black-out curtains (oh, it was a sad farewell to those Sanderson-esque organza swathes, but I've learned to prioritize sleep.)
- When I commute into our London office, I need to find an extra four hours per day. Adding in gym time would be a challenge, so my optimized process is to blend exercise with the commute itself. I deliberately choose the route that offers the maximum amount of walking, so despite it being a non-exercise day, my iPhone reports that I still generally walk around three miles, which ticks my 5k box neatly.

BIG IMPACT REFLECTION: THE POWER OF PROCESS

How can you integrate processes in your life that will enable you to delegate or optimize your daily and weekly routine to create space for time, energy and thus generative output, which will contribute to your wealth? Spend ten minutes brainstorming ideas, factoring in your No Room For Compromise Life Mandatories for Big Impact as well as the unmoveable demands. Get creative in your solutioning and design some inspired processes!

Soaring into Success and Satisfaction

"The question to contemplate is: Who is wealthier, the one with money or the one who serves?"

— Jay Shetty

Success and happiness are not the same thing. They can coexist, but they are not dependent on each other and it's entirely possible to be happy without being conventionally successful. You, my Darling, need to define what success means to you and where your happiness lies. Top tip – it's never just about money.

When it comes to success and happiness at work, there's a theory I love, which I learned about through the lens of "not making work feel like prison", which is pretty damn important for us all, eh?! It's called the Self-Determination Theory, developed by psychologists Edward Deci and Richard Ryan, and posits that we'll only ever feel satisfied, successful and happy with our work when we meet three basic psychological needs – autonomy, competence and relatedness.[137] Without these three things, work feels like entrapment, which of course won't lead to Big Impact and will more likely lead to burnout.

Autonomy. When we're operating with autonomy, able to control how and when we work, where and with whom, making decisions independently, we produce higher quality, higher volume, satisfying-to-produce work, which inevitably leads to better job performance/products/services/ etc., and thus contributes to financial security and an ever-increasing bank balance.

Competence. When we're operating with competence, feeling adept, effective and skilled, productivity is positively impacted and our self-esteem keeps tingling with every bolstering step forward.

Relatedness. When we're operating "relatedly" (especially with that Positive Relational Energy we learned in the Connection Strategy), we form and maintain meaningful connections with colleagues, relishing a supportive work environment, which we know improves overall wellbeing and motivation.

If all these non-prison-like states abound, we flourish. Intrinsic motivation effervesces, there's consistent satisfaction linked to output, happiness during the work itself is high, fulfilment intertwines professional and personal life realms, and it all builds to more likely financial success. And as we well appreciate, being comfortable financially is essential to our psychological sense of security – shelter and food forming the baseline of Maslow's hierarchy of needs. So, self-determination theory is a good model to follow both individually and with regards to any culture you're responsible for shaping. Think about this when designing work goals and mission statements.

Feeling Successful Won't Come from Sales Numbers

Things will get tough at times. It's how life inevitably rolls. But if when pursuing your Big Impact wealth goals like status and meritocratic achievements, you recognize that you are also collecting life experiences as part of your spiritual, emotional and intellectual growth, then any suffering that arises as you love, serve, learn, give and connect along the way, will ensure you more capably roll with the punches when they hit. There will be bad days as well as good ones, but having the certitude to philosophize that it's all part of the journey, to ground yourself in your self-worth, your intrinsic motivation and your sense of purpose, will make the bad feel more tolerable and provide the fortitude to continue (plus stimulate more reflective journal entries or fodder for your blockbuster movie script, *The Courageous Comeback,* at the very least).

As 20th-century theologian Paul Tillich said, "Suffering introduces you to yourself and reminds you that you're not the person you thought you were."[138] In other words, the mask comes off. Your innermost self stirs. You go back to the beginning. You start to come home. As my client Suzanne peeled away the surface layers of her self-identity, which had been warped by financial obsession and externalities, she rooted more healthily back into her innate, less egoically drenched wishes and wants. And from this place her healing and renewed growth could begin.

A eulogy doesn't move a congregation to tears because it reflects a LinkedIn profile charmingly detailing roles and how much money the deceased made for her company. Nope, a funeral celebrates the character of the individual. The virtues that person shone on the world. How they made people feel. How they cared, loved, laughed, gleamed. Their radiance, their luminosity, their light. Of course, that twinkles through work, yes, but so much more than work accolades, what's remembered is their devotion to family, friends and colleagues, their ability to connect and spread joy. The magic of you, the essence of your spirit, that is what will be remembered, that is who you are, not what.

So, when we ponder success in these terms, how does it change your focus? How do you want to be remembered? For the promotions you scaled or the cuddles you gave? A delicious serenity shimmers when we blend both. We'll feel a whole lot more balanced when what we do is infused with who we are, when ambition is chased in honour of our values, not despite them. Then every day bursts with riches.

Remember the Hedonic Treadmill we learned about earlier in the book (page 6)? Well, be cognisant of the happiness set-point constantly reverting back to baseline. No matter how juicy the carrot, how Nobel Prize-esque the award, how dreamy the date, eventually it will feel less special as we adapt to it. Apparently even during massages, the pleasure fades and it's less of a treat 30 minutes in compared with 10 minutes in. Think of the first bloom of romance with a new partner and how it eventually settles into contented companionship, with less fizz. The rush of a new home and how it's soon not enough and you need an extension. The new baby and questions about a sibling. More, more, more. Next, next, next. But when is enough enough?

When is it time to say no to the next project, the next night out, the next HIIT class, the next truffle parmesan chip or even the next meditation? When is more going too far in pursuit of the next high? When is more gluttonous, excessive and inappropriate? When is more harmful to you in some way? The answer is: before you compromise your values. In caps, bold and underlined: **DO NOT COMPROMISE YOUR VALUES.** Ever.

Ultimately, it won't feel like success if you're squashing one aspect of what's important to you while over-indexing concurrently on another. Loving hard is better than working hard if love is higher than work on your values list. Laughing lots is better than winning lots if laughter is more important to you. Sleep is more important than a workout if rest is more important than fitness. It's all relative to our values list and what's at the top of that list. If you keep striving to achieve something disconnected from a priority value, only dis-satisfaction will swirl, throughout the climb and at the peak.

There's also a subtle connection between risk and reward when it comes to success, satisfaction and happiness. We each have a personal risk tolerance and if Big Impact is a desire, evaluate the correlation between the size of your dream and size of risk you're prepared to take. The bigger the risk, the bigger the potential impact.

The individuals who risk it all do often lose it all, but if and when they gain, oh they gain. They reach those heady heights they dreamt of way back when the seeds of their idea first started sprouting. But the most devoted of entrepreneurs, employees and creators gain, regardless of whether or not their idea succeeds, because they themselves soared throughout the toil, the thrill of taking the risk, of stepping closer to their dreams each day, of living with hope, optimism and energized motivation, all of which was a form of wealth in itself. They were promotion-oriented, relishing the pursuit and the acquired wisdom and experience, irrelevant of the outcome.

So, play with this and take steps to gradually extend your risk tolerance. Play with little things that challenge you like eating brussels sprouts, or making a phone call on a train, going out without makeup on, whatever you identify as something you feel uncomfortable doing. Reassure yourself through small daily acts that you're not afraid to chase success, while remembering it needs to be meaningful success. There's no point doing risky stuff that holds no intrinsic value to you.

Satisfaction Doesn't Necessarily Lie in the Extra-Ordinary

Devoting our lives to striving for that epic tomorrow or trying to relive the best of the past is a surefire way to eliminate our chances of happiness in this moment, and this one, and this one ... Strong emotions arise when thinking about the past or the future, but emotions are always fleeting, always flitting onward, and it's emotionally healthier (and wealthier) to reorient ourselves into the emotions of the present (especially if any pervasive emotions are unpleasant). It's better to ground ourselves in the here and now, celebrating what's right in front of us, however ordinary it may be. Instead of retrospective mental meanderings, celebrate how far you've come in the past one, five or 50 years, and how much more evolved and consistently happier you feel today.

Understand that a quest for wealth solely as a means for material gain may often misdirect us away from savouring riches immediately in front of us. So, open your eyes to the unexpected joy of the ordinary to be found glinting in the garland of sparkling dew drops on a spider's web, a baby's giggle, a cool breeze on a stifling day, the random book you were meant to find, the last seat on the train. Look and look again and stop obsessing over attaining the extra-ordinary. Instead, re-enchant the ordinary, or as Catherine Gray, lyrical wordsmith and sobriety queen, puts it, "The overwhelming and inevitable life-lean towards the ordinary is why true deep-pile contentment is found when you re-enchant the everyday."[139] Stop feeling dissatisfied with the ordinary. Just stop it.

Interestingly, there's an actual personality type labelled a Satisficer.[140] Satisficers make decisions quickly and simply, feeling immediately content and, well, satisfied. They live in a state of mellow satisfaction, replete in choices well made, lives well lived. They feel successful because they are satisfied with their decisions made. By contrast, their opposites, Maximizers, spend too much of life in mental turmoil, deliberating over decisions, scrutinizing various scenarios, ruminating endlessly and ruing decisions made, even once committed. There's little peace for a Maximizer, yet so much simplicity and satisfaction for those Satisficers. Is it that simple to feel successful? To make peace with our decisions? Try it!

BIG IMPACT REFLECTION: REDEFINING WEALTH

Let's bring all your learnings together to redefine what wealth and success mean to you. Contemplate 1. Happiness, 2. Satisfaction, 3. Wealth, and 4. Success. Explore how abundant and fulfilling each state feels, detailing how, where, when, why and so on. Write your own definition for each term and establish any actions you'd like to take to confidently stride into a life of Big Impact Wealth. Envisage your Big Impact future as truly magnificent.

Your Big Impact Wealth Expansion Grid

You now understand the key components to create your bespoke Wealth Strategy for Big Impact; you know how multifaceted wealth is and how it extends beyond the financial into all life realms, you know how to recognize money blocks and gain tighter control over managing your finances, how to maximize your value and to orient your success toward that which is intrinsically motivated. The grid below is what you now know how to manage.

It's time to translate this into solid action to make your expansion a reality.

Grab your journal and review the statements below, focusing on the "Expanding To" column. Now spend 30 minutes freewriting on everything that comes up for you when you read the expansion statements. Elaborate on them where you see fit and make them entirely yours. As well as writing the "what", dive into the "how" and "why". Really explore the statements, applying your newfound knowledge, and have fun exploring all the life-altering ways you're going to feel and how you're going to get there. Let the inspiration pour forth and capture everything that comes to mind.

FROM	EXPANDING TO...
I have a self-identity focused on extrinsically motivated achievements like status and financial symbols of wealth and I am competitively driven in my pursuit.	I have redefined success based on what inner wealth means to me, removing adopted or inherited unconscious success ideologies and tuning into my self-worth primarily.
I have low self-worth which impacts what I charge or how effectively I negotiate my value.	I know how to maximize my sense of self-worth and how to "premiumize" my value.
I have negative money beliefs blocking my abundance potential and recognize I live with a scarcity mindset.	I have positive money beliefs with an abundance mindset and approach money management positively and effectively.
I fear my own greatness and hold myself back from my full potential in terms of income and stepping into the arena.	I understand how to push my own boundaries into success and how to use process to maximize my wealth potential.
I don't know my own limits.	I am clear when enough is enough and never to compromise my values.
I have no idea what state my finances are in.	I am tightly in control of my money.
I never take risks and am stuck.	I find the courage to take small risks connecting to my ambitions daily.
I never feel satisfied.	I am grateful to live every day feeling satisfaction and happiness and take pleasure in the ordinary.

Wealth Strategy Priority Actions

It's time for serious action. Now bring your reflections together and organize them into priority areas of focus that you identify as integral to your master Wealth Strategy for Big Impact Without Burnout across the next 12 months.

Drawing the grid below in your notebook or in a spreadsheet, list as many reflections and actions with deadlines per theme as you can based on all you've learned. Then distil all of these action ideas into three Wealth Strategy Priority Actions, which we'll incorporate into your master plan at the end of the book. Remember to always tune into your values and overarching impact goals as you create your plans. Make the three action priorities realistic, achievable and inspiring, and rigorously tied to firm deadlines.

ONE-YEAR BIG IMPACT WITHOUT BURNOUT MASTER PLAN			
WEALTH STRATEGY	REFLECTIONS	ACTIONS	DEADLINE
1. The Psychology of Wealth			
Who are you?			
2. The Power of Money Management			
The World of Abundance			
Releasing Money Blocks and Resentment			
Money Goals			
Premiumizing You			
The Power of Process			
3. Soaring into Success and Satisfaction			
Redefining Wealth			
	My 3 Wealth Strategy Priority Actions are...1...2...3...		

YOUR BIG IMPACT STRATEGY NO. 8: FULFILMENT

"Keep one still, secret spot where dreams may go, and sheltered so, may thrive and grow where doubt and fear are not. O keep a place apart, within your heart, for little dreams to go!"

— Louise Driscoll

We've arrived at our final strategy and by now you've reflected lots, made firm decisions and perhaps implemented adjustments here and there already. Hopefully, you're energized by an all-pervasive sense of right now marking a moment of transitionary and transformational growth in your life. This final strategy is about accountability. It's about owning how you lean into "no more struggle" consistently, in the most powerful and sustainable ways for you. It's about conclusively accepting that the only one responsible for the shape of your life, the pace of your progress, the magnitude of your impact or indeed your burnout, is you. It's about committing to the radiant You who you have visualized throughout this book. It's about taking charge of the breadth of your overall life fulfilment, so you sleep peacefully each night regardless of the velocity of life's cyclically, spiralling swirls. It's about loving your work and your lot and never deviating from a flow of graceful productivity. It's about living your truth purposefully, respectfully and excitedly. There are lifelong gifts held within this final strategy, about to be unlocked within you.

The Cambridge Dictionary defines fulfilment as "a feeling of pleasure because you are satisfied with what you are doing or have achieved". I see it as even grander. I see that feeling of happiness arising from more than the mere doing, but also from feeling what you intended to feel in life and being how you envisaged you would be. It's a sense of wonder and awe, of joy and gratitude. Fulfilment to me encompasses rushing with the whisper of divine creation within and all around. It's the glowing potential shimmering on every horizon, the beauty behind the veneer of life, and the endless possibilities rippling when creation is our status quo. It's dancing in the moonlight, it's splashing in the bathtub, it's smiling at the stranger. Fulfilment is a sense of thankfulness and bliss. It's bursting with excitement at the thrill of it all, at the ordinary miracles astonishing with their magnificence, the spectacular in the everyday, the wow in the now, life as a veritable starburst.

In these pages, you're going to effusively step into fulfilment along a path of integrity. You're going to route back to who you absolutely, really are (freed from any self-created, external identity you may have started peeling away in previous chapters). You're going to honour your soul's desires and ensure your journey into Big Impact is a spiritually enlivened one, where you feel that electrifying tingle of being aptly plugged into your destiny, bubbling with optimism, hope and a calm sense of internal certainty. By functioning in the world from a place of integrity as your mainstay, you will be able to easily notice when and where dissonance occurs and course-correct back onto the right path, into your truest self.

We can meditate, eat clean, avoid toxicity and practise doing good till the cows come home, but if we are not living each day authentic to our true, inner selves, and if we are compromising our values through action, word or deed, and if we are spending too much time in our heads not our hearts, we won't feel peaceful. We just won't.

Instead, what we'll feel is niggled. We'll feel out of sorts. Things will irritate us, people will trigger us, situations won't feel quite right or comfortable. Falling asleep may become a challenge, or drifting back off after we've awoken. Life will feel like a struggle, because it is a struggle when we're silencing our souls, our personalities, our way of being. Waking up each day to progress onward with an agenda, person or job we've now outgrown is tiresome and draining. We ache. We feel sore. This is not how life is meant to feel. We are meant to soar. I really believe that.

That free-spirited you who sat on the beach collecting shells as a child, immersed in the cornucopia of chipped cones and cracked coral treasures, is still who you are. You were inwardly still and content then. You were able to pursue what interested you and relish what washed up next into your sandy palms, inquisitively exploring the curved ridges of a new shell. That accepting, curious, calm little girl has the right to reemerge in you today, to navigate this messy and beautiful world with the same intrigue and wonder as she did way back when. It's your right to reconnect with her as your inner teacher, integrate her into this Big Impact ambitious woman you now are, and embrace life from this point onward with the spring of integrity in your every step.

So, if your reality today presents as a distortion of the one you dreamt of, then this point of dissatisfaction is your turning point. Your Eureka moment.

Because, when this moment arrives, you can now lift the veil to peek into what a reality in congruence with what you really want looks like. You can gaze back into that dream you had for your best life, for how you had intended to make your splash into the world, who you would be and how you would show up – your truth. At last, you can finitely draw your heart up into your head, your energetic self into alignment, step into a flow of integrity and click into living life as authentic You.

If you reach a state where the discomfort and pain of staying stuck suddenly feels worse than the discomfort and pain of changing, then you're ready to stride more completely into your congruent chapter where all the puzzle pieces slot into place, click, click, click. Getting clear on the wishes you want fulfilled is the starting point. Then living intentionally, honouring those wishes and blossoming from a sturdy place of integrity is how all the resplendent fulfilment beautifully manifests. Let's begin.

The Way of Integrity

It took me many years to understand the enormity of integrity. Now, I revere it as the only route to peace. Getting divorced after 26 years, with four little souls to bring on the journey, felt so contradictory. How could I be honouring integrity if I was ripping the family foundations from beneath my children's little feet? Who was I to cause such destruction, to shatter the family unit, to stimulate an unfamiliar new chapter? My brain, like an Edgar Allan Poe raven, screeched that I was selfish, despicable, vile. I was petrified of taking action for a long, long time. Six years, in fact. Six years of bemused oscillations of shall we, shan't we, rings off, then on, we will, we won't, therapy, conversations, round and round we went, endlessly debating if separation was the way of integrity.

Only at the point when I looked the decision and that wretched raven directly in the eyes did I know. In my belly, in my heart, in my soul, the way of integrity was to accept and honour the stark truth. We were evolved people, our relationship had changed and it was time for us to carefully and kindly move into the next phases of our lives separately, delicately and protectively carrying the children on the fragile wings of this momentous decision. And so, in this certitude that integrity was the best and only way, we painfully, lovingly, amicably divorced, acknowledging it not as failure but as evolution.

Life is indeed dynamic. Life will always keep moving onward. Staying in integrity can be the most simple and powerful way for you to exist positively in its flow without cackling ravens inhibiting your absolute right to joy, abundance and fulfilment. And ultimately, to exist as your true self.

My path to integrity, and thus peace, which I hope will become yours, centres on five essential ways of being, with yourself and others:

1. Truthful
2. Contractual
3. Intuitive
4. Present
5. Kind

1. Being Truthful

"A breach of integrity stops the flow of energy, just as a pebble jammed in a garden hose stops the flow of water."

— Gay Hendricks

My children, and anyone who knows me, will tell you that if you start or end a sentence with "to be honest", as in "No, it wasn't a great day at school to be honest", or "To be honest, I prefer London to Paris", I will invariably say "Thank you. Yes, please do always be honest." It's my stock reply, and I tell you this because it is representative of what I hope for and expect from everyone around me and, importantly, a standard I set myself, my team and my clients. It's a no-quibble part of my way of integrity. It's also a nonnegotiable aspect of having Big Impact Without Burnout. When honesty is not upheld, life is exhausting, complicated, stressful, jarring. Honesty matters. Do be honest. Please. Always.

Let's be clear why honesty matters.

- It's gruelling upholding lies. Secrets are stressful. Dishonesty is debilitating.
- Unclear boundaries through murky mistruths or unspoken clarity lead to complicated and disappointing relationships.
- Life is simpler and progress quicker when the truth is articulated.
- You cannot exit life's struggle if you're operating inauthentically.
- Honesty, even if it hurts, is always best (and can be delivered graciously).

We are taught not to lie as children. Lying is wrong. Thou shalt not lie is a premise in every religion, from Christianity's ten commandments and other Bible references, to one of Buddhism's five precepts, "I refrain from telling lies", to Judaic forbidding of lying "unless to save a life".[141] It's unanimously agreed that lies are not on.

Now, I might ask you if you are a liar and you will tell me: no way, I don't condone lying in any form. And then I ask you if you ever tell white lies? When I ask clients this, I tend to get the squirmy, nervous response of, "I don't lie, but I will admit that I exaggerate", accompanied by a shaking head and ironic eye roll, as if to acknowledge an unspoken consensus that lying is different from white lies and exaggeration. We all bend the truth here and there, don't we, Officer?

Well, yes and no. Most of us draw an invisible line between what constitutes a lie and what is an acceptable bend, an exaggeration or a white lie. I do it myself and I'm penning a chapter about honesty. I admit that I do exaggerate and expand stories for dramatic effect, working the crowd and all that, but with the big stuff that matters, the words that affect other people or influence situations or feelings, dishonesty is a serious no-go zone. I am always impeccable with my word, as Don Miguel Ruiz encourages in *The Four Agreements*, and I will not tolerate, nor will I ever spread lies. Neither should you. Stepping fully into your integrity means examining your relationship with the truth, both inwardly and outwardly, and honouring firm truth boundaries consistently.

A life spent trying to navigate or uphold muddied realities, unclear versions of what is or isn't, ominous silences, distorted facts, is ludicrously challenging. The truth keeps life simple, relationships healthy and progress straightforward. My experience at work, in my private life, within my wellbeing practice, in all interactions, has taught me time and time again that being truthful makes life easier, not always, but generally so. Secrets make life hard and make it impossible for you to soar and feel fulfilled.

Blurred Lines

We generally exaggerate to get attention, making a tale all the more engaging for its embellishment and don't maliciously mean any harm. But the extent of truth distortion and the circumstance in which it's been stretched can create unnecessary complexity. Think about an exaggerated CV or job interview. The person booms with apparent experience and smashed goals that are way beyond what was actually achieved. The employer risks hiring someone not necessarily capable. The employee joins in a paranoid state of being found out, most likely incapable. It's all a sorry mess.

And so it is with white lies. They can be messy too (quite literally in this example!). "Did you eat all the cake, darling?" the mother asks, smiling as she kneels opposite her child, observing his cream-smeared chops and chubby fingers powdered with icing sugar. "No, Mama," he fibs as he shakes his cheeky little head, looking down at his feet, unable to meet her gaze, empty plate clutched behind his back. We have to work harder to either deliver or decipher white lies. When deciphering, people are hard to figure out. Are they telling you facts or distortions? Should you trust or distrust? When should you probe deeper to gain clarity for your own peace of mind? (Here's a hint: Starts with A, ends in LWAYS.)

It works both ways. When you're sharing your wants and goals, how do you bend the truth versus communicate factually and clearly? When you tell your partner, "I want to work all day", what do you mean? Seventeen hours from dawn to dusk alone, uninterrupted and in your blissful solitary zone of genius, or a standard workday of eight hours punctuated with meal breaks together, or just three hours of working plus gym, pub lunch and movie night? What do you actually mean? It's kinder (and makes relationships a whole lot easier) to express the details and avoid ambiguity when sharing what you want with others.

What about the little lies we tell ourselves? "No, I don't like eating meat," says the religiously conditioned vegetarian, instructed by her parents not to eat flesh since birth, who in fact would love to try a bacon sandwich, triple layered with cheese and ketchup. But her mind doesn't wander there because it's conditioned to believe sets of rules and ways of being, so the truth, "I love bacon" is never to be admitted out loud or, more dangerously, even privately acknowledged.

What about being honest about our weaknesses? Or how we feel about a certain situation or someone? There's real peril afoot if we don't acknowledge what we feel or subconsciously know to be true – if we let an inner shame like "I'm letting my parents down if I eat meat" contort our innards into tangly knots. Likewise, if we feel it's too contentious to admit we don't like the gift or want to visit that house or see those people. Whenever we are functioning in ways born of fear not love, destruction instead of creation, and behaving such that we satisfy others – our boss, the world or whoever – rather than honouring our own wishes and wants, our very heart's desires, we're getting into murky waters. If something doesn't feel right and we're drawn away in a different direction, we need to delve deeper and check out what's going on.

In the work arena, being untruthful hampers both business relationships and our impact. So, strive to clean up your cloudy thoughts and words immediately. Unblur your lines.

BIG IMPACT REFLECTION: LIVING IN TRUTH

Reflect on a recent situation where you felt tempted to bend the truth or tell a white lie. How did that choice impact your feelings about yourself and your relationships with others? Imagine how the situation might have unfolded if you had chosen to be completely honest. Write about the potential benefits of embracing honesty in all aspects of your life, including being honest with yourself, and consider the ways in which living with integrity could lead to deeper, more fulfilling connections and a stronger sense of self-worth. What small steps can you take today to practise greater honesty and integrity?

Secrets Prohibit the Soul from Soaring

Doing something to serve another's need above our own, or suppressing an inner desire, is effectively keeping a secret. By definition, secrets are when something is kept unseen or unknown. Secrets are also acts made with an ulterior motive, thus manipulating a situation or person to suit your own gain. Unequivocally, secrets are exhausting and extremely hard to live with. "The main thing that is known about secrets is that keeping them is unhealthy for the brain", neuroscientist David Eagleman has written.[142] Secrets stress our bodies as well as our minds, weakening our immune systems, veering us toward burnout. It takes a lot of precious energy to maintain them. When our brains are forced to divert energy toward hiding something you need to keep buried within, you're shrinking cognitive focus in other, healthier aspects of your life. So, by locking yourself in your own secrecy prison, you risk harming your work, your relationships and your very survival. Within secrecy, we falter.

If you can't admit it out loud, it's a secret. (And corporate playgrounds are rife with managers battling this challenge.) Silence itself can be dishonest. Silence is not always kind. Silence holds the unsaid, unseen, unshared. Read this again and absorb please. Not saying something can be just as deceitful as a lie spoken aloud. Master manipulators artfully withhold information, trying to convince themselves they are not liars as nobody asked. This is subtle and nasty deception. Silence can be dishonest and the best liars around love it as a tool. So, be very wary of what is unsaid when your hackles are up and trust issues are at play. Ask pertinent questions.

Strategies to Communicate Honestly

- Use "I" statements to express your feelings without blaming others. For example, "I would prefer not to eat there."
- Be clear and specific to avoid misunderstandings. For example, "When I say I want to work all day, I mean don't interrupt me for 12 hours unless to bring me food ;-) !"
- Practice active listening by attentively hearing and reflecting on what others say. For example, "I understand you would rather we offer him a freelance gig for four weeks only."
- Ensure your tone and body language align with your verbal message to convey sincerity.
- Acknowledge and take responsibility for your mistakes to build trust and accountability. For example, "That one is on me, I apologize."
- Give feedback directly, clearly and earnestly. For example, "That should have been completed on Monday so it's delayed our project and I expect you to avoid this happening again."
- Ask for clarity if there is any ambiguity. For example, "Do you mean you want this to happen this year or this decade?"
- When silence hangs ask, "Is there anything not being said here?" You have every right to probe if you sense concealment.
- If you are harboring a secret, yours or someone else's, and it is weighing heavily on you, seek professional guidance about how to move forward.
- Always respect work confidentiality to the letter.
- Check yourself and your truth lines – when are you harmlessly exaggerating versus dangerously causing ripples of untruths to cascade, which may impact yourself and others? Stop the latter.

Living Your Truth

"Authenticity means erasing the gap between what you firmly believe inside and what you reveal to the outside world."
— Adam Grant

The word "integrity" is deeply linked to the concept of wholeness, since the root of the word "integer" means a whole number. Living, then, in integrity means expressing what's true for you, for the wholeness of you, for your complete "one-ness" in all situations. If you depart from your integrity and behave in any way outside of your wholeness, you're creating duplicity, "two-ness". The fake smile, the compliment you don't mean, marrying for money, partying to be in the cool gang, the sycophantic relationship you have with your boss despite finding her abhorrent: this is all duplicity. When you're duplicitous, you become what Martha Beck calls "the truth knower and the lie actor" all at once. That is duplicity. And, as Martha continues "... duplicity, not social noncompliance, is the real enemy of joy."[143] Her point is that you'll suffer more in the long run from the inner disquiet of not being true to yourself way more than any discomfort of being shunned by a community.

So, don't conform if it doesn't feel right. Don't alter yourself to be what's expected of you. Stay in your integrity. Conforming to meet societal expectations could mean staying in an unhappy marriage because divorce is culturally frowned upon. Cutting a fringe, wearing a pinstripe suit and carrying a duffel bag because your coworkers do doesn't make you a better hedge fund manager. And just because your partner would rather you put cooking dinner before working on your business each night, it doesn't mean you should.

When you're in duplicity, you're losing that authentic, non-pinstriped, business-not-kitchen-first, true version of you. You'll feel inauthentic and you'll be oozing inauthenticity too. When we are operating with a metaphorical mask on, whether we've donned it by choice or at someone else's behest, we vibrate with what I call Imposter Frequencies. If we feel the need to mask our real selves, we're hiding some essence within. Knowing we're concealing something, we're less confident, we're more shaky, nervous, shrunk, and afraid. Others sense our incongruence, our Imposter Frequencies. We're less likely to be hired when we're pretending we're good or experienced in something we are not. The interviewer will see right through us.

I believe any secret, however big or small, will impact your vibe and others will sense it. Even if you're in a bluster tap-dance and over egging something, dripping with bravado and boastfulness, if you're not being honest, your vibe is askew. When you're in full integrity, pure and congruent in body, mind and soul, you emit infectiously uplifting, what I call Magnificent Frequencies. You are magnetically earnest. These are the ones that will ensure you and your life keep expanding positively, growing in all the best and most fulfilling ways.

To tune into and experience your Magnificent Frequencies, which feels flipping amazing by the way, you need to learn to distinguish your desire from what others believe you should desire. For example, do you really want to marry that doctor or are you conforming to a desire your family holds? Equally, you need to distinguish a true desire from a false desire. A true desire is exciting, positive, expansive and good for you – "Let's get a puppy!" A false desire is fearful, urgent, desperate, crazed and bad for you – "I need to get hammered". It can be all too easy to slip into a situation, relationship or action without realizing it's not what you want but that you're being swept up by a need to please, a hope, a despondency, a childish want that you've since evolved away from, a way of satisfying society or family or your other half.

BIG IMPACT REFLECTION: TUNING INTO YOUR MAGNIFICENT FREQUENCIES

Find a quiet space where you can sit comfortably and undisturbed. Close your eyes and take a few deep breaths, focusing on the rise and fall of your chest. Visualize a warm, glowing light emanating from your heart, filling your chest with a sense of peace and love. Now, think of a goal or aspiration that truly excites you. As you focus on this goal, imagine the warm light from your heart travelling up to your head, merging with your thoughts and intentions. Feel the alignment between your heart's desires and your mind's plans. Sit in this energizing state for several minutes. Then open your eyes and write down everything you just experienced – how the goal expanded, the emotions stirred, the thoughts provoked. Reflect on how this alignment of heart and mind makes you feel more vibrant, motivated, and in tune with your true self. Practise this regularly so you can enter this state throughout your day, especially before big meetings or moments.

Buddha taught us all suffering is desire. However, I'm teaching you that desire is not a cause for suffering but a delicious clue to your life of integrity. Within each desire uncoils values, passions, optimism, excitement. It's not as simple as listing your desire and then your guiding light shines forth, illuminating the immediate path to follow, actions to take, when to set off. Neither is it as simple as figuring out the initial why behind the want and the conundrum is solved. It's more around trusting your feelings, thoughts and emotions, examining them from every angle, peeling layer upon layer away to reveal the soft core and richness within the true desire. Within this nectar lies the opportunity to embellish the desire with all the detail to design the path, elaborate on the how and when, and unleash motivation and energy to attain the desire with zeal.

For example, "I want the Dyson Airwrap. Why? So my hair curls quickly," does not get us close to authentic desire. Nor does "I want to get a job in the city. Why? So I earn a fat salary." Nor, "I want to go travelling. Why? Because I'm against corporate traps." No, where our wants are concerned, as with our triggers, there's juice behind each statement that needs squeezing out.

The magic starts to bubble up when we apply "And then?" questioning. Once your hair has curled, then what? So that I'm ready quicker. And then? So that I can have curly hair every workday. And then? So that I feel more confident in the office. And then? So I get promoted. And then? So I earn more. And then? So I can buy that flat. And then? So I can move out from my parents. And then? I can have a relationship. Aha! Gold. This isn't about a rapid, hair-twirling piece of electrical kit, this is about your desire to start finding love. That desire for a Dyson Airwrap is connected to evolving into independent adult life with a partner, not parents. Likewise, the seemingly inconsequential desire to work in the city is peeled away, layer by layer, to reveal an urgent desire to make Dad proud before it's too late. The travelling wish, an admission that we've not yet found the career path to follow so want a year of vox-pop stimulus to kickstart our imagination. There's always more than meets the eye when you ask the never-ending "And then?"

BIG IMPACT REFLECTION: TRUE OR FALSE DESIRES

Reflect on your current desires and aspirations, considering their alignment with your core values and long-term aspirations. Ask yourself what is motivating each desire and whether it leads to genuine fulfilment or temporary gratification. Tune into your inner wisdom and intuition to discern between true desires that resonate deeply with your authentic self and false desires driven by external influences or societal expectations. Write down actionable steps to pursue your true desires with clarity and purpose, releasing any desires that do not serve your highest good with compassion and understanding.

An expansive self-development reframe I encourage you to think about is this; the question isn't "What would I do if I wasn't afraid?", it's "What would I do if I was truly being myself?" What indeed would you do? How would you show up? What work would you do? What work would you do more of? Who would you be with? Where would you be? How would you feel? Don't ponder what life could look like when we bravely combat fear, starting from a place of negativity, but instead flip the question to start from the more powerful and positive abundance of who you really are, how damn incredible she is and the difference you know she's destined to make to the world. It's a simple reframe that invites more inspired and inspiring reflection.

2. Being Contractual

Honouring our commitments is an integrity imperative. Whether to ourselves, our community, our colleagues, our families, whoever, once we've agreed to do something, the wheels of expectation are set in motion. Your reputation hinges on this, as does respect, reliability and trust. If we don't uphold our promises to others, faith in us quickly fades and opportunities, and potentially friends, dry up. If we fail ourselves, constantly making excuses or repeatedly resisting requisite action, our self-worth shrivels, and we know how damaging this is. When broken inside, the outside can't sustain. If you deliver on business promises, but keep letting friends and family down, with personal integrity seemingly less of a priority than business integrity, you need to urgently do more inward reflection. Why are you selectively commitment-phobic? What does this say about you?

You know the six-degrees of separation idea, that we're all interconnected in some way, by six or fewer handshakes? Well, I like to think beyond the physical into the spiritual, envisaging invisible, gossamer threads between us, with chords thickening per the agreements we make with others, inferred or explicit. I like to believe in a spiritual dimension of souls connecting with other souls, our inner realms as well as our physical bodies attaching, our journeys intertwining for a fragment of time, however fleeting or enduring. This often subtle, energetic entanglement is experienced by so many of us as a web of connection keeping our lives alive with multitudinal filaments in a million and one different directions simultaneously.

When you make a promise to someone, you're designing a spiritual contract with them, or what Caroline Myss calls a "sacred contract". Her work teaches that our souls evolve from the interactions we have across our lifetimes and that each relationship, however peripheral, marks a potential growth opportunity of some form. She says, "A Contract is your overall relationship to your personal power and your spiritual power."[144] So, how we honour the promises we make influences our energetic vibrancy. When we break our word, we deplete both our personal and spiritual power.

Some chords and contracts will be stronger than others. Sometimes threads need to be cut to evolve separately, but there are always ways to uphold integrity when severing ties or ending contracts. An amicable divorce or a generous redundancy package are examples of positive partings, contracts (physically and spiritually) mutually disbanded. Dishonourable contract breaking where you renege on a decision pledge or an agreed plan, or painted an illusory picture that never materialized, are harmful both to yourself and others.

When you disappoint another by breaking a promise, you wound them (yes, even if we're talking about a professional agreement). You created a belief centred on collaborative creation, co-creation, on doing something together, which you reneged on without having overtly renegotiated the contract. That is dishonourable, that is not integrity and you need to do inner work to understand why you're making false promises to yourself and others. Is there a self-centred gain you are prioritizing? Is there a fear of the potential held within the magnitude of the contract's possibilities that is holding you back? If you break your word, investigate what is going on inside.

If you've been disappointed, I'm sorry. I know how hurt and upset you feel, how much your heart aches with the heaviness of the bullet lodged in your core. I know you'll perambulate through a series of difficult thoughts and emotions. When we're disappointed, we feel the pop of a bubble burst, its iridescent vision fragmenting and disappearing into nothingness.

When we accept the contract was ripped up behind our backs, we have two options: kick, scream and attack violently, verbally or otherwise, depending on how aggrieved we are. Or, preferably, surrender to what has happened, graciously and gracefully seeking out some karmic lesson. Did we miss a detail? Did we misinterpret the plan? Did we mishear something? Or were we duped? What was our role in this? Which part of us sat vulnerable and distracted, permitting this to occur, this person to manipulate us so? Were we asleep? Were we naive and silly, or sweetly innocent and taken advantage of? Either way, what can we learn? Caroline Myss views these moments as invitations to awaken our divine potential, advising, "Manipulation is the art of making another person's spirit dance for personal amusement, and only through honoring oneself do we become strong enough to refuse to dance."[145] Please pirouette only when you choose. Never when another instructs, "Spin!", however sweetly. Never.

BIG IMPACT REFLECTION: KARMIC DISAPPOINTMENT

Reflect on a recent disappointment you experienced. Write about how it made you feel and why it affected you so deeply. Then, shift your perspective to consider what this disappointment might be teaching you about yourself, your actions, or your expectations. What is the deeper karmic lesson here? How can this experience guide you toward growth and a more balanced approach to similar situations in the future? Use this reflection to uncover hidden insights and embrace the opportunity for personal development.

When it comes to honouring what you've promised yourself – like the decision pledges in this book – it can be as simple as the following four steps.

1. Write the decision down.
2. Elaborate on the commitment detail.
3. Strategize for handling wobbly moments of potential derailment.
4. Organise your life to ensure maintaining commitment is as easy as possible.

Boundary Setting

"Burnout is overwhelming and boundaries are the cure."
— Nedra Glover Tawwab

Protecting ourselves to minimize disappointment that we create or experience requires boundaries. Boundaries are the rules we construct for successfully playing our personal game of life. They preserve our ability to have Big Impact and not burn out. But they are ineffective if we don't communicate them. They are pointless if we don't honour them. They are fantastic superpowers when used well. As a recovered people-pleaser, I can attest that boundaries 100 per cent changed my life, my relationships, my vitality and my work, all for the better.

To establish boundaries with yourself and others, take the following steps:

- **Know your limits.** Based on your needs, values and priorities, understand where you need to set them in the first place.
- **Communicate clearly.** Be respectful and assertive, following the tips earlier in the chapter.
- **Be firm and consistent.** Don't bend your boundaries to accommodate others' demands if they don't chime with your values, ever.
- **Practice self-care.** Honour all the strategies designed throughout this book as a priority, relishing how saying "no" can be kind.
- **Set boundaries early.** Establish ways of working or being together at the start of any relationship, romantic, business or otherwise.
- **Trust your intuition.** Pay attention to discomfort and examine how a boundary has been crossed, if it needs asserting or establishing, and so on.
- **Reevaluate and adjust.** Regularly assess your boundaries as life is dynamic and evolving constantly.
- **Stay strong but be flexible.** Boundaries are fabulously empowering and such simple ways to glide through life with everyone knowing where they

stand. Rigidity isn't always necessary, so be smart, but don't ever cancel boundaries out of fear or pressure. Use them well and often!

3. Being Intuitive

"In thinking about miracles, I believe that our frame of reference has been too dramatic. We have been looking for the burning bush, the parting of the sea, the bellowing voice from heaven. Instead, we should be looking at the ordinary day-to-day events in our lives for evidence of the miraculous, maintaining at the same time a scientific orientation."

— M Scott Peck

Think about how you saw the world as a child, with miracles and wonder everywhere. The awe at a rainbow's opalescence majestically arcing the sky, the glee at raindrops pelting soft cheeks, face upturned, eyes blinking, giggling, a yellow petal on the dusty ground with no obvious origin, the ocean's froth melting the sandy shore. It was all mesmerizing.

We also knew what felt safe or not. We knew who we felt comfortable being around. Who expanded our energy and who contracted it. What we wanted to do next. How to be here now, effortlessly. We just were.

But, we gradually learned to desensitize ourselves to those guiding feelings as rational thinking took over. We started to process what we should or shouldn't do or say or feel. We stopped discovering that effusive wonder everywhere and instead began to take it all for granted. And as we shut down our awe, we relaxed into a more orderly universe, which happened to be peppered with coincidences. Well, hear me: there are no coincidences. Coincidences are the universe's signs you're in full alignment, congruent in heart and mind, living life, plugged into the magic, supported, doing the right thing and progressing in the right direction.

I can't explain it. I feel something and it makes me swoon with peaceful serenity, buttered in reassurance that I'm not alone in some inexplicable way, that there *is* something greater than me out there and that I am invisibly tuning into a form of divinity, a field of energy, something. You will also have noticed these coincidences in your life. When a white feather flutters into your path just as you're thinking "that" thought, or know a friend will call, or you dream a dream that then happens, or see symbols in patterns, or ask a book for random wisdom and there's poignance in the sentence your eyes settle upon. Synchronicities demonstrate we are on the correct path, in our expansion zone. We become more alert to potential and trust the things that are happening as part of some grand destiny. So, with childlike wonder, I invite you to open all of your senses wide, and invite the waves to stream in.

Jung described synchronicity as "an ever-present reality for those who have eyes to see",[146] teaching that occurrences labelled as coincidences are not due to chance. He vigorously defended his belief that synchronous events are directly related to the observer's mind and serve to provide powerful insight, direction and guidance to assist you on your "path of individuation". His principles were grounded in the science that once the psyche connects to an apparent coincidence, life is infused with greater meaning and purpose, so psychologically, we evolve. In other words, pay attention: significance is in the air, open your eyes and tune in to the force that is working to support you.

When we do tap into this invisible potency, we feel into what is right or wrong. I firmly believe we do always know the answer. We just have to learn how to shut down the rational, overthinking, overanalysing logical mind, get out of our heads and into our hearts where our soul is busy beating in tune with our integrity. That quickening, hyper-alertness accompanied by surging emotions means we need to pay attention to something. You're either heading in the wrong direction or the right one. How you feel is giving you the answer. (And as we've learned is true for every Big Impact Without Burnout Strategy, we're always guided best by going within first.)

So, if something doesn't feel right, it isn't. But you need to examine what exactly. Please trust your instincts. I've had two people in my life who I have "sensed" dark clouds above. Their energy seemed "grey thickening to black". I read their vibe as sinister and felt incomprehensibly repulsed and afraid of the shadowy energy. Nothing felt good about them from the very first encounter. However, for various reasons our lives intertwined, and despite managing engagements logically, warmly and compassionately with each individual, my instinctive inner feedback eventually proved right. I still shudder to recall those two eerie souls.

Likewise with situations, if it doesn't feel quite right, tune into why not? In what way? How? Examine the situation from every angle. Go to sleep pondering it and see what your dreams tell you. Once, the night before signing a contract with a new business partner, about to share one of my companies for the first time, I awoke with this voice saying: "Don't do it, don't do it." This was at a point when I had four young children, and to wake to anything other than a baby's want was highly irregular. I didn't pay attention to the nocturnal rumbling, did sign the next day, and two years later, debt-ridden and distant-friended, we parted. I should have trusted that inner voice.

A medium would call that clairaudience: tuning into an inexplicable, mysterious message we hear as a spoken sentence, or song lyrics, phrases, van signs, words floating between dreams. I lost a precious ring once, hunting for weeks around the house. When I briefed my subconscious to help me find it, I awoke to the dreamy, imagined sound of Seal's song "Kiss from a Rose" and knew instantly it was in a little trinket box adorned with a red rose. And indeed, there it was. As my favourite spiritual intuitive, author and friend Tanya Carroll Richardson teaches, "Sleep can be a time of mystical awakening. At dawn, quickly record the vivid, memorable nuances of your nocturnal adventures."[147]

It's not for me here to dissect intuition's distinguishing features as separate from conscious, analytical thought. However, it is for us to embrace intuition as a way of honouring our own integrity and staying on our path of magnificence, trusting there is a guiding light for each of us that is our golden compass. I believe that dumbing down of our intuitive powers as we become socialized as children is a waste. Some of us burn the sixth sense to cinders, rationally relegating it to nonsense, others tap back into it more prominently later in life once the synchronicities become too common to ignore, and others trust it faithfully throughout their life.

My invitation here is for you to rekindle your relationship with your own sixth sense and weave intuition back into your life. If only 5 per cent of our thoughts are conscious, 95 per cent of what's driving us is the subconscious, so tapping into this should surely be a prerequisite to an abundant power. Once you start using your inner compass, you'll get more adept at trusting it, and decision-making on a more instinctive, soulful basis will become second nature. Your intuition always has your best interests at heart and is a muscle for you to strengthen. Start listening to it and your superpower will evolve. Test it standing in front of the fridge before you next eat something: what does your body want right now? I doubt it will be the cheesecake, but listen carefully as it might be. Test it before you accept that new job. Test it before you make that sales call. Test it. Listen.

BIG IMPACT REFLECTION: REACTIVATING YOUR SIXTH SENSE

Each day, begin with a ten-minute meditation to calm your mind and tune into your inner voice, noting any thoughts or impressions that arise. Throughout the day, consciously observe your environment, paying attention to sights, sounds and feelings, and recording anything significant in your journal. Before sleep, write down a question you seek guidance on and note any dreams or thoughts that come to you overnight. Tune into your body's responses to different situations, recognizing gut feelings or physical sensations and reflect on their meanings. Surround yourself with positive influences, minimize interactions with naysayers, practise creative visualization, and end your day by reflecting on how your intuition guided your decisions, documenting these insights to strengthen your intuitive abilities.

Curiosity and Imagination

"Your Imagination and Reality are the same. Which you choose is up to you!"
— Declan Joyce

When we awaken our intuition, we permit ideas to flow and tune into them unconsciously, listening to them without interrogation. With imagination, we start to elaborate on this intuitive inspiration with details, adding colour and form to our ideas. Protect and nourish your imagination and play with those flashes of creativity. Don't sculpt and hone them, but stay light and exploratory, expand and stretch the flashes into prisms of varying possibilities, in whatever form they come. Be curious about it all. Everything around you once started from a seed in imagination. This little seed of yours burning bright right now may lead to something phenomenal. It may not. It doesn't matter. You're amassing experience regardless, stimulating brain tissue with new information. You're expanding.

Play with the visualization techniques you've practised throughout the book and make a deliberate shift from thinking, "This is a wish" or "I will ..." to "I am already where I intend to be." Before this book was even signed to a publisher, I had a visual of the cover designed and it was my screensaver everywhere, the book's title a Spotify playlist, the book's purpose printed out and stuck on walls all over my house, tucked into my work notebooks, on my bedside table, pinned to my makeup mirror, to the fridge. The idea for the book took shape visually and then more fully in thrilling intention statements, structure, objective. I added so much colour and positive energy to the concept of this book that, in my mind, it already existed. I felt its power. I experienced the creative process of writing abundantly with words streaming forth, a fountain of useful wisdom, training my subconscious via my nightly meditations that this had already happened, the book had come to fruition, was successfully serving women around the world transformatively and I was ensconced in glee, grace and giddy gratitude. And so it shall be.

So, like me, like every inventor, creator and intuitive before us, trust and protect your intuition and imagination and never let others taint your divine creative potential. You hold true wonder within.

4. Being Present

"Learn to think in moments, rather than in days, weeks, months, years, decades, or a lifetime. All we ever get is right now – that's it."

— Wayne W Dyer

When you concentrate on one activity exclusively, your mind is able to rest from its constant chatter, giving your chaotic brain a break and allowing a feeling of calmness to caress you. But serenity through distraction of a hobby, pastime or person is only one aspect of stilling our minds.

If we're swimming in seas of discombobulating thoughts, we'll more than likely be surging with undulating emotions at the same time and thus be energetically disordered. This isn't conducive to great work, relationships or sleep. We are not our best when our minds are perpetually erratic.

Michael A Singer is one of the great masters of the mind, as esteemed a businessman as he is spiritual guru, teaching us techniques to quieten thoughts and emotions to be free of inner pain and commotion, and to untether our very souls. He writes, "There is nothing more important to true growth than realizing that you are not the voice of the mind – you are the one who hears it."[148] In other words, there's peace on the other side of your negative thoughts when you detach from them and realize that you are not your thoughts. Your thoughts arise from within and can float away just as readily as they arrived.

This is way easier said than done, however, especially if we are not meditating monks devoted to practising this skill. Holy monks or otherwise, it's essential we take heed of Singer's and other sacred ones' advice and understand this as our route to freedom, learning not to be afraid of inner pain and disturbance, but instead to bear witness to it. Pragmatically, he suggests, "When a problem is disturbing you, don't ask, 'What should I do about it?' Ask, 'What part of me is being disturbed by this?'"[149] When we observe the parts of our psyche making noise, he invites us to get excited by that uncomfortable trigger as a moment to ignite the "dynamite" within, to break down that protective armour we've spent our lives caging ourselves inside. Once we observe our thoughts as separate from The Self and let them go, we liberate ourselves.

The process is a repetitive cycle of "observe and let go, observe and let go, observe and let go", staying detached from any neurotically cycloning thoughts because they are separate from our seat of consciousness. This is hard to comprehend I know and even harder to implement, especially during a tough mental swirl, but if we do spend time honing this inner work, there's respite and lightness as the reward.

If the mental model we created as children, of who we are and how the world functions, is suddenly disrupted by a new and different reality, presented by a person or situation, an "other", it threatens the sturdy fortress we've built around us. Rather than being a protective haven, this fortress of rigid beliefs then works as a prison, keeping us stuck in that psyche we built as little people, making us resistant, defiant and cross, opposing the reality we're now faced with that doesn't match our suppositions. Detachment and enquiry is the only route to freedom at this point.

Blowing unhelpful thought patterns into smithereens, using the dynamite Singer speaks of, is perhaps more accessibly epitomized in the myth of a Hindu deity we can all relate to I'm sure – The Goddess of Never Not Broken. Akhilandeshwari is a powerful symbol of strength and resilience through transformation. She rides an endlessly spinning crocodile representing life's chaotic swirls. Atop it, she learns to roll with swirling uncertainties, lurching through crisis after ensuing crisis, and instead of crumpling into a heap of panic and fear, she learns to adapt to ever unstable foundations. She learns that in each crisis, new strength can arise when, instead of allowing disaster to destroy our pure essence – through vengeance, helplessness or anger, for example – we gradually adapt to our cyclically wobbly base, each time emerging more insightful, more empathic and more creative. Each time life breaks us, we put ourselves back together again wiser, stronger, expanded. She's not dizzy, she's strong. As are you.

Letting Go

Most spiritual guides agree that surrender and practising the art of letting go is the path to both enlightenment and ecstasy. It is never easy, of course. My favourite writing teacher, Anne Lamott, once said about letting go of expectations, that "Everything I've let go of has claw marks on it."[150] I hear her. However, there comes a moment when letting go is the best, or perhaps only, option.

In *Letting Go: The Pathway of Surrender*, David R Hawkins teaches, "Letting go is like the sudden cessation of an inner pressure or the dropping of a weight. It is accompanied by a sudden feeling of relief and lightness, with an increased happiness and freedom. It is an actual mechanism of the mind, and everyone has experienced it on occasion."[151] His process of emotional liberation invites us to identify an active emotion, seemingly shackled and chained into our minds, to feel into it fully, welcoming it in, then let it move along, scraping and clanking away, part of our history, no longer our present.

Then repeat the process. And repeat once again. And repeat and repeat and repeat until we no longer feel the acute intensity of the emotion and eventually shift into the relief and lightness he speaks of. It is hard, gruelling work, but the relief on the other side of the pain is a gift.

BIG IMPACT REFLECTION: THE PRACTICE OF LETTING GO

The principle of the Letting Go method is deliberately separating thought from emotion, zoning in on the emotion by fully observing it, detaching from negativity, attachments and resistance to ultimately free oneself from the uncomfortable emotion. It's a pathway to surrender and can mark the beginning of a transformative journey toward emotional liberation and spiritual growth. Certain emotions are harder than others to let go of but persevere as I can attest to huge energy surges when the lightness arrives.

Step 1: Embrace Understanding. Begin by immersing yourself in the concept of letting go. Allow the knowledge to seep into your consciousness. Recognize that surrendering emotional attachments, judgements, and resistance paves the way for inner peace and acceptance.

Step 2: Identify and Acknowledge. Take a reflective moment to identify the emotions and attachments you desire to release. Is it anger, fear, guilt, resentment, or attachments to specific outcomes or relationships? Acknowledge their presence within you without judgement, for this is the first step toward liberation.

Step 3: Embrace Full Experience. Wholeheartedly embrace the emotions that arise within you. Allow yourself to feel their intensity. Understand that emotions are transient and do not define your essence. By accepting and experiencing them fully, you open the door to letting go.

Step 4: Observe with Detachment. Take a step back and observe your emotions as if you are a witness separate from them. Understand that you are not the emotion itself but a conscious observer. This newfound perspective empowers you to detach and create a space for transformation.

Step 5: Release with Intent. Consciously choose to release the emotions you have acknowledged and observed. This act of surrender involves a willingness to let go and trust in a higher power or a greater sense of being. Use affirmations or intentions to support this process. For example, you might say, "I release this anger and invite peace into my life."

Step 6: Cultivate Mindfulness and Meditation. Embrace the practice of mindfulness and meditation to deepen your awareness of the present moment. By nurturing this state of mindfulness, you strengthen your ability to detach from attachments and cultivate the art of letting go.

Step 7: Shower Yourself with Compassion. Throughout this journey, remember to be kind and compassionate toward yourself. Letting go is a gradual process, and setbacks or resistance may arise. Shower yourself with love, understanding and patience, for you deserve it.

Step 8: Seek Support, If Needed. Should you encounter difficulties along the way, do not hesitate to seek support. Reach out to therapists, counsellors or spiritual mentors who can offer guidance and additional tools to aid you in your letting-go practice.

Letting go is a transformational, freeing and ongoing practice that requires dedication and perseverance. Be gentle with yourself, trusting that the process of surrender will grant you inner peace and newfound freedom.

The thing about life is that so much of it, probably most of it, will unfurl with forces beyond our control, thrust to the winds of fate blowing in one direction or another. We cannot, nor should we ever try to, change another person. All we can ever do is try to understand them, and understand that which has happened. Likewise, situations will arise that aren't the glossy image we had tattooed all over our vision board but we won't be able to alter them. Opportunities may burst into our lives, then disappoint us. We will experience sadness and grief and a whole load of stuff we didn't order in the manifestation mantra. But when we experience life as a landscape of lessons, encouraging us to dissolve our self-protecting and too often self-harming psyches, it all becomes rather exciting. When we step away from blame and into curiosity and compassion instead of fear and tantrums, life expands limitlessly. When we surrender to what is, without emotion clouding what we're experiencing, we achieve a spiritual serenity.

That is not to say surrendering is about passively rolling over. It's about knowing when surrender is your power move. As one of my favourite surrender goddesses, Judith Orloff, puts it "Surrender is a state of living in the flow, trusting what is, and being open to serendipity and surprises."[152] Who doesn't like serendipity and surprises?!

Resistance on the other hand is our soul's doorbell. "I'm your growth moment, inner work ahead!" Resistance shows up as procrastination, distraction, insomniac thoughts, self-sabotage and more. But when you dare to embrace it in a headlock, the liberation on the other side is as sweet as honeysuckle scents on a balmy breeze. A feeling that is not resisted will disappear as the energy behind it dissipates. However, when it is, get excited, because when you feel resistance arising, your soul is a' knocking!

BIG IMPACT REFLECTION: SITTING IN STILLNESS

If there's resistance to stillness and your mind simply cannot be alone with itself, take the time to really question what you are hiding from yourself. There is serious work to be done if you cannot entertain ten minutes of quiet time.

Practicing Stillness as Stress Relief

Silencing our wild mental meanderings, both the good and the bad, takes effort, and one of the emptiest condolences you can proffer someone in pain is "try not to think about it". It's as nonsensical as asking them to stop their hair from growing while they're at it! It is not easy to quieten the mind, especially when thoughts are piercing. But, as we've explored throughout this book, the whole world is seeking mental quiet and we're at an interesting societal juncture where the spiritual is coalescing with the intellectual, the ancient with the modern, the East with the West and we have an abundance of tools we can access to oil our inner crankings.

The favourites I invite you to dive into here are Mindfulness and Meditation. While meditation typically entails a dedicated practice, mindfulness is a quality you can embody, not only while meditating, but also through every moment of your life, from the most mundane to raucous!

Meditation, Hypnosis and Visualization

Growing up, I used self-hypnosis regularly, borrowing cassettes off my mother, or borrowing them from the library (yes, I am from a different era!). I started as young as 12, falling asleep while listening to ocean waves crashing, piano music interspersed with pan pipes, scanning my body for tension, contracting muscles from toes to jaw then releasing, following the subliminal instructions, and breathe ... I dabbled in everything from straighter posture to better memory to more confidence. Self-hypnosis was accepted in my family as normal, so I've always embraced it. I'm sure later, successfully, beautifully and miraculously, birthing all four of my children at home, including the twins, was due to the reliability of my self-hypnosis practice – I knew the births would go well as I had rehearsed them in my sleep. Subliminal programming is powerful.

You can mix and match to suit your mood and intention. One thing I will say is that having an objective to a meditation, as with the suggestive mental-programming nature of hypnosis, or vivid emotional stimulus of a visualization, can negate the purity of the empty calm. If you go into meditation with a to-do list, like meeting your future self in a crystal cave ceremony, you're visualizing not meditating. True meditation is simply watching the breath flow in and out, thoughts flow in and out; it is not structured, purposeful, or intentional. So, distinguish the type of meditation you're choosing when you go into your practice.

The commonalities between hypnosis, subliminal visualization and meditation are slowing cognition down from beta brain waves (thinking and analytical) to alpha brain waves (serene, steady, stable). In the latter state, whether the aim is simply to still the mind, to be still, through meditation, to re-programme your neural pathways through hypnosis, or to enrich intention with emotion with a visualization exercise, all varieties free the mind from day-to-day contemplations and relax body as well as brain. I'm a huge advocate for all three. Experiment with what serves you best and build a practice ideally morning and night to go within.

Some meditation teachers advise never to meditate lying down as you risk falling asleep, but for me, that's how I fit meditation in twice daily and I absolutely love it. I can't wait to settle into my calm mind, be entirely private and pause the outer world momentarily when in bed. It's a gift I give myself. The entirety of my life is better when I honour this practice and I notice less ability to manage myself and life's day-to-day undulations without it. So, sorry experts that I'm not textbook perfect, but I've found my way and feel amazing for it. I encourage you to do the same. If you have a meditation corner, candles, crystals and can do a yoga pose, cool; if you reserve five minutes morning and night after waking and before sleep, equally cool; if it's closing your eyes on a commuter train, also cool. Do it your way, in your time.

Pleasingly, nowadays you don't need library membership for assisted relaxation. Nor do you need to go to an ashram to learn to "*om*". Guided meditations are available via a multitude of apps and services online. I also produce my own meditations, visualizations and hypnosis audios, varying content for a range of positive Big Impact intentions – download at biancabest.com.

Mindfulness

A paramedic once told me the way they soothe patients possessed by a frightening, ever-spiralling panic attack is to get them to narrate a simple familiar task like making a cup of tea. So, while the patient is hyperventilating, ravaged with terrifying thoughts, as they start working through the mechanics of the task and vocalizing them, their mind whirl slows and then recedes. Once the task has been completed, invariably the patient has calmed down. The moment they pause again and go back into the mental fog of worry and panic and the negative thoughts that triggered the excessive reaction in the first place, they risk veering right back into the epicentre of the storm. So, another task needs conducting. Empty all the mugs out of the cupboard and reorganize them, mindfully. Unstack the dishwasher, mindfully. Deadhead your petunias, mindfully. Whatever shifts focus away from the hard-to-bear thoughts into manageable, safe and steady ones.

That's the basic premise of mindfulness. Come into the very present moment and observe what is happening without judgement, observing every action and experience as it occurs. Just observe it and be here now. Like a child collecting pebbles on the beach with fastidious concentration. Observe, be. That's it.

You can do this in the shower, pausing to feel the water on your skin or watching the light sparkle off the tiles. You can do it as you walk to the office, step by step, pace by pace, feeling into your body as you saunter on. You can do it by breathing attentively in a toilet cubicle, away from the melee of the conference. You can be mindful anywhere and anytime.

Once again, I encourage you to experiment and work out how and where you can bring more mindfulness into your life. I religiously ground myself with a mindful moment when I feel that cortisol surge starting to cloud my decision-making or if I'm starting to lose my footing in my day. It only needs to be 60 seconds of conscious mindfulness and the brain is reset. Watch running water flowing over your hands. Feel your fingertips touching each other, caressing each bumpy tip. Fully contemplate three objects in your immediate vicinity. Mindfulness can be a neat emergency trick, even more powerful when practiced as a daily, or even hourly, life skill.

Perfection in the Present

Sometimes time will cheat you. Sometimes it will be stolen. Sometimes it will bend. Always it will keep on passing as right now becomes just then. Herald time, please. Savour presence when you remember. Of course, it is wonderful to be inspired by tickles of hope, motivated by our resplendent imagination and excited about our future, pregnant with its tantalizing possibilities, but there's such wonder to be found in the very ordinary richness of right now that it's worthy of a moment's respectful regard. So, stop please. Put this book down and look around you, feel into this moment, suck it up, touch it with all your senses and devour it before it's gone. I bet it's perfect, exactly as it is.

5. Being Kind

"Your inner growth is completely dependent upon the realization that the only way to find peace and contentment is to stop thinking about yourself."
— Michael A. Singer

It's well documented that acts of kindness ease anxiety and have the power to eradicate depression. When you focus on others instead of yourself you can't help but feel better as there's no room to wallow. You cannot be sad when you're being kind. Fact. It's one of the loveliest things about life. When you're being kind, you're released from your own negative feelings. So, why aren't we kind more often?

Well, we are kind by natural design, spiritually and genetically. Humans help other humans, just like animals will protect their own for the main part. But kindness disappears when we're too locked in survival emotions and prioritizing self-preservation over orientation around others. It's not very nice to be this way, both for ourselves and others. But we're not necessarily deliberately unkind; we're just over-indexing on our own pain or stress, allowing it to become too all-consuming for us to put anyone else first. Narcissists and chronic depressives suffer this most acutely, often even prioritizing themselves over their dependents, including their children. It's our psyches and those fortresses, the belief systems, we built around us when we were little that keep us festering in selfishness.

Selflessness, by contrast, is pure generosity, and is a healthier, more joyful state to be in. When we are giving, we feel good. There's a ripple effect, and we often have little idea how one kind word, one caring gesture, one smile can transform another's day. We create pure enchantment as we sprinkle our kindness dust into the world.

Being kind doesn't always necessitate grand gestures like giant charitable donations, as phenomenal as they are, but can be as simple as sending a "Thank you, you were amazing today!" email to a colleague on the commute home, or dropping off bread and milk for your neighbour to return home from their holiday to. It can be opening the door for someone, sending someone a spontaneous heart emoji, or domestic acts of service, like making an extra cup of tea for your partner when you brew your own.

It feels good to be kind and is the quickest way to jolt yourself out of any "Oh woe is me" suffering thought swirls. I always recommend this strategy when clients are doused in sad storms. Focus on giving, caring, doing something for someone else – make an "I love you" card, pick wildflowers and give the posy to a stranger, write an affectionate "Why you're special" letter, tidy your daughter's bedroom for her. The act of thinking fondly about someone else, anyone else, alleviates the weight dragging down our sorry shoulders and creates a shift of emotional energy. It's liberating. And there is always the opportunity to shift our thoughts into kinder ones, beneficial for yourself and others, when we are conscious of the mind chatter. For example, as Byron Katie, enlightened ex-depressive-cum-spiritual-leader, evangelizes, "If you judge what other people have done to you, you miss the opportunity to see the hurt child in them."[153] Et voila. The kindness of looking for the wounded child in even your fiercest opponent, in those most fraught moments in life, makes space for a far more constructive and fulfilling way of flowing through each moment.

Acts of generosity tend to spread across communities with a prosocial impact too, uplevelling the society collectively.[154] In the Blue Zones project, which examined behavioral commonalities across populations with the highest proportion of centenarians in the world, caring for each other was a key component to flourishing every time. Out of nine power attributes, number eight is entitled "Loved Ones First"[155]. Across the Blue Zones, looking after family is consistently a respected normality (which includes parents and siblings as well as children), and in Okinawa, the Japanese island famed for its buoyant and bendy older inhabitants (going from seated on the floor to standing up 60 times per day), this extends to friends too. Here, villagers created *moai* – allocated groups of five friends for life, supporting each other through thick and thin, to ensure the community unwaveringly thrives. How do you nurture your equivalent moais? Could you be more kind to your gang? Do something lovely now for them, right this second, go on!

Another heart-warming Japanese concept is that of *wabi-sabi*, a philosophy that celebrates imperfection and impermanence. *Wabi-sabi* encourages us to find beauty in the flawed and imperfect and to embrace life's ebbs and flows with wonder and gratitude. So the heirloom family plate is cracked, aha well, it tells a story of the cheeky little boy banging his spoon too hard one mealtime, and so on. It adds a dimension of calm acceptance to life, a philosophical sigh of "It's okay ...", on it rolls and on and on it shall always roll, transient, perfectly imperfect. Let's take a moment here to embrace the power of gratitude for what is ...

BIG IMPACT REFLECTION: COUNTING YOUR BLESSINGS

Without doubt, gratitude makes you feel vibrationally marvellous! I round off every night before I sleep, recalling my favourite moment with each child that day. Before that, in my journal, I close off my entry with the most dominant thing I'm thankful for that day. I literally sign my diary "Thank you" after every entry, with kisses and hearts too! I have clients who send me ten things they are grateful for at the end of each week via text. Whatever practice you wish to adopt, start recording the blessings you appreciate from the simplicity of a pretty flower to a generous act to a warm breeze drying your laundry quickly. Be gleefully grateful!

I also recommend using gratitude lists as emergency stress busters if you're in a mental swirl, upset, cross or generally low. Gratitude unquestionably lifts the spirits.

Moving beyond the individual, powerfully into the collective, I invite you to further take gratitude and acts of kindness into the workplace to champion, celebrate and embody a management style I am a huge advocate of – Kind Leadership. Kindness is infectious and the more we demonstrate it by calling out unkind, selfish or thoughtless behaviour and exemplifying the reverse, the more we foster organizations that encourage work as joyful. As it should be. Create a culture of service as opposed to self-serving and it's this other-centredness that the world, businesses and individuals will prosper upon. As the inspiring leader dedicated to marginalized group recruitment, Lord James Timpson, stated in his inaugural speech in Britain's House of Lords, "Trust and kindness are vital for leadership. ... when you care for people, they care back."[156] Indeed, as psychological safety abounds, so it diminishes risk of burnout, with the scene set for impact.

Reclaiming Ourselves

"Peace is your home. Integrity is the way to it. And everything you long for will meet you there."

— Martha Beck

Of course, kindness extends to ourselves, too. Self-compassion is a core tenet of your Big Impact life henceforth. In the workplace, try retiring any battle mode or combative stances you may have adopted as part of your self-protective working style. The warrior within can be released as you embrace your new chapter, embalmed in grace and wonder. Kindness is not weakness, kindness is simply, magnificently kind!

BIG IMPACT REFLECTION: RELEASING THE WARRIOR

I invite you to do an experiment for one week and observe your emotional undulations in your workplace and at home.

- Look at what provokes a trigger state that rouses your defences versus those moments you feel compassionate and in flow.
- Watch what happens when you release an aggressive stance and soften into kindness.
- Test the impact it has on your relationship dynamics, be it with your children, your team or your clients.
- Likewise, what happens when you expose your vulnerability?
- When you release your fear instead of hardening around it, do you notice different outcomes?
- Try journalling nightly to capture your reflections and learnings, or at the very least, jot notes on your phone during your commute.

You will find that as we take any self-protective armour off, kindly and gently moving back into our essential selves, we relax. We come home, often gliding back into reconnection with youthful wishes and wants. In my teens, I would lie on my bed, writing journals and short stories, envisaging myself as a Jane Austen-esque writer, romantic, intelligent and wistful, capturing events and feelings in prose. I had an old-fashioned typewriter and would clackety-clack away, immersed in my ambition to write. I was obsessed with books, reading them and also organizing them on my bookshelves, by author, by colour, by theme, by title – oh, the endless fun. From Enid Blyton to Virginia C Andrews to Jackie Collins (of course, I'm an 80s child), to the classics, to the stoics, and more. You already know how Barbara Taylor Bradford inspired my "woman of substance" ambition. But despite envisioning myself as a writer my entire childhood, life got in the way and the dream shrunk, faded and was suppressed until reignition later in life. It was and still is where I feel bountiful fulfilment, but I had to do the work to reconnect to it, many years later, to relight the fires of my purest ambition, to be kind to myself by once again listening to my soul's whispers. Let's now relight your fires.

BIG IMPACT REFLECTION: TRUE YOU

Find a photo of yourself aged between five and ten to inspire this exercise. Meditate on the photo for a few minutes before you begin journalling. Now contemplate: when you were little, what did you dream of doing? What did you love doing? What were the activities that made time expand and disappear, made you melt into the present and absorb into the task? What did you do? Collect feathers? Press flowers? Weave? Catch spiders? Draw, sing or dance? What was your favourite creative outlet and how did it make you feel? Note down key characteristics of your youthful personality, dominant emotions, happiness triggers, unhappiness triggers, where you liked to play, who with, doing what ... Next, contrast this to the You present in the world today and reflect on any obvious similarities and any glaring gaps. What could you do to invite more of carefree child You into who you are today? Visualize yourself embodying more of your youthful passion and spirit.

As you meet your younger self and she reminds you of her vibrancy, passion and abundance, know that this purity is, in fact, who you still are, and as you step into your evolved vision of Big Impact, Big Girl You, hold her close. Integrate her burning wishes and wants, and her unencumbered dreams and hopes into the actions you take, the decisions you make, the vibe you emit, the inspiration you radiate, all the ways you show up today. Bring her back up to the surface, excited, optimistic, curious and bursting with love. Blend her wide-eyed gorgeousness with your wisdom, experience and even bigger, bolder and more hopeful intentions. Fully embrace who you truly are and let your soul sparkle.

Your Big Impact Fulfilment Expansion Grid

You now understand the key components to create your bespoke Fulfilment Strategy for Big Impact; you know how to recognize if you're operating in your integrity, buzzing with your Magnificent Frequencies (never Imposter Frequencies). You understand the importance of living your truth, honouring your contracts, trusting intuition, being present and effusing with kindness and gratitude. You have reconnected with your inner child.

In the grid below is what you now know how to manage.

It's time to translate this into solid action to make your expansion a reality.

Grab your journal and review the statements below, focusing on the "Expanding To" column. Now spend 30 minutes freewriting on everything that comes up for you when you read the expansion statements. Elaborate on them where you see fit and make them entirely yours. As well as writing the "what", dive into the "how" and "why". Really explore the statements, applying your newfound knowledge, and have fun exploring all the life-altering ways you're going to feel and how you're going to get there. Let the inspiration pour forth and capture everything that comes to mind.

FROM	EXPANDING TO...
I blur the truth and am sometimes deceptive and manipulative. I don't know why I lie.	I am honest, always. I speak the truth and behave honourably. I have no secrets. I communicate scrupulously.
I wobble with Imposter Frequencies and don't always keep my word.	I radiate Magnificent Frequencies and always honour my promises made.
I can't distinguish my true desires from false desires.	I am clear how my true desires support me and how to distinguish harmful false desires.
I never protect myself with any boundaries.	I know how to design and convey healthy boundaries.
I feel empty. I don't feel compassionate.	I am full of grace and gratitude, compassion and kindness and relish the present moment.
I feel detached from my soul, too ego-dominant and unsure even of who I am.	I am intuitive and more awake, tapping into the unseen, trusting my heart and soul, my guiding light within and embracing the coincidences abounding.
I feel niggled, lacking in integrity and on the brink of a life crisis.	I live peacefully with all my values honoured consistently and practise presence techniques regularly.
I an exhausted by my inauthenticity, so tired of being someone I'm not.	I am totally, utterly, magnificently me!
I don't know how to manage my disappointment.	I know how to practise letting go.
I am always in battle mode.	I have released my warrior self and I am gentler in how I operate in the world, both toward myself and others.
I feel taut with resistance.	I lean into resistance as a signal to grow.
I oscillate from making decisions, then forgetting to honour them.	I honour my decisions as contracts to uphold. Most importantly, I honour being my True Self.

Fulfilment Strategy Priority Actions

It's time for serious action. Now bring your reflections together and organize them into priority areas of focus that you identify as integral to your master Fulfilment Strategy for Big Impact Without Burnout across the next 12 months.

Drawing the grid below in your notebook or in a spreadsheet, list as many reflections and actions with deadlines per theme as you can based on all you've learned. Then distil all of these action ideas into three Fulfilment Strategy Priority Actions, which we'll incorporate into your master plan at the end of the book. Remember to always tune into your values and overarching impact goals as you create your plans. Make the three action priorities realistic, achievable and inspiring, and rigorously tied to firm deadlines.

ONE-YEAR BIG IMPACT WITHOUT BURNOUT MASTER PLAN			
FULFILMENT STRATEGY	REFLECTIONS	ACTIONS	DEADLINE
Being Truthful			
Being Contractual			
Being Intuitive			
Being Present			
Being Kind			
	My 3 Fulfilment Strategy Priority Actions are...1...2...3...		

YOUR BIG IMPACT WITHOUT BURNOUT MASTER PLAN

You're a goddess, a wonder woman, a victor, a superstar, you rock! Wowzers, we've come a long way. You have reflected and journalled and visualized your way through a lot of content, a lot of strategies, a lot of concepts and awakenings. I'm proud of you. But mostly, I'm excited for you!

You have made 12 decision pledges about how you will build foundational solidity to prevent burnout and be gracefully productive. You have planned 12 actions to expand out into the world with your work, making the impact you desire, magnetizing relationships, wealth and fulfilment to you as your every day. Let's bring the inner and outer, the decisions and actions together now into your grand master plan. Here is where your expansion becomes a firm reality as you step into your Biggest Impact Without Burnout. This is the culmination of your excellent work (and probably the best bit of it all!).

Step 1: Get a large piece of paper and title it "My Magnificent Expansion" and, as shown on the opposite page, draw four concentric circles from the middle of the page, enlarging to just within the periphery of the paper's edges.

Step 2: In the smallest circle, write your Purpose statement (page 120).

Step 3: In the next circle, describe the Vision of You that you designed back in the Purpose chapter (page 122) – summarize in the words that feel most evocative and inspiring.

Step 4: The next circle is all about the foundational decision pledges you made to commit to no burnout. Write "I will not burnout because I will ..." and summarize the essence of your 12 pledge from Part One: The Foundational Imperatives, using single words or full sentences – all of them, or just the most pertinent, however creatively inspired you best want to capture their intentions.

Step 5: The largest circle is all about your impact out in the world. Write "I will have impact by ..." and summarize the essence of those 12 actions you created in Part Two: The Expansion Phenomenon, again using single words or full sentences, all of them, or just the most pertinent, however creatively inspired you best want to capture their intentions.

Step 6: Now really study what you've just created. This is your map to magnificence. Start drawing arrows from the centre out to the very edges of the paper. These arrows represent your expansion, the journey you're now on; the limitless present and abundant future you're now in. Even use a glitter pen if you fancy! Make this feel flipping special! You're expanding. You're amazing! You're doing this!! This is real! Have fun!

Step 7: Embracing this joy and these optimistic feelings of excitement and potentiality, lock in these inner and outer commitments, who you are and what you're driven by, and embellish your creation by adding in starbursts of captions around the page, indicating what your Big Impact expansion will unleash ...

Here's an example below to inspire you. Design yours with relish and who cares how juvenile and frivolous this exercise feels. Nobody is judging you except you. You're the creator of your life and, right now, you're the creator of a giant sparkly star-bursty visual of your fantasticness!

If you did all the work while reading this book, you are 35 steps closer to Big Impact Without Burnout and have a solid one-year master plan! Congratulations and very well done you!

If you read the book end-to-end and now plan to go back and do the reflection exercises, great, go for it! I definitely encourage doing this to avoid missing out on any richness the power of this book invites. Each exercise is designed to evoke transformation by vibrantly envisioning yourself in the positive intention. Do it! You'll see! The more powerful women in the world living Big Impact Without Burnout, the better our world will be.

MANIFESTING YOUR MAGIC

"Magic exists. Who can doubt it, when there are rainbows and wildflowers, the music of the wind and the silence of the stars? Anyone who has loved has been touched by magic. It is such a simple and such an extraordinary part of the lives we live."

— Nora Roberts

My son stood in our newly decorated living room. "Mummy!" he exclaimed. "You made a rainbow room!" I giggled with joy, then exclaimed, "Oh yes! Oh my, I did! I made a rainbow room!" In the indulgence of my freshly independent, divorced mid-life, I had decided to create a baby pink-themed living room (don't judge me please, it looks lush!). What I hadn't yet noticed as I turned the lights on that evening to show my littlest one the updated décor is that the new crystal droplet wall lights and central pendant chandelier created hundreds and thousands of twinkling, cascading prisms. We stood in a peony-pink room, alive with dancing rainbows. We were rapt, surprised, delighted, spellbound and serene at this unexpected moment.

It felt mesmerizing and mystical, special and spine-tingly supernatural. It felt like a fairy godmother had waved her glitter-sprinkling magic wand directly over us, giving the room a Cinderella makeover and like actual, dancing mice might have appeared with a golden pumpkin-shaped carriage to boot.

It makes me smile to recall that moment. And even now, I love to stand in that very spot whenever I feel life's overwhelming onslaught of triggering stress surges, or upset, or panic, or fear, or pressure, or any of the other inevitable realities that will arise.

That rainbow room was an unexpected, precious impact, borne from one little dream. It felt like a mini miracle, that the ordinary suddenly became extra-ordinary, another life gem to add to the gratitude list. I trusted my vision, I took action and boom, wow, the end result far exceeded my expectations! That surprise room represents everything I believe each one of us is capable of. I am convinced we are all empowered to create our own magic once we blend true-self integrity with active intention. It's then that not only do our plans materialize, but miracles occur too, popping up like satin ribbon-embellished gifts, tokens from the universe, reminding us that not only do wishes come true, but they often appear gleaming with rainbows and twinkles.

The unforeseen will always eventually, inevitably appear. Sometimes good, sometimes not so. Life is unpredictable. We cannot control its undulations. Occasionally, the unexpected will thwart our plans detrimentally, dashing dreams and creating disappointments, but at other more generous times, it will magnificently better plans, the gold we touch glinting evermore brightly, the opportunities far exceeding our initial hopes. Life will chuck us those curveballs. We will need to duck and dive, sometimes swerve or retreat, bravely compete at other times, but when we have our foundations sturdy, our hearts directing our expansion, these eight Big Impact Strategies buttoned down, we will remain strong, stoic, stable and able to soar. And when we are in our high vibe, positively purposeful, integral wholeness ... oh my, get ready for the majesty of how the unforeseen will unfurl then.

There's many a client of mine who laments the apparently lusher, greener grass over the fence: the friend's happier marriage, the colleague's more attentive boss, the competitor's healthier pipeline, the more scholarly child, heck, the shiner kitchen granite top even. My (sage, if unoriginal, I know) advice is: always water your own garden first, cultivate your own patch and carefully prioritize which seeds and flowers you dote on. As life shows us, time and time again, where your attention is focused, so your energy flows and expands, and that's the stuff that will grow. Don't waste your energy on diversions that pull you away from nurturing your essential self. Ultimately, that is what matters most in your life best lived. To love yourself, your passions and others hard. And when you are nourishing your private ground, never forget that often the impact that nobody sees can be even more fulfilling than the most publicly lauded impact we create. So, nurture your grass seeds as well as the towering sunflowers.

Thank you for joining me on this transformational journey of combining impact with peace, and eradicating strife from progress, for understanding how to remove the struggle from our modern, demanding but so possibility-enriched lives. We've gone deep. There's a lot to remember. I know. Please don't self-chastise if you veer off course here and there. It's okay. I will too.

Let's know our best is fabulous and more than enough. Let's agree to exemplify that the way of integrity is the best and only way and that kind impact is the best impact. Pay all the stuff that works for you forward, paving the path for colleagues, children, friends and beyond to get it too. Spread the word. Life does not need to be (and should not be) the struggle too many modern women find it. Big Impact is beautiful, fun and super-rewarding, something we all deserve. Be the star of your one magnificent life story. The world is waiting for your twinkly treasure. Go shine.

One Final Thought on Making Big Impact Without Burnout

If you happened to ask me who I would invite to my dream dinner party, I would seat Albert Camus at the head of the table. I started this book with my favourite quote of his, about our invincible summer within, our internal sunshine, so it's apt that he joins us as we conclude it.

Algerian philosopher, WWII Resistance hero, Camus is a man whose literature melts into my brain like syrup. Famed for his work on life's absurdity, one of his great works is *The Myth of Sisyphus*. Now, poor old Sisyphus was a strapping, loin-clothed Greek mythological figure, condemned to forever repeat the same futile task of pushing a boulder up a mountain, only to see it roll down again just as would near the top. Camus concludes his essay stating, "The struggle itself toward the heights is enough to fill a man's heart. One must imagine Sisyphus happy." And thus, life's absurdity according to Camus is that there is satisfaction, contentment, and perhaps even a swirl of joy in the pursuit of a goal that is personally, uniquely meaningful to us, a goal resonant with the depths of our souls.

And there it is. In the simplicity of pushing our Big Impact boulders uphill, within servitude and steady progress, we find patience as power, we discover private purpose as fulfilment, and we reach a sublime state of serenity. In my version of the Sisyphus myth though, for the visionary among us, there would be flower garlands aplenty and blossom trees lining the hill, celestial music would resound, glitter would rain from the sky, moonbeams would dance, sunbeams would sparkle, abundant rainbows would glint, and there would be, without doubt, a touch of magic to it all.

ENDNOTES

1   Deloitte, "Women Continuing to Face Alarmingly High Levels of Burnout, Stress in the 'New Normal' of Work," *Forbes*, April 26 2022, www.forbes.com/sites/deloitte/2022/04/26/women-continuing-to-face-alarmingly-high-levels-of-burnout-stress-in-the-new-normal-of-work

2   www.merriam-webster.com/dictionary/compromised

3   "Mental Health at Work," World Health Organization, September 2 2024, www.who.int/news-room/fact-sheets/detail/mental-health-at-work

4   "88% of UK Workforce Have Experienced Burnout in the Past Two Years, Reveals Research by LumApps," *EmployerNews*, September 2 2022, www.employernews.co.uk/news/88-of-uk-workforce-have-experienced-burnout-in-the-past-two-years-reveals-research-by-lumapps

5   Cotton, Jill, "How to Avoid Burnout as an Employee," Glassdoor, July 2 2022, www.glassdoor.co.uk/blog/how-to-avoid-burnout-as-an-employee

6   "Rising ill-health and economic inactivity because of long-term sickness, UK: 2019 to 2023", Data and Analysis from Census 2021, July 2023, www.ons.gov.uk/employmentandlabourmarket/peoplenotinwork/economicinactivity/articles/risingillhealthandeconomicinactivitybecauseoflongtermsicknessuk/2019to2023

7   Snyder, Kristy, and Cassie Bottorff, "Key HR Statistics and Trends in 2024," *Forbes Advisor*, May 17 2023, www.forbes.com/advisor/business/hr-statistics-trends

8   "The unused holiday & burnout epidemic: Breathe's 2024 holiday report", Breathe, www.breathehr.com/en-gb/resources/holiday-burnout-report-2024

9   dictionary.cambridge.org/dictionary/english/ambition

10 www.globalcitizen.org/en/

11 McKinnell, Neil, "Treating Depression After Leaving the Military," *Evoke Wellness*, February 18 2022, www. evokewellnesstx.com/blog/depression-after-leaving-the-military

12 "Gender Equality Is Stalling: 131 Years to Close the Gap", World Economic Forum, June 2023, www.weforum.org/press/2023/06/gender-equality-is-stalling-131-years-to-close-the-gap/

13 "Half the World's Women Have Given Up on Their Dreams: Kids Challenge Them to Dream Again," *PR Newswire*, June 21 2016, www.prnewswire.com/

news-releases/half-the-worlds-women-have-given-up-on-their-dreams-kids-challenge-them-to-dream-again-300288272.html

14 Corbett, Holly, "Women Are More Ambitious Now than Before the Pandemic, Finds a New Study," *Forbes*, October 5 2023, www.forbes.com/sites/hollycorbett/2023/10/05/women-are-more-ambitious-now-than-before-the-pandemic-finds-a-new-study/?sh=4e29766763c5

15 "The Careers After Babies report | That Works for Me," WeAreTheCity, March 3 2023, www.wearethecity.com/the-careers-after-babies-report-that-works-for-me/

16 Schafler, Katherine Morgan, *The Perfectionist's Guide to Losing Control: A Path to Peace and Power*, Orion Publishing, 2023

17 Ibid.

18 ereserve.library.utah.edu/Annual/EDPS/5960/Farr/pursuit1.pdf

19 Pignatiello, G A, Martin, R J, and Hickman, R L Jr, "Decision Fatigue: A Conceptual Analysis," *Journal of Health Psychology*, 25(1), 2020, pp 123–135, www.ncbi.nlm.nih.gov/pmc/articles/PMC6119549/

20 Bryant, Ben, "Judges Are More Lenient After Taking a Break, Study Finds," *The Guardian*, April 11 2011, www.theguardian.com/law/2011/apr/11/judges-lenient-break

21 "How Many Neurons Are in the Brain?", Brain Facts, December 2018, www.brainfacts.org/in-the-lab/meet-the-researcher/2018/how-many-neurons-are-in-the-brain-120418

22 www.discprofile.com

23 The Theodore Roosevelt Centre, www.theodorerooseveltcenter.org/Learn-About-TR/TR-Quotes

24 Reddit, "Career or Baby: When is the Right Time?" Reddit, www.reddit.com/r/workingmoms/comments/wbkv43/career_or_baby_when_is_the_right_time/?rdt=42569&onetap_auto=true

25 "Reporting Year 2023: Childcare and Early Years Survey of Parents," UK Government, July 25 2024, explore-education-statistics.service.gov.uk/find-statistics/childcare-and-early-years-survey-of-parents

26 Dyer, Wayne W, *Wishes Fulfilled: Mastering the Art of Manifesting*, Hay House, 2012

27 Miller, Michael, "State of the Heart: Global Human Energy Crisis," *Six Seconds*, August 2 2023, www.6seconds.org/2023/08/02/state-of-the-heart-global-human-energy-crisis/

28 Hammerschlag, R, er al. "Biofield Physiology: A Framework for an Emerging Discipline," *Global Advances in Health and Medicine*, 4, 2015, pp 35–41, www.ncbi.nlm.nih.gov/pmc/articles/PMC4654783

29 Solan, Matthew, "The Book of Neurogenesis," *Harvard Health*, August 1 2021, www.health.harvard.edu/mind-and-mood/the-book-of-neurogenesis

30 Golen, Toni, "Does exercise really boost energy levels?", *Harvard Health,* July 1

2021, www.health.harvard.edu/exercise-and-fitness/does-exercise-really-boost-energy-levels

31   Brower, Tracy, "For Pay, Productivity, and Wellbeing, Data Points to the Power of Exercise," *Forbes*, September 24 2023, www.forbes.com/sites/tracybrower/2023/09/24/for-pay-productivity-and-wellbeing-data-points-to-the-power-of-exercise/

32   "Confronting the Dangers of Ultra-Processed Food," *The Economist*, July 24 2023, www.economist.com/culture/2023/07/24/confronting-the-dangers-of-ultra-processed-food

33   Zuryn, Steven, "How Your Brain Makes and Uses Energy," University of Queensland, www.qbi.uq.edu.au/brain/nature-discovery/how-your-brain-makes-and-uses-energy

34   Centers for Disease Control and Prevention (CDC)

35   Terry, Natalie & Margolis, Kara Gross, "Serotonergic Mechanisms Regulating the GI Tract: Experimental Evidence and Therapeutic Relevance", *Handb Exp Pharmacol*, 2017; pp.319-342, pmc.ncbi.nlm.nih.gov/articles/PMC5526216/

36   Kogevinas, Manolis, "Probable carcinogenicity of glyphosate", *BMJ*, April 2019, www.bmj.com/content/365/bmj.l1613

37   "Exposing the Hidden Enemy: The Importance of Managing Chronic Inflammation across Different Specialties," *Science*, www.science.org/content/webinar/exposing-hidden-enemy-importance-managing-chronic-inflammation-across-different

38   Porter, William, *Alcohol Explained,* CreateSpace Independent Publishing, 2015

39   Harrell, Eben, "How 1% Performance Improvements Led to Olympic Gold," *Harvard Business Review*, October 30 2015, www.hbr.org/2015/10/how-1-performance-improvements-led-to-olympic-gold

40   Wilson, Clare, "Hot Baths Could Improve Depression as Much as Physical Exercise," *New Scientist*, October 22 2018, www.newscientist.com/article/2183250-hot-baths-could-improve-depression-as-much-as-physical-exercise/

41   Brad Stulberg and Steve Magness, *Peak Performance*

42   "Taking Breaks," UNC Learning Center, 2023, learningcenter.unc.edu/tips-and-tools/taking-breaks/

43   Blakely, Sara, Instagram, August 3 2023, www.instagram.com/sarablakely/reel/Cvdl8J3J3Ce

44   Reynolds, Gretchen, "Why an Outdoor Workout is Better for You Than Indoors," *The Washington Post*, April 12 2023, www.washingtonpost.com/wellness/2023/04/12/outdoor-exercise-benefits

45   Brown, Brené, *The Gifts of Imperfection: Let Go of Who You Think You're Supposed to Be and Embrace Who You Are*, Hazelden Publishing, 2018

46 Melanie Greenberg, *The Stress-Proof Brain: Master Your Emotional Response to Stress Using Mindfulness and Neuroplasticity*, New Harbinger, 2017

47 Yousafzai, Malala, *I Am Malala: The Story of the Girl Who Stood Up for Education and Was Shot by the Taliban*, Little, Brown and Company, 2013

48 Tolle, Eckhart, *A New Earth: Awakening to Your Life's Purpose*, Viking, 2005

49 Dweck, Carol S, *Mindset: The New Psychology of Success*, Random House Publishing Group, 2007

50 Frankl, Viktor, *Man's Search for Meaning*, Rider, 2004

51 Wiest, Brianna *The Mountain Is You: Transforming Self-Sabotage into Self-Mastery*, Thought Catalog Books, 2020

52 Ibid.

53 "Trigger," Merriam-Webster Dictionary, merriam-webster.com/dictionary/trigger

54 Mohr, Tara, *Playing Big: For Women Who Want to Speak Up, Stand Out and Lead*, Arrow, 2014

55 www.quotefancy.com/quote/879594/Oprah-Winfrey-Anything-you-can-imagine-you-can-create

56 Dunbar, R I M, Marriott, Anna, and Duncan, N D C, "Human Conversational Behavior," *Human Nature*, 8, 1997, 231–46, academia.edu/48337557/Human_conversational_behavior?uc-g-sw=5824931

57 Hilgemann, Brandon, "Thomas Edison's Reaction to His Lab on Fire" *ProPreacher*, August 25 2016, www.propreacher.com/thomas-edisons-reaction-lab-fire

58 Branson, Richard, "Don't See Obstacles, See Opportunities", *Huffpost*, May 2013, www.huffingtonpost.co.uk/richard-branson/richard-branson-business-advice_b_1931712.html

59 McKay, Matthew, and Fanning, Patrick, *Self Esteem: A Proven Program of Cognitive Techniques for Assessing, Improving, and Maintaining Your Self-Esteem*, New Harbinger Publications, 2016

60 Ibid.

61 Waterman, Alan, "The Relevance of Aristotle's Conception of Eudaimonia for the Psychological Study of Happiness," *Journal of Theoretical and Philosophical Psychology*, vol. 10 (1990), 39–44. 10.1037/h0091489.

62 Norton, David L, "According to Self-Actualization Ethics, It Is Ever," *Quote Park*, June 3 2021, quotepark.com/quotes/1857420-david-l-norton-according-to-self-actualization-ethics-it-is-ever/

63 Lembke, Anna, *Dopamine Nation: Finding Balance in the Age of Indulgence*, Headline, 2021

64 Robson, David, A brief history of the brain, *New Scientist*, September 2011, www.newscientist.com/article/mg21128311-800-a-brief-history-of-the-brain

65 Lembke, Anna, *Dopamine Nation: Finding Balance in the Age of Indulgence*, Headline, 2021

66 Ibid.

67 McClure, Samuel M, et al., "Time Discounting for Primary Rewards," *Journal of Neuroscience*, 27(21), 2007, pp 5796–5804, www.jneurosci.org/content/27/21/5796.short

68 Lembke, Anna, *Dopamine Nation: Finding Balance in the Age of Indulgence*, Headline, 2021

69 Strecher, Victor J, *Life On Purpose: How Living for What Matters Most Changes Everything*, HarperOne, 2016

70 Fredrickson, Barbara L, et al., "A Functional Genomic Perspective on Human Well-Being," *Proceedings of the National Academy of Sciences*, 110(33), 2013, pp13684–13689, www.pmc.ncbi.nlm.nih.gov/articles/PMC3746929/

71 Strecher, Victor J, *Life On Purpose: How Living for What Matters Most Changes Everything*, HarperOne, 2016

72 Ware, Bronnie, *The Top Five Regrets of the Dying: A Life Transformed by the Dearly Departing*, Hay House UK, 2012

73 Sinek, Simon, *Start With Why: How Great Leaders Inspire Everyone to Take Action*, Portfolio, 2011

74 Schafler, Katherine Morgan, *The Perfectionist's Guide to Losing Control: A Path to Peace and Power*, Orion Publishing, 2023

75 Pressfield, Steven, *The War of Art: Break Through the Blocks and Win Your Inner Creative Battles*, Black Irish Entertainment, 2012

76 Campbell, Joseph, *The Power of Myth,* Bantam Doubleday Dell Publishing Group 1988

77 Wharton Staff, "Why Older Entrepreneurs Have the Edge," Knowledge at Wharton Podcast, November 12, 2019, knowledge.wharton.upenn.edu/podcast/knowledge-at-wharton-podcast/age-of-successful-entrepreneurs/

78 Duckworth, Angela, *Grit: The Power and Passion of Perseverance*, Scribner Book Company 2016

79 Gladwell, Malcolm *Outliers: The Story of Success,* Penguin, 2009

80 Pilkington, Ed, "Just Mercy: New Film that Captures the Start of a Brilliant Civil Rights Career," *The Guardian*, January 18 2020, www.theguardian.com/film/2020/jan/18/just-mercy-bryan-stevenson-racial-injustice.

81 Lartey, Jamiles, "Bryan Stevenson: the lawyer devoting his life to fighting injustice", *The Guardian*, June 2019, www.theguardian.com/tv-and-radio/2019/jun/26/bryan-stevenson-lawyer-true-justice-just-mercy

82 Ibid.

83 Robinson, Marilynne, *The Givenness of Things: Essays*, Picador USA, 2016

84 Eliot, T S, *The Waste Land and Other Poems*, Faber, 2002

85 Robinson, Marilynne, *The Givenness of Things*, Virago, 2015

86 Covey, Stephen R, "Habit 3: Put First Things First," *FranklinCovey*, www.franklincovey.com/the-7-habits/habit-3/

87 Lembke, Anna, *Dopamine Nation: Finding Balance in the Age of Indulgence*, Headline, 2021

88 Morley, Phil, "Is information overload killing employee engagement?", *The Drum*, October 2017, www.thedrum.com/opinion/2017/10/20/information-overload-killing-employee-engagement

89 "Thinking vs Feeling: The Psychology of Advertising", University of South Carolina, November 2023, appliedpsychologydegree.usc.edu/blog/thinking-vs-feeling-the-psychology-of-advertising

90 Ruiz, Don Miguel, *The Four Agreements*, Amber-Allen Publishing, 1997

91 Green, Robert, and 50 Cent, *The 50th Law*, Harper Studio, 2009

92 Newport, Cal, *Deep Work: Rules for Focused Success in a Distracted World,* Grand Central Publishing, 2016

93 Goleman, Daniel, *Focus: The Hidden Driver of Excellence,* Harper, 2015

94 King, Stephen, *On Writing: A Memoir of the Craft,* Scribner, 2010

95 Csíkszentmihályi, Mihály, *Flow: The Psychology of Happiness*, Rider, 2002

96 Bhikkhu, Thánissaro, "One Tool Among Many: The Place of Vipassaná in Buddhist Practice", *Buddho* buddho.org/one-tool-among-many-the-place-of-vipassana-in-buddhist-practice/

97 Burkeman, Oliver, *Four Thousand Weeks: Time Management for Mortals*, Picador USA, 2023

98 Waddell, Martin (author), Austin, Virginia (illustrator), *Sailor Bear*, Candlewick, 1994

99 Kane, Brendan, *One Million Followers: How I Built a Massive Social Following in 30 Days*, BenBella Books, 2018

100 Shaw, Lucas, "'ABBA Voyage' Is Making $2 Million a Week With an Avatar Band", *Bloomberg*, Seotember 2023, www.bloomberg.com/news/newsletters/2023-09-04/-abba-voyage-tour-makes-2-million-a-week-with-an-avatar-band

101 www.bookey.app/quote-author/astro-teller

102 Pressfield, Steven, *The War of Art: Break Through the Blocks and Win Your Inner Creative Battles*, Black Irish Entertainment, 2012

103 Amabile, Teresa M, and Kramer, Steven J, "The Power of Small Wins," *Harvard Business Review*, May 2011, hbr.org/2011/05/the-power-of-small-wins

104 Ng, Kate, "Philosophers Have a Theory About Men and Household Chores," *The Independent*, December 23 2022, www.independent.co.uk/life-style/women/household-chores-men-women-split-b2250419.html

105 McClelland, T, and Sliwa, P, "Gendered affordance perception and unequal domestic labour," *Philosophy and Phenomenological Research*, vol. 107, 2023, 501–524. doi.org/10.1111/phpr.12929

106 "Gender Differences on Household Chores Entrenched from Childhood," Gender Equality Index 2021: Health, European Institute for Gender Equality, eige.europa.eu/publications-resources/toolkits-guides/gender-equality-index-

2021-report/gender-differences-household-chores?language_content_entity=en

107 Allen, Jules, and Stevenson, Imogen, "BSA 40: Gender Roles," *National Centre for Social Research*, September 21 2023, natcen.ac.uk/publications/bsa-40-gender-roles

108 Rodsky, Eve, *A Game-Changing Solution for When You Have Too Much to Do (and More Life to Live)*, G P Putnam's Sons, January 5 2019

109 Moore, Catherine, "Resilience Theory: A Summary of the Researc," *Positive Psychology*, December 30 2019, positivepsychology.com/resilience-theory

110 from a printed resource provided at the Co-Active Training Institute Professional Coach Training programme © 2019 Co-Active Training Institute

111 Taylor, Jill Bolte, *My Stroke of Insight: A Brain Scientist's Personal Journey*, Penguin Publishing Group, 2009

112 Dispenza, Dr Joe, "Back to Basics", August 2020, drjoedispenza.com/dr-joes-blog/back-to-basics

113 Greenberg, Melanie, *The Stress-Proof Brain: Master Your Emotional Response to Stress Using Mindfulness and Neuroplasticity*, New Harbinger, March 2017

114 Grant, Adam, *Give and Take: Why Helping Others Drives Our Success*, Penguin Publishing Group, 2014

115 Shetty, Jay, *Think Like a Monk: The Secret of How to Harness the Power of Positivity and be Happy Now*, Thorsons, September 2020

116 NASA Johnson, "4-H and NASA - Cultural Competency", *YouTube*, www.nasa.gov/stem-content/expeditionary-skills-embarking-on-pilgrimages

117 NASA stretegic Plan 2024, www.soma.larc.nasa.gov/mmx/pdf_files/FY2014_NASA_StrategicPlan_508c.pdf

118 Cardoso, Ricardo, et al., "Associations Between Posture, Voice, and Dysphonia: A Systematic Review," *Journal of Voice*, 33(1), 2019, pp124.e1–124.e12, www.sciencedirect.com/science/article/abs/pii/S0892199717301832

119 Seppälä, Emma, and Cameron, Kim, "The Best Leaders Have a Contagious Positive Energy," *Harvard Business Review*, April 18 2022, hbr.org/2022/04/the-best-leaders-have-a-contagious-positive-energy

120 "COVID-19 Blew Up the Epidemic of Loneliness," *UC Irvine News*, September 2 2020, news.uci.edu/2020/09/02/covid-19-blew-up-the-epidemic-of-loneliness

121 Covey, Stephen, *The 7 Habits of Highly Effective People*, Free Pr, 2004

122 Kluger, Avraham N & Itzchakov Guy, "The Power of Listening at Work", Annual Review of Organizational Psychology and Organizational Behavior, 9(1), January 2022, www.researchgate.net/publication/353573217_The_Power_of_Listening_at_Work

123 Edmondson, Amy C, *The Fearless Organization: Creating Psychological Safety in the Workplace for Learning, Innovation, and Growth*, Wiley, 2018

124 Christakis, Nicholas, "The Hidden Influence of Social Networks," *TED*, Feb 2010, www.ted.com/talks/nicholas_christakis_the_hidden_influence_of_social_networks/

125 Grant, Adam, *Give and Take: Why Helping Others Drives Our Success,* Penguin Publishing Group, 2014

126 Tobaccowalla, Rishad, *Restoring the Soul of Business: Staying Human in the Age of Data,* HarperCollins Leadership 2020

127 Marcus, Bonnie, *The Politics of Promotion: How High-Achieving Women Get Ahead and Stay Ahead,* John Wiley & Sons, 2015

128 www.merriam-webster.com/dictionary/influence

129 Chance, Zoe, *Influence is Your Superpower: How to Get What You Want Without Compromising Who You Are,* Vermilion, 2021

130 Covey, Steven, *7 Habits of Highly Effective People,* Free Pr. 2004

131 Landry, Lauren, "Why Emotional Intelligence is Important in Leadership," *Harvard Business School Online,* April 3 2019, online.hbs.edu/blog/post/emotional-intelligence-in-leadership

132 Lavinsky, Dave, "The Two Most Important Quotes in Business," *Growthink,* www.growthink.com/content/two-most-important-quotes-business

133 Walker, Aisha, "Public Speaking vs. Death: Which Do You Fear More?", A-G Associates, a-gassociates.com/career-change/public-speaking-vs-death-which-do-you-fear-more/

134 Robins, TOny, "Guide to personal relationships", www.tonyrobbins.com/blog/guide-to-personal-relationships

135 Strong, Rebecca, "Why Self-Worth and Self-Esteem Are Both Important, Plus 5 Expert-Approved Tips to Build Them Up," *Business Insider,* November 11 2022, businessinsider.com/guides/health/mental-health/self-worth?r=US&IR=T

136 Williamson, Marianne, *A Return to Love, : Reflections on the Principles of "A Course in Miracles",* Harper One, 2015

137 www.selfdeterminationtheory.org/theory/

138 Morisse, Barry, "Some Brief Thoughts on Suffering", January 2023, www.barrymorisse.com/blog/some-thoughts-on-suffering

139 Gray, Catherine, *The Unexpected Joy of the Ordinary,* Aster, 2019

140 Schwartz, Barry, *The Paradox of Choice: Why More Is Less,* Harper Perennial, 2004

141 www.torah.org/learning/integrity-lifeordeath/

142 www.marthabeck.com/2016/09/be-honest/

143 Beck, Martha, *The Way of Integrity: Finding the Path to Your True Self,* Piatkus, 2021

144 Myss, Caroline, *Sacred Contracts: Awakening Your Divine Potential,* Three Rivers Press, 2003

145 Ibid.

146 www.artsofthought.com/2020/05/30/carl-jung-synchronicity/

147 Richardson, Tanya Caroll, *Awakening Intuition: Using Your Mind-Body Network for Insight and Healing,* Harmony, 1999

148 Singer, Michael A, *The Untethered Soul: The Journey Beyond Yourself*, New Harbinger, 2007

149 Ibid.

150 Lamott, Anne, *Bird By Bird: Some Instructions on Writing and Life*, Vintage, 1995

151 Hawkins, David R, *Letting Go: The Pathway of Surrender*, Hay House UK, 2014

152 Orloff, Judith, *The Power of Surrender: Let Go and Energize Your Relationships, Success, and Well-Being*, Harmony, 2015

153 Katie, Byron, *A Mind at Home with Itself : How Asking Four Questions Can Free Your Mind, Open Your Heart, and Turn Your World Around*, HarperOne, 2017

154 University of Texas at Austin, "Acts of Generosity Are Contagious," *Blue Zones*, www.bluezones.com/2021/11/acts-of-generosity-are-contagious

155 Buettner, Dan, "Power 9," *Blue Zones*, www.bluezones.com/2016/11/power-9/

156 Peat, Jack, "James Timpson lauded for compassionate maiden speech in House of Lords", *The London Economic*, July 2024, www.thelondoneconomic.com/politics/james-timpson-lauded-for-compassionate-maiden-speech-in-house-of-lords-379670/

ACKNOWLEDGEMENTS

Writing this book has been a gift. I have cherished every moment lovingly creating the magic I hope *Big Impact Without Burnout* now sprinkles out into the world. I wish to thank my nearest and dearest for allowing me to soar, not struggle, as each chapter materialized, tolerating the tables and floors strewn with Post-it notes, the study door shut when concentration was required and the weeks I disappeared altogether to complete the manuscript in my creative paradise, the Maldives.

So, Ashley, Scarlett, Sebastian and Beau, thank you for giving me the space to write and for being endlessly supportive, encouraging and genuinely interested throughout this creation process. You are my sunshines, my joy bursts, my everythings.

My darling Ruud, my forever love, thank you for always having faith in me, from Day One introducing me to the world as "a writer", and seeing into my soul. I cherish you and I hope to make you proud as we stay young together.

Thank you to my endlessly supportive parents for believing in me. To my mother, for raising me to spot the magic everywhere, for our family's holistic approach to healing and teaching me kindness and gentleness always. To my father, for role modelling joviality and endless optimism, how to positively foray into entrepreneurialism and to always be 100% honest. I love you both.

To my besties Charlotte, Katherine, Solance, Tarina, Zoe, Helen, Emma and my unwaveringly encouraging sister Melissa for the laughter, the cuddles, the guidance, the listening, the fun and the constant love. You are my rocks.

Thank you to the wonderful team at Watkins for working patiently with me throughout the publishing process, the dream team! I'm especially grateful to Ella for seeing the potential in me and my Big Impact vision. Thank you from the bottom of my heart.

Thank you Emmaclare for journeying alongside me into the Big Impact adventure with your warmth, energy and inspiring excellence. I'm so excited!

To every client, reader, event attendee, talent agent, YouTube viewer, social media follower, friend, colleague and mentor, you give me the courage and confidence to honour my Big Impact dreams and I send you love, gratitude and the twinkly-star embellished promise to keep on serving you to the best of my ability. Here's to many more shared chapters together as we star in our magnificent stories. Thank you.

ABOUT THE AUTHOR

Bianca Best is a woman of impact. She is an award-winning global business leader, bestselling author, certified Success Strategist, entrepreneur, speaker and single mother of four, eradicating burnout one twinkle at a time. "I've sparkled my way through life reaching my stars and then some. For a long while I was in boom-bust mode, achieving my dreams then crashing, soaring but struggling, excited but exhausted. Until I perfected the route to Big Impact Without Burnout, mastering a 'no compromise' recipe for success, peace and power through graceful productivity and integrity always. I now sprinkle my Big Impact Way out into the world with the intention that more ambitious individuals star in their own stories with a twinkle not a twizzle!"

Bianca describes her CV as a chronology of passions explored and includes a decade as a techpreneur, running The Bespoke Gift Company which changed the personalised gift industry forever, a decade of corporate ascendency running vast digital divisions in the world's largest comms conglomerates from WPP to Publicis Groupe, to certifying in healing modalities from hypnotherapy to executive coaching (ICF accredited), to her international impact, exciting the working world through her keynotes, workshops and corporate programmes in organizations like Google, Amazon and Snap, her books, vlogs and editorial in publications like *Thrive Global* and her own blog, where she illuminates, inspires and ignites.

Her organization BIANCA BEST. is dedicated to infusing the working world with graceful productivity, kind leadership and unlocked human potential whereby individuals and organizations flourish and Big Impact Without Burnout is the mainstay.

For more of her work and sparkle visit: www.biancabest.com